CHARMING SMALL HOTEL GUIDES

BRITAIN
&
IRELAND

CHARMING SMALL HOTEL GUIDES

BRITAIN
&
IRELAND

EDITED BY
Tamara Grosvenor and Patti Kemp

Interlink Books
An imprint of Interlink Publishing Group, Inc.
New York • Northampton

15th expanded edition

First American edition published in 2004 by
Interlink Books
An imprint of Interlink Publishing Group, Inc.
46 Crosby Street, Northampton, Massachusetts 01060
www.interlinkbooks.com

Copyright © Duncan Petersen Publishing Ltd 2004, 2001, 2000,
1999, 1998, 1997, 1996, 1995, 1994, 1993, 1992, 1991, 1990, 1989, & 1988

This series is conceived, designed and produced by
Duncan Petersen Publishing Ltd.,
31 Ceylon Road, London W14 OPY

Editorial Director Andrew Duncan
Editors Tamara Grosvenor and Patti Kemp
Contributing Editors Fiona Duncan and Leonie Glass
Production Editors Sarah Boyall and Sophie Page
Art Editor Keith Davis
Maps Map Creation Ltd
Picture research Leo Mills

Library of Congress Cataloging-in-Publication Data available
ISBN 1-56656-536-7

Printed and bound in Slovenia

To request our complete 48-page full-color catalog, please call us toll
free at 1-800-238-LINK, visit our website at www.interlinkbooks.com,
or send us an e-mail: info@interlinkbooks.com

CONTENTS

INTRODUCTION

IN THIS INTRODUCTORY SECTION

Welcome to this 2004 edition of *Charming Small Hotel Guides Britain.* It was the first of the hotel guides that we expanded to 336 pages and the changes we have made seem to have gone down well with our readers:

• *Every hotel now has a colour photograph and a full page of its own. No more half-page entries without a photograph.*

• *The maps have been upgraded.*

• *The layout has been changed in order to take you more quickly to essential booking information.*

We hope that you will think these real improvements, rather than change for its own sake. In all other respects, the guide remains true to the values and qualities that make it unique (see opposite), and which have won it so many devoted readers. This new edition has been expanded again, to 384 pages, giving full coverage of Ireland, rather than the highly selective coverage in earlier editions. This is the guide's fifteenth consecutive update since it was first published in 1986. It has sold hundreds of thousands of copies in the U.K., U.S.A. and in five European languages.

WHY ARE WE UNIQUE?

This is the only independently-inspected (no hotel pays for an entry) UK-originated accommodation guide that:

- has colour photographs for every entry;

- concentrates on places that have real charm and character;

- is highly selective;

- is particularly fussy about size. Most hotels have fewer than 20 bedrooms; if there are more, the hotel must have the feel of a much smaller place. We have found that a genuinely warm welcome is much more likely to be found in a small hotel;

- gives proper emphasis to the description, and doesn't use irritating symbols;

- is produced by a small, non-bureaucratic company with a dedicated team of like-minded inspectors.

See also *'So what exactly do we look for?',* page 8.

So what exactly do we look for? — Our selection criteria

• A peaceful, attractive setting. Obviously, if the entry is in an urban area, we make allowances.

• A building that is handsome, interesting or historic; or at least with real character.

• Adequate space, but on a human scale. We don't go for places that rely too much on grandeur, or with pretensions that could be intimidating.

• Good taste and imagination in the interior decoration. We reject standardized, chain hotel fixtures, fittings and decorations.

• Bedrooms that look like real bedrooms, not hotel rooms, individually decorated.

• Furnishings and other facilities that are comfortable and well maintained. We like to see interesting antique furniture that is there to be used, not simply revered.

• Proprietors and staff who are dedicated and thoughtful, offering a personal welcome, but who aren't intrusive or overly effusive. *The guest needs to feel like an individual.*

• Interesting food. There are few entries in this guide where the food is not of a high standard.

• A sympathetic atmosphere; an absence of loud people showing off their money; or the 'corporate feel'.

A FATTER GUIDE, BUT JUST AS SELECTIVE

In order to accommodate every entry with a whole-page description and colour photograph, we've had to print more pages. *But we have maintained our integrity by keeping the selection to around 350 entries.*

Over the years, the number of charming small hotels in Britain and Ireland has increased steadily, not dramatically. We don't believe that there are presently many more than about 350 truly charming small hotels in Britain and Ireland, and that, if we included more, we would undermine what we're trying to do: produce a guide which is all about places that are more than just a bed for the night. Every time we consider a new hotel, we ask ourselves whether it has that extra special something, regardless of category and facilities, that makes it worth seeking out.

TYPES OF ACCOMMODATION IN THIS GUIDE

Despite its title, the guide does not confine itself to places called hotels or places that behave like hotels. On the contrary, we actively look for places that offer a home from home (see page 10). We include small and medium-sized hotels; pubs; inns; restaurants-with-rooms; guest-houses and bed-and-breakfasts. Some places, usually private homes which take guests, operate on house-party lines, where you are introduced to the other guests, and take meals at a communal table. If you don't like making small talk to strangers, or are part of a romantic twosome that wants to keep itself to itself, this type of establishment may not be for you. On the other hand, if you are interested in meeting people, perhaps as a foreign visitor wanting to get to know the locals, then you'll find it rewarding.

NO FEAR OR FAVOUR

To us, taking a payment for appearing in a guide seems to defeat the object of producing a guide. If money has changed hands, you can't write the whole truth about a hotel, and the selection cannot be nearly so interesting. This self-evident truth seems to us to be proved at least in part by the fact that pay guides are so keen to present the illusion of independence: few admit on the cover that they take payments for an entry, only doing so in small print on the inside.

Not many people realize that on the shelves of British bookshops there are many more hotel guides that accept

payments for entries than there are independent guides. This hotel guide is one of the few that do not accept any money for an entry.

HOME FROM HOME
Perhaps the most beguiling characteristic of the best places to stay in this guide is the feeling they give of being in a private home – but without the everyday cares and chores of running one. To get this formula right requires a special sort of professionalism: the proprietor has to strike the balance between being relaxed and giving attentive service. Those who experience this 'feel' often turn their backs on all other forms of accommodation – however luxurious.

OUR PET DISLIKES
Small hotels are not automatically wonderful hotels; and the very individuality of small, owner-run hotels, makes them prone to peculiarities that the mass-produced hotel experience avoids. For the benefit of those who run the small hotels of Britain - and those contemplating the plunge - we repeat once more our list of pet hates.

The Hushed Dining Room This commonly results when an establishment falls between two stools of a really small place, where the owner makes sure the ice is broken, and the not-so-small hotel, where there are enough people to create a bit of a hubbub.

The Ordinary Breakfast Even hotels that go to great lengths to prepare special dinners are capable of serving prefabricated orange juice and sliced bread at breakfast.

The Schoolteacher Mentality People tempted to set up small hotels should perhaps undergo psychometric testing to determine whether they are sufficiently flexible and accommodating to deal with the whims of travellers; some of them certainly are not.

The Excess of Informality At one not-cheap London address (which did not find its way into the guide) we were shown around by a young man in jeans (which might be acceptable) and socks (which is not). A recent reader's letter about an establishment (which has been dropped) recounted the owner greeting him in shabby gardening clothes, with a pack of unruly dogs at her heels. When she brought him tea, she was still in Wellington boots, and her hands were still encrusted with mud.

The Inexperienced Waiter Or waitress. Running a small operation does not excuse the imposition on the paying public of completely untrained (and sometimes ill-suited) staff who can spoil the most beautifully cooked meal.

The Imposing Name An unimportant one, this, but an irritant nonetheless. A charmingly cosy whitewashed cottage in the Lake District does not, in our view, constitute a 'county house hotel'.

The Lumpy Old Bed Surely, every hotel proprietor knows that they should occasionally sleep in each of the beds in each of their rooms? Otherwise its the easiest thing in the world to fail to spot the gradual decay of a mattress.

The Eratic Boiler There is nothing worse than arriving, chilled and tired at your chosen destination, only to step into a tepid bath. Lashings of hot water (and decent towels, not drying-up cloths) is a prerequisite of a decent establishment.

CHECK THE PRICE FIRST

In this guide we have adopted the system of price bands, rather than giving actual prices as we did in previous editions. This is because prices were often subject to change after we went to press. The price bands refer to the approximate price of a standard double room (high season rates) with breakfast for two people. Prices for Ireland are quoted in euros. They are as follows:

£	under £70		under 100 euros
££	£70 – £120		100 – 170 euros
£££	£120 – £180		170 – 260 euros
££££	more than £180		more than 260 euros

To avoid unpleasant surprises, always check what is included in the price (for example, VAT and service, breakfast, afternoon tea) when making the booking.

HOW TO FIND AN ENTRY

In this guide, the entries are arranged in geographical groups. First, the whole of Britain and Ireland are divided into five major groups, starting with Southern England and working northwards to Scotland; Ireland comes last.

Within these major groups, the entries are grouped into smaller regional sub-sections such as the South-West, Wales, the Midlands and the Highlands and Islands – for a full list, see page 5. Within each sub-section, entries are listed alphabaetically by nearest town or village; if several occur in or near one town, entries are arranged in alpha order by name of hotel.

To find a hotel in a particular area, use the maps following this introduction to locate the appropriate pages.

To locate a specific hotel, whose name you know, or a hotel in a place you know, use the indexes at the back, which list entries both by names and by nearest place name. The name of the county follows the town name in the heading for each entry.

The three main sections of the book (England and Wales, Scotland and Ireland) are introduced by area introductions.

HOW TO READ AN ENTRY

THE SOUTH-WEST

EVERSHOT, DORSET

SUMMER LODGE
~ COUNTRY HOUSE HOTEL ~

Summer Lane, Evershot, Dorset DT2 0JR
TEL (01935) 83424 **FAX** (01935) 83005
E-MAIL reception@summerlodgehotel.co.uk **WEBSITE** www.summerlodgehotel.com

THE CORBETTS ARE the living evidence that not all 'professional' hoteliers are mediocre; we don't know what contribution they made to guests' happiness when they were at the Savoy, but the dedication they have applied to that cause since they escaped to Dorset is remarkable indeed. A recent inspection confirmed that their standards, and enthusiasm, remain unchanged. Our only quibble: the lack of a non-smoking sitting room.

For many visitors, Summer Lodge is all that a country house hotel should be. The Georgian/Victorian building is on just the right scale to give a sense of slight extravagance without being intimidating, and the Corbetts and their staff are masters at making guests feel at home in it. French windows lead from the public rooms (William Morris fabrics, open fires) to the beautiful flowery garden. Charming bedrooms range from the merely delightful to the quite grand. Bathrooms are spacious and have large white fluffy towels.

The surrounding countryside has retained its rural beauty and there are many places of interest to visit, and some good pubs for lunch. The hotel's cream tea (included in half board rates) is a tempting reason to return there in the afternoon, and dinner remains a highlight.

~

NEARBY Minterne and Maperton Gardens; Montacute, Melbury deer park.
LOCATION 15 miles (24 km) NW of Dorchester, off A37 on edge of village; ample car parking
FOOD breakfast, lunch, dinner; room service
PRICE ££££
ROOMS 17; 13 double, 3 single, 1 suite, all with bath; all rooms have phone, TV, hairdrier, radio **FACILITIES** dining room, sitting room, bar, reading room; garden, croquet, heated swimming pool, tennis court **CREDIT CARDS** AE, DC, MC, V
CHILDREN accepted **DISABLED** access good to ground-floor bedrooms
PETS accepted by arrangement (£7.50 per night) **CLOSED** never
PROPRIETORS Nigel and Margaret Corbett

Name of hotel

Type of establishment

Description – never vetted by the hotel

Places of interest within reach of the hotel

This sets the hotel in its geographical context and should not be taken as precise instructions as to how to get there; always ask the hotel for directions.

Rooms described as having a bath usually also have a shower; rooms described as having a shower only have a shower.

Essential booking information.

Always let the hotel know in advance if you want to bring a pet. Even where pets are accepted, certain restrictions may apply, and a small charge may be levied.

City, town or village, and region, in which the hotel is located.

Some or all the public rooms and bedrooms in an increasing number of hotels are now non-smoking. Smokers should check the hotel's policy when booking.

Postal address and other key information.

Where children are welcome, there are often special facilities, such as cots, high chairs, baby listening and high teas. Always check whether children are accepted in the dining room.

Breakfast, either full or continental, is normally included in the price of the room. We have not quoted prices for lunch and dinner. Other meals, such as afternoon tea, may also be available. 'Room service' refers to food and drink, either snacks or full meals, which can be served in the room.

We list the following credit cards:
AE   American Express
DC   Diners Club
MC   Mastercard
V   Visa

This information is only an indication for wheelchair users and the infirm. Always check on suitability with the hotel.

In this guide we have used price bands rather than quoting actual prices. They refer to a standard double room (high season rates, if applicable) with breakfast for two people. Prices for Ireland are quoted in euros. Other rates – for other room categories, times of the year, weekend breaks, long stays and so on – may well be available. In some hotels, usually out-of-the-way places or restaurants-with-rooms – half-board is obligatory. Always check when booking. The price bands are as follows:

£	under £70
£ £	£70 – £120
£ £ £	£120 – £180
£ £ £ £	more than £180

	under 100 euros
	100 – 170 euros
	170 – 260 euros
	more than 260 euros

REPORTING TO THE GUIDE

Please write and tell us about your experiences of small hotels, guest houses and inns, whether good or bad, whether listed in this edition or not. As well as hotels in Britain, we are interested in hotels in France, Spain and the Balearics, Austria, Germany, Switzerland, the U.S.A and Greece. We assume that reporters have no objections to our publishing their views unpaid.

Readers whose reports prove particularly helpful may be invited to join our Travellers' Panel. Members give us notice of their own travel plans; we suggest hotels that they might inspect, and help with the cost of accommodation.

The address to write to us is:

Editor, *Charming Small Hotel Guides*,
Duncan Petersen Publishing Limited,
31 Ceylon Road,
London W14 0PY.

Checklist
Please use a separate sheet of paper for each report; include your name, address and telephone number on each report.

Your reports will be received with particular pleasure if they are typed, and if they are organized under the following headings:

Name of establishment
Town or village it is in, or nearest
Full address, including postcode
Telephone number
Time and duration of visit
The building and setting
The public rooms
The bedrooms and bathrooms
Physical comfort (chairs, beds, heat, light, hot water)
Standards of maintenance and housekeeping
Atmosphere, welcome and service
Food
Value for money

We assume that in writing you have no objections to your views being published unpaid, either verbatim or in an edited version. Names of major outside contributors are acknowledged, at the editor's discretion, in the guide.

Hotel location maps

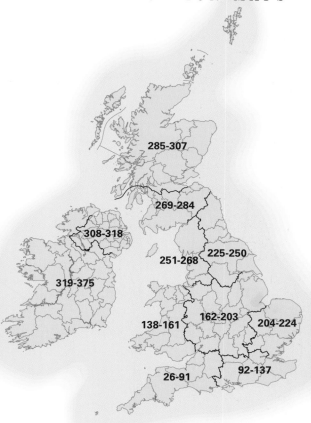

285-307

269-284

308-318

251-268 225-250

319-375

138-161 162-203 204-224

26-91 92-137

Amlwch

Carmel Head

Holyhead • Valley • Benllech
Beaumaris
Rhosneigr • Llangefni

Llanddeiniolen 149

Portmeirion 158
Talsarnau 160
Aberdaron • Abersoch 139

Dolgellau 143
Penmaenpool 156,157

Cardigan
Bay
Eglwsfach 144

Aberystwyth

Aberaeron
Tregaron •

St. George's Channel

Cardigan
Strumble Head • Newport
Lampeter •

Fishguard 145,146
Brechfa 140

St. David's
Carmarthen

Haverfordwest • Narberth
Pontarddulais

Pembroke • Llanelli •
Penally 155 *Carmarthen* **SWANSEA**
Bay
Reynoldston 159

Bristol

Barnstaple

Hartland Pt.
Hartland
Great
Torrington

Bude • Holsworthy 55
Ashwater 27
Virginstow 85
Lewdown 59
Lifton 60 Chagford 42

St. Martin 78
Padstow 67 • Rock 71
Liston 60
Wadebridge Callington Gulworthy 52
Hugh Town
St. Blazey 75 St. Keyne 77
St. Austell 74 **PLYMOUTH**
Fowey 48
St. Ives Redruth • Truro
Ruanhighlanes 73 Bigbury-on-Sea 37
Penzance 68, 69, 70 • St.Hilary 76 Rosevine 72
Land's End *Mount's* St.Mawes 79
Bay Gillan 50
Black Head
Lizard Pt. Lizard 61

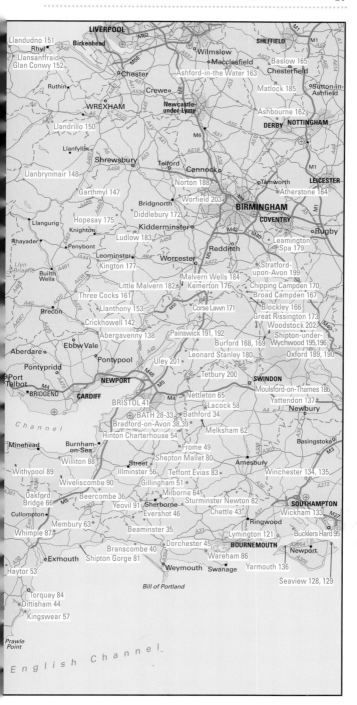

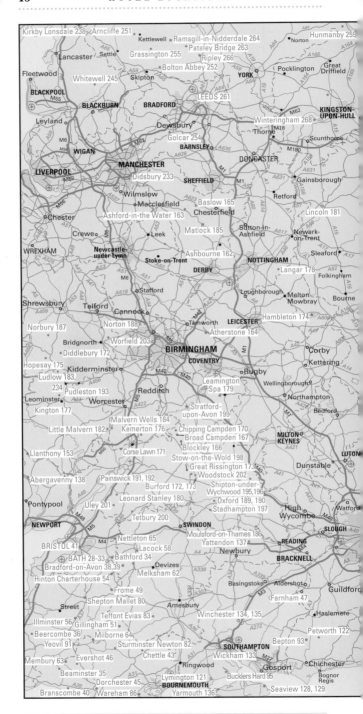

North

Sea

rnsea

Withernsea

Grimsby

Louth   Mablethorpe

Horncastle
A158   A158

ningsby   Skegness

Holkham 209   Cley-next-
Morston 215   the-Sea 208
Boston   Hunstanton   Cromer
Burnham Market 205
ngton   Fakenham
A151

palding   King's Lynn 210   Wroxham

Wisbech   Swaffham 223   Norwich 218, 219   Great
Yarmouth

March   Mundford   Lowestoft
Brandon
atteris   Thetford   Diss
Ely   Bury   Southwold 221
St. Edmunds 206, 207
Burwell   Newmarket   Beyton 204   Snape 220
Cambridge   Needham Market 217
Long Melford 213   Claydon   Woodbridge 224
ston   Lavenham 211, 212
Melbourn 214
Nayland 216   Stoke by Nayland 222
tevenage
Braintree   Colchester
Stansted
A414   Clacton-on-Sea

Chelmsford   Maldon
Chigwell
Rayleigh
DON 103-120   SOUTHEND-ON-SEA
Thames Estuary
Sheerness   Herne   Margate
Dartford   Bay
Whitstable 132
Banstead   Maidstone   Canterbury
gate   Ringlestone 123
Tunbridge   St. Margret's at Cliffe 127
East   Wells 130   Ashford   Dover
stead 98   Frant 101   Cranbrook 96   Folkestone
field 97   Fletching 100   Rye 125, 126   Littlestone 102
Uckfield 131   Rushlake Green 124   Dungeness
East Hoathly 99   Battle 92
RIGHTON   Brighton 94   Bexhill   Hastings
HOVE
Eastbourne

Strait of Dover

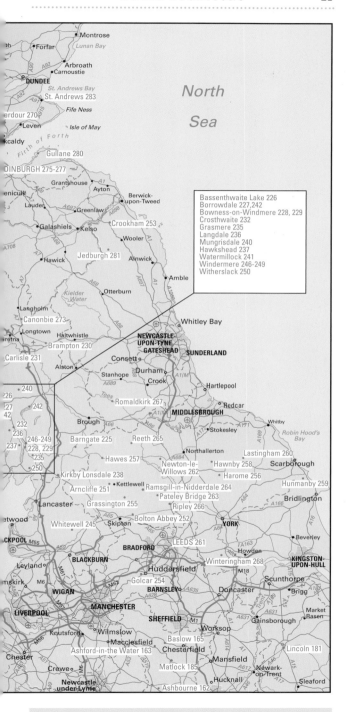

Montrose
Forfar
Lunan Bay
Arbroath
Carnoustie
DUNDEE
St. Andrews Bay
St. Andrews 283
Fife Ness
erdour 270
Leven
Isle of May
kcaldy
Firth of Forth
Gullane 280
DINBURGH 275-277
Grantshouse
Ayton
Berwick-upon-Tweed
enicuik
Lauder
Greenlaw
Crookham 253
Galashiels
Kelso
Wooler
Hawick
Jedburgh 281
Alnwick
Kielder Water
Otterburn
Amble
Langholm
Canonbie 273
Longtown
Haltwhistle
Whitley Bay
retna
Brampton 230
NEWCASTLE-UPON-TYNE
Carlisle 231
Consett
GATESHEAD
SUNDERLAND
Alston
Stanhope
Durham
Crook
A1/M
Hartlepool
226
240
Romaldkirk 267
Redcar
227
242
MIDDLESBROUGH
42
232
Brough
Stokesley
Whitby
236
246-249
Barngate 225
Reeth 265
Robin Hood's Bay
237
228, 229
Northallerton
Lastingham 260
235
Hawes 257
Newton-le-Willows 262
Hawnby 258
Scarborough
250
Kirkby Lonsdale 238
Harome 256
Arncliffe 251
Kettlewell
Ramsgill-in-Nidderdale 264
Hunmanby 259
Lancaster
Grassington 255
Pateley Bridge 263
Bridlington
twood
Whitewell 245
Skipton
Bolton Abbey 252
Ripley 266
YORK
CKPOOL M55
Beverley
BLACKBURN
BRADFORD
LEEDS 261
Howden
Leyland
Winteringham 268
KINGSTON-UPON-HULL
Huddersfield
M18
Scunthorpe
mskirk
M6
Golcar 254
BARNSLEY
Doncaster
Brigg
WIGAN
MANCHESTER
Market Rasen
LIVERPOOL
SHEFFIELD
M1
Worksop
Gainsborough
Knutsford
Wilmslow
Baslow 165
Chester
Macclesfield
Chesterfield
Lincoln 181
Ashford-in-the-Water 163
Crewe
Matlock 185
Mansfield
Newark-on-Trent
Newcastle-under-Lyme
Hucknall
Sleaford
Ashbourne 162

North Sea

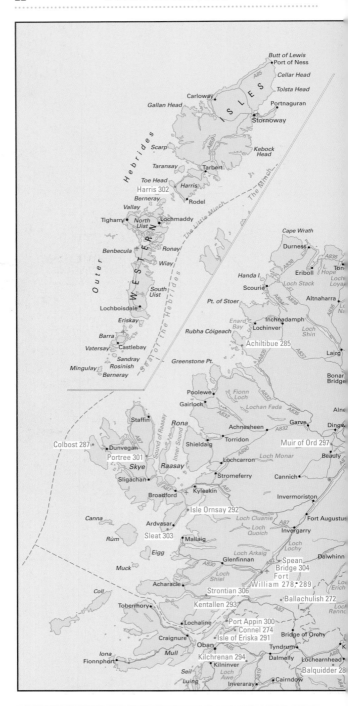

Atlantic

Ocean

Aran Island

Gweebarra

Ardara 3

Rossan Pt.　Killybe

Dunkineely

Donegal Bay

Benwee Hd.　*Downpatrick Head*　*Inishmurray*

Erris Hd.

Belmullet　　　*Killala Bay*　*Sligo Bay*　S

Inishkea　　Bangor Erris　　Dromore West　Ballysa

Blacksod Bay　Crossmolina　N59　Ballina

Ballycroy　L.Conn　　　Tobercurry

Achill Island　Mulrany 369　M A Y O　Riverstown 374　*L. Gara*

Newport　Castlebar　Swinford　B

Clare　*Clew Bay*　Westport　Ballymote 328　Ballaghaderre

Castlebar

Inishturk　　Ballyhaunis　Ca 335

Inishbofin　　*L. Mask*　Claremorris　N60

Kylemore 360　*R.Carra*

Inishark　Leenane 361, 362　Caherlistrane 330

Clifden 337-340　　Tuam

C O N N E M A R A　Recess 373　*ugh*

Slyne Head　　N59

Ballyconneely　　　　G A L W A

324　Cashel Bay 334　Ballinas

Galway 349, 350

Inishmore　　*Galway Bay*　Loughrea

Aran Islands　*Inishmaan*

Inisheer　　　　Gort　Portu

N67　Lisdoonvarna

Hags Head　363, 364 mon　*Lough Derg*

Liscannor Bay　Milltown　C L A R E

Malbay

Ennis　Newmarket-on-

Corofin 342　Fergus 371　Nen

Kilkee　　　　37

Kilrush　*Shannon* ✈

Loop Head　　　　　　Limerick

Mouth of The Shannon　Foynes

Ballybunion　Glin 351

Kerry Head　Listowel　Rathkeale

Abbeyfeale　L I M E R I C K　Tipper

Brandon Head　*Tralee Bay*　Rath Luirc　Kilmallock

Castlegregory 336　Tralee　Ballingarry 322

Dingle 343　Castleisland

Slea Head　*Dingle Bay*　K E R R Y　Kanturk 357　Mitchelstown

Killorglin

Caragh Lake *L. Leane*　Killarney　　Fermoy

331,332　　　　Mallow 365　N72

Valencia I.　Cahirciveen　Aghadoe 319

Bray Head　　　　　　　C O R K　Cloyne

Kenmare 358　　　　　Midleton

Bolus Head　　Macroom　　Cobh

Shanagarry

Glengarriff　Innishannon 356

Ballylickey 325, 326　　Bandon Kinsale *Cork Harbo*

Dursey Head　*Bantry Bay*

Clonakilty　　Butlerstown 329

Goleen 352, 353　Skibbereen

Mizen Head　　　*Galley Head*

ENGLAND & WALES

This section covers the largest geographical area in the guide, from the sheltered coves and sunken lanes of Devon and Cornwall in the south-west to the stark peaks and tranquil lakes of Cumbria in the north, and from the rugged moorland hills, windswept headlands and bays of the west Pembrokeshire coast to the flat east Norfolk fens. In both England and Wales, you can scarcely travel a mile without discovering something worth seeing: whether a historical sight, a picturesque village, a Georgian town or a spectacular view. For this edition of the guide, we have made many new discoveries throughout the country: among them, sophisticated townhouse B&Bs, comfortable country manors and guest-houses, seaside family hotels, stylish retreats and cosy village inns. All are within a wide range of prices and all have the special qualities of character and charm that we prize. Hotels new to the guide in Southern England include elegant Driftwood House on the rugged south Cornish coast (page 72); The Museum Inn, a popular Dorset pub (page 47); and Dorian House, a tasteful B&B overlooking Bath's Royal Crescent (page 31). In Sussex, the latest Hotel du Vin has opened in a series of Gothic-style buildings in Brighton (page 94), and The Old Railway Station (page 122) is our most unusual find. Always on the look-out for different London hotels, we have found three for this edition: The Colonnade in Little Venice (page 104), The Knightsbridge Green (page 113) and Twenty Nevern Square (page 120).

Wales

Among our most interesting new Welsh hotels are Tan-y-Foel, a country house with a distinctive style (page 141); Tyín Rhos, a secluded, comfortable farm (page 149); and Pen-y-Gwyrd, a favourite with climbers (page 154). In the Welsh Border town of Ludlow (but in our Central England section) we welcome Bromley Court (page 183) to the guide, a clever and charming conversion of Tudor cottages. On page 193, Ford Abbey occupies an 800-year-old Herefordshire farmhouse; and (page 216) the White Hart is a 15thC Suffolk coaching inn. In Northern England, surrounded by stunning Lakeland scenery, our new recommendations include The Drunken Duck Inn, full of character and charm (page 225); one of Wordsworthís haunts, The Samling (page 248); and in North Yorkshire, the cosy 14thC Star Inn, an archetypal English pub, which also serves Michelin-starred food.

THE SOUTH-WEST

ASHWATER, DEVON

BLAGDON MANOR
∼ COUNTRY HOUSE HOTEL ∼

Ashwater, Beaworthy, Devon EX21 5DF
TEL (01409) 211224 **FAX** (01409) 211634
E-MAIL stay@blagdon.com **WEBSITE** www.blagdon.com

DON'T BE PUT OFF by Blagdon Manor's isolated situation: it lies plum in the middle of the West Country, so no place of interest is really very far away.

This Grade II listed former farmhouse, surrounded by rolling countryside, was derelict when previous owners Tim and Gill Casey discovered it and brought it back to life. Successors Steve and Liz Morey purchased Blagdon Manor because, between them, they had worked in the hotel industry for 40 years and thought "it was time to do it themselves"

They told us that their goal isn't to make money, but to use their experience to provide quality. With that in mind, they have already embarked on a refurbishment plan and four bedrooms have been completely redone, while plans are in place for the remaining three.

The new conservatory makes an ideal spot for breakfast and lunch and with views toward the north side of Dartmoor, definitely adds to the place. Liz makes her own jam, marmalade and bread, but what can't be made on the premises comes from local businesses. Bedrooms are comfortable, with pretty fabrics.

The Morey's assured us that they will be at Blagdon for many years to come, "We want to be here until we retire." We would welcome comments on how they are doing.

∼

NEARBY National Trust Coast; golf courses.
LOCATION just off A388 Launceston – Holsworthy road, 4 miles (6.5 km) S of Holsworthy, in 20 acres; ample car parking and helicopter pad
FOOD breakfast, dinner
PRICE ££
ROOMS 7; 5 double, 2 twin, all with bath; all rooms have phone, TV, hairdrier
FACILITIES sitting room, library, dining room, bar; terrace, garden, croquet
CREDIT CARDS MC, V **CHILDREN** welcome over 12
DISABLED access difficult **PETS** not accepted
CLOSED 2 weeks in Nov and 2 weeks in Jan **PROPRIETORS** Steve and LIz Morey

THE SOUTH-WEST

APSLEY HOUSE
~ TOWN HOTEL ~

Newbridge Hill, Bath BA1 3PT
TEL (01225) 336966 **FAX** (01225) 425462
E-MAIL info@apsley-house.co.uk **WEBSITE** www.apsley-house.co.uk

ONCE UPON A TIME this was a grand house with huge grounds leading down to the River Avon. It was built for the Duke of Wellington in 1830, thus missing the flourishing Georgian period for which Bath is famous. The grounds were sold off long ago to make way for the houses which now surround Apsley House, leaving enough garden to ensure privacy for the occupants.

There are, however, still remnants of its eminent past within, from the grand sweeping staircase to the high ceilings of the spacious rooms. There is a large, comfortable drawing room, with a grand piano, for guests' use, as well as a licensed bar. New owners Claire and Nicholas Potts have updated the bedrooms and bathroom, added some new furniture and generally set about making the place "a lot cleaner". Bedroom No. 9 is fashioned from the old kitchen, complete with bread oven and a splendid marble fireplace. They have also turned their attention to the grounds and put some well-needed love into the gardens.

Claire is particularly proud of her cooked breakfasts, although the classical radio piped in over breakfast may not be to everyone's liking.

More reports please.

~

NEARBY Bath centre.
LOCATION on A431 to NW of city; ample car parking
FOOD breakfast, light supper in quieter times
PRICE ££
ROOMS 9 double, 8 with bath, 1 with shower; all rooms have phone, TV, hairdrier
FACILITIES sitting room, bar, breakfast room; garden
CREDIT CARDS AE, MC, V
CHILDREN accepted over 5
DISABLED access difficult **PETS** not accepted
CLOSED Christmas
PROPRIETORS Claire and Nicholas Potts

THE SOUTH-WEST

BATH PRIORY
~ EDGE-OF-CITY HOTEL ~

Weston Road, Bath BA1 2XT
TEL (01225) 331922 Fax (01225) 448276
E-MAIL bathprioryhotel@compuserve.com **WEBSITE** www.thebathpriory.co.uk

UNLIKE MANY OF ITS BREED of manicured country house hotels with health spas, the Bath Priory has a feeling of small-scale intimacy – which makes it, we feel, appropriate for our guide, despite the high prices.

Within walking distance of the centre, the hotel is shielded from the suburbs of Bath by a large park-like garden, while inside, the *atmosphere* of a gracious country house has been artfully created. The 'superior' bedrooms are seriously comfortable and very pretty (particularly Carnation with a four-poster in palest green silk, and Orchid, with an oriental theme)

Chef Robert Clayton has gained a Michelin star for his cooking, inspired by Nico Ladenis, and dinner is served in an intimate, candlelit room hung with oil paintings. Sink side by side into the deliciously squashy red velvet banquette, and don't miss the risotto – of lobster, perhaps, or wild mushroom. When you aren't exploring Bath, you can curl up in front of the drawing room fire, attended by a discreet fleet of charming ladies and white-aproned French and Italian waiters, or slip downstairs to the health spa for a beauty treatment, a session in the well-equipped gym, and a swim in the inviting and elegant indoor pool.

~

NEARBY Bath centre.
LOCATION 1 mile (2.5 km) W of centre; in grounds with car parking
FOOD breakfast, lunch, dinner; room service
PRICE ££££
ROOMS 28; 22 double and twin, 5 suites, 1 single, all with bath; all rooms have phone, TV, fax/modem point, hairdrier **FACILITIES** drawing room, 2 dining rooms, library, indoor swimming pool, leisure spa, beauty treatment rooms, gym; terrace, garden, croquet, outdoor swimming pool
CREDIT CARDS AE, DC, MC, V **CHILDREN** accepted
DISABLED 1 bedroom on ground floor specially adapted **PETS** not accepted
CLOSED 3 nights early Jan **MANAGER** Sue Williams

THE SOUTH-WEST

BLOOMFIELD HOUSE
~ TOWN GUEST-HOUSE ~

146 Bloomfield Road, Bath BA2 2AS
TEL (01225) 420105
E-MAIL bloomfieldhouse@compuserve.com **WEBSITE** www.bloomfield-house.co.uk

EVEN THE BLANK WINDOWS overlooking the car park have been painted with *trompe l'oeil* books and flowers, hinting at the visual treats in store for the visitor to Bloomfield House. The rounded hall, with hand-painted fresco of flowers and peacocks, positively confirms the initial impression that this is somewhere out of the ordinary.

Bridget and Malcolm Cox bought Bloomfield House from a talented producer of opera and his architect partner who had poured money and artistry into the Georgian building. The Coxes have wisely kept the grand interior they inherited – decorative paint finishes, French crystal chandeliers, superb heavy silk curtains – but they continue to update and add their own touches.

There was a seductive smell of oranges when our inspector called, as the Coxes were both busy making marmalade for their guests' breakfasts, served in the elegant dining room overlooking the garden. The bedrooms are beautifully decorated and, although not all can be described as spacious, they are without exception comfortable. Furniture is antique and fine, but not so refined that guests feel intimidated. In the evening, you can help yourself to sherry and relax in one of the gold damask-covered armchairs in the drawing room in front of the fire. In summer, a seat in the garden makes a peaceful alternative, with views across Bath. Smokers should note that this is a non-smoking establishment.

~

NEARBY Bath centre.
LOCATION off A367 to S of city; ample car parking
FOOD breakfast
PRICE ££
ROOMS 8; 6 double, 4 en suite, 3 with bath, 3 with shower, 1 twin with bath, 1 single with bath; all rooms have phone, TV, hairdrier **FACILITIES** sitting room, dining room; terrace, garden **CREDIT CARDS** MC, V **CHILDREN** accepted over 8 **DISABLED** access difficult **PETS** not accepted **CLOSED** never **PROPRIETORS** Bridget and Malcolm Cox

THE SOUTH-WEST

DORIAN HOUSE
~ BED-AND-BREAKFAST ~

1 Upper Oldfield Park, Bath, Avon BA2 3JX
TEL (01225) 426336 **FAX** (01225) 444699
E-MAIL dorian.house@which.net **WEBSITE** www.dorianhouse.co.uk

ALTHOUGH BATH has a large number of hotels, Dorian House, new to the guide this edition, stands out as a place of elegance and charm. Tim and Kathryn Hugh have made the most of this Victorian building built in 1880 of Bath stone, standing on a hill overlooking the city centre – bedrooms have splendid views towards Royal Crescent.

With high ceilings and large windows (including some impressive bay windows), rooms are drenched in light and, with tan, beige and cream tones, have a feeling of airiness. The house retains all of its original features and many rooms have fireplaces and fine antiques.

Breakfast is taken in a tastefully decorated breakfast room also with views of the city. The sitting room (with honesty bar) is equally refined. You can't have dinner here, but there are plenty of good restaurants in Bath and Tim and Kathryn provide a book of menus collected from the better restaurants in town. Tim happens to be a cellist for the London Symphony Orchestra and his concert recordings form part of Dorian House's own-label cd. His artistic flair is evident in this smart bed and breakfast.

~

NEARBY Bath centre.
LOCATION from Bath, take A367 signposted Shepton Mallet, after 1 minute's drive, take first road on the right; with car parking
FOOD breakfast
PRICE ££
ROOMS 11 doubles; all with bath or shower, all rooms have TV, phone, hairdrier
FACILITIES sitting room, dining room, honesty bar; garden
CREDIT CARDS MC, V
CHILDREN accepted by arrangement
DISABLED access difficult
PETS not accepted
CLOSED never
PROPRIETORS Tim and Kathryn Hugh

THE SOUTH-WEST

FOURTEEN RABY PLACE
~ TOWN GUEST-HOUSE ~

14 Raby Place, Bath, Northeast Somerset BA2 4EH
TEL (01225) 465120 **FAX** (01225) 465283

Bath has more than its fair share of hotels and guest-houses that exact a heavy toll from the many visitors who come to view the Roman Baths and splendid Georgian architecture. The few that manage to keep their prices reasonable are usually either far from the centre, or uninspiring, and we don't know of any that can match Muriel Guy's delightful Georgian house on the lower slopes of Bathwick Hill.

The house is in a typical Bath terrace, single-fronted, and not overly spacious. The railway runs close behind too, but offset these minor detractions against the price, comfort and richly decorated interior, and you will soon be persuaded by its advantages.

Mrs Guy is an inveterate traveller and collector, who has furnished her home with mementoes of her travels. Bedrooms are tastefully done in an interesting mix of colours and styles: white Portuguese bedcovers, crewel work curtains, embroidered peasant materials and handsome rugs are used to great effect throughout. Books on every conceivable subject fill the shelves, adding to the cosmopolitan feel of the place.

Breakfast (mainly organic produce is served) is taken around a large mahogany table in the kitchen/dining room. Don't automatically expect bacon with your free range eggs – it has to be specially requested. Smoking is not allowed. On our most recent visit, no one was home, so be sure to ring first.

~

NEARBY Bath centre.
LOCATION on S side of city; street parking
FOOD breakfast
PRICE £
ROOMS 4; 2 double, both with shower; 1 twin with separate shower; 1 family room with shower; all rooms have TV, hairdrier
FACILITIES dining room; garden **CREDIT CARDS** not accepted
CHILDREN accepted **DISABLED** not suitable
PETS by arrangement **CLOSED** never **PROPRIETOR** Muriel Guy

THE SOUTH·WEST

QUEENSBERRY
〜 TOWN HOUSE HOTEL 〜

Russel Street, Bath, Northeast Somerset BA1 2QF
TEL (01225) 447928 **FAX** (01225) 446065
E-MAIL reservations@bathqueensberry.com **WEBSITE** www.bathqueensberry.com

THIS BATH HOTEL is slightly large for our purposes, but cannot be allowed to escape the net. Its owners, Stephen and Penny Ross, opened it in 1988 and transformed three Georgian terraced houses into one of the most sophisticated and yet personal places to stay in the city. When we visited in early 2000, the hotel staff were on a high: the Queensberry had just been voted 'Hotel and Restaurant of the Millenium' by The Times.

The Queensberry is a discreet, quiet and beautifully decorated haven right in the centre of Bath. It has the advantage of a lift to all levels, which cuts down on confusion in the maze of stairwells and corridors which link the three buildings. Despite the small-scale appearance of the hotel, the majority of the bedrooms are surprisingly spacious, and are kitted out to the highest standards of comfort and elegance. Double beds generally mean king-size here, almost guaranteed to give you a good night's sleep, and made up with lovely cotton sheets. Rooms on the first floor are largest, with armchairs and breakfast tables; bathrooms are lavish, with quality toiletries and proper towels.

Downstairs, the principal sitting room is beautifully furnished in muted colours. The hotel's relaxed basement restaurant, the Olive Tree, has a life of its own: it's one of the most popular places to eat in Bath.

〜

NEARBY Assembly Rooms; Museum of Costume; The Circus.
LOCATION in middle of city, close to main shopping area; paved gardens behind; daytime car parking restricted
FOOD breakfast, lunch, dinner; room service
PRICE £££
ROOMS 29, 1 with shower, rest with bath; all rooms have phone, TV, hairdrier
FACILITIES sitting room, bar, restaurant; courtyard, valet parking
CREDIT CARDS AE, MC, V **CHILDREN** welcome
DISABLED access possible, lift/elevator
PETS guide dogs only **CLOSED** Christmas **PROPRIETORS** Stephen and Penny Ross

THE SOUTH-WEST

EAGLE HOUSE
~ VILLAGE GUEST-HOUSE ~

Church Street, Bathford, Bath, Somerset BA1 7RS
TEL (01225) 859946 FAX (01225) 859430
E-MAIL jonap@eagleho.demon.co.uk **WEBSITE** www.eaglehouse.co.uk

A STALWART OF OUR GUIDE, Eagle House provides a tranquil alternative to the bustle of staying in nearby Bath. Despite its outwardly grand Georgian exterior - the house was designed by John Wood the Elder - this is above all a family home, where John and Ros Napier go out of their way to provide a relaxed welcome to their guests.

Aquila the black Labrador wanders about and toys are readily available for the children, yet John's early training at the Ritz underpins informality with an innate professionalism. Personal service is the watchword here, but not in the nannying sense. As there is no licence to serve alcohol, the Napiers are quite happy for people to bring their own to drink in the large, elegant drawing room hung with family heirloom portraits which include Mary Queen of Scots and Charles 1 and II.

The bedrooms are decorated in pretty wallpapers and comfortably furnished in country style. There is also the option of the Walled Garden Cottage for those who value complete privacy. Equipped with kitchen, sitting room and two bedrooms each with bath, guests can still have breakfast in the main house. As ever at Eagle house, there is no pressure.

~

NEARBY Bath.
LOCATION 2.5 miles (4 km) E of Bath, off A363, in village; in 2-acre gardens, with ample car parking
FOOD breakfast
PRICE ££
ROOMS 8; 4 double with bath, 2 single with shower, 2 family with bath; all rooms have phone, TV, hairdrier **FACILITIES** breakfast room, drawing room; garden, lawn tennis, croquet. treehouse and swings for children
CREDIT CARDS MC, V **CHILDREN** welcome
DISABLED access difficult
PETS accepted **CLOSED** I0 days over Christmas
PROPRIETORS John and Rosamund Napier

THE SOUTH-WEST

BEAMINSTER, DORSET

BRIDGE HOUSE
COUNTRY HOTEL

Beaminster, Dorset DT8 3AY
TEL (01308) 862200 **FAX** (01308) 863700
E-MAIL enquiries@bridge-house.co.uk **WEBSITE** www.bridge-house.co.uk

DATING FROM THE 13TH CENTURY, Bridge House is reputedly a former monastery or clergy house and the oldest building in Beaminster. Whatever its antecedents, it is certainly a venerable and charming building and has been run as a hotel by Peter Pinkster and his wife for the past 16 years. He is ex-Navy, very jovial, and says he looks on Bridge House as a hobby. All the signs, however, are of a professional operation.

The sitting room and bar areas are cheefully decorated in cherry and green tartans; daughter Anna Pinkster's paintings, some of which are for sale, hang on the cream walls. Lunch and dinner are served in the pretty pink-panelled dining room or the conservatory which looks out on to the walled gardens. Chef Linda Pagett has been with the Pinkster's for several years. Young and enthusiastic, her cooking has made waves in an area blessed with quality local produce: fish, meat and cheese all come from nearby. Bread, biscuits, ice-cream and chocolates are all made in the Bridge House kitchens; even the marmalade that accompanies the satisfying breakfasts is made on the premises.

Bedrooms are all different, as would be expected in a building so full of nooks and crannies, with a priest's hole to boot. Those in the converted coach house are more modern, but equally comfortable.

NEARBY Mapperton Gardens; Forde Abbey.
LOCATION on A3066 in centre of town; ample car parking
FOOD breakfast; lunch; dinner
PRICE ££
ROOMS 14; 12 double and twin, 1 family all with bath, 1 single with shower; all rooms have phone, TV
FACILITIES sitting room, bar, restaurant, conservatory; walled garden
CREDIT CARDS AE, DC, MC, V **CHILDREN** accepted
DISABLED 4 bedrooms with easy access **PETS** accepted
CLOSED never **PROPRIETOR** Peter Pinkster

THE SOUTH-WEST

BEERCROCOMBE, SOMERSET

FROG STREET FARM
~ FARM GUEST-HOUSE ~

Beercrocombe, Taunton, Somerset TA3 6AF
TEL (01823) 480430 **FAX** (01823) 480430

VERONICA COLE has been running her farmhouse retreat, a flower-bedecked 'longhouse' hidden deep in the Somerset countryside, for over 20 years now. Her husband has recently leased the farmland and is now able to give Veronica a helping hand.

The house has considerable character and warmth, with a handsome oak-beamed inglenook in the sitting room and some very antique panelling. Guests walk through the front door straight in to the highly polished dining room. Veronica, an accomplished cook, makes as much as she possibly can for her carefully-prepared set dinner menus, from soups to ice-creams. Eggs come from her own hens, vegetables from Henry's organic garden, beef from the farm.. The couple also own a successful National Hunt stable, and horse-racing features prominently in their lives. The stables at the back of the farm invariably hold a variety of brood mares, hunters and young horses, guarded by the farm collie.

Bedrooms look out on to farmland, cider apple orchards and the pretty garden. They are all spacious and comfortable, with floral duvets, and a mix of antique furniture. One is virtually self-contained, having its own staircase and sitting room, separated from the shared sitting room by superb Jacobean panelling. The atmosphere is friendly, restful and unpretentious.

~

NEARBY Barrington Court; Vale of Taunton.
LOCATION on SW side of village, 10 miles (16 km) SE of Taunton; in gardens, with ample car parking
FOOD breakfast, dinner
PRICE £
ROOMS 3 double, 2 with bath, 1 with shower; all rooms have hairdrier, radio
FACILITIES 3 sitting rooms, dining room; terrace, garden **CREDIT CARDS** not accepted
CHILDREN accepted by arrangement
DISABLED not suitable **PETS** not accepted **CLOSED** Nov to Mar
PROPRIETORS Veronica and Henry Cole

THE SOUTH-WEST

BIGBURY-ON-SEA, SOUTH DEVON

THE HENLEY
~ COASTAL HOTEL ~

Folly Hill, Bigbury-on-Sea, South Devon TQ7 4AR
TEL(01548) 810240 **FAX** (01548) 810240
E-MAIL enquiries@thehenleyhotel.co.uk

RECOMMENDED TO US by an astute reader, The Henley, new to this edition, was described to us as 'the sort of place that I always hope to discover on holiday, and alas, rarely do.' Originally built as a holiday cottage during Edwardian times, the hotel has a beach-house feel and spectacular views that stretch from the Avon Estuary around to Burgh Island. And if simply looking at the sea isn't enough, you can climb down the private cliff path to a stretch of pristine beach.

Although owner Martyn Scarterfield was a PE and Art teacher in a previous life, he comes from a family hotel in Sidmouth and has been in the trade for many years. Co-owner Petra Lampe brings both charm and a sense of warmth and elegance to the hotel. Together, they create a relaxing atmosphere that is, above all, unpretentious.

Bedrooms are simple, yet comfortable and spacious. The dining room has Lloyd Loom furniture and overlooks the sea. Martyn does the cooking and it can be described as "real home cooked food" – excellent quality without any artificial presentation. The menu features a choice of three starters and two mains, one of which will be fresh, locally caught fish.

With its winning combination of great food, beautiful views and friendly owners, we are delighted to welcome The Henley to the guide.

~

NEARBY Burgh Island, Avon Estuary.
LOCATION 20 minutes from A38 beyond Bigbury-on-Sea towards sea; ample car parking
FOOD breakfast, dinner
PRICE ££
ROOMS 6 double and twin, 4 with bath, 2 with shower; all have phone, TV, radio
FACILITIES conservatory/dining room; garden, private cliff path, beach
CREDIT CARDS MC, V **CHILDREN** by arrangement **DISABLED** not suitable
PETS welcome **CLOSED** Nov to March
PROPRIETORS Martyn Scarterfield and Petra Lampe

THE SOUTH-WEST

BRADFORD OLD WINDMILL
~ TOWN GUEST-HOUSE ~

4 Masons Lane, Bradford-on-Avon, Wiltshire BA15 1QN
TEL (01225) 866842 **FAX** (01225) 866648
E-MAIL priscilla@distinctlydifferent.co.uk **WEBSITE** www.bradfordoldwindmill.co.uk

A RECENT VISIT to Peter and Priscilla Robert's extraordinary home confirms that this old windmill still provides guests with a unique experience. Built in 1807, the windmill functioned for only 20 years but left a memorable building in its stead. It boasts a 4-story Cotswold stone tower, conical tiled roof, pointed Gothic windows and restored sail galley.

The rooms, with curved walls and odd-angled corners, offer excellent views over old Bradford and beyond. The suite includes a minstrel gallery and the smallest room has a waterbed. Each room contains curiosities and guidebooks from the Roberts' extensive travels. Bathrooms could be updated.

There is a pretty terrace that also overlooks old Bradford, where breakfast and dinner are served, weather permitting. You get breakfast at a communal table, but special provision is made for honeymoon couples who wish to eat late and alone.

Priscilla will cook dinner if given notice. Recent dinner menus include Caribbean, Thai, Nepalese and other exotic influences. The breakfast menu is extensive and creative. Meals tend to be vegetarian and ingredients are 90 per cent organic. This is a very different kind of guest-house, and one with great character. See also our other windmill B&B on page 208.

~

NEARBY Bath; Kennet and Avon Canal.
LOCATION just N of town centre; with cottage garden and parking for 3 cars
FOOD breakfast, dinner (Mon, Thur, Sat only)
PRICE ££
ROOMS 3; 2 double, 1 suite, all with bath; all rooms have TV
FACILITIES sitting room, dining room; terrace
CREDIT CARDS MC, V
CHILDREN welcome over 6 **DISABLED** access difficult
PETS not accepted **CLOSED** Jan, Feb, Christmas
PROPRIETORS Peter and Priscilla Roberts

THE SOUTH-WEST

BRADFORD-ON-AVON, WILTSHIRE

PRIORY STEPS
~ TOWN GUEST-HOUSE ~

Newtown, Bradford-on-Avon, Wiltshire BA15 1NQ
TEL (01225) 862230 **FAX** (01225) 866248
E-MAIL priorysteps@clara.co.uk **WEBSITE** www.priorysteps.co.uk

HIGH ABOVE the lovely little wool town of Bradford-on-Avon, Carey and Diana Chapman's converted row of weavers' cottages look out over the predominantly Georgian houses interspersed with a smattering of Saxon and medieval buildings. Although only three minutes walk from the centre, Priory Steps is not easy to find. It is so discreetly signposted that it looks like a private home – which it is for the Chapmans and their children. As a result, the pictures and pieces that decorate the house have family connections and the atmosphere is informal and easy-going, especially in the book-lined sitting room.

Each of the bedrooms has a theme – Indian, Chinese and so on. In spite of the cottage architecture, there is nothing cramped about them: they are light and airy, with wonderful views. Beautifully decorated by Diana's mother-in-law, each has its own character and is furnished mainly with antiques.

Diana is a keen cook and dinner is served either at a communal table in the elegant dining room or, on fine days, out on the terrace of the garden looking down over the town. Dinners are three courses, with no choice, but special requirements are happily met, given notice. You will be made to feel like a house guest in a particularly well-run home. On our most recent inspection trip, Priory Steps was closed; be sure to ring ahead.

~

NEARBY Barton Tithe Barn; Bath.
LOCATION off A363 on N side of town; in 0.5 acre garden, with car parking
FOOD breakfast, dinner
PRICE ££
ROOMS 5 double and twin, all with bath; all rooms have TV
FACILITIES sitting room, dining room; terrace, garden
CREDIT CARDS MC, V
CHILDREN accepted
DISABLED access difficult **PETS** not accepted
CLOSED occasionally **PROPRIETORS** Carey and Diana Chapman

THE SOUTH-WEST

MASONS ARMS
~ SEASIDE VILLAGE INN ~

Branscombe, Devon EX12 3DJ
TEL (01297) 680300 **FAX** (01297) 680500
E-MAIL reception@masonsarms.co.uk **WEBSITE** www.masonsarms.co.uk

BRANSCOMBE IS A PICTURESQUE little Devon village, at the end of a winding lane, surrounded by steep, wooded hillsides and overlooking the sea. The National Trust owns most of the land around, and the South Devon Coastal Path passes through it. In other words, this village is a hive of activity, inspiring visits from walkers in winter and beachcomers in summer, many of whom pitch up at the Masons Arms. Welcoming, yes; popular, certainly. It's just what a village pub should be, although its success has meant that the owners have expanded to meet the demand. So what was a simple inn, converted from four cottages, now has two restaurants (one non-smoking), a large function room, 22 rooms spread out over two buildings and eight Garden Cottages.

The bedrooms have a cottagey feel, with pretty fabrics, beamed ceilings and sloping floors, although, on a recent visit we found rooms in the main building tired and dated. On the other hand, the recently upgraded Cottage Rooms are modern and stylish, which one would expect with the increase in price. The bathrooms are a smart slate grey. Food is good pub grub, with the restaurants offering a more up-market, and therefore more costly, menu. As long as you aren't expecting a superabundance of silence or suavity, then the Masons Arms will do.

~

NEARBY South Devon coastal path; Sidmouth.
LOCATION in village 8 miles (11 km) S of Honiton, off A3052 between Sidmouth and Seaton; with ample car parking
FOOD breakfast, lunch, dinner
PRICE £-££
ROOMS 22; 20 double, twin and family with bath ensuite, 2 with separate bath; self-catering cottages; all rooms have phone, TV, hairdrier
FACILITIES sitting room, bar, restaurants; terrace, garden **CREDIT CARDS** MC, V
CHILDREN welcome **DISABLED** access easy to self-catering cottages
PETS accepted **CLOSED** never **PROPRIETOR** Murray Ingles

THE SOUTH-WEST

BRISTOL

HOTEL DU VIN
~ TOWN HOTEL ~

The Sugar House, Narrow Lewins Mead, Bristol, Avon BS1 2NU
TEL (0117) 925 5577 **FAX** (0117) 925 1199
E-MAIL admin@bristol.hotelduvin.com **WEBSITE** www.hotelduvin.com

AFTER ITS REJUVENATING appearances first in Winchester and then in Tunbridge Wells, the Hotel du Vin, concept of hotelier Robin Hutson and wine expert Gerard Basset, has brought style and panache to the hotel scene in Bristol. Converted from a collection of derelict 18thC sugar warehouses, the hotel's gracious Queen Anne frontage belies the wizardry behind its façade. Open brickwork, black-painted girders and sweeping stairs with a curving steel bannister combine traditional industrial elements with contemporary glamour to great effect.

Sponsored by and named after different wine houses, the huge bedrooms contain custom-made, superbly comfortable beds, alongside equally huge bathrooms with dazzling showers and free-standing baths. Though it fronts on to Bristol's main thoroughfare, the hotel's double glazing effectively blocks any traffic noise. Many of the staff who serve in the hotel's Bistro have been imported from the sister hotels at Winchester and Tunbridge Wells, and are well-versed in the Hotel du Vin's ethos of relaxed, unpretentious service of imaginative dishes cooked with a sure hand. The aptly-named Sugar Bar is dominated by a large mural of grapes on the vine, while whitewashed walls, big squashy sofas, wood flooring and rugs contribute to the unhurried, plantation house feel.

~

NEARBY city centre; docks; Christmas steps.
LOCATION in city centre, residents only car parking
FOOD breakfast, lunch, dinner
PRICE £££
ROOMS 40 double and twin, all with bath; all rooms have phone, TV, CD player, minibar, hairdrier
FACILITIES sitting room, billiards room, dining room, bar, humidor, courtyard
CREDIT CARDS AE, DC, MC, V **CHILDREN** accepted
DISABLED access possible, lift/elevator **PETS** guide dogs only
CLOSED never **MANAGER** Lesley Skelt

THE SOUTH-WEST

CHAGFORD, DEVON

GIDLEIGH PARK
~ COUNTRY HOUSE HOTEL ~

Chagford, Devon TQl3 8HH
TEL (01647) 432367 **FAX** (01647) 432574
E-MAIL gidleighpark@gidleigh.co.uk **WEBSITE** www.gidleigh.com

THIS QUINTESSENTIAL COUNTRY HOUSE HOTEL, created 25 years ago by Americans Paul and Kay Henderson, has a low-key, very British appeal. It's all about ticking clocks and curled-up Siamese cats, and enveloping, understated luxury. Take your walking boots and your Labrador and prepare for the very rich, highly-praised cooking of Michael Caines (which merits two Michelin stars) and Paul Henderson's legendary wine cellar. For complete seclusion, take the Thatched Cottage that stands in the grounds.

On the edge of Dartmoor, lost in woods, the house is situated at the end of a long, bumpy, tree-lined lane which opens out to present an idyllic park setting. Behind the house are attractive terraced gardens, giving way to woods; in front, the rocky River Teign.

Inside, the oak-panelled sitting room is large, with a log fire and comfortable furniture, and well stocked with current magazines and periodicals. Bedside books include volumes of Ted Hughes' poetry (he lived nearby and was a frequent visitor). All the bedrooms give an immediate feeling of comfort and friendliness. Two especially attractive ones are next to the main building in a converted chapel. If you are prepared to pay its heart-stoppingly high prices, you will find Gidleigh Park above all relaxing and friendly.

~

NEARBY Castle Drogo; Dartmoor; Rosemoore, Knighthayes Court gardens.
LOCATION 2 miles (3 km) W of Chagford; in 45 acre grounds with ample car parking
FOOD breakfast, lunch, dinner; room service
PRICE ££££
ROOMS 14 double, all with bath; 1 cottage in the grounds; all rooms have phone, TV, hairdrier **FACILITIES** sitting room, bar, loggia, 2 dining rooms; terrace, garden, croquet, fishing, tennis, bowls, putting **CREDIT CARDS** DC, MC, V
CHILDREN accepted; under 7 not allowed in dining room for dinner
DISABLED no special facilities **PETS** welcome
CLOSED never **PROPRIETORS** Paul and Kay Henderson

THE SOUTH-WEST

CHETTLE, DORSET

CASTLEMAN
~ COUNTRY HOUSE HOTEL ~

Chettle, near Blandford Forum, Dorset, DT11 8DB
TEL (01258) 830096 **FAX** (01258) 830051
E-MAIL chettle@globalnet.co.uk **WEBSITE** www.castlemanhotel.co.uk

CHETTLE IS ONE OF THOSE RARE estate villages that has hardly changed in the 150 years it has been in the benign ownership of one family – who live in the fine Queen Anne manor house, open to the public during summer months. Teddy Bourke, one of the family, took on the decrepid ex-dower house ('locals all thought it was haunted') in 1996, together with his partner, Barbara Garnsworthy, transforming it into a charmingly eccentric and very reasonably priced hotel and restaurant. Part of the building dates back 400 years, but it was much altered in Victorian times when it was tricked out with a galleried hall; a richly carved oak Jacobean fireplace was also installed in one of the reception rooms (the other is Regency style) with bookcases to match. Upstairs, the elegant proportions of the rooms have been left intact, and bedrooms are just right: comfortable and in good taste, but without room service or unnecessary frills so as to keep prices sensible; several of the bathrooms have Victorian roll top baths. The 'large' rooms are enormous, one with a huge bay window overlooking the fields, whilst the smaller ones are still spacious. The garden could do with some love.

The Castleman's restaurant – a long, rather plain room at the rear – serves straightforward traditional and modern British dishes – and the bill is not indigestible, either. 'Superb value', say regular guests.

~

NEARBY Kingston Lacy House; Cranborne Chase; Salisbury.
LOCATION in village, signposted off A354, 6 miles (9 km) NE of Blandford; ample car parking
FOOD breakfast, Sunday lunch, dinner
PRICE ££
ROOMS 8 double, all with bath; all rooms have phone, TV, hairdrier
FACILITIES dining room, 2 sitting rooms, bar; garden **CREDIT CARDS** MC, V
CHILDREN welcome **DISABLED** access difficult
PETS not accepted in house; 2 stables available for guests' horses and dogs
CLOSED Feb **PROPRIETORS** Edward Bourke and Barbara Garnsworthy

THE SOUTH-WEST

DITTISHAM, DEVON

FINGALS
~ MANOR HOUSE HOTEL ~

Old Coombe Manor Farm, Dittisham, near Dartmouth, Devon Q6 OJA
TEL (01803) 722398 **FAX** (01803) 722401
E-MAIL richard@fingals.co.uk **WEBSITE** www.fingals.co.uk

FINGALS IS DIFFERENT, and those who love it will really love it – which sums up why we remain enthusiastic about this manor farmhouse in a secluded valley, close to the River Dart. Owner Richard Johnston, calls it a 'hotel and restaurant', but in practice, Fingals comes much closer to the 'country house party' type of guest-house, where it is normal (though not obligatory) for guests to share a table in the wood-panelled dining room at mealtimes.

The house – 17thC with Queen Anne front additions – has plenty of charm, with a stylish blend of new and old furniture, pine and oak. An adjacent self-catering barn is ideal for a family or for those wanting extra space and privacy.

Fingals is an exceptionally relaxed place – you pour your own drinks, eat breakfast whenever you like, be it morning or afternoon – and those who insist on everything being just so are likely to be disappointed. The four-course dinners, chosen from a short menu, are modern in style, competent in execution, and ample in quantity. A laid-back place with a laid-back yet thoroughly professional proprietor.

~

NEARBY Dartmouth Castle.
LOCATION 4 miles (6 km) N of Dartmouth, 1 mile (1.5 km) from village; with garden and ample car parking
FOOD breakfast, snack lunch, dinner
PRICE ££
ROOMS 13; 11 double, 2 family rooms, all with bath; all rooms have phone; some have TV **FACILITIES** dining room, bar, library, TV room, swimming pool, jacuzzi, sauna, snooker, croquet, tennis, table-tennis; sailboat available
CREDIT CARDS AE, MC, V
CHILDREN accepted
DISABLED access difficult
PETS accepted but not in public rooms
CLOSED New Year to Easter **PROPRIETOR** Richard Johnston

THE SOUTH-WEST

DORCHESTER, DORSET

CASTERBRIDGE
∾ TOWN HOTEL ∾

49 High East Street, Dorchester, Dorset DT1 1HU
TEL (01305) 264043 **FAX** (01305) 260884
E-MAIL reception@casterbridgehotel.co.uk **WEBSITE** www.casterbridgehotel.co.uk/

YOU MIGHT EASILY drive straight past the Casterbridge, assuming it to be just another one of those dreary country town hotels which seem to dominate British high streets. However, when you learn that it is owned by the same family as the Priory (see page 86) you might stop and wisely think again. The hotel has been in the Turner family since 1930, but in the 1980s family scion Stuart and wife Rita took it over and started on the monumental task of updating its moribund interior.

They succeeded in bringing life to an old Georgian building that remains faithful to its origins, but incorporates the modern touches we all crave; above all it is a very comfortable place in which to stay. A drawing room has been decorated in soft blue-greys and pink, with several large, pleasing oil paintings and an abundance of reading matter. The Georgian furniture is all in keeping. A well-stocked bar next door leads into a delightful conservatory and to a little courtyard with fountain beyond. Unlike the Priory at Wareham, the Casterbridge only offers bed and breakfast. The bedrooms are prettily decorated, with delightful wallpapers, quality fabrics and pleasant bathrooms. Bedrooms in the modern annexe beyond the courtyard are equally comfortable, but have less charm than those in the main building. The Turners are charming hosts and happy to help their guests.

∾

NEARBY Hardy country; Dorset coast.
LOCATION on main road in centre of town; limited street parking
FOOD breakfast
PRICE ££
ROOMS 15; 10 double, 5 single, all with bath or shower; all rooms have phone, TV, hairdrier **FACILITIES** sitting room, bar, conservatory/breakfast room; patio garden
CREDIT CARDS AE, DC, MC, V **CHILDREN** welcome
DISABLED 2 rooms on ground floor **PETS** not accepted
CLOSED Christmas Day and Boxing Day **PROPRIETORS** Stuart and Rita Turner

THE SOUTH-WEST

EVERSHOT, DORSET

SUMMER LODGE
~ COUNTRY HOUSE HOTEL ~

Summer Lane, Evershot, Dorset DT2 0JR
TEL (01935) 83424 **FAX** (01935) 83005
E-MAIL reception@summerlodgehotel.co.uk **WEBSITE** www.summerlodgehotel.com

THE CORBETTS ARE the living evidence that not all 'professional' hoteliers are mediocre; we don't know what contribution they made to guests' happiness when they were at the Savoy, but the dedication they have applied to that cause since they escaped to Dorset is remarkable indeed. A recent inspection confirmed that their standards, and enthusiasm, remain unchanged. Our only quibble: the lack of a non-smoking sitting room.

For many visitors, Summer Lodge is all that a country house hotel should be. The Georgian/Victorian building is on just the right scale to give a sense of slight extravagance without being intimidating, and the Corbetts and their staff are masters at making guests feel at home in it. French windows lead from the public rooms (William Morris fabrics, open fires) to the beautiful flowery garden. Charming bedrooms range from the merely delightful to the quite grand. Bathrooms are spacious and have large white fluffy towels.

The surrounding countryside has retained its rural beauty and there are many places of interest to visit, and some good pubs for lunch. The hotel's cream tea (included in half board rates) is a tempting reason to return there in the afternoon, and dinner remains a highlight.

~

NEARBY Minterne and Maperton Gardens; Montacute, Melbury deer park.
LOCATION 15 miles (24 km) NW of Dorchester, off A37 on edge of village; ample car parking
FOOD breakfast, lunch, dinner; room service
PRICE ££££
ROOMS 17; 13 double, 3 single, 1 suite, all with bath; all rooms have phone, TV, hairdrier, radio **FACILITIES** dining room, sitting room, bar, reading room; garden, croquet, heated swimming pool, tennis court **CREDIT CARDS** AE, DC, MC, V
CHILDREN accepted **DISABLED** access good to ground-floor bedrooms
PETS accepted by arrangement (£7.50 per night) **CLOSED** never
PROPRIETORS Nigel and Margaret Corbett

THE SOUTH-WEST

FARNHAM, DORSET

THE MUSEUM INN
⟶ VILLAGE HOTEL ⟵

Farnham, Blandford Forum, Dorset DT11 8DE
TEL(01725) 516261 **FAX** (01725) 516988
E-MAIL themuseuminn@supanet.com **WEBSITE** www.museum.inn.co.uk

THE CASTLEMAN HOTEL in Chettle is now joined by another really excellent place in which to eat and stay in the neighbouring, and equally delightful, village of Farnham on Cranbourne Chase. It was built by the father of modern archaeology, General Augustus Henry Lane-Foxx Pitt-Rivers, as accommodation for visitors to his nearby museum. It is exceedingly clean and the food is good.

Today, the museum has undergone a complete refurbishment after a long spell as a low-key, rather dismall pub, and it now combines a popular inn, with imaginative bar food served in several different areas, a more formal restaurant, and eight guest bedrooms. These are simple and stylish, with attractive prints on cream walls, and *toille-de-jouey* or checked fabrics for bedspreads, curtains and upholstered chairs. Owners Mark Stephenson and Vicky Elliot ensure a laid-back atmosphere, employing friendly young staff from Australia and New Zealand. There's always a buzz around the bar, and Mark Treasure's food in the restaurant is making waves. A great new place.

⟶

NEARBY Blandford Forum; Cranbourne Chase; Dorchester, Salisbury.
LOCATION in village, 7.5 miles NE of Blandford Forum, off A354 to Salisbury
FOOD breakfast, lunch, dinner
PRICE ££
ROOMS 8 double and twin, all with bath and shower; all rooms have phone, TV, modem point, hairdrier
FACILITIES bar, conservatory, sitting room, dining room
CREDIT CARDS DC, MC, V
CHILDREN accepted over 5
DISABLED 4 rooms on ground floor
PETS accepted
CLOSED never; restaurant open Fri dinner, Sat dinner, Sun lunch
OWNERS Mark Stephenson and Vicky Elliot

THE SOUTH-WEST

FOWEY, CORNWALL

FOWEY HALL

~ SEASIDE FAMILY HOTEL ~

Hanson Drive, Fowey, Cornwall PL23 1ET
TEL (01726) 833866 **FAX** (01726) 834100
E-MAIL info@foweyhall.com **WEBSITE** www.foweyhall.com

FOR A HOLIDAY HOTEL that caters to the whims of children and adults in equal measure, look no futher than Fowey Hall. The idea is to keep the children happy with a long list of activities, and adults likewise content with good food and luxurious accommodation.

On a hill overlooking Fowey Harbour, the imposing building was allegedly Kenneth Graham's inspiration for Toad Hall in *Wind in the Willows*. Built over 100 years ago by a former Lord Mayor of London, it is a turreted white mansion with the feel of a small French château and none of the oppressiveness associated with Victorian domestic architecture. Public rooms are warm and welcoming, some with log fires, and most with a view over the harbour. There are two dining rooms, one in the style of a Palm Court, which serves a brasserie menu, the other an elegant adult-only affair. Bedrooms are impressively furnished with the needs of a family in mind; those with sitting areas in the turrets are great fun for children. During the day, parents can relax, while their offspring cavort in Four Bears Den and The Garage, staffed by nannies.

~

NEARBY Fowey; Looe.
LOCATION at the top of the town; ample car parking
FOOD breakfast, lunch, dinner; room service
PRICE £££
ROOMS 24; 12 double and twin, 12 suites, all with bath; all rooms have phone, TV, hairdrier **FACILITIES** 2 dining rooms, sitting room, TV room, video games room, indoor swimming pool, crèche, games room; terrace, garden, croquet, badminton
CREDIT CARDS AE, DC, MC, V **CHILDREN** welcome
DISABLED access limited **PETS** accepted **CLOSED** never
DIRECTORS Tim and Hazel Brocklebank

THE SOUTH-WEST

FROME, SOMERSET

BABINGTON HOUSE

◆ COUNTRY HOUSE HOTEL ◆

Babington, near Frome, Somerset BA11 3RW
TEL (01373) 812266 **FAX** (01373) 812112
E-MAIL reservations@babingtonhouse.co.uk **WEBSITE** www.babingtonhouse.co.uk

BABINGTON WAS THE BRIGHT IDEA of Nick Jones, owner of the trendy Soho Club in London, and bought as a country retreat for club members. There is still talk about 'members' and 'non-members' but in practise anyone can stay here, although it might be better if you were young, or at least young at heart, street-wise, and preferably in the media business. Having said that, everyone is made to feel welcome, in an atmosphere which is so laid-back that it's almost horizontal yet at the same time professional (much helped by the manager, Bodo, who has run some of London's finest hotels). If you are tired of stuffy country house hotels, with too many swags and drapes and no concessions to children, you will find Babington enormously refreshing: a contemporary hotel set in an elegant country house that offers metropolitan chic and unpretentious luxury. Bedrooms are wonderful, with huge bottles of complimentary lotions in the bathrooms (no mean sachets here) and 24-hour room service. You can have any number of beauty treatments in the Cow Shed, where there is also an indoor pool and a gym. Small children are kept occupied in the well-equipped crèche. We would particularly welcome feedback on Babington: how does it feel staying here if your face doesn't fit?; how did you cope with life in the bar/sitting room?

◆

NEARBY Bath; Bradford-on-Avon.
LOCATION in countryside, 15 miles (24 km) S of Bath; ample car parking
FOOD breakfast, lunch, dinner; room service
PRICE ££££
ROOMS 28 double and twin, all with bath; all rooms have phone, TV, DVD player, CD player, fax/modem point, minibar, hairdrier **FACILITIES** sitting room/bar, snooker room, dining room, bistro, computers, indoor and outdoor swimming pools, health club, crèche, cinema, chapel; terrace, garden, tennis court
CREDIT CARDS AE, DC, MC, V **CHILDREN** welcome
DISABLED bedrooms on ground floor and adapted WC
PETS accepted **CLOSED** never **PROPRIETOR** Nick Jones

The South-West

Gillan, Cornwall

Tregildry
∼ Coastal Rural hotel ∼

Gillan, Manaccan, Helston, Cornwall TR12 6HG
Tel (01326) 231378 **Fax** (01326) 231561
E-MAIL trgildry@globalnet.co.uk **WEBSITE** www.tregildryhotel.co.uk

Getting to Tregildry through twisting country lanes is something of a challenge; it's well off the beaten track and you should be sure to ask the hotel for directions before you set out. What's special about it? Certainly not the pebbledash building itself, which owners Lynne and Huw Phillips readily agree is unexciting. The view, on the other hand, is unforgettable. On a high point above the Lizard Peninsula, Tregildry commands a magical panorama over the Helford River and Falmouth Bay.

Lynne and Huw could do little to change the exterior, beyond painting it, but they have transformed the interior, which could never be called unexciting. It's all very sunny, using bright, bold colours such as apricots and yellows, with rattan and Indonesian furniture lending a vaguely colonial look. The bedrooms are attractive and well-equipped, and they all have views of the sea, though No 3, with its double aspect, is the favourite. Behind the hotel, a footpath leads down to what is effectively a private beach – a great bonus.

Our inspector commented on the helpfulness and professionalism of its owners, and also enjoyed Huw's (modern British) cooking.

∼

Nearby National Trust Coast; Cornish garden; coastal walks and beaches.
Location 12 miles from Helston on Lizard Peninsula, overlooking Helford River and Cornish coast; ample car parking
Food breakfast, dinner; full licence
Price ££
Rooms 6 double, 3 twin, 1 single, all with bath; all rooms have phone, TV, radio, tea/coffee kit, hairdrier
Facilities sitting room, library, dining room; terrace
Credit cards MC, V **Children** welcome over 8
Disabled access difficult **Pets** accepted
Closed Nov to Feb
Proprietors Huw and Lynne Phillips

THE SOUTH-WEST

GILLINGHAM, DORSET

STOCK HILL HOUSE

~ COUNTRY HOUSE HOTEL ~

Gillingham, Dorset SP8 5NR
TEL (01747) 823626 **FAX** (01747) 825628
E-MAIL reception@stockhillhouse.co.uk **WEBSITE** www.stockhillhouse.co.uk

THIS RESTORED VICTORIAN MANOR HOUSE, reached up a long drive through wooded grounds, has been immaculately furnished and decorated in indivual, opulent and somewhat heavy turn-of-the-century style by its hands-on owners, the Hausers, who have been at the helm for the past 17 years. Bedrooms are luxurious, and although the atmosphere is definitely formal, one is relieved to discover that it is also genuinely warm and friendly. Three of the bedrooms are in a separate coach house, and are more contemporary in style.

Peter Hauser does all the cooking and produces superb results. His Austrian roots are reflected in the varied, generous menu, which changes daily. Fruit and vegetables come from his impressive walled kitchen garden. While he works away in the kitchen, guests are apt to pop in for a chat or to see what he is planning for dinner that evening. Many of the hotel's staff are recruited from Germany and they are attentive and friendly.

The extensive grounds include formal gardens and a tennis court. More reports would be appreciated.

~

NEARBY Shaftesbury; Stourhead House and Gardens.
LOCATION 5 miles (8 km) NW of Shaftesbury on B3081; in 11-acre grounds with ample car parking
FOOD breakfast, lunch, dinner
PRICE ££££
ROOMS 9 double, 8 with bath, 1 with shower; all rooms have TV, phone, hairdrier
FACILITIES sitting room, dining room, breakfast room, parkland, kitchen garden, tennis court, croquet, putting green
CREDIT CARDS MC, V
CHILDREN welcome over 7
DISABLED 1 suite on ground floor **PETS** not accepted
CLOSED restaurant only, Sat and Mon lunch
PROPRIETORS Peter and Nita Hauser

THE SOUTH-WEST

GULWORTHY, DEVON

HORN OF PLENTY

~ COUNTRY RESTAURANT-WITH-ROOMS ~

Gulworthy, Tavistock, Devon PL19 8JD
TEL *(01822) 832528* **FAX** *(01822) 832528*
E-MAIL enquiries@thehornofplenty.co.uk **WEBSITE** www.thehornofplenty.co.uk

THE HORN OF PLENTY has long featured in the pages of this guide, despite the several changes of ownership which it has undergone in recent years. Readers' letters told us that the standard of the bedrooms was not high enough during the last regime, but a recent inspection reassured us that the enthusiastic new owners, Paul and Andie Roston, had largely put things right .

Built in 1830 by the Marquess of Tavistock, the secluded, creeper-covered house is approached down a short avenue of tall trees and has a splendid location overlooking the Tamar Valley, a view shared by the bedrooms, some of which have small terraces. The majority are in a converted coach house 50 yards from the main house; they are comfortable and well-equipped, decorated in modern style, with light floral fabrics and pine furniture and a host of minor luxuries. Best however, are the two rooms above the restaurant in the main house which the Rostons have recently refurbished.

The Horn of Plenty is primarily a restaurant, and dinner is the main event, skilfully prepared by chef, and now co-owner, Peter Gorton (well-known now, thanks to a recent television series) and served in front of picture windows in the two-part dining room.

~

NEARBY Cotehele House; Dartmoor; Plymouth.
LOCATION 3 miles (5 km) W of Tavistock on A390; with ample car parking
FOOD breakfast, lunch, dinner
PRICE £££
ROOMS 10; 8 double and twin, 6 with bath, 2 with shower, 2 suites with bath; all rooms have phone, TV, video, minibar, hairdrier
FACILITIES sitting room, bar, restaurant; terrace, garden
CREDIT CARDS MC, V **CHILDREN** accepted; over 7 in restaurant for dinner
DISABLED 2 suitable bedrooms **PETS** accepted by arrangement
CLOSED Christmas **PROPRIETORS** Paul and Andie Roston and Peter Gorton

THE SOUTH-WEST

BEL ALP HOUSE
~ COUNTRY HOTEL ~

Haytor, near Bovey Tracey, Devon TQ13 9XX
TEL (01364) 661217 **FAX** (01364) 661292

PEACEFULLY SET IN eight lush acres, this is a fine, white-painted Edwardian house high above Haytor, enjoying magnificent views over a patchwork of fields and woodland and the rolling foothills of Dartmoor.

Bel Alp House was once owned by the tobacco millionairess Dame Violet Wills; with its present owners, Jack and Mary Twist, it has fallen into very caring hands. We are delighted to see that they have fulfilled the much needed promise they made when they took to upgrading the bedrooms and improving all the facilities. Consequently, the guest rooms, which are furnished and decorated with an emphasis on quiet, restful colours, are now among the largest and most comfortable that you are likely to come across. 'Our smallest room', according to Jack, has an area double the size of many hotel bedrooms. Bathrooms are equally spacious, with modern fittings, except for the two which feature original Edwardian basins and baths mounted on marble plinths.

Public rooms are light and airy, with large bay windows looking south over the moor. Dinner comprises a set menu, with a few daily changing choices. A recent visitor enthuses about the food and the warm welcome. A quiet, steady place.

~

NEARBY Haytor Rocks; Lustleigh; Dartmoor National Park; Castle Drogo; Torquay.
LOCATION in countryside, E of Haytor, 2.5 miles (4 km) W of Bovey Tracey off B3387; ample car parking
FOOD breakfast, lunch by arrangement, dinner
PRICE ££
ROOMS 8 double and twin, all with bath; all rooms have phone, TV, hairdrier
FACILITIES 2 sitting rooms, dining room; garden.
CREDIT CARDS AE, DC, MC, V
CHILDREN accepted **DISABLED** access possible
PETS accepted **CLOSED** Christmas and New Year
PROPRIETORS Jack and Mary Twist

THE SOUTH-WEST

HINTON CHARTERHOUSE, AVON

HOMEWOOD PARK

~ COUNTRY HOUSE HOTEL ~

Hinton Charterhouse, nr Bath, Avon BA2 7TB
TEL (01225) 723731 **FAX** (01225) 723820
E-MAIL res@homewoodpark.com **WEBSITE** www.homewoodpark.com

HOMEWOOD PARK, has been in these pages for over a decade and has undergone several changes of ownership in this time, most recently, in 1998. It used to be in the hands of Stephen and Penny Ross (now at the Queensberry – see page 33). Homewood Park still uses the formula of mixing the informal with the solicitous in supremely elegant surroundings.

The large Georgian building is surrounded by award-winning gardens and parkland. Flowers from the garden and the restored greenhouses are used to decorate the hotel. Bedrooms are individually decorated in country house style – matching curtains, bedcovers and canopied bedheads in soft prints – while in the bathrooms Italian tiles and stencilling give a slightly exotic air.

Chef Jean de la Rouzière, new to Homewood Park, has brought a blend of French and English food to the menu. Some recent comments from visitors imply that the hotel has 'lost its spark', with bedrooms which are beginning to look tired. We would welcome further reports.

~

NEARBY American Museum; Bath.
LOCATION 6 miles (8 km) S of Bath, close to A36; in 10-acre grounds with ample car parking
FOOD breakfast, lunch, dinner; room service
PRICE £££
ROOMS 17 double, 2 suites, all with bath; all rooms have phone, TV, hairdrier, most have fax/modem points
FACILITIES sitting room, bar, study, 3 dining rooms; garden, tennis, croquet, swimming pool
CREDIT CARDS AE, DC, MC, V
CHILDREN accepted
DISABLED access easy; 2 ground-floor bedrooms
PETS not accepted
CLOSED never **PROPRIETOR** A. Moxon

THE SOUTH-WEST

COURT BARN

⟶ COUNTRY HOUSE HOTEL ⟵

Clawton, Holsworthy, Devon EX22 6PS
TEL (01409) 271219 **FAX** (01409) 271309
E-MAIL courtbarnhotel@talk21.com **WEBSITE** www.hotels-devon.com

COURT BARN LACKS any trace of stuffiness or pretentiousness; and it has an abundance of easy-going warmth. It is a four-square house, dating from the 16th century but partly rebuilt in 1853, where antiques, souvenirs, books and games jostle with sometimes unusual furnishings in a carefree medley of patterns. The result is reassuring: this home-like environment spells comfort far beyond the meretricious harmony of hotels colour-matched by designers. And its owners, Susan and Robert Wood, spare no effort to make you feel at home and welcome.

Downstairs, there is a drawing room with open log fire and views over the garden, a breakfast room which looks out on to the croquet lawn, and an elegant dining room which is candlelit in the evenings. The food, on our most recent visit, was satisfying, accompanied by an extensive wine list, annotated by Robert ('Norwegian wines are terrible and may account for the country's lowest wine consumption in Europe').

Beautifully kept park-like grounds surround the house; croquet hoops, putting holes, badminton and lawn tennis suggest plenty to do outside. Beyond are gently rolling hills; and Court Barn is perfectly placed for exploring both Devon and Cornwall.

⟶

NEARBY Bude, Boscastle, Tintagel, Hartland Abbey, Dartmoor.
LOCATION on A388 from Launceston to Holsworthy, at Clawton; ample car parking
FOOD breakfast, lunch, dinner
PRICE ££
ROOMS 8; 7 double and twin, 1 suite, all with bath; all rooms have phone, TV, hairdrier **FACILITIES** dining room, breakfast, drawing room, TV room; garden, croquet, badminton, lawn tennis, 4-hole pitch and putt
CREDIT CARDS AE, DC, MC, V **CHILDREN** accepted
DISABLED access difficult
PETS accepted by arrangement
CLOSED never **PROPRIETORS** Robert and Susan Wood

THE SOUTH-WEST

ILMINSTER, SOMERSET

THE OLD RECTORY

~ COUNTRY HOUSE BED-AND-BREAKFAST ~

Cricket Malherbie, Ilminster, Somerset TA19 0PW
TEL (01460) 54364 **FAX** (01460) 51374
E-MAIL theoldrectory@malherbie.freeserve.co.uk **WEBSITE** www.malherbie.freeserve.co.uk

New to the guide this year, The Old Rectory at Cricket Malherbie lies down a winding road in the Somerset countryside. The main building dates from the mid-16th century, although the old barns on the site started as workman's cottages and could possibly be even older. A thatched roof and carved Tudor beams lend character to the oldest part of the house. Owners Patricia and Michael Fry-Folley are particularly proud of the Strawberry Hill Gothic windows and the Georgian shuttered windows and original paintings in the dining room.

Decorated in soothing creams, beiges and greens, the five bedrooms feature pretty floral fabrics and have charmingly uneven floors. One bed has a headboard made of plaster casts taken from carved Taunton church pew ends. Smaller bathrooms have been made roomier by creative fixtures.

You can have dinner by arrangement, served at a communal table. The menu features all-local produce, for example, free range Langport chicken marinated in lime with risotto, smoked eels, vegetables from the garden, soft fruits when in season (and dried in the winter). The West Country cheeses are all produced within 15 miles of here.

A calming retreat, professionally run, but friendly.

~

NEARBY Montacute, Barrington Court Gardens, Lyme Regis.
LOCATION off A358, turn left at road signposted Ilminster, after 1 mile take lane on right signposted Cricket Malherbie – on left 200 yards past the church
FOOD breakfast, dinner by arrangement
PRICE ££
ROOMS 35, 4 double, 1 twin, all with bath; all rooms with TV, clock radio; some have VCR **FACILITIES** sitting room, dining room; garden
CREDIT CARDS MC, V **CHILDREN** not accepted
DISABLED access difficult **PETS** not accepted
CLOSED 4 days over Christmas
PROPRIETORS Patricia and Michael Fry-Foley

THE SOUTH-WEST

KINGSWEAR, DEVON

NONSUCH HOUSE
~ RIVERSIDE VILLAGE GUEST-HOUSE ~

Church Hill, Kingswear, Dartmouth, Devon TQ6 0BX
TEL (01803) 752829 **FAX** (01803) 752357
E-MAIL enquiries@nonsuch-house.co.uk **WEBSITE** www.nonsuch-house.co.uk

THE NOBLE FAMILY are old friends of this guide, having for many years run Langshott Manor near Horley in Surrey with great warmth and professionalism. Their most recent venture takes us from Gatwick to Devon, which is primarily run by their son, Christopher (Kit).

Nonsuch House in fact combines two tall, slim houses which stand, rather unprepossessingly, on a hairpin bend in a one-way system high above the Dartmouth ferry at Kingswear. The views, looking across the river towards Dartmouth, are superb, and can be had from all the windows. Bedrooms are named after shipping forecasts and are smart, comfortable and well-equipped – certainly a cut above the normal guest-house. They are also in the process of refurbishing the bedrooms and making them all en suite. The sitting room is decorated in rich, warm colours and furnished with large, comfy sofas and an open fire. The dining room is a deep green, small yet intimate, leading on to a conservatory that also has stunning views to the sea. This in turn leads down the hill to a lovely little garden for residents to use.

Kit's cooking is simple yet delicious, with fresh seafood every day and an award-winning breakfast. The family are also able to organise any of the varied activities around Dartmouth, such as sailing, river trips, or recommending bracing walks.

~

NEARBY Dartmouth; Dartmoor; Torquay.
LOCATION from Dartmouth ferry to Kingswear, take Fore Street, then turn sharp right after 100 yards on to Church Hill; street car parking
FOOD breakfast, dinner
PRICE ££
ROOMS 3 double, 2 with shower, 1 with bath; all rooms have TV
FACILITIES sitting room, dining room, conservatory; terrace, garden
CREDIT CARDS MC, V **CHILDREN** accepted over 10
DISABLED 1 room suitable **PETS** not accepted **CLOSED** never
PROPRIETOR Kit Noble

THE SOUTH-WEST

LACOCK, WILTSHIRE

AT THE SIGN OF THE ANGEL

~ VILLAGE INN ~

6 Church Street, Lacock, near Chippenham, Wiltshire SN15 2L[ ]B
TEL (01249) 730230 **FAX** (01249) 730527
E-MAIL angel@lacock.co.uk **WEBSITE** www.lacock.co.uk

LACOCK AND THE SIGN OF THE ANGEL go hand-in-hand: the 'perfect' English village (almost entirely in the preserving hands of the National Trust) and the epitome of the medieval English inn – half-timbered without, great log fires, oak panelling, beamed ceilings, splendid old beds and polished antique tables within.

There are many such inns sprinkled around middle England, but most are better enjoyed over a beer or two, or a meal, than overnight. Even here, the rooms vary in comfort and none could be called spacious. But they are all cosy and charming nonetheless, and full of character. The Angel is emphatically run as a small hotel rather than a pub – tellingly, there are no bars, and the residents' oak-panelled sitting room on the first floor is quiet. It has belonged to the Levis family for over 40 years, and is now jointly run by daughter-in-law Lorna Levis and George Hardy with the help of village ladies. Lorna and George also share the traditional cooking (best for Sunday lunch). Breakfast offers old-timers such as junket and prunes, as well as a huge cooked meal if you want it.

If the rooms in the inn itself are booked, don't turn down the cottage annexe, which is equally attractive and pleasantly secluded. The Angel's gardens are somewhat scruffy – probably due to the ducks.

~

NEARBY Lacock Abbey; Bowood House; Corsham Court; Sheldon Manor.
LOCATION 3 miles (5 km) S of Chippenham off A350, in middle of village; with gardens, and some car parking
FOOD breakfast, lunch, dinner
PRICE ££
ROOMS 10; 8 double, 2 twin, all with bath; all rooms have phone, TV, rooms in main inn have fax/modem points **FACILITIES** 3 dining rooms, sitting room; terrace, garden
CREDIT CARDS AE, DC, MC, V **CHILDREN** accepted **DISABLED** 1 room on ground floor
PETS accepted **CLOSED** Christmas; restaurant only, Mon lunch
PROPRIETORS George Hardy and Lorna Levis

THE SOUTH-WEST

LEWDOWN, DEVON

LEWTRENCHARD MANOR

~ MANOR HOUSE HOTEL ~

Lewdown, near Oakhampton, Devon EX20 4PN
TEL (01566) 783256 **FAX** (01566) 783332
E-MAIL s&j@lewtrenchard.co.uk **WEBSITE** www.lewtrenchard.co.uk

DRIVING EAST DOWN the narrow road from Lewdown, on the edge of Dartmoor, nothing quite prepares you for the first sight of Lewtrenchard Manor, a magnificent 16thC stone manor house, with some Victorian additions, approached by an avenue of beech trees and set in stunningly beautiful grounds which lead down to a lake studded with swans.

The interior is equally impressive. The massive reception rooms are rich in ornate ceilings, oak panelling, carvings and large open fireplaces. Despite its size, however, the hotel has the warm and hospitable atmospher of a much humbler building, engendered in great part by its hostess, Sue Murray. Peek into the drawing room on your arrival, and you'll be hopping to get in there and curl up with a good book.

On the first floor, a splendid long gallery, full of family paintings and portraits, leads to the spacious bedrooms, all of which have extensive views through leaded windows and over the Devon countryside.

A former owner of Lewtrenchard was the Reverend Sabine Baring Gould (who wrote, amongst others, the hymn Onward, Christian Soldiers). Mercifully, he largely resisted the Victorian habit of embellishing an already beautiful building.

~

NEARBY Dartmoor; Tintagel; Exeter; Boscastle.
LOCATION from old A30 at Lewdown, take road signposted Lewtrenchard; in 11-acre grounds with ample car parking
FOOD breakfast, light weekday lunch, Sun lunch, dinner
PRICE ££–£££
ROOMS 9; 7 double and twin, 2 suites, all with bath; all rooms have phone, TV, hairdrier **FACILITIES** sitting room, bar lounge, restaurant, breakfast room, ballroom; garden, croquet, fishing lake **CREDIT CARDS** AE, DC, MC, V
CHILDREN under 5 by arrangement **DISABLED** access difficult **PETS** accepted
CLOSED never **PROPRIETORS** Sue and James Murray

THE SOUTH-WEST

ARUNDELL ARMS
~ FISHING INN ~

Lifton, Devon PL16 0AA
TEL (01566) 784666 **FAX** (01566) 784494
E-MAIL reservations@arundellarms.com **WEBSITE** www.arundellarms.com

A 200-YEAR-OLD COACHING INN, on a site that dates back to Saxon times, which is famous for fishing and food. Traditional country pursuits are taken seriously here: the hotel runs a series of courses on fly fishing for both beginners and the experienced, but people also come to the Arundell Arms for riding, golf, bird watching and to enjoy some of the loveliest country in England. Anglers have 20 miles of private fishing and a 90-feet -deep lake at their disposal.

Then there is the food, for which resident chef Philip Burgess has established a fine reputation. You might start with a homemade soup followed by pan-fried salmon with a ginger and chilli salsa, and end with basil ice-cream with poached pears and raspberries. Almost all the staff are local people and tend to stay for a long time, following the example of the proprietor Anne Voss-Bark who has managed the hotel since 1961.

From the sitting room you can see the garden and the 250-year-old former cockpit, now a tackle room. There are two rather grand interconnecting dining rooms and, of course, a bar. Bedrooms are homely rather than sophisticated, and those in the old part of the building are preferable to those in the annexe. A friendly, welcoming traditional country inn.

~

NEARBY Dartmoor; Tintagel; Boscastle, Port Isaac, Exeter.
LOCATION 3 miles (5 km) E of Launceston, just off A30 in Lifton; with ample car parking
FOOD breakfast, lunch, dinner
PRICE £££
ROOMS 27; 20 double and twin, 7 single, all with bath; all rooms have phone, TV, hairdrier, fax/modem points **FACILITIES** 2 restaurants, 2 bars, games room, drying room; garden, salmon and trout fishing (20 miles of private rights), fishing lake, fly fishing lessons, organise shooting parties **CREDIT CARDS** AE, DC, MC, V
CHILDREN accepted **DISABLED** access possible **PETS** dogs accepted
CLOSED 3 nights at Christmas **PROPRIETOR** Anne Voss-Bark

THE SOUTH-WEST

THE LIZARD, CORNWALL

LANDEWEDNACK HOUSE
~ COUNTRY HOUSE BED-AND-BREAKFAST ~

Church Cove, The Lizard, Cornwall TR12 7PQ
TEL (01326) 290909 **FAX** (01326) 290192
E-MAIL landewednackhouse@amserve.com

A BEAUTIFUL 17THC former rectory which has been skilfully and sympathetically restored by owners Peter and Marion Stanley to become a warm and elegant private home to which they welcome paying guests. The parish of Landewednack, at the end of the Lizard peninsula, is the most southerly in England and is fortunate enough to have a climate mild enough for most of the year to encourage a wide variety of trees, plants and shrubs to flourish. Marion has made the most of this opportunity and her gardens are a delight.

Inside, the house is equally enchanting. Leading off the flagstoned hall is the dining room with a beamed ceiling and massive granite fireplace where guests can dine by candlelight (by prior arrangement with Marion) in front of a crackling log fire. Breakfast is taken in a separate, smaller room. House guests can relax in the elegant drawing room at any time of the day, or in the evening for pre-dinner drinks. The three bedrooms are all different, and all charming. The best view is from the Yellow Room, with a mahogany half-tester. Through its large bay window you can see across the garden to the church and the sea beyond – a wonderful sight at sunset. This is a non-smoking establishment.

~

NEARBY The Lizard peninsula; St Ives; Isles of Scilly.
LOCATION from Helston take A3083 to Lizard; before entering village turn left to Church Cove, then left towards lifeboat station
FOOD breakfast; other meals by arrangement
PRICE ££
ROOMS 3 double and twin, 1 with bath, 2 with shower; all rooms have phone, TV, hairdrier **FACILITIES** dining room, drawing room, breakfast room; garden, swimming pool **CREDIT CARDS** MC, V **CHILDREN** not accepted
DISABLED access difficult
PETS accepted by arrangement
CLOSED Christmas **PROPRIETORS** Peter and Marion Stanley

THE SOUTH-WEST

MELKSHAM, WILTSHIRE

SHURNHOLD HOUSE
~ MANOR HOUSE GUEST-HOUSE ~

Shurnhold, Melksham, Wiltshire SN12 8DG
TEL (01225) 790555 **FAX** (01225) 793147

Y ET ANOTHER GRAND old house rescued from decay in the late
1980s and put to new use – in this case, a bed-and-breakfast
guest-house. The house is a beautifully proportioned stone-built
Jacobean affair dating from 1640. It sits quite close to a busy main road
on the outskirts of an unremarkable town, but is well shielded by trees
(look for the signs, because you will not spot the house) and well placed
for touring in several directions.

Inside, all is as you would wish. A flagstone floor in the bar/sitting
room, oak beams, log fires and pretty floral fabrics here and in the
breakfast room and sitting room, which is full of books. Period furnishings
are used wherever the opportunity arises and the budget allows. The
beamed bedrooms are spacious, with restrained decoration – perhaps rich
floral drapes against plain white walls – and several different styles of
bed; several have fireplaces. There is a proliferation of cute teddy bears.

Prices have been set at just the right level – higher than your
typical B&B, but at half the rate of many 'country house hotels'
occupying similarly splendid buildings. The licensed bar is an unusual
feature for a B&B establishment.

~

NEARBY Lacock; Bradford-on-Avon.
LOCATION in countryside, 1 mile (1.5 km) NW of Melksham on A365 to Bath; in
large garden with ample car parking
FOOD breakfast
PRICE ££
ROOMS 6 double, 1 family room, all with bath or shower; all rooms have TV
FACILITIES dining room, sitting room, bar/sitting room
CREDIT CARDS AE, MC, V
CHILDREN welcome
DISABLED no special facilities **PETS** accepted by arrangement
CLOSED never **PROPRIETOR** Sue Tanir

THE SOUTH-WEST

MEMBURY, DEVON

LEA HILL

~ COUNTRY BED-AND-BREAKFAST ~

Membury, near Axminster, Devon EX13 7AQ
TEL (01404) 881881 **FAX** (01404) 881890
E-MAIL reception@leahill.co.uk **WEBSITE** www.leahill.co.uk

LEA HILL HAS CHANGED a good deal since our last visit. It used to be a country hotel, but new owner Sue Avis has cut it back to a four-room bed-and-breakfast. Because of the charm of both the building and its owner, and its stunning location, we're glad to keep it in the guide.

The setting really is enchanting: on a prominent hilltop with views over woodland and meadows. The building itself is a prime example of a thatched Devon longhouse with parts dating from the 14th century when it was a farmhouse. Three bedrooms are located in a 400-year-old converted barn. Decorated with chintzy fabrics, they have a country farmhouse feel. The fourth room is located in the main house with exposed beams and charming uneven floors.

You eat a generous breakfast in the Willow Room overlooking the Membury Valley. Dinner is not served, but Sue will produce, if asked, a plate of smoked trout (caught in the trout farm just up the road).

This picturesque B&B is above all friendly and cosy: we received a warm welcome from both Sue and Florrie, her collie cross rescue dog.

~

NEARBY Lyme Regis; Axminster; Sidmouth.
LOCATION in 8-acre grounds, 1 mile (2.5 km) S of Membury; ample car parking
FOOD breakfast, light dinner by arrangement
PRICE ££
ROOMS 4 double and twin, all with bath, 3 holiday cottages; all rooms have TV, hairdrier
FACILITIES breakfast room; terrace, garden, 6-hole par 3 gof course
CREDIT CARDS none
CHILDREN not accepted
DISABLED access difficult
PETS dogs accepted
CLOSED never
PROPRIETOR Sue Avis

THE SOUTH-WEST

MILBORNE, DORSET

OLD VICARAGE
~ COUNTRY HOTEL ~

Milborne Port, Sherborne, Dorset DT9 5AT
TEL (01963) 251117 **FAX** (01963) 251515
E-MAIL theoldvicarage@milborneport.freeserve.co.uk **WEBSITE** www.milborneport.freeserve.co.uk

THE SOMEWHAT FORBIDDING Gothic frontage belies the colourful interior of this interesting venture on the Somerset/Dorset borders. Jörgen Kunath and Anthony Ma (German and Vietnamese in that order) ran a successful restaurant in West London for 13 years. Thus the Old Vicarage is essentially a weekend house-party place, particularly for fans who knew the couple in London, rather than a typical roadside hotel.

Displayed to great effect in the mango-coloured hall, the delightful drawing room and the bedrooms upstairs, Anthony's skill as a painter/decorator is exemplary. The drawing room is stuffed with an eclectic mix of comfortable sofas, gold-painted Russian icons, polished pewter plates, a Vietnamese coffer and a Broadwood baby grand piano. Large mullioned windows look over the park-like gardens and fields beyond.

The south-facing dining room is more simple, with solid bamboo chairs and boat-shaped pine sideboard. It's Anthony's cooking that takes centre-stage here, blending exotic and traditional local flavours. Dinner is only served on Fridays and Saturdays, but both pubs in the village are recommended for their food. The bedrooms in the coach house have recently been enlarged and refurbished.

~

NEARBY Yeovil; Glastonbury; Dorchester.
LOCATION in town on A30; in 3-acre garden with ample car parking
FOOD breakfast, dinner (Fri, Sat, only)
PRICE ££
ROOMS 6; 2 double, 1 twin, 3 family, 1 with shower, rest with bath; all rooms have phone, TV, hairdrier **FACILITIES** sitting room, restaurant; terrace, garden, croquet
CREDIT CARDS AE, MC, V **CHILDREN** accepted over 5
DISABLED 1 room with limited access
PETS accepted in coach house (£5 per night)
CLOSED early Jan to early Feb
PROPRIETORS Jörgen Kunath and Anthony Ma

THE SOUTH-WEST

NETTLETON, WILTSHIRE

FOSSE FARMHOUSE
~ COUNTRY HOTEL ~

Nettleton Shrub, Nettleton, near Chippenham, Wiltshsire NS14 7NJ
TEL (01249) 782286 **FAX** (01249) 783066
E-MAIL CaronCooper@compuserve.com **WEBSITE** www.fossefarmhouse.8m.com

CARON COOPER, former presenter of BBC's *Cooking with Confidence*, presides over a small corner of France in the Wiltshire countryside. She has decorated Fosse Farmhouse with some style, mainly *à la française*. The sitting room is in a provincial Normandy style, while across the courtyard the converted stables feature a low, uneven beamed ceiling modelled on a house Caron owned in France. Antiques, including many French pieces, fill the house and Caron runs a small antique shop out back during the summer months. (The pieces in the house are also for sale.)

Bedrooms in the main house feel very much a part of Caron's home. The two doubles are a good size, while the single is small with a shower that could use an update. In the stable block, original cobbled flooring in the downstairs sitting room and light airy bedrooms, makes a pleasing alternative.

Caron's food blends French with English influences. The menu is no-choice, but guests can let her know beforehand of any special needs. You might get rack of lamb with a mint and port wine sauce or chicken *basquaise*; dessert might be sticky toffee pudding or crème brulée.

We have had some readers' reports letters questioning the quality of the food. More reports welcome.

~

NEARBY Castle Combe; Cotswolds.
LOCATION in countryside off B4039, 6 miles (9.5 km) NW of Chippenham, in 1.5 acres of garden with car parking
FOOD breakfast, lunch, dinner
PRICE ££
ROOMS 6; 4 double and twin with bath or shower, 1 single with shower, 1 family room with bath; all rooms have TV, hairdrier
FACILITIES sitting room, dining room, tea room; terrace, garden
CREDIT CARDS MC, V **CHILDREN** accepted **DISABLED** access difficult
PETS accepted by arrangement
CLOSED never **PROPRIETOR** Caron Cooper

THE SOUTH-WEST

BARK HOUSE
~ COUNTRY GUEST-HOUSE ~

Oakford Bridge, Near Bampton, Devon EX16 9HZ
TEL (01398) 351236
WEBSITE www.barkhouse.co.u

OUR MOST RECENT visit to Bark House confirmed our impressions of this delightful guest-house. Alastair Kameen and his assistant, Justine, make a gentle, friendly pair and have created a welcoming and relaxing place to stay. Tucked away in the beautiful Esk Valley, the building is about 200 years old and was originally used to store bark for tanning. It's everyone's idea of a Devon cottage, particularly in spring when the facade is smothered by a magnificent old wisteria. By day, you can explore the woodland paths and gardens behind the house and, opposite the building, a sitting area provides a sunny spot for afternoon tea. By night, the tiny hamlet of Oakfordbridge sparkles in the velvet-black valley while the only sounds are the trickling of a small cascade in the garden and the burbling River Exe.

Inside, the cosy and intimate sitting room, with an open fire, is the perfect place to relax and anticipate dinner. Alastair, whose training includes a prestigious Relais and Châteaux establishment, looks after the cooking and our inspector recently enjoyed a 'heavenly' meal that included ham, mushroom and Gruyère pancakes and a 'divine' sticky date pudding.

The bedrooms reflect the essential simplicity of Bark House. You could almost be at home. Alastair's breakfasts are delicious.

~

NEARBY Exmoor; Knightshayes House; Marwood and Rosemoor gardens
LOCATION in own grounds, on A396 near Bampton; car parking
FOOD breakfast, dinner
PRICE ££
ROOMS 5 double and twin with bath or shower; all rooms have phone, TV
FACILITIES sitting room, dining room; garden, garden croquet
CREDIT CARDS not accepted
CHILDREN accepted **DISABLED** access difficult
PETS accepted
CLOSED for a short period during winter, Mon and Tues in main season
PROPRIETOR Alastair Kameen

THE SOUTH-WEST

PADSTOW, CORWALL

SEAFOOD RESTAURANT & ST PETROC'S HOTEL

~ RESTAURANT-WITH-ROOMS ~

Riverside, Padstow, Cornwall PL28 8BY
TEL (01841) 532700 **FAX** (01841) 532942
E-MAIL reservations@rickstein.com **WEBSITE** www.rickstein.com

RICK STEIN'S PADSTOW EMPIRE now extends to three different places to stay, at varying prices, and three places to eat: his flagship Seafood Restaurant, the Bistro in St Petroc's Hotel, and the Café in Middle Street.

If you are intent on eating at the quayside Seafood Restaurant (superb seafood, straight from the fishing boats, served by friendly staff in a lively dining room) then the bedrooms above make the best choice for a night's stay. They are spacious and more than comfortable in an understated way, with superb estuary views from Nos 5 and 6. What the place lacks in public rooms, it makes up for in laid-back atmosphere and its prime position on the quay. St Edmund's House, behind the restaurant, has six new pricey suites. Less expensive, but no less tasteful, are the rooms in St Petroc's Hotel just up the hill, a little removed from the bustle of the quayside. This is an attractive white-painted building with views across the older parts of town as well as of the estuary. Some rooms are on the small side. The place exudes a friendly ambience, not least in the Bistro, where a short, very reasonably priced menu features meat and vegetable dishes as well as seafood. There are also three attractive, inexpensive rooms above the Café in Middle Street.

~

NEARBY surfing beaches; Trevose Head.
LOCATION in village centre, 4 miles (6 km) NW off A39 between Wadebridge and St Columb; car parking
FOOD breakfast, lunch, dinner
PRICE ££
ROOMS 35 single, double and twin in 3 different buildings, most with bath, some with shower; all rooms have phone, TV, hairdrier; some have minibar
FACILITIES 3 restaurants, bar, sitting room, conservatory **CREDIT CARDS** MC, V
CHILDREN welcome in St Petroc's Hotel and the Café, over 3 in restaurant
DISABLED access possible.
PETS dogs accepted in rooms except St Edmund's House
CLOSED Christmas and New Year **PROPRIETORS** Rick and Jill Stein

THE SOUTH-WEST

PENZANCE, CORNWALL

THE ABBEY

~ TOWN HOTEL ~

Abbey Street, Penzance, Cornwall TR18 4AR
TEL (01736) 366906 **FAX** (01736) 351163
E-MAIL booking@abbey-hotel.co.uk **WEBSITE** www.abbey-hotel.co.uk

W HEN WE LAST VISITED the Abbey, one of our over-riding impressions was of consistent good management. We don't often get reports about it, but this doesn't change our continuing belief that it is one of the most exceptional places to stay in the West Country. Jean and Michael Cox have taken a house with character in the heart of old Penzance (it was built in the mid-17thC and given a Gothic façade in Regency times); they have decorated and furnished it with unstinting care, great flair and a considerable budget; and they have called it a hotel. But they run it much more as a private house, and visitors who expect to find hosts eager to satisfy their every whim may be disappointed.

For its fans, the absence of hovering flunkies is of course a key part of the appeal of The Abbey. But there are other attractions – the confident and original decoration, with abundant antiques and bric-a-brac, the spacious, individual bedrooms (one with an enormous pine-panelled bathroom); the welcoming, flowery drawing-room and elegant dining-room (both with log fires burning 'year-round'); the delightful walled garden behind the house. Dinner can be had at the restaurant next door, owned by the hotel and holder of a Michelin star. Front rooms overlook the harbour and the dry dock.

~

NEARBY Tregwainton Garden; St Michael's Mount; Land's End.
LOCATION in middle of town, overlooking harbour; parking for 6 cars in courtyard
FOOD breakfast, dinner; room service
PRICE ££-£££
ROOMS 7; 4 double and twin, 1 suite, 2 single, 4 with bath, 3 with shower; all rooms have TV, hairdrier
FACILITIES sitting room, dining room; walled garden
CREDIT CARDS AE, MC , V **CHILDREN** accepted
DISABLED access difficult **PETS** accepted in bedrooms only
CLOSED never **PROPRIETORS** Jean and Michael Cox

The South-West

PENZANCE, CORNWALL

PENZANCE ARTS CLUB

~ TOWN HOTEL ~

Chapel Street, Penzance TR18 4AQ
TEL (01736) 363761 **FAX** (01736) 363761
E-MAIL reception@penzanceartsclub.co.uk **WEBSITE:** www.penzanceartsclub.co.uk

NEW TO THE GUIDE this edition, the Penzance Arts Club provides accommodation with artistic flair. Built as the Portuguese Embassy in 1781, the building is a Grade II listed Georgian house. The Club offers a variety of painting and writing courses for members, but non-members can stay too. The focus on local art is evident, with a fortnightly-changing show in the entry hall exhibit space and a plethora of paintings lining the stairwells and rooms. For those who are interested in the South Cornwall art scene or who want a break to restore their creative juices, this is the place.

Although not luxurious, the rooms are light and airy in cheerful blue, peach and lemon hues and hold an eclectic collection of furniture and floral fabrics. Four rooms have free standing showers and wash basins in the corner. Several rooms have views of the harbour.

Dinner and lunch are available in the member's restaurant. You can eat downstairs in rooms which used to be the kitchens of the original house. Mrs Rhubarb, a healthy and feisty cat, presides over the club. Rooms fill up quickly, so be sure to book in advance. The club produces an events guide and some of the activities maybe non-member friendly. It's worth enquiring.

The building isn't particularly well signposted. Keep an eye out for it on the left as you pass by the church.

~

NEARBY Tate at St Ives, Newlyn Gallery, Barbara Hepworth Museum, St Michael's Mount.
LOCATION in centre of town at the lower end of Chapel Street, across from the church
FOOD breakfast, lunch; dinner in summer
PRICE ££
ROOMS 7 double, 1 with bath, rest with shower; all rooms have TV
FACILITIES bar, sitting room, restaurant, exhibit space; writing and art courses
CREDIT CARDS MC, V **CHILDREN** welcome
DISABLED not accessible **PETS** small dogs by arrangement, £10 per week
CLOSED never **PROPRIETOR** Belinda Rushworth-Lund

THE SOUTH-WEST

PENZANCE, CORNWALL

SUMMER HOUSE
～ TOWN RESTAURANT-WITH-ROOMS ～

Cornwall Terrace, Penzance, Cornwall TR18 4HL
TEL (01736) 363744 **FAX** (01736) 360959
E-MAIL reception@summerhouse-cornwall.com **WEBSITE** www.summerhouse-cornwall.com

LINDA AND CIRO ZAINO moved to the tip of Cornwall from London, where Ciro had managed some of the capital's top restaurants, to open this restaurant-with-rooms in a Grade II listed Georgian house close to the sea front. They run it with great panache, reports our inspector, who considers it a 'great find'. He describes it as Mediterranean in colour and feel, quirky in style and breezy in atmosphere. Brighton meets the Neapolitan Riviera.

The former home of one of Cornwall's leading naïve artists, the house is still full of paintings, indiosycratic furniture and lush pot plants. Downstairs there is a little cosy sitting room as well as the most important room in the building, the restaurant. Here blues and yellows predominate in a room that spills out in to a small walled garden burgeoning with terracotta pots and palm trees. Ciro's sunny cooking, using fresh local ingredients, has become a great draw.

Upstairs, the five simple bedrooms are highly individual with a diverse mix of family pieces and collectables. Fresh flowers are everywhere. Linda is charming and her front-of-house presence is just right: enthusiastic, friendly and welcoming. More reports please.

～

NEARBY Trengwainton Garden; St Michael's Mount; Land's End; St Ives; Newlyn School art colony.
LOCATION close to the harbour; drive alongside the harbour and turn right immediately after the Queen's Hotel; car parking
FOOD breakfast, dinner
PRICE ££
ROOMS 5; 4 double, 2 with bath, 2 with shower, 1 twin with shower
FACILITIES sitting room, dining room; small walled garden
CREDIT CARDS MC , V **CHILDREN** not accepted
DISABLED access difficult
PETS not accepted **CLOSED** Jan; restaurant closed Sun or Bank Holiday Mon
PROPRIETORS Ciro and Linda Zaino

THE SOUTH-WEST

ROCK, CORNWALL

ST ENODOC
~ SEASIDE HOTEL ~

Rock, Wadebridge, Cornwall PL27 6LA
TEL (01208) 863394 **FAX** (01208) 863970
E-MAIL enodochotel@aol.com **WEBSITE** www.enodoc-hotel.co.uk

WELL-HEELED BRITISH FAMILIES have flocked to Rock for their bucket-and-spade holidays for generations, but hotels which are both stylish and child-friendly have been thin on the ground hereabouts – until, that is, the emergence in 1998 of the old-established St Enodoc Hotel from a change of ownership and total makeover.

The imposing building is typical of the area: no beauty, but solid and purposeful, with pebbledash walls and slate roof. Emily Todhunter's interior decoration suits its seaside location, with its bright colours (paint, fabrics, painted furniture, modern art), clean lines, and easy-going comfort. The Californian-style Porthilly Bar and split-level Grill is popular with non-residents, although reports indicate that the Pacific Rim food could improve. It has panoramic views, with a wide terrace for outdoor dining. Bedrooms feel like bedrooms rather than hotel rooms, with marvellous views across the Camel Estuary.

With its child-friendly facilities, the hotel is particularly popular during holidays and half terms. Although the hotel has been recently been sold, the management and staff remain unchanged. More reports please.

~

NEARBY Polzeath 2 miles; Padstow (by ferry).
LOCATION overlooking the Camel Estuary, bordering St Enodoc golf course in Rock, 2 miles off B3314 from Wadebridge; car park
FOOD breakfast, lunch, dinner
PRICE £££
ROOMS 15 double, all with bath, 4 suites, 1 with shower, rest with bath; all rooms have phone, TV, radio, hairdrier, fan
FACILITIES sitting room, library, dining room, bar, billiard room, gym, sauna; outdoor heated swimming pool
CREDIT CARDS AE, DC, MC, V
CHILDREN welcome **DISABLED** ramp side entrance; adapted WC on ground floor
PETS not accepted **CLOSED** Jan to mid Feb **MANAGER** Mark Gregory

THE SOUTH-WEST

ROSEVINE, SOUTH CORNWALL

DRIFTWOOD HOTEL

~ COASTAL HOTEL ~

Rosevine, near Portscatho, South Cornwall, TR2 5EW
TEL (01872) 580644 **FAX** (01872) 580801
E-MAIL info@driftwoodhotel.co.uk

'SITUATED ON seven glorious acres of Cornwall's finest heritage coastline,' says the brochure – and Driftwood does indeed provide all you could want on a seaside break. It's a whitewashed converted family house that has been refurbished and renovated into a stylish yet comfortable haven by interior designer Fiona and husband Paul. All ten bedrooms, including the cabin overlooking the beach, have a clean, fresh style that helps maximise the space, as do the cosy sitting and drawing rooms.

Those who love seafood will be happiest here, but the rest of the food is good too. The menu is concentrated on well prepared dishes with fresh local ingredients. The restaurant has spectacular views of the rugged Cornish coastline and you can eat outside, weather permitting. For children there is a TV room with computer games and video library. If you fancy getting out and about there are numerous small pubs and restaurants nearby St Mawes; or hampers can be made up for lazing on the beach.

All around Driftwood there are varied activities that suit different tastes. Great walks and gardens such as Trelissick, the Eden Project, within a short drive; for art lovers, the Tate Gallery at St Ives; or for the energetic, watersports, riding, tennis and golf.

~

NEARBY Eden Project, Tate Gallery, the gardens of Heligan, Glendurgan and Trebah.
LOCATION in countryside just off A3078, S of Truro; ample parking for cars and boats
FOOD breakfast, lunch, dinner
PRICE £££
ROOMS 10 double, 3 with bath, 1 with shower; rest with bath and shower, cabin with double and twin; all rooms have phone, TV, hairdrier
FACILITIES sitting room, drawing room, dining room, bar; garden, beach
CREDIT CARDS AE, MC, V
CHILDREN welcome **DISABLED** access difficult
PETS not accepted **CLOSED** Jan **PROPRIETORS** Paul and Fiona Robinson

THE SOUTH-WEST

RUANHIGHLANES, CORNWALL

CRUGSILLICK MANOR

~ MANOR GUEST-HOUSE ~

Ruanhighlanes, Truro, Cornwall TR2 5LJ
TEL (01872) 501214 **FAX** (01872) 501214/501228
E-MAIL barstow@adtel.co.uk **WEBSITE** www.adtel.co.uk

A RECENT VISIT TO CRUGSILLICK MANOR confirmed our impression that this guest-house is well-maintained and personally, yet profesionally, run. Situated on the lovely Roseland Peninsula, with its many coves and harbours, Crugsillick is a beautiful listed Grade II* Queen Anne manor house. Lying in a sheltered hollow twenty minutes' walk from the Coastal Path and Pendower beach, it has a truly peaceful atmosphere, with views across the attractive gardens to a wooded valley beyond.

The antique-filled house is the home of the Barstows, who are superb hosts, treating their visitors as house guests whilst at the same time recognizing their desire for privacy. Their elegant drawing room, with its log fire and its highly unusual ceiling and scalloped friezes – reputedly moulded by French prisoners during the Napoleonic wars – is for the use of guests, and a four-course dinner is served by candlelight at a communal table in the 17thC dining-room with beautiful flagstone floor. Ingredients often include fruit and vegetables from the garden. Communal dining seems to work well here, with Rosemary expressing her enjoyment at watching previously unacquainted guests exchange telephone numbers upon departure. Bedrooms are extremely comfortable, with cosy beds, prettily decorated and furnished with antiques. A cottage sleeping four (suitable for disabled) is available to rent.

~

NEARBY St Mawes; gardens of Heligan; Trelissick and Trewithin, Eden Project, National Maritime Museum.
LOCATION on road to Veryan off A3078; in extensive garden with ample car parking
FOOD breakfast, picnic lunch on request, dinner
PRICE ££
ROOMS 3 double or twin, 2 with bath, 1 en suite, 1 adjacent, 1 with shower; all rooms have hairdrier **FACILITIES** drawing room, dining room, large hall
CREDIT CARDS MC, V **CHILDREN** accepted over 12 **DISABLED** access difficult
PETS not accepted **CLOSED** never **PROPRIETORS** Oliver and Rosemary Barstow

THE SOUTH-WEST

St Austell, Cornwall

BOSCUNDLE MANOR

～ COUNTRY HOUSE HOTEL ～

Tregrehan, St Austell, Cornwall PL25 3RL
Tel (01726) 813557 **Fax** (01726) 814997
E-MAIL stay@boscundlemanor.co.uk **WEBSITE** www.boscundlemanor.co.uk

DAVID AND SHARON PARKER have recently taken over Boscundle Manor. Although a mainstay of the guide for many years, the hotel was becoming tired and frayed around the edges. The Parkers have stepped in with a full-scale refurbishment plan, which they are pursuing with plenty of enthusiasm. The previous owners took most of the antiques with them, so new furniture, mainly oriental mahogany, features throughout. Carpets and curtains are being replaced, fresh coats of paint are brightening the walls and the bathrooms and bedrooms are gradually being updated.

The grounds, although slightly smaller than they were (and without the converted barn), still have two holes of golf and several pleasant walks through woodlands with badger sett, ponds and old tin mine remains.

The Parkers intend to change the sunny conservatory into a brasserie for casual dining. The formal dining room has a daily-changing menu using Cornish produce whenever available. The butter on the table comes from hand-milked cows and is hand-packed at the local dairy. Sharon looks after the cooking and David eagerly seeks guests' reactions to new dishes.

Reports welcome on how the upgrades eventually turn out.

Nearby Eden Project, Heligan Gardens, Lanhydrock House
Location 2.5 miles (4 km) E of St Austell, close to A390; in 8 acre woodland gardens; ample car parking
Food breakfast, dinner
Price £££
Rooms 14; 7 double and twin, 2 suites, all with bath; 1 single with shower, 1 garden room, 1 cottage with 3 doubles; all rooms have phone, TV, minibar, safe, fridge **Facilities** 1 sitting room, bar, 1 dining room, conservatory/breakfast room; heated indoor and outdoor pool; garden, croquet, 2 practice golf holes, woodland walks, helicopter landing pad, civil wedding licence **Credit cards** AE, MC, V
Children welcome **Disabled** access possible to cottage **Pets** welcome
Closed Jan 1 to Feb 14 **Proprietors** David and Sharon Parker

THE SOUTH-WEST

ST BLAZEY, CORNWALL

NANSCAWEN MANOR HOUSE

~ COUNTRY GUEST-HOUSE ~

Prideaux Road, Luxulyan Valley, near St Blazey, Cornwall PL24 2SR
TEL (01726) 814488
E-MAIL keith@nanscawen.com **WEBSITE** www.nanscawen.com

DATING FROM THE 16THC, Nanscawen Manor has been carefully extended in recent years and sits amidst five acres of mature and very pretty gardens and grounds, with a 'wonderfully located' outdoor swimming pool. Its seclusion is enviable: approached by a fairly steep uphill track from the road, you can't see the house until you are almost upon it. As well as the pool, you can also sink into the whirlpool spa, and there is a terrace on which to sit in the sunshine amongst palm trees and hydrangeas. A recent inspection confirmed readers' reports that the Martin's family home is an excellent bed-and-breakfast guest-house.

The entrance hall, with polished parquet floor, leads to a large, attractive sitting room with an honesty bar. Breakfast is taken in a sunny, cane-furnished conservatory; it's very good, and includes dishes such as locally smoked salmon with scrambled eggs. A semi-spiral staircase takes you up to the three bedrooms, described by one reader as 'charming, but perhaps a touch too feminine for some tastes.' Rashleigh, in the newer part of the house, is vast, while the two in the original wing have large beds, one a four-poster, and views of the garden to the south. With ongoing refurbishments, Keith told us they are "making things better as they go along". A non-smoking establishment.

~

NEARBY Fowey; Lanhydrock House; the Eden Project; Polperro; Looe.
LOCATION in countryside, 0.5 mile (1 km) off A390, NW of St Blazey, 3 miles (5 km) NE of St Austell; in 5-acre grounds, with car parking
FOOD breakfast
PRICE ££
ROOMS 3 double and twin, all with bath; all rooms have phone, TV, hairdrier
FACILITIES drawing room, conservatory; terrace, garden, heated outdoor swimming pool, whirlpool spa **CREDIT CARDS** MC, V **CHILDREN** accepted over 12
DISABLED access difficult **PETS** not accepted
CLOSED never **PROPRIETORS** Keith and Fiona Martin

THE SOUTH-WEST

St Hilary, Cornwall

ENNYS

~ COUNTRY HOUSE BED-AND-BREAKFAST ~

St Hilary, Penzance, Cornwall TR20 9BZ
TEL (01736) 740262 **FAX** (01736) 740055
E-MAIL ennys@ennys.co.uk **WEBSITE** www.ennys.co.uk

TRAVEL JOURNALISTS don't often move over into the hospitality business themselves, but Gill Charlton is one who has, and she has brought her considerable knowledge of what makes an intersting place to stay to this excellent country guest-house.

Ennys is a beautiful, creeper-clad 17thC Cornish manor house situated at the end of a long tree-lined drive in little St Hilary, a few miles from Penzance. The sheltered gardens are full of shrubs and flowers and include a swimming pool and grass tennis court. The fields stretch down to the River Hayle, along which you can walk and picnic.

Bedrooms in the main house are prettily decorated, furnished in country house style, and all have window seats with garden or country views. Two family suites are in an adjacent converted stone barn near which self-catering accommodation is also available. Proper cream teas are laid out in the rustic farmhouse-style kitchen. Afterwards, you can curl up in the large comfotable sitting room with open log fire. Gill is the perfect hostess, and a mine of information on the surrounding area.

~

NEARBY Lands End; Penzance; Lizard peninsula.
LOCATION in gardens with car parking; from B3280 from Marazion turn left into Trewhella Lane, just before Relubbus
FOOD breakfast
PRICE £
ROOMS 5; 3 double, 1 with bath, 2 with shower, 2 suites, all with bath; all rooms have TV, hairdrier **FACILITIES** breakfast room, sitting room; garden, grass tennis court, heated outdoor swimming pool
CREDIT CARDS MC, V
CHILDREN accepted over 3
DISABLED access difficult **PETS** not accepted
CLOSED Nov 1 to March 15
PROPRIETOR Gill Charlton

THE SOUTH-WEST

ST KEYNE, CORNWALL

WELL HOUSE

~ COUNTRY HOTEL ~

St Keyne, Liskeard, Cornwall PL14 4RN
TEL (01579) 342001 **FAX** (01579) 343891
E-MAIL wellhse@aol.com **WEBSITE** www.wellhouse.co.uk

WE'VE HAD CONSISTENTLY satisfied feedback on this hotel in recent years. Attention to detail is part of Nicholas Wainford's policy of providing a comfortable and restful background at this Victorian hill-top house with an outdoor heated swimming pool. Everything here has been carefully chosen to create an atmosphere of calm and stylish luxury – up to country-house standard, but on a smaller scale (and at lower cost).

The house itself was built by a tea-planter in 1894, obviously with no expense spared. The beautifully tiled entrance hall, the staircase and all the woodwork are as new. The dining room, terrace and most of the richly decorated bedrooms look out over wooded grounds to the Looe valley. The sitting room, with its roaring log fire, offers warmth and peace on a cold night.

The contemporary decoration and paintings on the walls are in no way at odds with the atmosphere of the old stone house. Nor is the modern style of the dishes on the daily changing menu. This is one of the best places to eat at in Cornwall. It is also one of the most attractive, with its soft yellow colour scheme. The wine list is extensive and largely French, with a heavy slant towards prestigious clarets. The lunch and dinner menus change daily. 'Mouthwatering, inventive and great value for money', says our most recent inspector.

~

NEARBY Looe; Plymouth; Bodmin Moor; Eden Project.
LOCATION in countryside just outside village of St Keyne, 2 miles (3 km) S of Liskeard, off B3254; in 3.5-acre gardens with ample car parking
FOOD breakfast, lunch, dinner; room service
PRICE £££
ROOMS 9; 8 double, 1 family room, all with bath; all rooms have phone, TV, hairdrier **FACILITIES** sitting room, dining room, bar; garden, tennis, heated swimming pool, croquet **CREDIT CARDS** MC, V **CHILDREN** welcome
DISABLED no special facilities **PETS** accepted by arrangement, no snakes
CLOSED never **PROPRIETORS** Nicholas Wainford and Ione Nurdin

THE SOUTH-WEST

ST MARTIN, ISLES OF SCILLY

ST MARTIN'S ON THE ISLE

∽ ISLAND HOTEL ∽

St Martin, Isles of Scilly, TR25 0QW
TEL (01720) 422092 **FAX** (01720) 422298
E-MAIL stay@stmartinshotel.co.uk **WEBSITE** www.stmartinshotel.co.uk

AFFICIONADOS RETURN to this upmarket island hotel time and again, either for family holidays, or as a peaceful getaway in superb surroundings. In the sunshine, the Scillies can vie with many a 'paradise' archipelago: there are lovely colourings, fabulous beaches and endless uninhabited islands scattered across a deep blue sea. St Martin's, near Tresco, is virtually car-free, and the hotel is the only one on the island. The relaxed and friendly manager, Keith Bradford, usually meets guests at the quay.

The hotel is modern, built in the 1980s under the supervision of the Prince of Wales of local stone, with slate roofs to resemble a string of traditional fishermen's cottages. Scattered on the expansive lawn in front, which runs down to the private beach, are deck chairs and tables and chairs shaded by parasols. Boat trips, with picnics, can be arranged to uninhabited islands and to Tresco, and a Cornish Crabber is available for fishing trips.

Bedrooms, in modern style, with pine fittings and white bathrooms, are practical and comfortable; the best have sea views. The food, served in the first-floor dining room, is surprisingly rich and sophisticated; lighter meals are served in the bar.

∽

NEARBY boat trips to Tresco and other Scilly Isles.
LOCATION at N end of island, close to beach in own grounds; helicopter to St Mary's and boat to island; free transport from quay to hotel
FOOD breakfast, lunch, dinner; room service
PRICE ££££
ROOMS 30; 28 double, twin and family, 2 suites, all with bath; all rooms have phone, TV, hairdrier, radio **FACILITIES** sitting room, bar, dining room, snooker room, indoor swimming pool; garden, private beach, sailing, fishing, clay pigeon shooting, shark fishing, bird watching, scuba diving, snorkelling, windsurfing
CREDIT CARDS AE, DC, MC, V **CHILDREN** welcome
DISABLED hotel accessible but access to island difficult **PETS** accepted
CLOSED Nov to Feb **MANAGER** Keith Bradford

THE SOUTH-WEST

ST MAWES, CORNWALL

TRESANTON

~ SEASIDE TOWN HOTEL ~

St Mawes, Cornwall TR2 5DR
TEL (01326) 270055 **FAX** (01326) 270053
E-MAIL info@tresanton.com **WEBSITE** www.tresanton.com

IT'S EASY TO DRIVE PAST the hotel, as it has no obvious entrance, particularly for cars. Look closer and you will see a discreet sign and some steps next to a pair of white-painted garages. Stop, and within seconds someone will appear to welcome you, take your luggage and park your car. This is not any old seaside hotel.

Tresanton was opened in the summer of 1998 by Olga Polizzi, daughter of Lord Forte, and it is now well established as the West Country hotel for chic townies who prefer not to forego sophistication when by the seaside. Yet St Mawes is a happy-go-lucky holiday village, full in summer of chirpy families, bucket and spade in hand, and the two must rub along together. A whitewashed former sailing club and a cluster of cottages on the sea front make up the hotel, which was well known back in the 1960s, but had long lost its glamour before Olga Polizzi came across it. She set about redesigning it in minimalist, elegant style, using restful, muted tones of oatmeal and flax, accentuated by blues, greens, browns or yellows. Bedrooms are a study in understated luxury and have stunning sea views. The warm and comfortable sitting room and bar are more traditional.

Tresanton has become the most sought-after hotel in the South of England, and right so. The food, in particular, is gaining many plaudits.

~

NEARBY Trelissick, Glendurgan, Heligan and Trebah gardens; Truro; Eden Project; National Maritime Museum.
LOCATION in town, just below castle, 14 miles (22 km) S of Truro; car parking
FOOD breakfast, lunch, dinner; room service
PRICE ££££
ROOMS 26; 24 double and twin, 2 suites, all with bath; all rooms have phone, TV, video, fax/modem point, hairdrier **FACILITIES** sitting room, dining room, bar, cinema, terraces; boats, 8-metre yacht **CREDIT CARDS** AE, MC, V
CHILDREN welcome **DISABLED** 3 rooms on ground floor up several steps
PETS not accepted **CLOSED** never **PROPRIETOR** Olga Polizzi

THE SOUTH-WEST

SHEPTON MALLET, SOMERSET

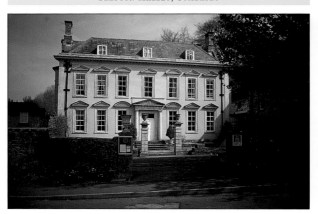

BOWLISH HOUSE
~ RESTAURANT-WITH-ROOMS ~

Wells Road, Shepton Mallet, Somerset BA4 5JD
TEL (01749) 342022 **FAX** (01749) 345311
E-MAIL reservations@bowlishhouse.fsnet.co.uk

OVER THE PAST few years, Bowlish House has changed ownership several times and was becoming increasingly tired and shabby. Then, in 2002, Darren Carter and Jason Goy took over. They are attempting to turn the trend with a major refurbishment: new fabrics and furniture and redecoration throughout. Although their plans are on a large scale, Darren and Jason assured us that the work won't affect guests' comfort. Improvements should be slow and steady.

On a recent inspection, we caught the two in mid-renovation. Bedrooms are comfortable and rather homey with chintzy bedspreads and curtains. While keeping the country house furniture, the bar has been rejuvenated, although we hope they ditch the muzak. The dining room is painted deep aubergine and opens onto a spacious, more relaxed conservatory. The lunch menu is 'bistro' style while dinners are traditional English. Five eating times are scheduled throughout the day, and we worry that this timetable (breakfast from 8 to 9:30, morning coffee from 10 to 11:30, lunch from 12 to 2:30, afternoon tea from 3 to 5 and dinner from 6:30 to 9:30) will be too rigid. Although Darren and Jason are enthusiastic about their project, we also worry that the size of the task could overwhelm them. We will welcome comments on how they fare.

~

NEARBY Wells; Glastonbury; Mendip Hills.
LOCATION just W of Shepton Mallet on A371; walled garden and parking for 15 cars
FOOD breakfast, morning coffee, lunch, afternoon tea, dinner
PRICE ££
ROOMS 4; 3 double, 1 twin, all with bath; all rooms have TV, phone, minibar
FACILITIES dining room, bar, sitting room, conservatory **CREDIT CARDS** MC, V
CHILDREN welcome
DISABLED access by arrangement **PETS** not accepted
CLOSED never
PROPRIETORS Darren Carter and Jason Goy

THE SOUTH-WEST

INNSACRE FARMHOUSE
~ FARM GUEST-HOUSE ~

Shipton Gorge, Bridport, Dorset DT6 4LJ
TEL (01308) 456137
E-MAIL innsacre.farmhouse@btinternet.com

SET ON THE SIDE of a steeply rising, hill, this 17thC farmhouse is surrounded by ten acres of its own land, conveniently placed three miles from the sea and National Trust coastal path. The Davies's own flock of Jacob sheep graze the hillside, contributing to the atmosphere of peace and rural charm.

The farmhouse itself is quite dark inside, with one main room serving the triple purpose of sitting room, bar and dining room. Warmed by a woodburning stove in winter, the beamed room is divided by screens to separate diners and drinkers. It is decorated in an eclectic mix of objects, including colourful Provençal fabrics and strikingly large arrangements of flowers.

Jayne Davies is responsible for cooking the excellent suppers. There is no choice, although she takes into account the various likes and dislikes of guests and the three courses are all freshly prepared using local ingredients. Jayne will also make up picnic lunches for the many walkers that come to stay. Sydney (previously a hairdresser) has painted the bedrooms in strong heritage colours and furnished them with provincial French furniture in keeping with the rustic appeal of the place. Informality is the keyword here.

NEARBY coastal path; Lyme Regis; Chesil Beach; Dorchester, Jurassic Coast.
LOCATION in quiet countryside, 2 miles (3km) E of Bridport, S of A35; with ample car parking
FOOD breakfast, dinner
PRICE ££
ROOMS 4; 3 double, 1 twin, all with bath; all rooms have TV
FACILITIES bar, sitting room
CREDIT CARDS MC, V **CHILDREN** accepted over 9
DISABLED no special facilities **PETS** accepted (small charge)
CLOSED Christmas Day to New Year
PROPRIETORS Sydney and Jayne Davies

THE SOUTH-WEST

PLUMBER MANOR
~ MANOR HOUSE HOTEL ~

Hazelbury Bryan Road, Sturminster Newton, Dorset DT10 2AF
TEL (01258) 472507 **FAX** (01258) 473370
E-MAIL book@plumbermanor.com **WEBSITE** www.plumbermanor.com

THIS IS A HANDSOME Jacobean manor house, 'modernized' in the early 20thC, that has been in the Prideaux-Brune family for well over 300 years. Since 1973, brothers Richard, Tim and Brian have been running it as an elegant but relaxed restaurant with comfortable bedrooms. Richard Prideaux-Brune is much in evidence front-of-house, as is his brother Tim. Together with Brian, who is responsible for the highly-regarded food, they draw in restaurant customers from far and wide – expect plenty of bustle on Friday and Saturday evenings, and non-residents in the dining room.

The brothers make charming hosts, and have created a very relaxed and welcoming atmosphere. Old family portraits hang in the house; labradors lounge in the bar; the decoration is homely and comfortable rather than smart. The large bar area might detract from the feeling of a family home, but it helps the Prideaux-Brunes' operation in a practical way (shooting parties are a feature in winter).

Bedrooms are divided between those in the main house (which lead off a gallery hung with portraits) and those in a converted stone barn and courtyard building which overlook the extensive gardens and stream. They are all spacious and comfortable.

~

NEARBY Thomas Hardy country; Shaftesbury; Sherborne.
LOCATION 2 miles (3 km) SW of Sturminster Newton; private car parking
FOOD breakfast, Sun lunch, dinner
PRICE £££
ROOMS 16; 14 double, all with bath, 2 small doubles with bath; all rooms have phone, TV
FACILITIES dining room, sitting room, bar; garden, croquet, tennis court
CREDIT CARDS AE, DC, MC, V **CHILDREN** welcome
DISABLED easy access to barn bedrooms and dining room
PETS accepted by arrangement
CLOSED Feb **PROPRIETOR** Richard Prideaux-Brune

THE SOUTH-WEST

TEFFONT EVIAS, WILTSHIRE

HOWARD'S HOUSE
∽ VILLAGE RESTAURANT-WITH-ROOMS ∽

Teffont Evias, Salisbury, Wiltshire SP3 5RJ
TEL (01722) 716392 **FAX** (01722) 716820
E-MAIL enq@howardshousehotel.com **WEBSITE** www.howardshousehotel.com

TEFFONT EVIAS, IN THE NADDER VALLEY, has been owned by the same family, father to son, since 1692. It is picturesque and has great charm without being twee. In the grounds stands Howard's House, opposite a marvellously knotty topiary hedge, and embellished by a Swiss gabled roof in the early 19th century – its then owner had fallen for all things Swiss on the Grand Tour. It is surrounded by two acres of pretty garden.

Its *raison d`être* is the food, created by chef Boyd McIntosh. A sample meal may consist of seared scallops with a saffron dressing, and steamed fillet of sea bass piled on a lemon and garlic mash, and topped by a ravioli of salmon. The smallish dining room, mint green with white tablecloths, is soothing but predictable, as is the decoration in the cosy sitting room and the bedrooms: pastel-coloured walls, floral fabrics, pine furnishings. The four-poster room is the prettiest; rooms 1 and 2 look out over the garden.

Breakfast here is above reproach: excellent coffee, warm croissants and toast wrapped in a white napkin, and the frothiest, creamiest fresh orange juice you can imagine. You might choose a boiled egg, or something more sophisticated such as poached egg tartlet with hollandaise sauce. Last year, Bill and Noële Thompson took over ownership and assure us the quality will remain unchanged.

∽

NEARBY Salisbury Cathedral; Wilton House; Stonehenge; Old Sarum.
LOCATION in village, off B3089 (signposted from Teffont Magna), 10 miles (16 km) W of Salisbury; car parking
FOOD breakfast, Sunday lunch, dinner
PRICE £££
ROOMS 9; 8 double and twin, 1 family, all with bath; all rooms have phone, TV, hairdrier **FACILITIES** dining room, sitting room; terrace, garden
CREDIT CARDS AE, MC, V **CHILDREN** welcome
DISABLED ground-floor dining room accessible
PETS accepted **CLOSED** Christmas **PROPRIETOR** Bill and Noële Thompson

THE SOUTH-WEST

TORQUAY, DEVON

ORESTONE MANOR
~ COUNTRY HOUSE HOTEL ~

Rockhouse Lane, Maidencombe, Torquay, Devon TQ1 4SX
TEL (01803) 328098 **FAX** (01803) 328336
E-MAIL enquiries@orestone.co.uk **WEBSITE** www.orestone.co.uk

ORESTONE MANOR, a grand colonial style house, sits high above Lyme Bay and boasts views of the sea from every room. The large conservatory filled with Lloyd loom furniture and palm trees on the lawn lend to the Mediterranean feel of this manor house of the English Riviera. Inside, Indian fabrics, Oriental prints and elephant-themed decorations tie the individually decorated rooms together. And although an elephant was a seemingly random choice for the logo, last summer, a gardener found an 18thC lady's smoking pipe shaped like an elephant in the flower bed. This chance finding reinforces the colonial feeling that pervades Orestone Manor.

New proprietors Rose and Mark Ashton welcome you with warm conversation and make you feel like a long-time friend. The friendly atmosphere continues through dinner, where excellent food and exceptional service relax the formal dining room. Our inspector recently enjoyed a superb lobster bisque, followed by well-presented seared local scallops with a roe tortellini and a heavenly pudding of khalua and marscapone cheese chocolate ravioli with a dark chocolate sorbet. Coffee and petit fours are served in the conservatory or, in colder months, in the sitting room beside an intricately carved fireplace dating from the early 1800s. Although all rooms are well-appointed, our favourite is number six because of its long bathroom with a clawfoot bath and balcony overlooking the sea.

~

NEARBY South Devon Coastal Path, National Trust properties, Dartmouth, Totnes.
LOCATION from Torquay follow the A379 signposted Teignmouth up Watcombe Hill, signposted at the top of Rockhouse Lane
FOOD breakfast, lunch, dinner, room service
PRICE ££
ROOMS 12 double or twin, all with bath; all have phone, TV, complimentary sherry
FACILITIES dining room, sitting room, bar, conservatory, private dining room, meeting room; terrace, heated swimming pool **CREDIT CARDS** AE, MC, V **CHILDREN** welcome
DISABLED 1 room **PETS** welcome **CLOSED** never **PROPRIETORS** Rose and Mark Ashton

THE SOUTH-WEST

VIRGINSTOW, DEVON

PERCY'S AT COOMBESHEAD
~ COUNTRY HOTEL AND RESTAURANT ~

Virginstow, Devon EX21 5EA
TEL (01409) 211236 **FAX** (01409) 211460
E-MAIL info@percys.co.uk **WEBSITE** www.percys.co.uk

THIS CHARMING PLACE was originally bought as their retirement home by the Bricknell-Webbs, who ran a restaurant in North London called Percy's. They decided to open the 16thC farmhouse in rural Devon as a hotel and restaurant, as well as running the 130-acre farm. The bedrooms, in an adjacent converted barn, are spacious, understated and simple in the best way: there are no frills, but everything is of a high standard: the showers are power showers, the beds are king-size, and the real coffee comes in cafetières. Two rooms, with stripped wood floors, pale wooden furniture, fresh flowers, candles on each table and a wood-burning stove make up the intimate and calming restaurant. Tina cooks in the modern English style, with almost all ingredients, such as salad, eggs, lamb and venison, coming from the estate. Fish features strongly, and it is very good, not surprisingly as Tony has a licence to bid directly at the Looe fish auction. The scallops are superb, or you might opt for squid sautéed and served on a bed of mixed leaves. The wine list is equally good, with bottles listed in ascending order of price regardless of country of origin, and almost all available by the glass.

A modern extension with two sitting rooms, a heated deck and patio and the Zinc bar has just been added. Although it's getting architectural praise, we would like reports as to whether the major developments result in a loss of charm.

~

NEARBY Dartmoor; Tintagel; Clovelly; Tamar Otter Sanctuay.
LOCATION from the A30, travelling W, turn off after Okehampton to Broadwidger, then follow signs to Virginstow
FOOD breakfast, lunch, dinner
PRICE £££
ROOMS 8 double and twin, all with bath or shower; all rooms have TV, hairdrier, minibar; some have DVD **FACILITIES** restaurant, bar, 2 sitting rooms; heated deck/patio; garden
CREDIT CARDS AE, MC, V **CHILDREN** over 12 **DISABLED** 4 ground-floor rooms, 1 specially adapted **PETS** in bedrooms only **CLOSED** never **PROPRIETORS** Tony and Tina Bricknell-Webb

THE SOUTH-WEST

THE PRIORY
~ COUNTRY TOWN HOTEL ~

Church Green, Wareham, Dorset BH20 4ND
TEL (01929) 551666 **FAX** (01929) 554519
E-MAIL reservations@theprioryhotel.co.uk **WEBSITE** www.theprioryhotel.co.uk

HIDDEN BEHIND THE CHURCH, this 16thC Priory is the perfect retreat for anyone who appreciates a sense of history, as well as peace, comfort and good food. It has been run for the last 27 years by the Turner family, and is currently under the guiding hand of Jeremy, who is maintaining everything, from the excellent antiques to the pretty fabrics in the bedrooms, has been done with taste and in keeping.

The bedrooms are all that should be expected from a 16thC priory: beams, sloping ceilings and floors, as well as being supremely comfortable and well-equipped with books (no *Reader's Digest* here) and attractive toiletries in the bathrooms. To keep up with the demand for rooms the boathouse has been converted to provide four extra bedrooms, or rather suites, equipped with luxury baths and French windows opening on to the River Frome. Indeed, by boat is the best way to arrive at the Priory: moorings are available and, after a quick walk through the stunning gardens (from which Mrs Turner gathers flowers for the arrangements) you can relax with a pre-dinner drink on the terrace. The food is richly sastisfying, with a mainland European flavour emanating both from the menu and the French staff.

~

NEARBY Poole Harbour; Swanage; Lulworth Cove.
LOCATION in town near market square; in 4.5 acre gardens with ample car parking
FOOD breakfast, lunch, dinner
PRICE £££
ROOMS 18; 14 double, 2 single, 2 suites, all with bath; all rooms have phone, TV, hairdrier, minibar
FACILITIES sitting room, bar, restaurant; terrace, garden, croquet, pontoon, organise gold and fishing outings
CREDIT CARDS DC, MC, V
CHILDREN accepted over 8 **DISABLED** access difficult
PETS guide dogs only **CLOSED** never **PROPRIETOR** Turner family

THE SOUTH-WEST

WHIMPLE, DEVON

WOODHAYES
~ COUNTRY HOUSE HOTEL ~

Whimple, near Exeter, Devon EX5 2TD
TEL (01404) 822237 **FAX** (01404) 822337
E-MAIL info@woodhayes-hotel.co.uk **WEBSITE** www.woodhayes-hotel.co.uk

WOODHAYES, LONG FEATURED in our guide, is the archetypal English country house hotel – comfortable, spacious and quiet. The gravel on the drive scrunches satisfyingly, the lawns are perfectly mown, nothing disturbs the peace of the countryside.

Having bought Woodhayes in 1998, Zimbabwean Eddie Katz and his English wife Lynda have altered the interior, replacing the inoffensive pastels with more zingy colours, updated bathrooms and generally given the place a facelift. They are, however, retaining the many architectural delights of the Georgian house, including the flagstone flooring in the bar and the wonderful white-painted Strawberry Gothic doors that are much in evidence throughout. Behind the main house, the Cottage has been completely revamped to provide a comfortable self-contained unit, perfect for four adults and a couple of children.

Lynda now serves only breakfast, which is carefully and freshly prepared; those seeking dinner will be directed to a local pub. More reports please.

~

NEARBY Exmoor and Dartmoor.
LOCATION in village, 5 miles (8 km) NW of Exeter; ample car parking
FOOD breakfast
PRICE ££
ROOMS 8; 3 double, 2 twin with bath en suite, 1 double with separate bath, 1 double, 1 twin with bath in Cottage; all rooms have phone, TV, hairdrier
FACILITIES sitting room, bar, dining room; gardens
CREDIT CARDS AE, DC, MC, V
CHILDREN accepted over 5
DISABLED access difficult
PETS not accepted
CLOSED Christmas and New Year
PROPRIETORS Eddie and Lynda Katz

THE SOUTH-WEST

WILLITON, SOMERSET

WHITE HOUSE
⟨ RESTAURANT-WITH-ROOMS ⟩

Williton, Somerset TA4 4QW
TEL (01984) 632777

DESPITE BEING in the same little country town for over 30 years, Dick and Kay Smith continue to gather up awards for outstanding food, demonstrating their unwavering commitment to quality, sheer skill and changing fashion in the kitchen. They both cook, are both self-effacing about what they do so well, and deserve every accolade that comes their way. When we revisited the White House recently, we were again struck by their affability and easy-going manner.

What can you expect to find on the daily-changing menu? Starters might be dressed seared scallops with diced tomato, grilled marinated breast of wood pigeon on hot beetroot; main courses: a boned-out saddle of venison or a grilled sea bass fillet with aubergine and tomato *coulis*; puddings are just as tempting. Dick Smith's wine list is equally fine, and to add to the vinous atmosphere, posters in the bar advertise auctions of historical wine cellars. Both bar and sitting room are informally furnished, large potted plants and ceramics made by the couple's potter son adding a jauntily artistic feel to the place. Soft colours, patchwork quilts and plain linens decorate the bedrooms. Those in the main house are the most spacious, while those in the converted stables and coach house are less exposed to traffic noise. Mediterranean plants in the garden include figs and palms in large pots.

⟨

NEARBY Exmoor, Cleeve Abbey; Quantock Hills.
LOCATION on A39 in centre of town; with ample car parking
FOOD breakfast, dinner
PRICE ££
ROOMS 10 double and twin, all with bath; all rooms have phone, TV
FACILITIES sitting room, bar, dining room **CREDIT CARDS** not accepted
CHILDREN accepted
DISABLED 1 room with possible access **PETS** not accepted
CLOSED Nov to May **PROPRIETORS** Dick and Kay Smith

THE SOUTH-WEST

WITHYPOOL, SOMERSET

ROYAL OAK
~ VILLAGE INN ~

Withypool, Somerset TA24 7QP
TEL (01643) 831506 **FAX** (01643) 831659
E-MAIL enquiries@royaloakwithypool.co.uk **WEBSITE** www.royalaokwithypool.co.uk

WITHYPOOL IS A CENTRE for hunting, shooting and fishing, hidden away in the middle of Exmoor in a highly photogenic landscape. History and charm have persevered: Gail Sloggett is very aware of what she has inherited (this is where R.D. Blackmore wrote his classic tale *Lorna Doone* in 1866, and also where Eisenhower stayed in 1944), and the Royal Oak remains first and foremost a country pub, with bars suitably kitted out in antlers and hunting scenes.

Gail has made some changes (all good and tasteful) to the wall colours that accomodate the humourous sporting prints all over the walls, on the stairs and the landings. The bedrooms are extremely comfortable, some beamed, the obviously traditional being subtly incorporated into the slightly more modern. Panelled walls surround the bathroom, and in one bedroom white and blue *toille de jouie* adorn the walls and furnishings.

Two cottages at the rear are used for overflow accommodation or for self-catering. Don't turn them down, they are delightful and immensely tasteful and cosy. The staff are helpful and friendly and the food goes from strength to strength, garnering Michelin stars and Egon Ronay recommendations.

~

NEARBY Exmoor; Minehead.
LOCATION in middle of village, just off B3223, 15 miles SW of Minehead; ample car parking
FOOD breakfast, lunch, dinner
PRICE ££
ROOMS 8 double and twin, all with bath; all rooms have phone, TV, hairdrier
FACILITIES sitting room, 2 bars, restaurant; terrace
CREDIT CARDS DC, MC, V
CHILDREN welcome
DISABLED not suitable
PETS accepted **CLOSED** never **PROPRIETOR** Gail Sloggett

THE SOUTH-WEST

WIVELISCOMBE, SOMERSET

LANGLEY HOUSE

~ COUNTRY HOUSE HOTEL ~

Langley Marsh, near Wiveliscombe, Somerset TA4 2UF
TEL (01984) 623318 **FAX** (01984) 624573
E-MAIL user@langley.in2home.co.uk

TAKING UP WHERE PETER AND ANNE WILSON left off, Stuart and Sue Warnock continue to run Langley House along well-ordered lines. Between them, they know what they are about.

The house is a modest building with a rambling garden in delectable, rolling Somerset countryside that is neglected by most visitors to the West Country. (The Warnocks are happy to advise guests on where to go touring during the day and provide them with maps.) It feels like a family home rather than a hotel. The drawing room, with deep pink walls and an open log fire, is relaxed and comfortable, while bedrooms have been redone in pretty floral fabrics. The dining room is still not ideally furnished – we would like to see more informality and less elegance – but the private dining room is cheerful with lemon yellow walls. The modern English menu could include quail egg salad or seared king scallops and has a vegetarian option. The Warnocks are happy to provide information on local fishing and shooting.

~

NEARBY Exmoor; National Trust houses.
LOCATION 0.5 miles (1 km) NW of Wiveliscombe, off B3227; in 4-acre gardens with ample car parking
FOOD breakfast, dinner
PRICE £££
ROOMS 9; 7 double, 6 with bath, 1 with shower; 2 single, both with bath; 1 family room with bath; all rooms have TV, phone, hairdrier
FACILITIES bar, 2 sitting rooms, restaurant; garden, croquet
CREDIT CARDS MC, V
CHILDREN welcome
DISABLED access to ground floor easy
PETS accepted by arrangement
CLOSED never
PROPRIETORS Stuart and Sue Warnock

THE SOUTH-WEST

YEOVIL, SOMERSET

LITTLE BARWICK HOUSE
～ RESTAURANT-WITH-ROOMS ～

Barwick, near Yeovil, Somerset BA22 9TD
TEL (01935) 423902 **FAX** (01935) 420908
E-MAIL reservations@barwick7.fsnet.co.uk **WEBSITE** www.littlebarwickhouse.co.uk

VERONICA AND CHRISTOPHER COLLEY built up Little Barwick's reputation for fine food over many years, so their many devotees will be reassured to know that their successors come armed with impeccable culinary pedigrees. Tim Ford is one of Britain's finest young chefs: he trained at Sharrow Bay and spent time in several top hotels refining his art. Latterly he has been head chef at Summer Lodge in Evershot (see page 46), and now he and his wife Emma, who was front-of-house there, have taken on their own place.

They should have no problems in attracting custom, old and new. Locally-sourced meat, game and fish provide the cornerstone of Tim's cooking (our inspector enjoyed pink roasted rump of Dorset lamb with aubergine caviar and black olive sauce), while the lunch menu is a simpler variation of the dinner menu.

Little Barwick has featured in these pages for years, recommended for its friendly informality, and this looks set to remain. However, the Fords have completed a programme of redecoration that has freshened up both the interior and exterior of this lovely listed Georgian dower house. The dining room is now a creamy yellow. Bedrooms remain cheerful with fresh flowers, real coffee in cafetières and homemade shortbreads.

～

NEARBY Brympton d'Evercy; Montacute House.
LOCATION 2 miles (3 km) S of Yeovil off A37; car parking
FOOD breakfast, lunch, dinner
PRICE ££
ROOMS 6 double and twin, all with bath or shower; all rooms have TV, hairdrier, phone **FACILITIES** sitting room, dining room, bar/private dining room; garden
CREDIT CARDS AE, MC, V
CHILDREN welcome
DISABLED access difficult
PETS accepted
CLOSED 2 weeks Jan **PROPRIETORS** Emma and Tim Ford

THE SOUTH-EAST

BATTLE, EAST SUSSEX

LITTLE HEMINGFOLD FARMHOUSE
~ COUNTRY HOTEL ~

Telham, Battle, East Sussex, TN33 0TT
TEL (01424) 774338 **FAX** (01424) 77535
WEBSITE www.smoothhound.co.uk/hotels/littlehem.html

DON'T BE MISLED BY the word 'farmhouse': apart from the setting there is not much that is agricultural about this substantial, rambling building, part 17thC, part early Victorian. The house has a peaceful setting in 40 acres of farm and woodland; it is surrounded by gardens, and overlooks a pretty 2-acre trout lake (the Slaters are happy to lend fishing rods). Inside, intriguing nooks and crannies give the house a special charm. The two sitting rooms and the cosy dining room all have log fires. So do four of the nine bedrooms, all individually furnished, and accommodated in the converted coach house and stables, grouped around a flowery courtyard.

Allison and Paul emphasize fresh ingredients in their traditional cooking, though we have received mixed reports from visitors about the food. One reader writes: 'the beef we ordered for dinner was quite the best ever and the puddings most unusual and delicious...on Sunday, after a walk through their lovely grounds, we indulged in a huge breakfast, which was again superb'. Another was less happy with the choice of bread at breakfast time, and was irritated by the slow service and having to share a table. We welcome further reports.

~

NEARBY Bodiam Castle; Great Dixter; Rye; Sissinghurst.
LOCATION 1.5 miles (3 km) SE of Battle, off A2100; in 40-acre garden, with trout lake, fields and woods; ample car parking
FOOD breakfast, light lunch, dinner
PRICE ££
ROOMS 13 double, 1 family room; 10 with bath; all rooms have phone, TV, electric blankets; 4 rooms have log-burning stoves **FACILITIES** 2 sitting rooms, dining room, bar; garden, boating, trout-fishing, tennis, croquet
CREDIT CARDS AE, MC, V **CHILDREN** accepted over 9
DISABLED access difficult **PETS** accepted **CLOSED** 1 Jan to 13 Feb
PROPRIETORS Paul and Allison Slater

THE SOUTH-EAST

BEPTON, WEST SUSSEX

PARK HOUSE
◇ COUNTRY HOTEL ◇

Bepton, Near Midhurst, West Sussex GU29 0JB
TEL (01730) 819000 **FAX** (01730) 819099
E-MAIL reservations@parkhouse.com **WEBSITE** www.parkhousehotel.com

PARK HOUSE HAS BEEN in the O'Brien family for over 50 years, and has always retained the atmosphere of a private country house – thanks first to the careful attention of Ioné O'Brien, and now to her son, Michael.

A 16thC farmhouse with Victorian additions, the hotel, with its cream-painted roughcast walls, at first looks rather suburban. Inside, however, the elegant public rooms strike a very different note. The honesty bar, festooned with mementoes and photographs of polo players (Cowdray Park is close at hand) is admirably well-stocked, while the drawing room, particularly appealing at night, gleams with polished parquet floor, velvet-backed alcoves filled with books and china, yellow walls, and table lamps which cast a golden glow. Bedrooms are traditional; best are the two in the annexe, one of which has a private patio. The dinner menu has been expanded (it used to be amazingly limited) and features traditional English food. Lunch can be as simple as sausage and mash or oxtail pie. We would welcome comments on the food.

◇

NEARBY Petworth; Goodwood; Cowdray Park; Chichester.
LOCATION in countryside, on the B2226 just N of Bepton village, 3 miles (5 km) SSW of Midhurst; ample car parking
FOOD breakfast, lunch, dinner; room service
PRICE £££
ROOMS 18, 10 double, 2 family rooms in main building, all with bath; 3 cottages, each with 2 doubles; all rooms have phone, TV, hairdrier, fax/modem point
FACILITIES dining room, sitting room, bar; garden, swimming pool, tennis, croquet, putting green, 9-hole pitch and putt course
CREDIT CARDS AE, DC, MC, V
CHILDREN welcome
DISABLED specially adapted ground-floor bedroom
PETS accepted **CLOSED** never
PROPRIETOR Michael O'Brien

THE SOUTH-EAST

BRIGHTON, WEST SUSSEX

HOTEL DU VIN
~ TOWN HOTEL ~

Ship Street, Brighton, West Sussex BN1 1AD
TEL (01273) 718588 **FAX** (01273) 718599
E-MAIL info@brighton.hotelduvin.com **WEBSITE** www.hotelduvin.com

DOWN A NARROW COBBLED street, tucked back from the seafront, a collection of part gothic-styled buildings make up the newest hotel in this stylish micro-chain (others include Bristol, page 41, Tunbridge Wells, page 130 and Winchester, page 134). In the main building, bizarre gargoyles watch over a double height hall and a heavily carved staircase. Just through the reception area, you can sink into the cosy leather armchairs or brown velvet sofas in the bar and enjoy a drink and a cigar. Black and white photos of celebrities and their favourite smokes line the walls, while wooden seagulls swoop and perch on the beams in the high timbered ceilings. Through glass windows and doors, you can see the Bistro, done out in wine-related pictures, floor-to-ceiling windows and bunches of dried hops. Bedrooms are each sponsored by and named after a wine house. Those facing the central courtyard (with a pretty vine-covered pergola) have chalky blue-green wood siding, beach-house style, and inside, are decorated in soft blue and sand tones. In the bathrooms, scroll top baths are mounted in driftwood and old railway sleepers. Two suites have telescopes for spying boats out at sea.

No apologies for including the fourth in the chain: all the Hotel du Vin are original in their own right, sympathetically adapting themselves to whatever building they choose to inhabit.
~

NEARBY seafront, The Lanes, Brighton Pier.
LOCATION from A23, take Kings Road to Middle street, then turn right into Ship Street, valet car parking
FOOD breakfast, lunch, dinner
PRICE ££–£££
ROOMS 37, 34 twin/double, 3 suites, all with bath; all rooms have TV, CD player, radio, minibar, trouser press, hairdrier **FACILITIES** bar, restaurant, wine cellar, walk-in cigar humidor, billiards, courtyard with pergola
CREDIT CARDS AE, DC, MC, V **CHILDREN** welcome **DISABLED** access possible
PETS not accepted **CLOSED** never **MANAGER** Nigel Buchanan

THE SOUTH-EAST

MASTER BUILDER'S HOUSE

~ RIVERSIDE HOTEL ~

Bucklers Hard, Beaulieu, Hampshire SO42 7XB
TEL (01590) 616253 **FAX** (01590) 616297
E-MAIL res@themasterbuilders.co.uk **WEBSTE** www.themasterbuilders.co.uk

THE SUPERBLY SITED Master Builder's Hotel had long been ripe for a carefully judged overhaul, and when its lease from Lord Montagu of Beaulieu came up for renewal, Jeremy Willcock and John Illsley, proprietors of the George in Yarmouth, Isle of Wight (see page 136) were just the right pair to step in. Lord Montagu's daughter, interior designer Mary Montagu Scott, undertook the redecoration, creating a straightforward traditional style with a maritime theme (plenty of old prints on the walls) in keeping with the spirit of Bucklers Hard, where some of Nelson's ships were built in the 18th century. Today it is a picturesque and popular marina, with a street of shipwrights' dwellings, a popular bar for visiting yachtsmen, and a maritime museum.

The 18thC Master Builder's House was lumbered some years back with an unsympathetic modern annexe, the Henry Adams Wing. Even the designer's best efforts cannot give the bedrooms here the character they lack, and although they are now comfortable and attractive, given their size, we feel they are somewhat ambitiously priced. Bedrooms in the main building have much more character. The sophisticated new reception area is a vast improvement on the old, and in the smart dining room, with absorbing views down to the river, 'modern classical' dishes are served.

~

NEARBY New Forest; Beaulieu; Lymington.
LOCATION overlooking Beaulieu river at Bucklers Hard, 2 miles (3 km) SE of Beaulieu, 9 miles (14 km) SE of Lyndhurst; ample car parking
FOOD breakfast, lunch, dinner
PRICE £££
ROOMS 25 double, all with bath; all rooms have phone, TV, hairdrier
FACILITIES sitting room, dining room, yachtsman's bar; terrace, garden, pontoon available **CREDIT CARDS** AE, MC, V **CHILDREN** welcome
DISABLED access difficult **PETS** not accepted **CLOSED** never
PROPRIETORS Jeremy Willcock and John Illsley

THE SOUTH-EAST

CRANBROOK, KENT

CLOTH HALL OAST

〜 MANOR HOUSE GUEST-HOUSE 〜

Cranbrook, Kent TN17 3NR
TEL (01580) 712220 **FAX** (01580) 712220

LOVERS OF MRS MORGAN'S previous guest-house will be happy to know that, although no longer running long-time favourite Old Cloth Hall, she has simply moved to the nearby Cloth Hall Oast. With 20 years of experience to support her new venture, Mrs Morgan describes it as "just as nice as the other – if not better" and it is already receiving positive reviews.

The house is situated on a 5-acre estate that is hidden from the road, slightly isolated and very quiet. A large pond with fish and a pretty tree in the middle provides a lovely view from lawn chairs on the half-moon shaped decking. For sunny summer days, you can enjoy a swim in the heated pool or simply relax in the nearby summer house. Two terraces with outdoor patio furniture, a superb croquet lawn and a pergola in the garden complete the picture.

The interior of Cloth Hall Oast is just as special as her previous place. The dining room, open to three galleried floors that include a grand piano, showcases a stunning custom-made chandelier. The bedrooms feel light and warm and one features a whirlpool bath. The sitting room has a fireplace that's perfect for curling up beside on a cool evening.

We welcome comments on the food.

〜

NEARBY Sissinghurst; Scotney Castle Gardens.
LOCATION in countryside 1 mile (1.5 km) E of Cranbrook on road to Tenterden, before cemetery; in grounds of 5 acres; ample car parking
FOOD breakfast, dinner by arrangement
PRICE ££
ROOMS 3 double, 2 with bath, 1 with shower; all rooms have TV and hairdrier
FACILITIES sitting room, dining room; 2 terraces, garden, heated outdoor swimming pool, summer house, croquet **CREDIT CARDS** not accepted
CHILDREN accepted by arrangement
DISABLED access difficult **PETS** not accepted **CLOSED** Christmas
PROPRIETOR Katherine Morgan

THE SOUTH-EAST

CUCKFIELD, WEST SUSSEX

OCKENDEN MANOR

~ MANOR HOUSE HOTEL ~

Ockenden Lane, Cuckfield, West Sussex RH17 5LD
TEL (01444) 416111 **FAX** (01444) 415549
E-MAIL ockenden@hshotels.co.uk **WEBSITE** www.hshotels.co.uk

A TELLING COMMENT FROM the inspector we sent recently: 'Anne Goodman oversees the decoration herself, so gives it the personal touch, rather than simply splashing out on the finest.' She has made many changes for the better here since taking over this attractive 16th/17thC manor house.

Bedrooms are spacious and individual (and crammed with giveaways); a superb master suite with sombre panelling relies on reds and greens to give a feeling of brightness. Several of the bathrooms are notably spacious, and they are equipped with Molton Brown toiletries. The main sitting room, though lavishly furnished, has a personal feel. Staff are friendly and obliging. (A notice in the hotel states that whatever a hotel's character and charm, it is only as good as its staff.)

Dinner, which is served in the oak-panelled restaurant with painted ceiling and stained glass windows, is another highlight. Food is based on local produce, with vegetables and herbs from the garden.

Although Ockenden Manor is popular with business people, it is a human, comfortable hotel, with a very pleasant young manager in Kerry Turner. 'Hidden away behind trees and a high wall; quiet; good value', says our inspector.

~

NEARBY Nyman's; Sissinghurst; Wakehurst Place; Gatwick; Brighton.
LOCATION 2 miles (3 km) W of Hayward's Heath close to middle of village, off A272; in 9-acre grounds, with ample car parking
FOOD breakfast, lunch, dinner
PRICE £££
ROOMS 21 double, 1 single, all with bath; all rooms have phone, TV, hairdrier
FACILITIES sitting room, bar, dining room; terrace, garden
CREDIT CARDS AE, DC, MC, V
CHILDREN welcome
DISABLED no special facilities **PETS** not accepted
CLOSED never **PROPRIETORS** Sandy and Anne Goodman

THE SOUTH-EAST

EAST GRINSTEAD, WEST SUSSEX

GRAVETYE MANOR
~ MANOR HOUSE HOTEL ~

Vowels Lane, near East Grinstead, West Sussex RH19 4LJ
TEL (01342) 810567 **FAX** (10342) 810080
E-MAIL info@gravetyemanor.co.uk **WEBSITE** www.gravetyemanor.co.uk

THE COUNTRY HOUSE HOTEL, now so much a part of the tourist scene in Britain, scarcely existed when Peter Herbert opened the doors of this serene Elizabethan house over 40 years ago. It is scarcely surprising that in that time he and his team have got their act thoroughly polished; but it is remarkable that Gravetye is not in the least eclipsed by younger competitors. Standards in every department are unflaggingly high. Service consistently achieves the elusive aim of attentiveness without intrusion, while the ambitious food is about the best in the county. A recent visitor, who has known the hotel for 30 years, remained as impressed as ever: 'A sleek operation that doesn't compromise.' However, another commented on 'lots of wealthy-looking people in sunglasses and strange-looking jogging suits'.

The pioneering gardener William Robinson lived in the house for half a century until his death in 1935. Great care is taken to maintain the various gardens he created; Robinson was also responsible for many features of the house as it is seen today – the mellow oak panelling and grand fireplaces in the calm, gracious sitting rooms, for example. Bedrooms – all immaculate – vary in size from the adequate to the enormous, and prices range accordingly.

~

NEARBY Wakehurst; Nyman's Gardens.
LOCATION 4.5 miles (7 km) SW of East Grinstead by B2110 at Gravetye; in 30 acre grounds with ample car parking
FOOD breakfast, lunch, dinner, room service
PRICE ££££
ROOMS 17 double, 1 single, all with bath; all rooms have phone, TV, hairdrier; 2 rooms have air-conditioning
FACILITIES 2 sitting rooms, bar, dining room; croquet, trout fishing
CREDIT CARDS MC, V **CHILDREN** welcome over 7 **DISABLED** access difficult
PETS not accepted (1 mile from kennel) **CLOSED** never **PROPRIETORS** Herbert family

THE SOUTH-EAST

EAST HOATHLY, SUSSEX

OLD WHYLY

~ COUNTRY HOUSE GUEST-HOUSE ~

East Hoathly, Sussex BN8 6EL
TEL (01825) 840216 **FAX** (01825) 840738
WEBSITE www.oldwhyly.co.uk

DRIVING UP to Old Whyly in the springtime is magical; owner Sarah Burgoyne has planted 4,000 tulip bulbs and at the right season, the lawn is ablaze with colour. Set in 40-acre grounds, with a duck-dotted lake, well-maintained gardens and walks that take in the nearby 600-acre stud farm, this Grade II listed 18thC manor has an enviable setting

Once you cross the well-gravelled drive and climb the front steps, you will be welcomed in Sarah's (and her dog, Noodle's) antique-filled home. The impressive family painting collection lines the walls, including a full-length portrait of Sarah herself. The sitting room has a roaring fire with inviting furniture – perfect for admiring the china collection or just reading a book. Bedrooms are spacious and comfortable. However, one of the best reasons to stay at Old Whyly is the food. Sarah, a passionate cook who trained in Paris, prepares excellent dishes and, although many of her customers tend to eat at Glyndebourne, Sarah is more than happy to provide lunch and dinner. On our first trip (Old Whyly is new to the guide), our inspector was highly impressed by dinner. 'A thoroughly enjoyable experience – and her pastry is divine.'

Breakfast, often accompanied by discussions of the previous night's opera, includes honey from Sarah's bees kept in the orchard and eggs from the hens that wander about on the lawn.

~

NEARBY Glyndebourne, Charleston Farm House, East Sussex National Golf Course, Batemans.
LOCATION just off A22 S of Uckfield on road to Halland, ample car parking
FOOD breakfast, lunch; dinner by arrangement
PRICE ££
ROOMS 3 double and twin, 2 with bath, 1 with shower **FACILITIES** sitting room, dining room; terrace, garden, croquet, hard top tennis court, heated swimming pool, lake, walking paths **CREDIT CARDS** none **CHILDREN** welcome **DISABLED** access difficult
PETS by arrangement **CLOSED** never **PROPRIETOR** Sarah Burgoyne

THE SOUTH-EAST

FLETCHING, EAST SUSSEX

GRIFFIN INN

~ VILLAGE INN ~

Fletching, near Uckfield, East Sussex TN22 3SS
TEL (01825) 722890 **FAX** (01825) 722810
E-MAIL thegriffininn@hotmail.com **WEBSITE** www.thegriffininn.co.uk

ON OUR LATEST visit to the Griffin Inn, the pub was packed, the dining room was almost full and the kitchen was bustling. Owner James Pullan was just ushering one set of wine tasters out of the door, while representatives from a prestigious Italian winery were expected at any minute. Successful? Evidently. But still welcoming and cosy? Definitely.

This 16thC village inn has been owned by the Pullan family for 20 years and it maintains its winning combination of good food and pretty bedrooms with beams, low ceilings and four-poster beds. Everything is a bit uneven, quaint, on a small scale – but endearing rather than cramped. Beds are inviting and bathrooms are in an attractive Victorian style, with funky porthole mirrors.

The pub has more beams, paneling, open fires and hunting prints, while the old public bar has been turned into the 'Club Room', with sofas, armchairs and a backgammon board. Good food is always at hand either in the pub or in the restaurant, which uses fresh seasonal ingredients and local organic vegetables. Both menus change daily. The wine list has over 100 wines, 70 percent of which are priced at under £20 per bottle.

On sunny days, you can take your drink out to the garden overlooking Sheffield Park and enjoy live jazz at the weekends. In summer, they set up what James calls "a proper BBQ", serving Pacific Rim dishes.

~

NEARBY Sheffield Park; Glyndebourne; Ashdown Forest.
LOCATION in village 1 mile (1.5 km) E of A275; with car parking
FOOD breakfast, lunch, dinner
PRICE ££
ROOMS 7 double and 1 twin, 4 with bath, 4 with shower; all rooms have TV, hairdrier
FACILITIES bars, restaurant, bar billiards; terrace, patio, garden
CREDIT CARDS AE, DC, MC, V **CHILDREN** welcome **DISABLED** 2 rooms on ground floor
PETS accepted in bar, but not in bedrooms or restaurant
CLOSED Christmas Day **MANAGERS** James Pullan and John Gatti

THE SOUTH-EAST

FRANT, KENT

THE OLD PARSONAGE
COUNTRY GUEST HOUSE

Frant, Tunbridge Wells, Kent TN3 9DX
TEL (01892) 750773 **FAX** (01892) 750773
E-MAIL oldparson@aol.com **WEBSITE** www.theoldparsonagehotel.co.uk

AT THE HEART OF the charming village of Frant, The Old Parsonage is set in 3 acres of gardens. This is a fine Georgian country house beautifully renovated by Tony and Mary Dakin. The tall and spacious reception rooms are filled with plants and decorated with lithographs and watercolours as well as Mary's unusual tapestries and Tony's evocative photographs of village scenes.

The centrepiece is the exceptionally large and airy atrium, which floods light on to the main staircase, landing and hall, and shows off the black and white photographic portraits in the picture gallery. The drawing room is delightful too, gracious in style, with Persian rugs, crystal chandeliers and antiques – impressive without being overpowering. The freshly decorated bedrooms (two with four-posters) have large bathrooms (one, with sunken bath, is almost a sitting room). Their decoration and furnishing are constantly under review.

The Dakins are evidently enthusiastic and dedicated: 'This is our home, so we want it to look its best,' says Mary. Tony is responsible for breakfast, and for the pleasant garden. (Free sherry on the terrace.) An excellent base for visiting the several famous National Trust properties in the area – see below.

NEARBY Bodiam, Leeds, Hever and Scotney Castles; Sissinghurst and Sheffield Park Gardens; Bateman's; Penshurst Place; Knole.
LOCATION next to church in village 2 miles (3 km) S of Tunbridge Wells, in large gardens with ample car parking
FOOD breakfast
PRICE ££
ROOMS 2 double and 2 twin, 2 with bath, 2 with shower; all rooms have TV, hairdrier, alarm clock/radio
FACILITIES sitting room, breakfast room, conservatory
CREDIT CARDS MC, V **CHILDREN** accepted over 7 **DISABLED** access difficult
PETS accepted in bedrooms **CLOSED** never **PROPRIETORS** Tony and Mary Dakin

THE SOUTH-EAST

LITTLESTONE, KENT

ROMNEY BAY HOUSE

~ SEASIDE HOTEL ~

Coast Road, Littlestone, New Romney, Kent TN28 8QY
TEL (01797) 364747 **FAX** (01797) 367156
WEBSITE www.uk-travelguide.co.uk/rombayho.htl

THE APPROACH THROUGH sprawling Littlestone is unpromising, particularly in the dark when you don't know where you're heading. But this dignified 1920s house, built by Clough Williams Ellis for American columnist Hedda Hopper, has a superb position between the sea and Romney Marsh. There's a smell of wood smoke and fresh flowers as you enter, and Jennifer Gorlich's interiors are reminiscent of a small hotel in Provence, with plenty of French furniture and fabrics. She is usually in the kitchen, whipping up her famous cream teas (they can be had at any time from breakfast onwards) and delicious four-course dinners. This is a thoroughly relaxed place: the cosy bar; the warm, firelit sitting room packed with groups of comfortable, inviting chairs; late breakfasts in the pretty conservatory; drinks on the terrace; and entertaining Helmut happily attending to everyone's needs. It was his idea not to have phones in the house.

Bedrooms have creamy cottons, fresh white bedlinen, bright checks, and antiques; an upstairs 'look-out' room has the feel of a beach house, with piles of towels for swimming, faded blue denim cushions on wicker chairs, and sea shells. An entry in the Visitor's Book records that the Gorlichs are great practitioners of the art of good living; all this, and the beach too. The house is quietly on the market, but it's business as usual until it sells.

~

NEARBY Rye; Dungeness Lighthouse; Sandwich.
LOCATION in New Romney, take Station Road to sea front, turn left, and follow hotel signs for 1 mile; car parking
FOOD breakfast, weekday sandwich lunch, weekend light lunch, dinner
PRICE £££
ROOMS 10 double and twin, all with bath or shower; all rooms have TV, hairdrier
FACILITIES sitting room, dining room, look-out room; terrace, garden, hard tennis court, croquet, boules, beach adjacent to golf course **CREDIT CARDS** DC, MC, V
CHILDREN accepted over 14 **DISABLED** access difficult **PETS** not accepted
CLOSED Christmas **PROPRIETORS** Jennifer and Helmut Gorlich

THE SOUTH-EAST

LONDON

THE BEAUFORT

~ TOWN BED-AND-BREAKFAST ~

33 Beaufort Gardens, London SW3 1PP
TEL (020) 7584 5252 **FAX** (020) 7589 2834
E-MAIL enquiries@thebeaufort.co.uk **WEBSITE** www.thebeaufort.co.uk

THREE HARRODS DOORMEN in a row gave our inspector unerring directions for the hundred-yard walk to The Beaufort, part of a Victorian terrace overlooking a quiet Knightsbridge cul-de-sac. Taken over by Ahmed and Sarah Jajbhay, this is still one of the few hotels in the world which surprises you with what doesn't appear later on your bill. Feel like a glass of champagne? No charge. Cream tea? Limo to or from the airport? Light meal in your room? The answer's still no charge. And, just when you have been made to feel so good that you want to give a tip, you fall victim to a no-tipping policy.

All the rooms are different, some decorated in muted pastels, others following in the cheerful footsteps of the public areas. Each room has a CD player, video and portable stereo and, for those who need added protection from the English weather, there are also chocolates, shortbread, brandy and umbrellas. And then there are the flowers. Plenty of them. Many are real, but most are hanging on the walls as part of the enormous collection of English floral watercolours. Noted for the friendliness of its staff, the Beaufort has many faithful regulars.

~

NEARBY Harrods; Victoria and Albert Museum.
LOCATION off Brompton Road, just W of Harrods; pay and display parking in street
FOOD breakfast; room service
PRICE ££££
ROOMS 28 double, twin, single and suites, all with bath or shower; all rooms have phone, TV, video, CD player, air-conditioning, fax/modem points, hairdrier; fax/answering machines on request
FACILITIES sitting room, bar **CREDIT CARDS** AE, DC, MC, V
CHILDREN accepted
DISABLED access difficult
PETS not accepted
CLOSED never **PROPRIETORS** Ahmed and Sarah Jajbhay

THE SOUTH-EAST

LONDON

THE COLONNADE
~ TOWNHOUSE HOTEL ~

2 Warringtom Crescent, Little Venice, London W9 1ER
TEL (020) 7286 1052 **FAX** (020) 7286 1057
E-MAIL res_colonnade@etontownhouse.com **WEBSITE** www.etontownhouse.com

SET IN LITTLE VENICE, with its canals and bridges, The Colonnade Townhouse manages to overcome the trappings of a large hotel to provide a private place to stay. The building itself occupies two Victorian townhouses that were built in 1865 as private residences. In the late 1800s, it was used as a girls' school and, in the early 1900s, it became a maternity hospital. Alan Turing, creator of the first computer and the man who solved the Enigma code, was born here, and you'll find a suite named after him. When the building later became a hotel, Sigmund Freud stayed here while waiting for his house in Hampstead to be finished. In his suite, a bed sits in a gallery above a sitting room with enormous floor-to-ceiling windows. In the JFK Suite, you can sleep in the four-poster bed built for President Kennedy's state visit in 1962. Another suite is named after James Wright, a builder in the early 1900s whose name was found scrawled, graffiti-style, on the walls that he helped to decorate. The rest of the bedrooms are done out in three smart colour schemes: black and gold, green and gold or red and gold. In the sitting room, comfy sofas, attractive stripy chairs, an open coal fire and complimentary sherry, port and lollipops offset the strange artificial topiary.

In the basement, the achingly hip Enigma bar and restaurant serves contemporary Mediterranean fare. Was that snakeskin-textured paneling we spotted beside the bar?

~

NEARBY Little Venice.
LOCATION 1-minute walk from Warwick Avenue tube, 3 car parking spaces in garage, £15 per night, must be pre-booked
FOOD breakfast, lunch, dinner, 24 hr room service
PRICE £££
ROOMS 43; 35 double, 5 twin, 3 single, most with shower, some with bath; all rooms have TV, stereo, phone, minibar, safe, hairdrier, trouser press, iron **FACILITIES** sitting room, restaurant with terrace **CREDIT CARDS** AE, DC, MC, V **CHILDREN** welcome
DISABLED not suitable **PETS** by arrangement **CLOSED** Christmas **MANAGER** Oliver Brown

THE SOUTH-EAST

LONDON

COVENT GARDEN

~ TOWN HOTEL ~

10 Monmouth Street, London WC2H 9HB
TEL (020) 7806 1000 **FAX** (020) 7806 1100
E-MAIL covent@firmdale.com **WEBSITE** www.firmdale.com

THE GROUP OF SEDUCTIVE London hotels owned by Tim and Kit Kemp includes five sprinkled across the city. They began with Dorset Square (see page 106) and then opened several more similar town house hotels, before becoming more expansive here in Covent Garden, but without losing any of their previous assurance.

Monmouth Street is an attractive, fairly quiet street ideally placed for theatre and media-land. The building was formerly a French hospital, which Tim and Kit (she is responsible for all the interior decoration) have transformed into a hotel that at once feels glamorous, yet at the same time welcoming and not in the least intimidating, A stunning drawing room stretches across the first floor, with a really well-stocked drinks-and-snack bar at one end, where guests can help themselves at any time. On the gound floor is a small bar/bistro, serving tasty, simply cooked dishes *à la mode*; or you can order from the well-balanced room service menu at any hour.

Bedrooms all look different, although each possesses a matching fabric-covered mannequin (the hotel is a favourite with models), and they all have superb granite bathrooms with double basins and excellent mirrors. One bedroom has a musical theme, another is split-level, another has a memorable four-poster bed. The cosy attic rooms are also delightful.

~

NEARBY Covent Garden; Royal Opera House; West End theatres.
LOCATION in fairly quiet street between Shaftesbury Avenue and St Martin's Lane; metered parking or public car park nearby
FOOD breakfast, lunch, dinner; room service
PRICE ££££ **ROOMS** 58; 46 double and twin, 6 suites; 6 single, all with bath; all rooms have phone, TV, video, CD player, fax/modem point, air-conditioning, minibar, hairdrier **FACILITIES** drawing room, restaurant, bar, library, work-out room, beauty treatment room, screening room, meeting rooms **CREDIT CARDS** AE, MC, V
CHILDREN accepted **DISABLED** access possible, lift/elevator
PETS not accepted **CLOSED** never **PROPRIETORS** Tim and Kit Kemp

THE SOUTH-EAST

LONDON

DORSET SQUARE
~ TOWN HOUSE HOTEL ~

39 Dorset Square, London NW1 6QN
TEL (020) 7723 7874 **FAX** (020) 7724 3328
E-MAIL reservation@dorsetsquare.co.uk **WEBSITE** www.dorsetsquare.co.uk

L OOKING OUT OVER the original site of Lord's cricket ground, this perfectly restored Regency house is like one of those impossible geometric shapes that are bigger on the inside than on the outside. Yet it is still cosy, and although it offers the services and technology of a new, purpose-built hotel, there is always a real person to welcome you home at any time of the day or night. Kit Kemp and her husband Tim (who also own the Covent Garden, page 105, among other hotels) have thought of just about everything in this, their original venture into hotel-keeping: fabrics and furniture of the style and age to complement the building, bathrooms of such marble splendour that even the most fanatical of critics would look forward to them, fresh flowers everywhere and, last but not least, real radios in all the (good-sized) rooms.

If you need more than a drink from the honesty bar in the sitting room there is the Potting Shed Restaurant and Bar in the basement, so-called because it was here that the Lord's groundsmen kept their pots. Today the restaurant is decorated with cricketing and ballooning scenes and serves modern English food. During the summer you can even ask the hotel to bring your drinks out to you in the square's gardens.

~

NEARBY Regent's Park; Madame Tussaud's; Oxford Street.
LOCATION close to Marylebone and Baker Street station, in square with access to 2-acre private gardens; meter car parking outside, public lot nearby
FOOD breakfast; room service
PRICE ££££
ROOMS 38; 32 double and twin, 6 single, all with bath or shower; all rooms have phone, TV, air-conditioning, minibar, hairdrier, safe; some have fax/modem point
FACILITIES sitting room, restaurant, bar **CREDIT CARDS** AE, MC, V
CHILDREN welcome **DISABLED** not suitable **PETS** not accepted
CLOSED never **MANAGER** Olivia Hetherington

THE SOUTH-EAST

DUKES

⮜ TOWN HOTEL ⮞

35 St James's Place, London SW1A 1NY
TEL (020) 7491 4840 **FAX** (029) 7493 1264
E-MAIL bookings@dukeshotel.com **WEB SITE** www.dukeshotel.co.uk

DISCREETLY SET BACK in its own gas-lit courtyard, this civilized Edwardian hotel makes an excellent address in a prestigious West End area, and is run with efficency and a marked thoughtfulness for its guests by manager Andrew Phillips and his young, friendly team. The place was in a creaky, frayed state by the time hotelier David Naylor-Leyland (who also owns the Franklin, page 109) bought it and gave it a new lease of life a few years ago. The clubby, animated bar is said to serve the best dry martini in London.

The feel of Dukes is of an English country house, mercifully decorated without resorting to excess. This is particularly evident in the restrained but charming bedrooms, which feel more like guest rooms in a private house than hotel rooms, with the bonus of excellent king-size beds. The penthouse, with superb views, would make a perfect romantic hideaway in which to hole up for a few days – finances permitting.

The hotel has recently added fitness and beauty treatment facilities, putting it on a par with much larger luxury establishments. Public rooms are small, but that's what gives the place its cosy feel. Staff are smiling and willing; we would welcome comments on the food.

⮜

NEARBY St James's; Piccadilly Circus; Royal Academy; Green Park.
LOCATION in West End, tucked off St James's Street; valet parking in nearby public car park
FOOD breakfast, lunch, dinner; room service
PRICE ££££
ROOMS 89; 78 double and single, 11 suites, all with bath; all rooms have phone, TV, fax/modem point, minibar, air-conditioning, hairdrier, safety deposit box
FACILITIES sitting room, restaurant, bar, gym, sauna, beauty treatment rooms
CREDIT CARDS AE, DC, MC, V
CHILDREN accepted
DISABLED access possible, lift/elevator
PETS not accepted **CLOSED** never **MANAGER** Andrew Phillips

THE SOUTH-EAST

FIVE SUMNER PLACE

∽ TOWN BED-AND-BREAKFAST ∽

5 Sumner Place, London SW7 3EE
TEL (020) 7584 7586 **FAX** (020) 7823 9962
E-MAIL reservations@sumnerplace.com **WEBSITE** www.sumnerplace.com

IF YOU HAVE SERIOUS SHOPPING in mind, or want to attend a Christie's auction at their sale rooms round the corner, and you are looking for a place to stay which is less hard on the purse than some of the neighbouring 'house hotels', consider Sumner Place. The rooms in this town house are freshly decorated, furnished in traditional style, and reasonably priced for the area. Despite its central location (a few yards from the hurly-burly of South Kensington), it is quiet and unpretentious, there are no signs outside, and you come and go as you please with your own key to the permanently locked front door. South Kensington is the place for buses and tubes to just about anywhere (including Heathrow airport) and boasts one of the few London cab-ranks that actually has taxis waiting on it. Inside, the lift is quite snug (as are the rooms) but in early Victorian houses like this, it is a fairly rare amenity.

Breakfast is a pan-European buffet with cold cuts and cheese as well as the more expected toast, cereal, fruit and yogurt. It is served in a quiet and (sometimes) sunny conservatory which takes up half the small garden. Manager Tom Tyranowicz runs the hotel with quiet efficiency from a minute office and will cheerfully bring you anything from a cup of tea to an ironing board.

∽

NEARBY Science Museum; Natural History Museum; Knightsbridge.
LOCATION in residential street off Old Brompton Road; with public car park and meters nearby
FOOD breakfast
PRICE £££
ROOMS 13; 10 double and twin, 3 single, all with bath or shower; all rooms have phone, TV, hairdrier, answering machine
FACILITIES conservatory, patio **CREDIT CARDS** AE, MC, V
CHILDREN accepted over 6 **DISABLED** bedrooms on ground floor, lift/elevator
PETS not accepted **CLOSED** never **MANAGER** Tom Tyranowicz

THE SOUTH-EAST

THE FRANKLIN
~ TOWN HOUSE HOTEL ~

28 Egerton Gardens, London SW3 2DB
TEL (020) 7584 5533 **FAX** (020) 7584 5449
E-MAIL bookings@franklinhotel.co.uk **WEBSITE** www.franklinhotel.co.uk

LONDON HAS MORE THAN a smattering of *bijoux* town house hotels, and it can be bewildering trying to decide which one to plump for, since they are all centrally located, all abound in acres of expensive fabric in their luxurious bedrooms and smart, rather formal public rooms, and all specialize in friendly yet professional service. The ones we least prefer are almost claustrophobic in their preciousness; the best have an easy-going lack of self-conciousness, while at the same time feeling protective and relaxing, and that's what we like about the Franklin, sister hotel to Dukes (see page 107).

What really sets the Franklin apart are the bedrooms. Some are enormous, some have original features such as plasterwork and panelling, some are split-level, with the bed above and a sitting area below. Best of all are the ground - floor Garden Rooms, which open directly on to private communal gardens, full of white roses in summer, and in which guests are allowed to wander. All the bedrooms are decorated in florals and stripes, flounces and swags, and have king-size beds, some canopied. The elegant, richly decorated public rooms also have garden views, with floor-length windows. Service is prompt and willing, and the young staff are charming. There is now a small 'internet room' that acts as a one-guest-at-a-time business centre.

~

NEARBY Victoria and Albert Museum; Natural History Museum; Knightsbridge; Hyde Park.
LOCATION in side street off Brompton Road, opposite Brompton Oratory; valet parking in public car park
FOOD breakfast; room service
PRICE ££££
ROOMS 47; 37 double and twin, 10 single, all with bath; all rooms have phone, TV, fax/modem point, minibar, air-conditioning, hairdrier **FACILITIES** sitting room, breakfast room, bar, internet room **CREDIT CARDS** AE, DC, MC, V
CHILDREN accepted **DISABLED** access possible, lift/elevator
PETS not accepted **CLOSED** never **MANAGER** Duncan Couper

THE SOUTH-EAST

THE GORE
~ TOWN HOUSE HOTEL ~

189 Queen's Gate, London SW7 5EX
TEL (020) 7584 6601 **FAX** (020) 7589 8127
E-MAIL reservations@gorehotel.co.uk **WEBSITE** www.gorehotel.co.uk

IN 1990 THE TEAM who opened Hazlitt's (see page 111) bought this Victorian town house (long established as a hotel) set in a wide tree-lined street near Kensington Gardens, and since then have given it the Hazlitt treatment: the bedrooms are furnished with period antiques, the walls are enlivened with pictures, and they have recruited a young and friendly staff, trained to give efficient but informal service.

It has character by the bucketload; walls whose every square inch is covered with prints and oil paintings; bedrooms furnished with antiques, each with its own style – a gallery in one room, Judy Garland's bed in another. There is also an impressive dossier in each room describing what to do locally – 'put together with verve and a feel for what the guest might really want'. The panelled bar on the ground floor is a popular rendezvous for non-residents as well as guests. Across the hallway is Bistrot 190 (same owners, same style) which opens from 7.30 am to 11.30 pm and, as well as breakfast, offers lighthearted modern dishes with an international spin.

Restaurant 190, which is famous for its ways with fish, is stylish with rosewood panels and deep red velvet chairs.

~

NEARBY Kensington Gardens; Hyde Park; Albert Hall; Harrods.
LOCATION just S of Kensington Gardens; metered parking and public car park nearby
FOOD breakfast, lunch, dinner
PRICE ££££
ROOMS 54; 31 double, 23 single (32 baths and 22 showers); all rooms have phone, TV, minibar, hairdrier, safe, fax/modem point
FACILITIES library/sitting room, bar, restaurant, bistro
CREDIT CARDS AE, DC, MC, V **CHILDREN** welcome
DISABLED access possible, lift/elevator **PETS** accepted by arrangement
CLOSED never
PROPRIETORS Peter McKay and Douglas Blaine

THE SOUTH-EAST

LONDON

HAZLITTS

◁≈ TOWN HOUSE HOTEL ≈▷

6 Frith Street, Soho, London W1D 3JA
TEL (01409) 211224 **FAX** (01409) 211634
E-MAIL reservations@hazlitts.co.uk **WEBSITE** www.hazlittshotel.com

THERE IS NO QUARTER of central London with more character than Soho; and there are few places to stay with more character than Hazlitt's, formed from three Georgian terraced houses off Soho Square. The sloping, creaking floorboards have been retained (it can be an uphill walk to your bed), and the rooms decorated with suitable antiques, busts and prints. Recent restoration work has revealed original fireplaces and Georgian paneling that's nearly 300 years old. The bedrooms, named after some of the people who visited or stayed in the house where the eponymous essayist himself lived, are delightfully different from most London hotel rooms, some with intricately carved wood headboards, one with a delightful four-poster, all with free-standing bath tubs and Victorian fittings in the bathrooms.

As befits an establishment with such literary connections, Hazlitt's is particularly popular with visiting authors, who leave signed copies of the works when they depart. Sadly, the dresser in the little sitting room in which they are kept is now locked to protect the books, which had a habit of going missing. Continental breakfast is served in the bedrooms, as well as light dishes such as pasta and filled baguettes. A hotel for people who like their comforts authentic, yet stylish.

◁≈▷

NEARBY Oxford Street; Piccadilly Circus; Covent Garden; theatres.
LOCATION in Soho, between Oxford Street and Shaftesbury Avenue; public car parks nearby
FOOD breakfast; room service
PRICE ££££
ROOMS 17 double (1 twin) all with bath; all rooms have phone, TV, fax/modem point, hairdrier, safe, minibars
FACILITIES sitting room **CREDIT CARDS** AE, DC, MC, V
CHILDREN welcome **DISABLED** not suitable **PETS** accepted by arrangement
CLOSED never **PROPRIETORS** Peter McKay and Douglas Blaine

THE SOUTH-EAST

LONDON

L'HOTEL
~ TOWN GUEST HOUSE ~

28 Basil Street, London SW3 1AS
TEL (020) 7589 6286 **FAX** (020) 7823 7826
EMAIL reservations@lhotel.co.uk **WEBSITE** www.lhotel.co.uk

A RECENT REVISIT CONFIRMED L'Hotel as a delightfully tranquil haven in busy Knightsbridge, especially considering that its chic little Metro restaurant in the basement has long made this a popular address with local residents and shoppers. The entrance is pleasantly understated, which gives it the look of a private house. Inside, hand-stencilled motifs embellish the striped colour-washed walls and wooden floor. The small but well-equipped bedrooms have padded fabrics on the walls, in soft creams and beiges, wooden shutters and antique pine furniture, as well as double glazing and cooling fans. Some rooms can be interconnected to form a suite, which is popular with families.

The restaurant has a bright, continental brasserie look and it is also where the hotel guests have breakfast. It is decorated in mellow woods and cosy reds, terracottas and plum shades; the seating combines banquettes, chairs at wooden-topped tables, and bar stools at the brown marble bar. The food is modern British. Guests can also eat at the Capital Hotel, L'Hotel's sister establishment and neighbour, where there is a smart, formal dining room which holds two Michelin stars.

~

NEARBY Knightsbridge; Hyde Park; Buckingham Palace.
LOCATION between Sloane Street and Harrods; public car park opposite and at Capital Hotel, if available
FOOD breakfast, lunch, dinner
PRICE £££
ROOMS 12; 11 double, 1 suite; all with bath; all rooms have phone, TV, minibar, safe
FACILITIES restaurant/bar; use of Capital Hotel facilities
CREDIT CARDS AE, DC, MC, V **CHILDREN** welcome
DISABLED not suitable
PETS accepted by arrangement
CLOSED restaurant only, Sun lunch and dinner
PROPRIETOR David Levin

THE SOUTH-EAST

LONDON

THE KNIGHTSBRIDGE GREEN
~ CITY HOTEL ~

159 Knightsbridge, London SW1X 7PD
TEL (020) 7584 6274 **FAX** (020) 7225 1635
EMAIL thekghotel@aol.com **WEBSITE** www.thekghotel.co.uk

OWNED BY THE SAME FAMILY as the St Enodoc (see page 71), theKnightsbridge Green is a comfortable yet affordable hotel halfway between Harrods and Harvey Nichols. The Marler family keep their prices lower than comparable hotels in the area by steering clear of pricy frills. There are no minibars, no restaurant, no breakfast room (breakfast is served in the large bedrooms) and no health club (guests can use the one at the Berkeley for a fee). There are, however, tea and coffee making facilities in all of the rooms, an ice machine and bar service (11am to 8pm).

Despite employing a charismatic manager, Paul Fizia, the Marlers are still very much involved with the day-to-day running of the hotel, and it shows. It has a cared-for feel, and a host of regular guests use it as a *pied-à-terre*. Downstairs the decoration is refreshingly modern: the entrance in cool mint-green, the large sitting areas in shades of green and blue. The attractive, well-lit bedrooms are all different, with bold printed fabrics, modern furniture and spotless marble bathrooms. Some rooms have pretty window seats, one has a sleigh bed, another a four-poster, and suites have sofa beds, so are ideal for families. Staff are friendly, and they serve an excellent full English breakfast with freshly squeezed orange juice and bacon from Harrods.

~

NEARBY Hyde Park; Victoria and Albert Museum; Harrods, Harvey Nichols.
LOCATION near junction with Brompton Road, opposite Knightsbridge Barracks; car park in Raphael Street
FOOD breakfast; drinks
PRICE £££
ROOMS 28; 5 double, 4 twin, 7 single, 12 suites, all with bath; all rooms have phone, TV, air-conditioning, hairdrier, safe **FACILITIES** sitting room
CREDIT CARDS AE, DC, MC, V **CHILDREN** welcome
DISABLED 2 specially adapted suites, lift/elevator
PETS accepted by arrangement **CLOSED** never **PROPRIETORS** Marler family

THE SOUTH-EAST

LONDON BRIDGE
~ TOWN HOTEL ~

8-18 London Bridge Street, London SE1 9SG
TEL (020) 7855 2200 **FAX** (020) 7855 2233
E-MAIL sales@london-bridge-hotel.co.uk **WEBSITE** www.london-bridge-hotel.co.uk

WHERE DO THEY PUT all those rooms? This large, comfortable, independently-owned hotel, opened in late 1998 and tucked away in a small street beside London Bridge station, manages to feel small, cosy and intimate. The enticing lobby sets the scene, with tartan sofas, pretty lamps, ornamental pillars, silver French chairs, Matisse prints and a smart little concierge's stand; the shiny, chrome luggage trolley gets parked behind some *faux* box trees. Extra executive rooms and a health club were added in 1999 and on the ground floor is The Georgetown restaurant, so this is a perfect base for business people who walk across London Bridge to the City. Right on the doorstep are all the attractions of Bankside, including the new Tate Gallery and Millenium Bridge to St Paul's, and the weekend rates are good value for central London.

Standard bedrooms are smallish and double-glazed; those to the rear of the hotel have views over rooftops, church spires and trees. Neat black and white bathrooms have power showers and granite-topped wash-basin units; rooms have checked fabrics, painted wood furniture and navy blue blankets on the beds. Stowed away in cupboards are special safes for laptops. On the way down to breakfast in the basement you can see Roman remains found under the building.

~

NEARBY The City; Tower of London; Globe Theatre; Bankside Tate.
LOCATION beside London Bridge station; public car park
FOOD breakfast, lunch, dinner, room service
PRICE ££££
ROOMS 138; 134 double and twin. all with bath, 4 single with shower, 3 self-catering apartments; all rooms have phone, fax/modem point, TV, air-conditioning, minibar, hairdrier, safe
FACILITIES lobby, dining room, restaurant, health club **CREDIT CARDS** AE, DC, MC, V
CHILDREN welcome **DISABLED** 6 bedrooms specially adapted, 2 lifts/elevators
PETS not accepted **CLOSED** never **MANAGER** Nicholas Cowell

THE SOUTH-EAST

LONDON

MILLERS
~ TOWN GUEST-HOUSE ~

111a Westbourne Grove, London W2 4UW
TEL (020) 7243 1024 **FAX** (020) 7243 1064
E-MAIL enquiries@millersuk.com **WEBSITE** www.millersuk.com

IF YOU ARE AN ANTIQUE LOVER who thinks your house is as full as it can be, a stay at Martin Miller's hotel (he is the author of the much respected Millers Antiques Guide) will be an educational as well as a comfortable experience. Only local knowledge or skilful map-reading will bring you to the hotel's maroon door in Hereford Road. The sedan chair in the hall and the oriental rugs and prints on the stairs do a poor job of preparing you for the eclectic (and some might say eccentric) splendour of the large first-floor drawing room. It is not so much full of antiques as stacked with them, and you can't help feeling that the addition of just one more snuff-box might cause a perilous situation. Lit in the evening by dozens of candles (helped here and there by a little electricity), a stay at Millers is an entirely unique experience.

Your welcome from the staff couldn't be warmer, and the bedrooms (all named after poets and up more stairs on the second floor) are elegantly, if less dangerously, furnished, each in a style appropriate to its poet. Breakfast, taken at one large table, is a do-it-yourself affair and there is a tremendous choice of restaurants within easy walking distance - but don't forget your key as the front door is always locked.

~

NEARBY Portobello Road Market; Notting Hill Gate; Kensington Gardens; Kensington High Street.
LOCATION on first floor above restaurant on corner of Westbourne Grove and Hereford Road (entrance in Hereford Road); car parking on meters
FOOD breakfast
PRICE £££
ROOMS 8 double and twin, all with bath; all rooms have phone, TV
FACILITIES sitting room, library **CREDIT CARDS** AE, MC, V
CHILDREN accepted **DISABLED** not suitable
PETS not accepted **CLOSED** never
PROPRIETORS Martin and Ioana Miller

THE SOUTH-EAST

NUMBER SIXTEEN

~ TOWN GUEST HOUSE ~

16 Sumner Place, London SW7 3EG
TEL (020) 7589 5232 **FAX** (020) 7584 8615
E-MAIL reservations@ numbersixteenhotel.co.uk **WEBSITE** www.numbersixteenhotel.co.uk

NUMBER SIXTEEN IS one of London's most characterful luxury bed-and-breakfast establishments. The original building has spread along its early Victorian South Kensington terrace, to encompass four adjoining houses – all extensively refurbished in the last few years.

Public rooms and bedrooms alike are brimful of pictures, including a huge eye-catching abstract in the reception room. Downstairs there are always big bowls of fresh flowers – sweet peas or roses perhaps – and the large rear patio garden is well kept and full of colour. Inside, the decoration is richly traditional and harmonious. A series of small sitting rooms with Victorian moulded ceilings, polished antiques and luxurious drapes, lead to an award-winning conservatory, from where, on summer days, you can sit and admire the profusion of flowers outside.

Bedrooms are generously proportioned, comfortable and stylish, largely furnished with period pieces or reproductions; some have French windows opening on to the garden. Breakfast is served in your room or in the public areas. The hotel has no dining room but there are plenty of restaurants on the Old Brompton Road nearby.

~

NEARBY South Kensington museums; Knightsbridge; Kings Road.
LOCATION off Old Brompton Road; no private car parking
FOOD breakfast; room service
PRICE £££
ROOMS 36; 27 double, 23 with bath 4 with shower; 9 single with shower; all rooms have phone, TV, minibar, hairdrier, safe, umbrellas
FACILITIES sitting room, bar, conservatory; small garden
CREDIT CARDS AE, DC, MC, V
CHILDREN accepted over 12
DISABLED access possible, lift/elevator
PETS not accepted **CLOSED** never
MANAGER Tristan McEwen

THE SOUTH-EAST

PEMBRIDGE COURT

~ TOWN HOUSE HOTEL ~

34 Pembridge Gardens, London W2 4DX
TEL (020) 7229 9977 **FAX** (020) 7727 4982
E-MAIL reservations@pemct.co.uk **WEBSITE** www.pemct.co.uk

MANAGED BY VIVACIOUS Nicola Green, but supervised by Churchill, a vast and presidential ginger cat, Pembridge Court is a 19thC town house guarded by bay trees and just far enough removed from the bustle, buses and tubes of Notting Hill Gate to be quiet. Long-established and much loved by its regular guests – many from the worlds of music, motor racing and antiques – the hotel is very much treated as a home from home. One faithful guest actually went so far as to buy it. Rooms vary in size and cost, but, unusually for a small hotel, those advertised as large are exactly that: substantial enough for a business meeting or a small party if you feel like it, and certainly smart enough and well-equipped enough for either. The smallest room is also honestly described: it is called The Last Resort.

On the ground floor is a comfortably furnished sitting room, dressed in yellow and blue, which can also be borrowed for private meetings. Hung everywhere in frames are Victorian lace gloves, fans, beadwork and other fascinating but less instantly recognizable items of millinery. Downstairs the bar and restaurant have now been converted into a breakfast room.

~

NEARBY Kensington Gardens; Kensington High Street; Portobello Road.
LOCATION in residential street just N of Notting Hill Gate; with garage for 2 cars
FOOD breakfast, lunch, dinner, snacks; room service
PRICE £££
ROOMS 20; 17 double and twin, 3 single, 4 with shower, rest with bath; all rooms have phone, TV, hairdrier, voicemail, modem points, air-conditioning; some have CD and video
FACILITIES breakfast room, sitting room with drink service, meeting room
CREDIT CARDS AE, DC, MC, V
CHILDREN welcome
DISABLED access difficult **PETS** accepted by arrangement
CLOSED never **MANAGER** Nicola Green

THE SOUTH-EAST

LONDON

PORTOBELLO
⤳ TOWN HOUSE HOTEL ⤳

22 Stanley Gardens, London W11 2NG
TEL (020) 7727 2777 **FAX** (020) 7792 9641
E-MAIL info@portobello-hotel.co.uk **WEBSITE** www.portobello-hotel.co.uk

OWNED BY TIM HERRING, who also owns the popular Julie's Bar in Clarendon Road, the Portobello has long been the darling of the film, fashion and music industries. You get the feeling that life no longer holds many surprises for the laid-back management. With so many night-owls and international time-travellers as regulars, its reception, bar and restaurant are open right round the clock. Pastel decoration with antique armchairs in the bar and cane chairs in the tiled dining room (the preserve of manager Johnny Ekperigin) give a fresh, light air. The back of the hotel looks out over quiet private gardens framed by a large mimosa tree. The sitting room is a mixture of styles, with Victorian sofas, a large leather-topped desk, parlour palms and stripped French doors draped with brilliant red livery. Military prints and mirrors in gilded frames deck the walls.

Bedrooms vary in size from the spacious (the Round Room has a large round bed and an Edwardian bathing machine in it) to the microscopic 'cabins' on the top floor that nevertheless have refrigerators and colour televisions with a bewildering selection of channels. There are two themed rooms in the basement, one in Japanese style, the other colonial.

⤳

NEARBY Portobello Road; Kensington Gardens; Kensington High Street
LOCATION in residential area of Notting Hill Gate, off Kensington Park Road; with pay and display and metered parking
FOOD breakfast, lunch, dinner; room service
PRICE £££
ROOMS 24; 18 double and twin, 6 single, all with bath or shower; all rooms have phone, TV, fax/modem point, minibar, hairdrier; some have air-conditioning
FACILITIES sitting room, dining room, bar
CREDIT CARDS AE, MC, V
CHILDREN accepted **DISABLED** not suitable
PETS accepted by arrangement
CLOSED Christmas and New Year **PROPRIETOR** Tim Herring

THE SOUTH-EAST

THE ROOKERY
~ TOWN HOTEL ~

Peter's Lane, Cowcross Street, London EC1M 6DS
TEL (020) 7336 0931 **FAX** (020) 7336 0932
E-MAIL reservations@rookery.co.uk **WEBSITE** www.rookeryhotel.com

OPENED BY the owners of the imaginative Hazlitt's and the Gore (see pages 111 and 110), this homely little hotel full of old curiosities and flights of fancy is in a traffic-free alleyway among the restaurants of fashionable Clerkenwell. Created from a row of converted listed Georgian cottages, it is packed with character and 'time-warp' detail: wood panelling; period shutters; open fires; flagged floors; even a special creaky sound put into the treads of the new stairs to make them seem old. Pretty bedrooms have little half-shutters, fresh Egyptian cotton sheets, summer and winter duvets. Minibars and 'workstations' are discreetly hidden behind antique doors. Bathrooms are delightful, with Victorian fittings, exposed copper pipes and wainscotting. The suite – on two floors – pushes the general style further. The rococo French bed, attendant blackamoor, and Edwardian bathing machine behind lace curtains, are in the same room, and an electronically controlled ceiling panel shuts off the upper floor for business meetings, so no rumpled sheets are visible.

A conservatory, with open fire, leather chairs and rustic pictures, serves as a day room, opening on to a tiny terrace garden. Breakfast, continental, is on trays: fresh orange juice, coffee and croissants prepared and baked in the kitchen early every morning by the hotel's own *pâtissier*.

NEARBY The City; St Paul's; Smithfield; Farringdon tube station.
LOCATION in pedestrian street in Clerkenwell, near Smithfield and City; parking in nearby public car park
FOOD breakfast, light meals; room service
PRICE £££££
ROOMS 31; 24 double, 6 single, 1 suite, all with bath; all rooms have phone, fax/modem points, TV, minibar, hairdrier, safe
FACILITIES conservatory; terrace **CREDIT CARDS** AE, DC, MC, V **CHILDREN** accepted
DISABLED 1 bedroom on ground floor **PETS** accepted by arrangement
CLOSED Christmas **PROPRIETORS** Peter McKay and Douglas Blaine

THE SOUTH-EAST

LONDON

TWENTY NEVERN SQUARE
~ TOWN HOUSE HOTEL ~

Twenty Nevern Square, London SW5 9PD
TEL (020) 7565 9555 **FAX** (020) 7565 9444
E-MAIL reservations@twentynevernsquare.co.uk **WEBSITE** www.twentynevernsquare.co.uk

PEACE AND TRANQUILITY aren't two words usually associated with London but, just around the corner from bustling Earl's Court, Twenty Nevern Square, new to this edition, is suprisingly calm and cosy. Set across from a graceful private square, this townhouse hotel is compact rather than cramped and intimate rather than uncomfortable.

Decorated in a combination of colonial and italian influences, rooms have a feeling of understated luxury. Natural fabrics have been used throughout; silk curtains, wooden floors and hessian carpets blend nicely with muted walls and smart patterned bedspreads. One hundred metres of silk has been used in decorating the Chinese room, with oriental-print cushions and floor-to-ceiling white and navy drapes and a unique hand-carved cabinet resembling a temple. Four bedrooms have delightful 'sleigh' beds and two others have terraces that look down into local backyard gardens. Bathrooms are brick, smart and done out entirely in marble.

Downstairs, the conservatory-style restaurant serves simple Mediterranean-style food at reasonable prices. Main courses all cost less than £10 - a rare find in London. In the small sitting room, two lovebirds in a wicker cage twitter happily to themselves. After our visit to Twenty Nevern Square, we felt pretty content, too.

~

NEARBY Earl's Court Exhibition Centre, Natural History Museum, Victoria and Albert Museum.
LOCATION 2-minute walk from Earl's Court tube station, with 4 car parking spaces on secure lot, £17.50 per night, must be pre-booked
FOOD breakfast, lunch, dinner, 24 hr room service
PRICE £££
ROOMS 19; 5 single, 14 double or twin, all with shower or bath; all rooms have TV, stereo, phone, hairdrier **FACILITIES** restaurant, sitting room
CREDIT CARDS AE, DC, MC, V **CHILDREN** accepted **DISABLED** access difficult
PETS not accepted **CLOSED** never **MANAGER** Aleksandra Turner

THE SOUTH-EAST

LYMINGTON, HAMPSHIRE

STANWELL HOUSE

TOWN HOTEL

High Street, Lymington, Hampshire, SO41 9AA
TEL (01590) 677123 **FAX** (01590) 677756
E-MAIL sales@stanwellhousehotel.co.uk **WEBSITE** www.stanwellhousehotel.co.uk

UNTIL ITS RECENT REINCARNATION, Stanwell House Hotel was a fading Georgian landmark in the prettiest part of Lymington's attractive High Street. When Jane McIntyre took over in 1995 the place was transformed: an Italianate stone-flagged courtyard now stretches the length of the building, affording inviting views from the street of a glass-roofed sitting room strewn with velvet cushions; on one side of the entrance is a smart country clothing shop, Stanwells, on the other a bar and a cosy bistro in simple 17thC style – dark walls, oak settles, pewter plates and a *trompe l'oeil* fireplace. Our meal here was delicious, in the modern English manner, and inexpensive.

In contrast to the bistro, the candle-lit restaurant – steel chairs upholstered in purple, cerise, pink and deep red velvet, swathes of silk curtains – and the bedrooms in the main house are theatrical, not to say over the top. The latter share a predeliction for dramatic walls, rich hangings in silk, velvet and brocade, piles of white cushions and baths, some of them roll top, swathed in yet more fabric. The bedrooms in the extension are a lesson in how to make undistinguished rooms look pretty and welcoming. This hotel attracts a laid-back youngish clientèle, especially for weekends away from the city.

We have had a quite serious letter from a reader regarding cleanliness and service; we hope it's a one off but we would welcome more comments.

NEARBY New Forest; Beaulieu; Isle of Wight.
LOCATION on High Street, close to the quay and marina; public car parks nearby
FOOD breakfast, lunch dinner
PRICE ££
ROOMS 11 double, 8 twin, 3 luxury suites; 2-bedroomed cottage; all with bath,
1 with shower; all rooms have phone, TV, hairdrier **FACILITIES** conservatory, bar,
dining room, bistro; garden **CREDIT CARDS** AE, DC, MC, V **CHILDREN** welcome
DISABLED access difficult **PETS** accepted **CLOSED** never **PROPRIETOR** Jane MacIntyre

THE SOUTH-EAST

PETWORTH, WEST SUSSEX

THE OLD RAILWAY STATION
~ BED-AND-BREAKFAST ~

Petworth, West Sussex GU28 0JF
TEL (01798) 342346 **FAX** (01798) 342346
E-MAIL mlr@old-station.co.uk **WEBSITE** www.old-station.co.uk

IF YOU'VE EVER DREAMED about stepping back in time and taking a great rail journey, now you can do just that – in West Sussex. The Old Railway Station, new to this edition, provides unique accommodation in either the original Petworth Railway Station building, dating from 1894, or in one of three Pullman Carriages rescued from the Cornish seaside.

The station building, now Grade II listed, is both impressive and welcoming. The former waiting-room, which now contains the breakfast room and sitting-room, has 20-foot vaulted ceilings, original ticket office windows and, in winter, a roaring log fire. In the summer, you can enjoy breakfast on the terrace, which was the station platform and sits above a grassy area that follows the old rail line's path under a nearby tunnel.

At the other end of the platform sit three early 20th century carriages, just like the ones used by the Orient Express. Because of the obvious space constraints, bedrooms and bathrooms are narrow, but very long. Original furnishings, marquetry in the walls and antique luggage and clocks all add to the charm, though bathrooms are modern. Beds are large – almost as wide as the carriages – and inviting.

Inside the main building, two bedrooms lie at the top of a book-lined spiral staircase (the library). Both rooms are spacious and well-fitted out and one has an original stained glass window in the bathroom that overlooks the waiting room. A romantic experience that's just a little bit different.

~

NEARBY Petworth.
LOCATION just S of Petworth off A285, ample parking
FOOD breakfast
PRICE ££–£££
ROOMS 8 doubles, all with bath; all rooms with TV, radio, hairdrier
FACILITIES breakfast room, sitting room with modem point; terrace
CREDIT CARDS MC, V **CHILDREN** accepted over 10 **DISABLED** by arrangement
PETS not accepted **CLOSED** end of Dec **PROPRIETOR** Mrs Lou Rapley

THE SOUTH-EAST

RINGLESTONE, KENT

RINGLESTONE INN

~ COUNTRY INN ~

Ringlestone Hamlet, near Harrietsham, Maidstone, Kent ME17 1NX
TEL (01622) 859900 **FAX** (01622) 859966
E-MAIL bookings@ringlestone.com **WEBSITE** www.ringlestone.com

AFFABLE MIKE MILLINGTON-BUCK (he used to run Leeds Castle) has this secluded little hamlet up on the downs buzzing with projects. The centrepiece is a 16thC inn, once used as a hospice for monks, with warm, traditional, oak-beamed bars offering good food, home-made pies, 32 English fruit wines, and French house and chateaux wines imported by Mike and his daughter, Michelle Stanley.

Quiet, very comfortable lodgings are over the road in a converted tile-hung Kentish farmhouse, where one entry in the Visitor's Book remarks 'You've thought of everything'. Indeed, these are delightful rooms, with cream natural fabrics, French rustic furniture, pretty white embroidered sheets and pillow cases and spotless bathrooms with power showers, but it is the thoughtfulness here that impresses. Summer and winter duvets, a whole tea-set in your room so you can invite friends in, a washing machine and ironing board on the landing, *three* kinds of breakfast, including a tray in your room, and a housekeeper, Jane, to look after any other needs. The rumoured expansion has yet to materialize and, in our opinion, Ringlestone Inn doesn't need it. One reader was disappointed with the quality of the food and was concerned that the price might be a bit high. Comments welcome.

~

NEARBY Leeds Castle; Sissinghurst; Canterbury; Rochester; Rye.
LOCATION in hamlet; off A20, between Harrietsham and Wormshill; car parking
FOOD breakfast, lunch, dinner
PRICE £££
ROOMS 3 double and twin, all with bath; all rooms have phone, TV, CD player, hairdrier, minibar, trouser press
FACILITIES dining room, sitting room; garden, terrace
CREDIT CARDS AE, DC, MC, V **CHILDREN** accepted
DISABLED access difficult **PETS** not accepted
CLOSED Christmas Day **PROPRIETORS** Mike Millington-Buck and Michele Stanley

THE SOUTH-EAST

RUSHLAKE GREEN, EAST SUSSEX

STONEHOUSE
∽ COUNTRY HOUSE HOTEL ∽

Rushlake Green, Heathfield, East Sussex TN21 9QJ
TEL (01435) 830553 **FAX** (01435) 830726
WEBSITE www.stonehousesussex.co.uk

OUR LATEST REPORTER enthusiastically agrees with everything we have said about Stone House in the past. It is Peter and Jane Dunn's ancestral family home, a glorious 16thC manor house. The delightful Jane ('old world and lovely manners') does what she enjoys most – cooking, and looking after her guests individually. Her relaxed and friendly demeanour belies a very sure touch, and Stone House is run with great competence – which means it is much in demand for house parties, Glyndebourne visitors (luxury wicker picnic hampers can be prepared), shooting weekends and even small executive conferences. They have recently created a Victorian walled vegetable garden and an 18thC-style rose garden. Wine has become a hobby for Peter and Jane, and they are justly proud of their wine list.

Bedooms are beautifully decorated; two have fine antique four-posters and are particularly spacious (the bathrooms can double as sitting rooms). Televisions are hidden so as not to spoil the period charm. An excellent place in which to sample authentic English country living at its most gracious – log fires and billiards, woodland walks and croquet – together with the atmosphere of a home.

∽

NEARBY Battle; Glyndebourne.
LOCATION just off village green 3 miles (4.5 km) SE of Heathfield, in large grounds with ample car parking
FOOD breakfast, lunch by arrangement, dinner
PRICE £££
ROOMS 6 double and twin, all with bath; all rooms have phone, TV, hairdrier
FACILITIES sitting room, library, dining room; billiards, snooker; gardens, croquet, fishing, shooting **CREDIT CARDS** MC, V
CHILDREN welcome over 9
DISABLED access difficult **PETS** accepted in bedrooms only
CLOSED Christmas to 6 Jan **PROPRIETORS** Peter and Jane Dunn

THE SOUTH-EAST

RYE, EAST SUSSEX

JEAKE'S HOUSE
TOWN HOUSE BED-AND-BREAKFAST

Mermaid Street, Rye, East Sussex TN31 7ET
TEL (01797) 222828 **FAX** (01797) 222623
E-MAIL jeakeshouse@btinternet.com **WEBSITE** www.jeakeshouse.com

THIS SPLENDID 17THC HOUSE – or rather three houses turned into one – has been lovingly restored to make a delightful small hotel: a verdict confirmed by many readers, who return time after time. It is the domaine of Jenny Hadfield, who used to be an operatic soprano, and although the place is essentially a charming small hotel, she has lent it a certain theatrical quality. Originally built as a wool store in 1689, it later became a Baptist school and, earlier this century, the home of American writer Conrad Potter Aiken, when it played host to many of the leading artistic and literary figures of the time.

The beamed bedrooms, which come in various shapes and sizes, overlook either the old roof-tops of Rye or Romney Marsh. Bedsteads are either brass or mahogany, bedspreads lace, furniture antique. There are plenty of thoughtful extras in the rooms. Downstairs, a galleried ex-chapel makes the grandest of breakfast rooms. A roaring fire greets guests on cold mornings, and Jenny will serve you either a traditional breakfast or a vegetarian alternative. There is a comfortable parlour with a piano and a bar, with books and pictures lining the walls. 'Situated on *the* street in Rye (the cobbled Mermaid Street) within walking distance of all the sights,' says our inspector. 'In all, a lovely place, and Jenny is bright, bonny and amusing.'

NEARBY Great Dixter; Ellen Terry Museum.
LOCATION in centre of Rye; private car parking nearby
FOOD breakfast
PRICE ££
ROOMS 11; 7 double and twin, 1 single, 2 family rooms, 1 suite; 9 rooms with bath, 1 sharing; all rooms have TV, phone
FACILITIES dining room, sitting room, bar **CREDIT CARDS** MC, V
CHILDREN accepted over 11
DISABLED access difficult **PETS** by arrangement **CLOSED** never
PROPRIETOR Jenny Hadfield

THE SOUTH-EAST

RYE, EAST SUSSEX

THE OLD VICARAGE
∼ TOWN GUEST-HOUSE ∼

66 Church Square, Rye, East Sussex TN31 7HF
TEL (01797) 222119 **FAX** (01797) 227466
E-MAIL oldvicaragerye@info.net **WEBSITE** www.oldvicaragerye.co.uk

THIS CHARMING, SUGAR PINK, listed Georgian house with a fenced front garden filled with roses is on a footpath leading to the churchyard of St Mary-the-Virgin. The church stands on top of the hill on which Rye is built, so it is quiet and secluded, away from the noise and traffic. It's a warm and welcoming house, and the experienced Masters have built up a faithful following; not surprisingly, their self-imposed high standards of hospitality have been rightly recognised. Paul, a former hotelier, cooks and has twice carried off a Best Breakfast in Britain competition with his hot scones, home-made jam, home-made yoghurt, local sausages and Romney Marsh mushroom morning spreads. Julia, who used to work for a tea importer, was recently a Landlady of the Year finalist. Her personal touches are everywhere: newspapers chosen for each guest (she's rarely wrong about who reads what); maps and guidebooks in every room for those who like exploring; home-made fudge and biscuits on the hot drinks tray. Her most popular room is the first floor front, overlooking the churchyard, with four-poster bed. She uses Laura Ashley prints and fabrics for a pretty effect and disguises shower rooms as cupboards. Regulars return again and again, giving a comforting sense of continuity. "A gem for those who like small, family-run places", says our reporter. This is a non-smoking house.

∼

NEARBY Great Dixter; Ellen Terry Museum; Romney Marsh.
LOCATION on footpath in centre of Rye (on A259); private car parking £2.50 a day
FOOD breakfast
PRICE ££
ROOMS 4; 3 double, 1 suite, 3 with shower, 1 with bath; all rooms have TV, hairdrier
FACILITIES sitting room, library, TV room, dining room
CREDIT CARDS not accepted **CHILDREN** accepted over 8
DISABLED access difficult **PETS** not accepted
CLOSED Christmas **PROPRIETORS** Julia and Paul Masters

THE SOUTH-EAST

ST MARGARET'S AT CLIFFE, KENT

WALLETT'S COURT

～ MANOR HOUSE HOTEL ～

Westcliffe, St Margaret's at Cliffe, Dover, Kent CT15 6EW
TEL (01304) 852424 **FAX** (01304) 853430
E-MAIL wc@wallettscourt.com **WEBSITE** www.wallettscourt.com

THE OAKLEYS STARTED doing bed-and-breakfast in their handsome old manor house in 1979, rescuing it from a poor state of repair. They developed in steps into a hotel with a restaurant that now has a reputation locally as well as with guests. Another recent expansion has brought the hotel to a total of 16 rooms. On a recent visit, we thought that the rooms in the outlying buildings (except for the Barn) were standardized – too much like hotel rooms for this guide; but the rooms in the main house and the converted barn retain their charm. The barn rooms each have individual character and a rustic feel while the bedrooms in the main house have four-poster beds, robust antique furniture and large bathrooms.

Dating from 1627 (but on much earlier foundations), the main house has abundant beams and brickwork in the best Kent tradition and the public areas include a panelled sitting room with period furniture and a grandfather clock ticking calmly away. The breakfast room is pleasantly in keeping and there is an impressive old staircase.

Wallet's Court also has a spa club available to members; the gym has good equipment and personal instructors and the pool looks out onto the rolling Kent countryside. Convenient for the ferry terminals and the Channel tunnel, the hotel plugs a gap in an area where there is a dearth of hotels.

～

NEARBY Walmer Castle; ferries and Eurotunnel.
LOCATION 3 miles (5 km) NE of Dover on B2058, off A258; ample car parking
FOOD breakfast, lunch dinner
PRICE ££
ROOMS 16 double, twin and family, all with bath; all rooms have phone, TV, hairdrier
FACILITIES sitting room, 2 dining rooms, children's playground, indoor swimming pool, sauna, solarium, gym; garden, tennis court, miniature golf, beauty and massage treatments **CREDIT CARDS** AE, DC, MC, V **CHILDREN** welcome
DISABLED 6 ground-floor bedrooms **PETS** not accepted **CLOSED** Christmas
PROPRIETORS Chris, Lea and Gavin Oakley

THE SOUTH-EAST

SEAVIEW, ISLE OF WIGHT

PRIORY BAY HOTEL
~ SEASIDE HOTEL ~

Priory Drive, Seaview, Isle of Wight PO34 5BU
TEL (01983) 613146 **FAX** (01983) 616539
E-MAIL reservations@priorybay.co.uk **WEBSITE** www.priorybay.co.uk

WHEN ANDREW PALMER'S motorboat broke down on the sweeping private beach of Priory Bay, he stumbled on an old-fashioned hotel with extensive grounds that he never knew existed, despite a lifetime of holidaying in the area. He bought it, and with the help of a talented friend, Annabel Claridge, effected a stunning transformation, opening in summer 1998. Bedrooms are decorated with charm and freshness, each different, some seaside simple, others more dramatic. The house itself has a colourful history and a quirky hotch-potch of styles with a Tudor farmhouse at its core and a Norman tithe barn in the grounds. Memorable details include the Gothic church porch brought from France in the 1930s, the Tudor fireplace depicting the *Sacrifice of Isaac*, and the delightful Georgian murals of pastoral island scenes in the dining room. Less lovely are the grounds – at present – and the scattered oubuildings, some barrack-like. The highlight is the wonderful sweep of beach where children can be kept happy for hours (this is an extremely child-friendly hotel), with a beach bar, serving grills and salads, cutting out the need to retreat to the hotel for lunch.

Dinner, on our visit, was very good. Andrew Palmer, who founded the New Covent Garden Soup Company, is settling into his role in life as a hotelier.
~

NEARBY Osborne House; Bembridge Maritime Museum; Cowes.
LOCATION in own grounds with private beach, on B3330 S of Seaview between Nettlestone and St Helens; ample car parking
FOOD breakfast, lunch dinner
PRICE ££ **ROOMS** 18 double and twin, all with bath; all rooms have phone, TV, hairdrier; also 10 self-catering cottages
FACILITIES drawing room, sitting room, bar, 2 dining rooms; garden, 9-hole golf course, tennis, swimming pool, private beach, sailing, fishing, windsurfing, beach restaurant **CREDIT CARDS** AE, MC, V **CHILDREN** welcome **DISABLED** access possible
PETS not accepted **CLOSED** never **PROPRIETORS** Andrew and James Palmer

THE SOUTH-EAST

SEAVIEW, ISLE OF WIGHT

SEAVIEW HOTEL
~ SEA TOWN HOTEL ~

High Street, Seaview, Isle of Wight PO34 5EX
TEL (01983) 612711 **FAX** (01983) 613729
E-MAIL reception@seaviewhotel.co.uk **WEBSITE** www.seaviewhotel.co.uk

IF YOU HAVE A PENCHANT FOR breezy, old-fashioned English seaside resorts, you will love sailing-mad Seaview, and probably this hotel, which also acts as the central pub of the village. The Haywards have been at the helm for 20 years, but there seems to be no let-up in their enthusiasm for keeping up high standards and for providing a really personal service. Their dedication has paid off: amongst the raft of awards they have won over the years, a great source of pride must be last year's for UK Quality in Business Excellence; and indeed when we last called Nick was carrying out staff appraisal. It certainly appears to be a happy team, if the staff's willingness is anything to go by, and extra touches, such as turning down the beds at night and serving freshly squeezed orange juice with the early morning tea are appreciated by guests, many of whom return each year.

There is a public bar, towards the rear of the building, and two restaurants, one smoking and one non-smoking, but serving the same menu. One, called the Sunshine Room, but actually painted blue, is an airy room with a contemporary feel, a showcase for Nick's collection of model ships. The other is more formal, with a nautical bar. New chef Michael Green, who came from a Michelin-starred restaurant, uses locally-caught seafood. Comments on the food would be welcome.

NEARBY Osborne House; Flamingo Park; Bembridge.
LOCATION near the beach in seaside village 3 miles (5 km) E of Ryde; car parking
FOOD breakfast, lunch, dinner; room service
PRICE ££
ROOMS 16; 14 double and twin, 12 with bath, 2 with shower; 2 suites both with bath; all rooms have phone, TV, hairdrier; 2 self-catering cottages
FACILITIES 2 sitting rooms, 2 dining rooms, 2 bars **CREDIT CARDS** AE, DC, MC, V
CHILDREN welcome **DISABLED** 2 ground-floor bedrooms, but doors narrow
PETS accepted, but not in public rooms
CLOSED Christmas **PROPRIETORS** Nick and Nicola Hayward

THE SOUTH-EAST

HOTEL DU VIN
~ TOWN HOTEL ~

Crescent Road, Tunbridge Wells, Kent TN1 2LY
TEL (01892) 526455 **FAX** (01892) 512044
E-MAIL info@tunbridgewells.hotelduvin.co.uk **WEBSITE** www.hotelduvin.co.uk

THE MUCH-PRAISED HOTEL du Vin & Bistro in Winchester (see page 134) has replicated itself twice over, first here in Tunbridge Wells, and more recently in Bristol (see page 41). They could now, therefore, be described as a group of chain hotels (more are planned), a species which this guide goes out of its way to ignore. However, such is the panache with which Robin Hutson, Gerard Besson and Peter Chittick have carried out their vision of an easy-going yet chic mid-price town hotel that we have no hesitation in including any of them: they are all great.

As in Winchester, once again the owners set their sights on a faded old hotel, ripe for conversion, in this case one with an elevated position, an abundance of space, and many period features such as the billiard room (its walls now charmingly decorated with hand-painted cigar designs), the staircase, fireplaces in the bedrooms and the delightful terrace overlooking Calverley Park. Bedrooms are stylishly restrained and extremely comfortable, with huge bathrooms and deliciously deep tubs and spacious showers. The Bistro is a faithful copy of Winchester's, right down to the garland of hops and the world-class *sommelier*. This one – Henri Chapon – came from Manoir aux Quat' Saisons. We asked him why. 'At the Manoir, it was a case of keeping everything the same; here, with a new venture, we can move forward.' The food has a sunny Mediterranean bias.

~

NEARBY Sissinghurst Castle Gardens; Rye.
LOCATION in centre of town, with car parking
FOOD breakfast, lunch, dinner
PRICE £££
ROOMS 36 double, 4 with shower, 32 with bath; all rooms have phone, TV, CD player, minibar, hairdrier **FACILITIES** sitting room, billiard room, bar, bistro; terrace
CREDIT CARDS AE, DC, MC, V **CHILDREN** welcome
DISABLED access possible, lift/elevator **PETS** not accepted
CLOSED never **MANAGER** Matthew Callard

The South-East

Uckfield, East Sussex

Hooke Hall
～ Town bed-and-breakfast ～

High Street, Uckfield, East Sussex TN22 1EN
Tel (01825) 761578 **Fax** (01825) 768025
website www.hookehall.co.uk

Hooke Hall has featured in these pages for years now, and it continues its policy of providing comfortable bed-and-breakfast accommodation in gracious surroundings, although we have heard one dissenting voice which talked of things being stuck in a rut. We prefer to think that owner Alister Percy's gentle humour and kind manner atones for the slightly dated furnishings and frayed carpets.

Hooke Hall is an elegant Queen Anne town house (built in the early 18th century), situated in the centre of Uckfield. Juliet, Alister's wife, runs her own interior design business and knows all about good taste in the traditional manner: family portraits, panelled rooms, log fires, gentle lighting, her own charming botanical paintings, mementos from foreign travels and plenty of flowers all contribute to the effect. The combination of home and guest-house is cleverly achieved; there is a domesticated, lived-in air about the place despite the presence of such chain hotel standbys as minibars and trouser-presses in the rooms.

The ten bedrooms vary in size, some richly decorated with four-poster beds, others with sloping ceilings.

～

Nearby Sheffield Park; Brighton; Glyndebourne.
Location on the A22, 10 miles (16 km) SW of Tunbridge Wells; in the centre of town; car parking
Food breakfast
Price ££
Rooms 10 double and twin, 8 with bath, 2 with shower; all rooms have TV, minibar hairdrier **Facilities** sitting room; garden
Credit cards MC, V
Children welcome over 12
Disabled access difficult **Pets** not accepted
Closed Christmas and New Year
Proprietors Alister and Juliet Percy

THE SOUTH-EAST

HOTEL CONTINENTAL
~ SEASIDE HOTEL ~

29 Beach Walk, Whitstable, Kent CT5 2BP
TEL (01227) 280280 **FAX** (01227) 280257
E-MAIL reservations@hotelcontinental.co.uk **WEBSITE** www.hotelcontinental.co.uk

WHITSTABLE, WITH ITS ROWS of cottages and beach huts strung along the shore, has recently achieved cult status. For trendy thirty-somethings, this inspired small 1920s hotel, restored in Art Deco style and opened in the summer of 1998, is *the* place to be beside the seaside. With bright colours, simple decoration and excellent brasserie food, James Green of the Whitstable Oyster Fishery Company family – a thirty-something marine biologist – has brought light, life and fun back to what was, for years, a sad, squalid building. Right on the beach, it is perfect for families, and the large mustard yellow and red bar room downstairs (kept cosy with a wood-burning stove) has tall windows overlooking the sea – ten of the bedrooms have sea views, too (four with balcony). Bedrooms are a bit too basic, with a minimum of furniture – you hang your clothes on a brass peg on the wall – but the framed photographs (one per room) by local photographer Mark Dimico are both suitable and stylish. Bathrooms are small, white-tiled with a smart blue stripe. At night, you can lie in bed, pull back the blue curtains to see the lights of the ships in the distance and listen to the sound of the sea. You can get even closer to the sea in one of the simply converted fishermen's huts (especially fun for children) which stand on the beach. There's a restaurant for dinner and the bar serves food all day Friday and Saturday, with a half dozen Whitstable Rock oysters – produced by the hotel's own fisherman - only £5.

~

NEARBY Canterbury; Margate; North Downs
LOCATION on seafront; with ample car parking.
FOOD breakfast, lunch, dinner
PRICE ££
ROOMS 23; 21 double and twin, 1 suite, 1 family room, all with bath; all rooms have phone, TV, hairdrier **FACILITIES** bar, brasserie/restaurant, sitting room
CREDIT CARDS AE, DC, MC, V **CHILDREN** welcome **DISABLED** no special facilities
PETS not accepted **CLOSED** never **MANAGER** James Green

THE SOUTH-EAST

WICKHAM, HAMPSHIRE

OLD HOUSE

~ VILLAGE HOTEL ~

The Square, Wickham, Hampshire PO17 5JG
TEL (01329) 833049 **FAX** (01329) 833672

THE OLD HOUSE, A STALWART of our guide for many years, possesses much
that we look for: an interesting setting – at a corner of the main square
of one of the finest villages in Hampshire; a superb building – Grade II
listed early Georgian; a delightful secluded garden; an immaculately kept
and welcoming interior, with antiques and *'objets'* arranged to the best
possible effect; and an attractive restaurant, created from the original
timber-framed outhouse and stables.

Nothing is over-stated – except perhaps the generous arrangements of
fresh flowers that adorn all the public rooms. Bedrooms vary
considerably – some palatial, others with magnificent beams, one or two
rather cramped – but again a mood of civilized comfort prevails. Our
reporter remarked on the imposing carved bar and the attractive
beamed dining room. However, times are changing for the Old House.
The Skipwiths, who had been here for nearly 30 years, 'declared their
innings closed' a couple of years ago, and since then the hotel has
changed hands three times. The decorations, the ambience and even the
French regional menu have happily stayed largely the same and so, it
seems, does the warmth of welcome. A reader writes: 'lovely bedrooms...
staff excellent... food delicious... they deserve to do well as so much
thought is put into providing a lovely experience.'

~

NEARBY Portsmouth (ferries); South Downs; Winchester, Chichester.
LOCATION 2.5 miles (4 km) N of Fareham, on square in middle of village; car parking
FOOD breakfast, lunch, dinner
PRICE ££
ROOMS 9; 7 double and twin, 2 single, all with bath; all rooms have TV, phone,
hairdrier **FACILITIES** sitting room, 3 dining rooms, bar
CREDIT CARDS AE, DC, MC, V
CHILDREN accepted **DISABLED** access difficult **PETS** not accepted
CLOSED never **PROPRIETOR** Mr P Scott

THE SOUTH-EAST

HOTEL DU VIN
~ TOWN HOUSE HOTEL ~

14 Southgate Street, Winchester, Hampshire S023 9EF
TEL (01962) 841414 **FAX** (01962) 842458
E-MAIL reception@winchester.hotelduvin.com **WEBSITE** www.hotelduvin.com

THERE IS AN ALLURING BUZZ in the air at this stylish, affordable Georgian town house, flagship hotel in the now burgeoning Hotel du Vin group (see pages 41 and 130). It's got panache, and the wood-floored, hop-garlanded Bistro sets the tone: staffed by a charming bunch of mainly French youngsters, it has the intimate, slightly chaotic yet professional air of the genuine article. Start with a bucket of champagne in the voluptuous mirrored and muralled bar, then choose a bottle from the inventive, kindly priced wine list to go with the inventive, sunny, Modern English food.

The bedrooms and bathrooms are every bit as appealing, with fresh Egyptian cotton bedlinen, CD players, capacious baths and huge showers. For maximum quiet, ask for a Garden Room, or splash out on the sensuous Durney Vineyards suite with a four-poster draped in maroon velvet, a black slate double shower and murals depicting famous paintings of nudes. 'Breakfast in Bed' has recently been introduced, but otherwise there is no room service, helping to keep prices remarkably reasonable. There is also a loftily proportioned sitting room, its walls decorated with *trompe l'oeil* panelling in delicious shades of caramel and pale green.

~

NEARBY Cathedral; Venta Roman Museum; Winchester College.
LOCATION in the town centre, a minute's walk from the cathedral; ample car parking
FOOD breakfast, lunch, dinner
PRICE £££
ROOMS 23; 22 double and twin,1 suite, all with bath; all rooms have phone, TV, CD player, minibar, hairdrier
FACILITIES sitting room, dining room/breakfast room, private dining room, bar, wine-tasting cellar; garden, boules
CREDIT CARDS AE, DC, MC, V
CHILDREN welcome
DISABLED several bedrooms on ground floor
PETS not accepted **CLOSED** never **MANAGER** Mark Huntley

THE SOUTH-EAST

WINCHESTER, HAMPSHIRE

WYKEHAM ARMS
~ TOWN INN ~

75 Kingsgate Street, Winchester, Hampshire SO23 9PE
TEL (01962) 853834 **FAX** (01962) 854411

'**E**NORMOUSLY CHARMING; tons of personality,' confirms our latest reporter. Tucked away in the quietest, oldest part of the city, with Winchester College only yards away and the Cathedral also close by, this is primarily a well-frequented local pub, and a first-rate one: 250 years old with four cosy bars furnished with old school desks, one engraved with the Winchester motto, *Manners Makyth Man*. Interesting objects – old squash rackets, peculiar walking sticks – line the warm brick-red walls. This quirky character runs to the bedrooms, which are small in proportion and low-ceilinged, but each furnished in its own style with a personal feel, and adapted to accommodate all the usual facilities.

Breakfast is served upstairs, over the pub, in a pleasant straightforward English country breakfast room with Windsor chairs and a fine collection of silver tankards. Hearty pub food at lunch time and in the evenings; real ales and an impressive list of 70 wines, changed regularly, 20 served by the glass. Outside is a cobbled courtyard. Over the road is the 'Saint George' annexe with seven pleasant bedrooms and a suite with a 'folly' bedroom in the old College Bakehouse.

~

NEARBY Cathedral; Venta Roman Museum; Winchester College.
LOCATION next door to College, on corner of Canon Street; small courtyard garden with some car parking
FOOD breakfast, lunch, dinner
PRICE ££
ROOMS 14, 9 double with bath, 2 twin with bath, 2 single with shower; all rooms have phone, TV
FACILITIES sitting room, 2 bars, patio
CREDIT CARDS AE, MC, V
CHILDREN welcome over 14
DISABLED access difficult **PETS** welcome
CLOSED Christmas Day **MANAGER** Kate and Peter Miller

THE SOUTH-EAST

YARMOUTH, ISLE OF WIGHT

GEORGE HOTEL
~ SEASIDE TOWN HOTEL ~

Quay Street, Yarmouth, Isle of Wight PO41 OPE
TEL (01983) 760331 **FAX** (01983) 760425
E-MAIL res@thegeorge.co.uk **WEBSITE** www.thegeorge.co.uk

IN MANY WAYS THE GEORGE is a perfect hotel: an atmospheric building in the centre of a breezy and historic harbour town, with welcoming rooms, a buzzing brasserie with tables spilling across the waterfront garden, and a quieter, more formal restaurant where good, inventive food is served. When they took over the peeling and faded 17thC former govenor's residence, owners John Illsley (former bass guitarist of Dire Straits) and Jeremy and Amy Willcock took great care to restore and renovate with sympathy. A panelled and elegantly proportioned hall sets the scene, leading to a cosy wood-panelled sitting room with thick velvet drapes at the windows, an amusing mid-Victorian evocation of the George above the fireplace and a roaring log fire in winter. Across the hall is the dark red dining room, and beyond the central stairs, the Brasserie and garden.

Upstairs, the bedrooms are all inviting and all different: one has a four - poster; another is a light and pretty corner room; two have wonderful teak-decked balconies with views across the Solent. (The hotel has its own motor yacht for outings.) 'It's a sheer pleasure,' writes a satisfied reader, 'to hop on the ferry at Lymington, alight at Yarmouth, and settle in to the George for two or three days.'

~

NEARBY Yarmouth Castle (adjacent); Newport 12 miles; ferry terminal.
LOCATION in town, close to ferry port overlooking Solent; long stay car park 3-min walk
FOOD breakfast, lunch, dinner; room service
PRICE £££
ROOMS 17; 13 double and twin, 2 suites, 2 single, all with bath; all rooms have phone, TV, hairdrier
FACILITIES sitting room, restaurant, brasserie; garden, private beach, 36 ft motor yacht available for charter **CREDIT CARDS** AE, MC, V
CHILDREN welcome over 8
DISABLED access difficult **PETS** accepted by arrangement **CLOSED** never
PROPRIETORS Jeremy and Amy Willcock and John Illsley

THE SOUTH-EAST

YATTENDON, BERKSHIRE

ROYAL OAK
~ VILLAGE INN ~

The Square, Yattendon, near Newbury, Berkshire RG18 0UG
TEL (01635) 201325 **FAX** (01635) 201926
E-MAIL royaloak@corushotels.com **WEBSITE** www.corushotels.co.uk

THIS INN HAS HAD A new lease of life in the past few years – attractive refurbishment of rooms and food by Robbie Macrae, which wins a steady stream of praise. It's not difficult to believe that the food is more stylish than when Oliver Cromwell dined there, as the hotel claims he did.

Lest you mistake it for a mere pub, the sign on the front of this cottagey, mellow red-brick inn announces 'Hotel and Restaurant'. Certainly, the Royal Oak is no longer a common-or-garden local. Its two restaurants have a style and elegance not usually associated with ale and darts. But there is still a small bar where residents and non-residents alike can enjoy a choice of real ales without having a meal.

Next to the smart/rustic informal dining area, with large open fireplace, is the light, relaxed and comfortable sitting room (with newspapers and books within easy reach of its sofas) and beyond that the formal restaurant with its elegant reproduction furniture. Bedrooms are prettily decorated and equipped with every conceivable extra. Another attraction is the walled garden, full of colour and a delight during the summer months.

~

NEARBY Basildon Park; Donnington Castle; Snelsmore Common.
LOCATION 7 miles (11 km) NE of Newbury, in middle of village; ample car parking
FOOD breakfast, lunch, dinner
PRICE £££
ROOMS 5; 4 double and twin, 1 suite, all with bath; all rooms have phone, TV, hairdrier
FACILITIES restaurant, sitting room, dining room, bar; walled garden
CREDIT CARDS AE, DC, MC, V
CHILDREN welcome
DISABLED access easy to restaurant and bar but otherwise difficult
PETS accepted by arrangement
CLOSED Christmas night; restaurant closed Sun eve
MANAGERS Corinne and Robbie Macrae

WALES

LLANWENARTH HOUSE
~ COUNTRY GUEST-HOUSE ~

Govilon, Abergavenny, Monmouthshire NP7 9SF
TEL (01873) 830289 **FAX** (01873) 832199
E-MAIL mandy@we;sh.hotel.co.uk

AMANDA WEATHERILL HAS PUT tremendous efforts into rescuing this dignified, mainly late 16thC house set in large grounds and have at the same time taken great care to keep the personal touches. Llanwenarth House is still very much a family home, where guests gather for drinks in the handsome drawing room (in front of a blazing log fire on chilly nights), dine as if at a dinner-party in the splendid candle-lit dining room, and must at all costs avoid tripping over the dog. Amanda, who is Cordon Bleu-trained, supervises the kitchen, where the emphasis is on fresh home-grown and local ingredients: home-produced meat and poultry, as well as vegetables from the garden. Wines are from the exceedingly well-stocked cellar.

The bedrooms and public rooms (heavy on hunting memorabilia) are notably bright, spacious and comfortable with period furniture, chintz fabrics and floor-to-ceiling windows, many of which reveal spectacular views of the peaceful Usk valley. The area attracts outdoors types, with trout and salmon fishing on the River Usk and riding, pony-trekking and golf all within easy reach. For the less sporty, there's croquet on the lawn and Abergavenny, a delightful market town.

~

NEARBY Brecon Beacons; Offa's Dyke; Raglan Castle; Chepstow Castle.
LOCATION 4 miles (6 km) SW of Abergavenny, off A465; with ample car parking
FOOD breakfast, dinner
PRICE ££
ROOMS 5 double with bath or shower; all rooms have TV
FACILITIES sitting room, dining room; garden
CREDIT CARDS not accepted
CHILDREN welcome over 10
DISABLED 1 ground-floor bedroom
PETS accepted by arrangement
CLOSED Jan **PROPRIETORS** Amanda Weatherill

WALES

ABERSOCH, GWYNEDD

PORTH TOCYN
SEASIDE HOTEL

Bwlchtocyn, Abersoch, Pwllheli, Gwynedd LL53 7BU
TEL (01758) 713303 **FAX** (01758) 713538
E-MAIL porthtocyn.hotel@virgin.net **WEBSITE** www.porth-tocyn-hotel.co.uk

THIS WHITEWASHED, SLATE-ROOFED establishment, looking out over the sea from the Lleyn peninsula towards Snowdonia, is a rare animal. The Fletcher-Brewers, who have owned it for over 50 years, call it a country house hotel; but it is not what most people would understand by the term. Porth Tocyn certainly contains as many antiques as the typical country house hotel and is run with as much skill and enthusiasm as the best of them. But the building – an amalgam of several old lead-miners' cottages, which has been much extended over the years – makes for a cosy, home-like atmosphere, emphasized by the chintzy decoration. And the seaside position has naturally encouraged the Fletcher-Brewers to cater for children as well as parents keen to enjoy the hotel's civilized attractions. Chief among these is the excellent dinner-party-style food; with seafood and temptingly sticky puddings as particular specialities, so don't go expecting to lose weight.

Bedrooms have been kept low key and simply furnished, but are excellent value. There are splendid all-round views towards the sea and to the peaks of Snowdonia.

NEARBY Plas Yn Rhiw; Criccieth Castle; Snowdonia.
LOCATION 2.5 miles (4 km) S of Abersoch; in 25 acres of farmland with ample car parking
FOOD breakfast, lunch, dinner, picnics
PRICE ££
ROOMS 17; 13 double, 3 single, 1 family room, all with bath; all rooms have phone, TV **FACILITIES** 6 sitting rooms, TV room, dining room, bar; garden, swimming pool, tennis
CREDIT CARDS MC, V **CHILDREN** welcome
DISABLED 3 ground-floor bedrooms
PETS accepted by arrangement
CLOSED early Nov to week before Easter **PROPRIETORS** Fletcher-Brewer family

WALES

TY MAWR

~ COUNTRY HOTEL ~

Brechfa, Carmarthenshire SA32 7RA
TEL (01267) 202332/202330 **FAX** (01267) 202437
E-MAIL info@tymawrhotel.co.uk **WEBSITE** www.tymawrhotel.co.uk

FIRMLY AT RIGHT ANGLES to the main street of this tiny village on the fringe of Brechfa Forest, and by the River Marlais, Ty Mawr has a pretty garden and fine views of the surrounding wooded hillsides. A warm welcome from the owners is guaranteed, and, once inside, the oak beams, stone walls and tiled floors proclaim the building's three and a bit centuries' tenure of this glorious spot. The public rooms are cosy and cheerful and include an immaculate bar with smart pine fittings, and a comfy, chintzy sitting room with an open log fire. The long slate-floored restaurant looks out on to the garden and, candle-lit in the evenings, is where the chef's skill in the kitchen shows in earnest: fresh, usually Welsh, ingredients are assembled without undue fuss but with plenty of imagination. A mouthwatering selection of fresh breads is served at breakfast. The wines are well-chosen and offered at eminently reasonable prices. Upstairs, the bedrooms are bright, comfortable and pleasantly rustic, and breakfast in the morning answers to appetites ranging from the merely peckish to the downright ravenous. The flowers in the garden tubs are quite impressive, but it's worth remembering that in spring 2000 the National Botanical Gardens of Wales opened a few miles away.

~

NEARBY Kidwelly Castle; Llansteffan Castle; Brecon Beacon, National Botanical Gardens of Wales.
LOCATION 10 miles (16 km) NE of Carmarthen, on B4310, in village; with ample car parking
FOOD breakfast, dinner
PRICE ££
ROOMS 5; 3 double, 1 twin, 1 4-poster, all with bath; all rooms have widescreen TV, DVD, minibar, hairdrier **FACILITIES** sitting room, dining room, bar; garden
CREDIT CARDS MC, V **CHILDREN** welcome **DISABLED** not suitable **PETS** by arrangement
CLOSED restaurant only, Jan **PROPRIETORS** John and Pearl Richardson

WALES

CAPEL GARMON, CONWY

TAN-Y-FOEL
COUNTRY HOTEL

Capel Garmon, nr Betws-y-Coed, Llanrwst, Conwy, LL26 0RE
TEL (01690) 710507 **FAX** (01690) 710681
E-MAIL enquiries@tyfhotel.co.uk **WEBSITE** www.tyfhotel.co.uk

TAN-Y-FOEL MEANS 'The house under the hillside' in Welsh and it lives up to its name. Surrounded by hills in the heart of Snowdonia, Tan-y-Foel is a beautiful example of a Welsh country house with wonderful views and lush countryside all around. Parts date back to the 16th Century; parts are highly contemporary – and it pulls it off remarkably well. The interior is a riot of vibrant colours cleverly kept in check with beautiful furnishings and distressed paint work. The intimate reception rooms are decorated in peaceful earth tones, for relaxing in with a drink before dinner. The gardens are secluded and well looked after, but not too manicured, perfectly in keeping with the ruggedness of the country beyond.

All the rooms are individually decorated, comfortable, out of the ordinary. Interesting *objets d'art* are placed on shelves or hang on the walls making you feel as if you should be somewhere more exotic, certainly farther afield than Wales. The food is adventurous and has earned many awards. Mediterranean influences contrast with traditional Welsh dishes and classic French ones. A highly original hotel for people who want something out of the ordinary.

NEARBY Conwy Castle, Caernarfon Castle, Bodnant Gardens, Llanberis.
LOCATION just off the A5, head towards Capel Garmon/Nebo, 1.5 miles (2.5 km) up the hill, Tan-y-Foel is on the left
FOOD breakfast, dinner
PRICE ££
ROOMS 6 doubles all with bath and shower; all rooms have TV, hairdrier, phone
FACILITIES dining room, sitting room; garden
CREDIT CARDS MC, V
CHILDREN accepted over 7
DISABLED not suitable **PETS** not accepted
CLOSED Dec and Jan
PROPRIETORS Mr & Mrs Pitman

WALES

CRICKHOWELL, POWYS

THE BEAR

~ TOWN INN ~

Crickhowell, Powys NP8 1BW
TEL (01873) 810408 **FAX** (01873) 811696
E-MAIL bearhotel@aol.com **WEBSITE** www.bearhotel.co.uk

IT REALLY DOESN'T MATTER what route you take into Crickhowell as, like most other travellers for the last 500 years or so, you're bound to end up at The Bear. Owned and very much run by Judith Hindmarsh and her son Steve, it's one of those versatile places that can turn itself into whatever you want: if you feel like a drink, it's an excellent bustling pub shining with polished brass and pewter. If you feel like an informal meal, you'll be given an excellent one in either bar or in the oak-beamed and flag-floored kitchen restaurant. If you want something more upmarket, all you need do is move to the smaller, smarter *à la carte* restaurant that looks out into the courtyard (flower-filled in summer). Here, provided you are more than eight years old, you will find flowers on the table and food open to international influences, prepared with an imagination and a lightness of touch that belies the traditional trappings outside.

If you need a hotel, The Bear can comfortably surpass your expectations as well: the bedrooms are a mixture of sizes and of styles – old and new – but all are furnished and equipped to uncompromisingly high standards. Finally, if you need to escape the hurly-burly, there is a quiet, beamed sitting room.

~

NEARBY Brecon Beacons; Offa's Dyke; Hay-on-Wye.
LOCATION in town centre on A40 between Abergavenny and Brecon; ample car parking
FOOD breakfast, lunch, dinner, bar snacks
PRICE ££
ROOMS 35 double and twin with bath or shower; all rooms have phone, TV, hairdrier **FACILITIES** sitting room, 2 dining rooms, bar; garden
CREDIT CARDS AE, MC, V **CHILDREN** accepted
DISABLED 2 ground-floor bedrooms
PETS accepted
CLOSED Christmas Day; restaurant only, Sun
PROPRIETORS Judith and Steve Hindmarsh

WALES

DOLGELLAU, GWYNEDD

PLAS DOLMELYNLLYN

~ COUNTRY HOUSE HOTEL ~

Ganllwyd, Dolgellau, Gwynedd LL40 2HP
TEL (01341) 440273 **FAX** (01341) 440640
E-MAIL info@dolly-hotel.co.uk **WEBSITE** www.dolly-hotel.co.uk

FOR LONGER THAN A DECADE the father-and-daughter team of Jon Barkwith and Jo Reddicliffe have been running 'Dolly' with considerable style. Parts of it are more than half a millennium old but there was still work going on when we visited. It sits in a very comfortable way on its own bench above Ganllwyd, taking in the beautiful views across the valley, and, in the principally Victorian interior, antiques mingle equally comfortably with more modern furnishings to create a warm, friendly atmosphere. China and crystal twinkle on all sides. The drawing room is elegant but the dining room is obviously where the team gets down to real business. Jo's award-winning cuisine, best described as 'imaginative modern British', has a widespread fan club and we could well understand people, even vegetarians, who might beg for an extension to their booking. There is an extensive wine cellar which is unlikely to lack the perfect complement to her food, and minor diners get an early sitting to themselves. Bedrooms are named after local rivers and individually furnished and decorated; most have splendid views. There is excellent walking from the front door and all guests have access to that essential Welsh facility, the drying room. This a passionately non-smoking hotel.

~

NEARBY Cymer Abbey; Snowdonia; Lake Vyrnwy.
LOCATION in countryside, on A470 5 miles (8 km) N of Dolgellau; ample car parking
FOOD breakfast, lunch by arrangement, dinner
PRICE ££
ROOMS 10; 9 double, 1 single, all with bath; all rooms have phone, TV, hairdrier
FACILITIES sitting room, dining room, conservatory bar; garden, fishing
CREDIT CARDS AE, DC, MC, V **CHILDREN** welcome over 8
DISABLED not suitable
PETS accepted in 2 bedrooms
CLOSED Nov to Mar
PROPRIETORS Jon Barkwith and Jo Reddicliffe

WALES

EGLWYSFACH, POWYS

YNYSHIR HALL

~ COUNTRY HOUSE HOTEL ~

Eglwysfach, Machynlleth, Powys SY20 8TA
TEL (01654) 781209 **FAX** (01654) 781366
E-MAIL info@ynyshir-hall.co.uk **WEBSITE** www.ynyshir-hall.co.uk

THE REENS HAVE BEEN at Ynyshir Hall for some years now and, happily, seem to know what they are about. Since our last publication they have joined Relais and Chateaux, which has meant extensive upgrades in all the rooms. Both are ex-teachers, Joan of geography, Rob of design and art – and his paintings now decorate the walls of the whole house. Given Rob's background, you might well expect the decoration of the hotel to be rather special, too – and you would not be disappointed. The colour schemes are adventurous, the patterns bold, the use of fabrics opulent, the attention to detail striking. The bedrooms – including two brand-new ones – are named after famous artists, which is paralleled in the colour schemes and fantastic replicas of Matisse, Hogarth and Monet that Rob has created.

The white-painted house dates from the 16th century, but is predominantly Georgian and Victorian. It stands in 12 glorious acres of landscaped gardens next to the Dovey estuary.

The Michelin-starred food is adventurous but not over-complex – modern British – based on fresh local ingredients, especially fish, game, shellfish and Welsh lamb.

~

NEARBY Llyfnant valley; Aberystwyth.
LOCATION 11 miles (18 km) NE of Aberystwyth, just off A487; ample car parking
FOOD breakfast, lunch, dinner
PRICE £££–££££
ROOMS 9; 5 doubles, 4 suites, all with bath and shower; all rooms have phone, TV, hairdrier **FACILITIES** sitting room, dining room, bar, conservatory in 1 room
CREDIT CARDS AE, DC, MC, V
CHILDREN accepted over 9
DISABLED 1 ground-floor room
PETS accepted in 1 bedroom
CLOSED Jan
PROPRIETORS Rob and Joan Reen

WALES

FISHGUARD, PEMBROKESHIRE

THREE MAIN STREET
~ RESTAURANT-WITH-ROOMS ~

3 Main Street, Fishguard, Pembrokeshire SA65 9HG
TEL (01348) 874275 **FAX** (01348) 874017

THE COLOURFUL OLD HARBOUR and this irresistable restaurant above it are the two best things about Fishguard. If you find that you're kicking your heels, waiting, say, for an early-morning ferry to Rosslare, then this three-storey Georgian town house with its stone-dressed façade and pretty hanging baskets is the place both to stay in and eat in. It's a two-woman show: Inez Ford and Marion Evans have teamed up to try 'to create the sort of restaurant we'd like to go to', and we admire their taste. Inez usually greets the guests and settles them into the small bar, where they can have pre-dinner drinks and peruse the menu, while Marion and a small, well-trained team slave at the stove.

The food is so imaginative and beautifully presented, without falling into the trap of being pretentious or over-complicated, that it has established the restaurant as one of the foremost in South Wales. As you'd expect, local fish and seafood are the specialities. During the day, coffee, tea, delicious home-baked cakes and light lunches are served in the two simply but stylishly furnished dining rooms. Upstairs, there are three equally stylish, well-equipped bedrooms that recall the Art Deco era.

~

NEARBY Pembrokeshire coast; Preseli Hills.
LOCATION in town centre; with limited car parking
FOOD breakfast, lunch by arrangement, dinner
PRICE ££
ROOMS 3; 2 double, 1 twin, all with shower; all rooms have TV, hairdrier
FACILITIES dining room, bar
CREDIT CARDS not accepted
CHILDREN welcome
DISABLED no special facilities
PETS not accepted
CLOSED Feb; restaurant only, Sun eve, Mon eve
PROPRIETORS Marion Evans and Inez Ford

WALES

FISHGUARD, PEMBROKESHIRE

TREGYNON

~ FARMHOUSE HOTEL ~

Gwaun Valley, Fishguard, Pembrokeshire SA65 9TU
TEL (01239) 820531 **FAX** (01239) 820808
E-MAIL tregynon@online-holidays.net **WEBSITE** www.online-holidays.net/tregynon

IN THE 6TH CENTURY, Saint Brynach was supposed to have communed with angels at the summit of nearby Carn Ingli, but you don't have to climb quite so high to reach the Heards' blissfully isolated retreat, which has matured nicely since its doors were opened in 1980. Set in unspoilt 'bluestone' country (where the raw material for Stonehenge was quarried), it actually has an Iron Age fort on the property by a 200-foot waterfall. In the house are beams and stone walls and in winter the huge inglenook fireplace must exercise a magnetic attraction for guests just in from the hill; furnishing throughout is suitably cosy-rustic.They have recently added three self-catering cottages, the smallest accomodating 2-3 people and the largest 6.

Only the smallest of the bedrooms is in the 16thC stone farmhouse, with the larger ones in nearby cottages. Jane learnt to cook at her French grandmother's knee, and it is around her skills that Tregynon's small, divided dining room revolves. Her food is a highlight: traditionally based, wholesome and imaginative, with proper care taken of vegetarians, and there is a well-rounded wine list. The Heards even have their own smokehouse where they cure their bacon and gammon. Children eat at tea-time, preserving adult peace at the dinner table. There is no smoking in the dining room or bedrooms.

~

NEARBY Pembrokeshire coast; Pen-Lan-Uchaf; Pentre Ifan (Burial Chamber); Carnhuan Farm Park.
LOCATION isolated in countryside 7 miles (11 km) SE of Fishguard, 3 miles (5 km) S of Newport (get directions); with car parking
FOOD breakfast, dinner
PRICE ££
ROOMS 6; 4 double and twin, 2 family, all with bath; all rooms have phone, TV, hairdrier **FACILITIES** sitting room, 2 dining rooms, bar; garden **CREDIT CARDS** MC, V
CHILDREN welcome over 8 **DISABLED** Farmhouse has access **PETS** not accepted
CLOSED in winter, Sun, Wed and Thurs, in Summer Sun and Thurs
PROPRIETORS Peter and Jane Heard

WALES

GARTHMYL, POWYS

GARTHMYL HALL
~ COUNTRY HOTEL ~

Garthmyl, near Montgomery, Powys, Wales SY15 6RS
TEL (01686) 640550 **FAX** (01686) 640609

IF YOU LEAVE THE HISTORIC TOWN of Montgomery behind you, and head directly towards Snowdonia, in a short space of time you will cross the upper reaches of the River Severn, which perversely flows north at this point. Just beyond it is Garthmyl Hall, a Georgian gem flanked by cedars, backed by a walled garden and woods, and with enough height to look back across gently cultivated countryside towards the river. The open stone-flagged hall and light stone staircase give you an idea of the architectural merits of the rest of the building, and you will not be disappointed. As well as restoring the original features, Nancy and Tim Morrow have carefully added sympathetic furnishings and decoration. The vast drawing room with its gilded ceiling is balanced by the smaller, more intimate library.

Dinner (pan-European, long on fresh produce and deliberately short on choice) and breakfast are both taken in the green dining room. The bedrooms show just as much thought and attention to comfort: a spectacular array of antique bedsteads, crisp sheets, bouncy towels, flowers, chocolates – even the bathrooms are fit to sleep in. This is a friendly, informal hotel which does more than tolerate children and where quality seems to be beating price pretty handsomely.

~

NEARBY Powis Castle; Welshpool, Llanfair Light Railway and Montgomery.
LOCATION 5.5 miles (9 km) S of Welshpool, on A483; with ample car parking
FOOD breakfast, dinner
PRICE ££
ROOMS 9; 8 double and twin, 1 single, all with bath or shower; all rooms have phone; TV, fax/modem lead on request
FACILITIES sitting rooms, bar, dining room; garden
CREDIT CARDS AE, MC, V
CHILDREN accepted
DISABLED not suitable **PETS** not accepted **CLOSED** never
PROPRIETORS Tim and Nancy Morrow

WALES

LLANBRYNMAIR, POWYS

BARLINGS BARN

~ SELF-CATERING BARN ~

Llanbrynmair, Powys SY19 7DY
TEL (01650) 521479 **FAX** (01650) 511414
E-MAIL barlbarn@zetnet.co.uk **WEBSITE** www.barlbarn@zetnet.co.uk

THE ONLY SOUNDS TO DISTURB the peace come from the sheep on the surrounding hillsides, and from the nearby brook. It is a rural idyll, with a garden full of roses and honeysuckle – a picturesque setting for the outdoor activities, such as walking, bird-watching, fishing and golf that you can enjoy in the surrounding countryside.

It is, in fact, the perfect peace of the place that keeps Barlings Barn in these pages despite the Margolis's move a few years ago towards a self-catering set-up. Home-made biscuits await your arrival in the secluded barns adjacent to Felicity and Terry's Welsh farmhouse – one with an oak-beamed stone fireplace and wood-burning stove. Their latest project has been to enclose the spring-fed, heated swimming-pool in a stunning new building, so guests can now make use of it, as well as the sauna, sunbed and squash court, all through the year.

The barns are well-equipped with fridge/freezers, microwaves and barbecues – even a dishwasher. Though it's basically self-catering, the local baker will deliver delicious warm bread to the door. There's a colourful market every Wednesday in Machynlleth.

NEARBY Snowdonia; Aberdovey beach;.
LOCATION 2 miles (3 km) NE of Llanbrynmair at end of private lane off road to Pandy; with ample car parking
FOOD self-catering
PRICE ££-£££
ROOMS barn sleeps between 14-16 people
FACILITIES garden, indoor swimming pool, squash, sauna, sunbed
CREDIT CARDS not accepted
CHILDREN welcome
DISABLED 2 ground-floor rooms
PETS accepted by arrangement
CLOSED never **PROPRIETORS** Terry and Felicity Margolis

WALES

LLANDDEINIOLEN, GWYNEDD

TY'N RHOS
~ COUNTRY HOTEL ~

Llanddeiniolen, Caernarfon, Gwynedd, LL55 3AE
TEL (01248) 670 489 **FAX** (01248) 670 079
E-MAIL enquiries@tynrhos.co.uk **WEBSITE** www.tynrhos.co.uk

L YNDA AND NIGEL Kettle are the proud owners of this unusual little establishment near Caernarfon. Ty'n Rhos (or 'house on the heath' in English) was a farm with 72 acres when Nigel and Lynda first bought it in 1972. Over the years, they have successfully transformed it into a small but comfy hotel with a relaxed rural atmosphere. Entering, you will be struck by the conservatory, which has magnificent views over the well-tended gardens and rolling country beyond: sit here and enjoy a light lunch or a cup of tea. Next door is a cosy little bar that serves canned beers, wine and soft drinks, curl up and read your book or socialize in front of the open fire. Next door is the dining room, which is light and airy and again offers spectacular views. Lynda and her team of chefs pride themselves on using local fresh fish and meat and vegetables and herbs straight from their garden in the summer and offer hearty traditional Welsh or more continental breakfast.

The bedrooms are all individually furnished with unfussy fabrics and furnishings, some with fantastic views; some are a little small. However, Lynda and Nigel have renovated some farm byres outside the main building that house three spacious bedrooms, with one especially suitable for disabled. The other big plus here is its location, with historic castles and towns, dry skiing, seaside and serious mountain walks nearby.

~

NEARBY Snowdonia; Bangor (horseracing); Conwy Castle; Llandudno dry ski slope.
LOCATION from the A5 turn onto the B4366 signposted Llanberis, take road on the right signed to Seion and the hotel is on the left
FOOD breakfast, dinner, light lunch from Tues to Sat
PRICE ££
ROOMS 3 in renovated farm buildings, 10 in main house with bath or shower; all rooms have phone, TV **FACILITIES** dining room, sitting room, bar, conservatory; croquet, garden **CREDIT CARDS** AE, MC, V **CHILDREN** accepted
DISABLED access to ground-floor rooms and public rooms **PETS** not accepted
CLOSED over Christmas and New Year **PROPRIETORS** Lynda and Nigel Kettle

WALES

LLANDRILLO, DENBIGHSHIRE

TYDDYN LLAN
∾ RESTAURANT-WITH-ROOMS ∾

Llandrillo, near Corwen, Denbighshire LL21 0ST
TEL (01490) 440264 **FAX** (01490) 440414
E-MAIL tyddynllan@compuserve.com **WEBSITE** www.tyddynllan.co.uk

A FIRM FAVOURITE WITH READERS since our first edition, this Georgian stone house has been decorated by the Kindreds with elegant flair, period antiques and fine paintings, creating a serene ambience. It is very much a home, despite the number of guests it can accommodate – there is a major extension to the building, cleverly complementary to the original, using slate, stone and cast-iron.

Our latest report of Tyddyn Llan glowed: 'No intrusive reception desk; spacious sitting rooms furnished with style; dining room shows great flair; bedrooms well equipped with original pieces of furniture; small but modern and very pleasing bathrooms; peaceful, comfortable stay, warm atmosphere provided by attentive hosts; great charm.'

Chef Sean Ballington is continuing in the footsteps of his talented predecessor, Jason Hornbuckle, producing a new angle on Welsh country house food with inventive and well-planned small menus using quality local ingredients, and keeping the kitchen's high reputation secure.

The place is surrounded by large grounds; the lawn is large enough to practise fly-casting; and the hotel has four miles of fishing on the Dee.

∾

NEARBY Bala Lake and Railway; Snowdonia.
LOCATION 5 miles (8 km) SW of Corwen off B4401; with ample car parking
FOOD breakfast, lunch, dinner
PRICE £££
ROOMS 12 double and twin, 10 with bath, 2 with shower; all rooms have phone, TV, radio
FACILITIES sitting room, bar, restaurant; croquet, fishing
CREDIT CARDS MC, V **CHILDREN** welcome
DISABLED 1 suite suitable
PETS accepted in bedrooms by arrangement
CLOSED never
PROPRIETORS Bryan and Susan Webb

WALES

LLANDUDNO, CONWY

ST TUDNO

⌒ SEASIDE HOTEL ⌒

Promenade, Llandudno, Conwy LL30 2LP
TEL (01492) 874411 **FAX** (01492) 860407
E-MAIL sttudnohotel@btinternet.com **WEBSITE** www.st-tudno.co.uk

THE BLANDS ARE METICULOUS in attending to every detail of this award-winning seafront hotel, which they have been improving for almost 30 years now. They could not, however, improve on its location: right on Llandudno's dignified promenade, opposite the carefully restored Victorian pier and sheltered from inclement weather by the Great Orme headland. Each of the nineteen rooms have been individually decorated in bright, cheerful colours with matching fabrics and furnishings: most have spectacular views of the sea. Thoughtful extras such as complimentary wine and fresh flowers add to the comfort. The two sitting rooms facing the Promenade are delightfully Victorian yet surprisingly light and spacious, perfect for reading or indulging in afternoon tea.

The air-conditioned Garden Room Restaurant is light and inviting, and suits its name with a profusion of plants and cane-backed chairs. The seasonal menu with daily changing carte, based on the best local ingredients, deserves serious study in the comfortable bar, and – though it's not cheap – the cooking is right on target. If you over-indulge, you can try to recover your figure by pounding up and down the lovely covered pool, decorated with murals. All of this would be difficult to resist even without the bonus of the hotel's young and helpful staff.

⌒

NEARBY Dry ski slope; Conwy Castle; Bodnant Gardens; Snowdonia.
LOCATION on seafront opposite pier and promenade gardens; with parking for 12 cars and unrestricted street parking
FOOD breakfast, lunch, dinner
PRICE ££-£££
ROOMS 19; 12 doubles and twins, 4 family, 2 suites, 1 single, all with bath or shower; all rooms have phone, TV, fridge, hairdrier **FACILITIES** 2 sitting rooms, dining room, bar; garden, indoor swimming pool **CREDIT CARDS** AE, DC, MC, V
CHILDREN welcome **DISABLED** not suitable; lift/elevator **PETS** accepted by arrangement **CLOSED** never **PROPRIETORS** Martin and Janette Bland

WALES

LLANSANFFRAID GLAN CONWY, CONWY

THE OLD RECTORY

~ COUNTRY RECTORY ~

Colwyn Bay, Conwy LL28 5LF
TEL (01492) 580611 **FAX** (01492) 584555
E-MAIL info@oldrectorycountryhouse.co.uk **WEBSITE** www.oldrectorycountryhouse.co.uk

THIS PRETTY FORMER Georgian rectory, home of the owners, enjoys an exceptional elevated position, standing in two-and-a-half acres of flowery gardens with lovely sweeping views across the Conwy Estuary to Conwy Castle and Snowdonia beyond. Most of the bedrooms, two of which are in a separate building, share this view. The rooms, despite the modern appliances, have an old-fashioned feel about them, with ponderous beds, mostly either half tester or four-poster, in walnut, mahogany and oak. Downstairs is an elegant panelled drawing room decorated with the Vaughans' collection of Victorian watercolours.

The couple's progression as hoteliers, and particularly Wendy's as a chef, has been remarkable. An ex-nurse with no culinary training whatsoever, she began by cooking for parties of visiting American tourists. As they started to take in bed-and-breakfast guests and then graduated to fully fledged hotel, so Wendy's culinary skills improved and they now hold several awards for their food, including three rosettes, six Good Food Awards and a Conde Nast Restaurant for Wales award. Wendy still produces a delicious and imaginative three-course dinner each night unaided, except for help with the washing up and the vegetable chopping (done by Michael, who also oversees the wine list to complement her food). Guests eat at separate mahogany candle-lit tables dotted round the room. No smoking, except in the coachhouse.

~

NEARBY Bodnant Gardens; Betws-y-Coed; Llandudno.
LOCATION on A470 half a mile (1 km) S of junction with A55; ample car parking
FOOD breakfast, dinner
PRICE £££
ROOMS 6 double, 5 with bath, 1 with shower; all rooms have phone, TV, hairdrier, tea and coffee making facilities **FACILITIES** sitting room, dining room; garden
CREDIT CARDS MC, V **CHILDREN** accepted over 5 **DISABLED** 2 ground-floor rooms
PETS in coachhouse ony **CLOSED** Dec to Feb **PROPRIETORS** Michael and Wendy Vaughan

WALES

LLANTHONY, GWENT

ABBEY HOTEL
~ COUNTRY INN ~

Llanthony, Abergavenny, Gwent NP7 7NN
Tel (01873) 890487 **Fax** (01873) 890844

FAR INTO THE BLACK MOUNTAINS, on the west bank of the Afon Honddu and overlooked by Offa's Dyke to the east, Llanthony Priory lies high and remote in the Vale of Ewyas. The most spectacular approach is southwards from the sloping streets and busy bookshops of Hay-on-Wye. One of the earliest Augustinian houses in Britain, it was endowed by the de Lacy family, but by the time of Henry VIII's dissolution of the monasteries had fallen into disuse. The Prior's quarters survived amongst the ruins and are now used as the hotel. Gothic horror enthusiasts will be delighted not only by the setting but also when they learn that the highest of the bedrooms can only be reached by climbing more than 60 spiral steps up into the south tower. This is not a hotel for the fastidious or the faint-hearted: it is a long way from anywhere and much used by walkers attracted to the stunning country that surrounds it. Unless you plan to arrive on foot yourself, you should remember that your fellow guests may have had their appetites sharpened by fresh air and their critical faculties dulled by fatigue. However, the chance to sleep in this unique piece of history (with a four-poster and half-tester available) and to wake up to the view from the tower also comes with a very modest price tag.

~

Nearby Offa's Dyke; Brecon Beacons; Hay-on-Wye.
Location off A465 from Abergavenny to Hereford, take mountain road heading N at Llanfihangel Crucorney; with ample car parking
Food breakfast, lunch, dinner
Price £
Rooms 5 double and twin
Facilities sitting room, dining room, bar; garden
Credit cards not accepted **Children** accepted over 10
Disabled access not possible **Pets** not accepted
Closed Sun to Thurs Nov to Easter; restaurant only, Mon eve
Proprietor Ivor Prentice

WALES

NANT GWYNANT, GWYNEDD

PEN-Y-GWRYD HOTEL
∽ CLIMBING HOSTEL ∽

Nant Gwynant, Gwynedd, LL55 4NT
TEL (01286) 870211
WEBSITE www.pyg.co.uk

A PILGRIMAGE PLACE for climbers: this is the home of British Mountaineering, where Edmund Hillary and his team set up their training base before the assault on Everest in 1953. Still in the same friendly family after 58 years, the charming old coach inn, set high in the desolate heart of Snowdonia, is just the sort of place you dream of returning to after a day outdoors: simple, unsophisticated, warm and welcoming, with good plain home cooking, including wickedly calorific puddings.

In keeping with the purpose of the place the bedrooms are simple with no frills, not all of them have en suite bathrooms, but they all have fluffy towels and warm embroidered bedding and linen; the best room is in the annexe and has a grand four-poster bed. One of the bathrooms houses a vintage Victorian bath that looks deep and inviting. For the less intrepid walkers there is still plenty to see in the vicinity, as it is littered with castles and gardens.

After a hard day on the hill you can soak your aching muscles in the natural pool in the garden or unwind in the new sauna. For children (or playful adults) there is a games room with a dart board and table tennis.

NEARBY Bodnant Gardens; Caernarfon, Beaumaris and Harlech Castles; Isle of Anglesey; Blackrock Sands.
LOCATION take the A5 to Holyhead, as you enter Capel Curig, turn left on to the A4086. 4 miles (6 km) on the hotel is on a T junction with the lake in front of it
FOOD breakfast, lunch, dinner, tea
PRICE £
ROOMS 15 double, 1 single; 6 with private bathroom, 1 ground floor annexe room with bathroom, 5 public bathrooms **FACILITIES** sitting room, dining room, smoke room, bar, sauna, natural swimming pool, games room, fishing
CREDIT CARDS none **CHILDREN** welcome **DISABLED** 1 ground-floor room
PETS by arrangement **CLOSED** Nov to Dec and mid week until the 1st of March
PROPRIETORS Mr and Mrs Pullee

WALES

PENALLY, PEMBROKESHIRE

PENALLY ABBEY
COUNTRY HOUSE HOTEL

Penally, near Tenby, South Pembrokeshire SA70 7PY
TEL (01834) 843033 **FAX** (01834) 844714
E-MAIL penally.abbey@btinternet.com **WEBSITE** www.penally-abbey.com

EVER SINCE THE MIDDLE AGES this has been recognized as one of the spots from which to appreciate the broad sweep of the Pembrokeshire coast and National Park from Tenby to Giltar Point. The links golf course which parallels the beach wasn't there, but the ruins of the medieval chapel which gave this Gothic country house its name are still in the secluded and well-tended gardens. The windows and doors (including the doors to the rooms) all have the characteristic double curve arches and Bela Lugosi himself would have been quite at home in the corridors and on the stairs. There is a comfortable and well furnished drawing room with an open fire, a welcoming bar far from the world's woes and weather, and a tall, candle-lit dining room for the well planned and prepared dinners, which include a wide choice of fresh Welsh game and produce. All the bedrooms are freshly-decorated and well equipped: some you could play cricket in and are furnished on an appropriately grand scale. Steve Warren and his family have made a smart but easy and informal hotel that is child friendly (babysitting *and* baby listening on tap). Children are welcome in the dining room for the (excellent) breakfasts but an early supper sensibly makes this a child-free zone in the evening.

NEARBY Tenby; Colby Woodland Garden; Upton Castle, Pembroke Castle
LOCATION in village 1.5 miles (2.5 km) SW of Tenby; with ample car parking
FOOD breakfast, dinner
PRICE £££
ROOMS 12 double and twin with bath; all rooms have phone, TV, fax/modem point, hairdrier
FACILITIES sitting room, billiards room, dining room, bar, indoor swimming pool; garden **CREDIT CARDS** AE, MC, V **CHILDREN** accepted
DISABLED access possible to 2 ground-floor bedrooms
PETS not accepted
CLOSED never **PROPRIETORS** Steve and Elleen Warren

WALES

PENMAENPOOL, GWYNEDD

GEORGE III

~ COUNTRY INN ~

Penmaenpool, Dolgellau, Gwynedd LL40 1YD
TEL (01341) 422525 **FAX** (01341) 423565
WEBSITE www.mortal-man-inns.co.uk

PENMAENPOOL CLINGS to the south bank of the Mawddach estuary; looking north across the water, crowded with enough birdlife to have persuaded the RSPB to establish a centre next door; you can see the Diffwys mountains in the distance. There was once a flourishing boat-building industry here (half the hotel was originally a chandlers), and until the 1960s there was a railway station. The line, which used to separate the hotel from the shore, was closed and its waiting room, ticket office and station master's house were later bought and turned into additional bedrooms. Still very much a busy pub, there is excellent bar food from a long and varied menu. If you've come from the north side of the estuary and just popped in for a drink, do remember that the long wooden toll bridge which shortens your journey back by several miles closes at 7pm. More 'serious' food is served in the restaurant which has French windows opening on to a long balcony overlooking the estuary.

Residents have a separate sitting room to themselves, complete with beams and an inglenook fireplace. Upstairs, most of the light, beamed bedrooms have the same view (some avid bird-watchers have been known to miss breakfast). Guests have free access to more than 12 miles of river and lake fishing and there are wonderful walks from the door.

~

NEARBY Fairbourne Railway; Snowdonia; Lake Vyrnwy.
LOCATION 2 miles (3 km) W of Dolgellau on A493, on edge of Mawddach estuary; with ample car parking
FOOD breakfast, lunch, dinner
PRICE ££
ROOMS 12 double and twin with bath or shower; all rooms have phone, TV, hairdrier
FACILITIES sitting room, dining room, 3 bars; fishing; mountain bicycle hire
CREDIT CARDS MC, V **CHILDREN** welcome
DISABLED access possible to Lodge bedrooms
PETS accepted by arrangement **CLOSED** never **PROPRIETORS** Mortal Man Inn Ltd

WALES

PENMAENPOOL, GWYNEDD

PENMAENUCHAF HALL
~ COUNTRY HOUSE HOTEL ~

Penmaenpool, Dolgellau, Gwynedd LL40 1YB
TEL (01341) 422129 **FAX** (01341) 422787
E-MAIL relax@penhall.co.uk **WEBSITE** www.penhall.co.uk

NOT FAR FROM THE MARKET town of Dolgellau, Penmaenuchaf Hall's drive winds steeply up a wooded hillside from the south bank of the Mawddach Estuary to this sturdy grey stone Victorian manor house. Set on terraces in 21 acres of grounds, the views across Snowdonia must have been top of the list of reasons that brought the original builder – a Lancashire mill owner – to this peaceful spot at the foot of Cader Idris. A rose garden and a water garden add a charm of their own to the beautiful setting.

Indoors, Mark Watson and Lorraine Fielding have saved but also softened the Victorian character of the house so that, from the imposing main hall you are drawn to the warmth and light of the ivory morning room, the sitting rooms and the library. The same sympathetic treatment carries through to the bedrooms – fine fabrics are married with fine furniture and only the beds are baronial. If you are not tempted by the excellent walking in the surrounding hills, you can revive the skills of a mis-spent youth in the billiards room or simply doze in the sunny conservatory. Dinner, a stylish modern British event, is served in the panelled dining room.

~

NEARBY Mawddach Estuary; Snowdonia; Lake Vyrnwy, Portmeirion.
LOCATION off A493 Dolgellau-Tywyn road; with ample car parking
FOOD breakfast, lunch, dinner
PRICE £££
ROOMS 14 double and twin with bath; all rooms have phone, TV, hairdrier; superior and deluxe rooms have minibar **FACILITIES** sitting rooms, library, billiards room, 2 dining rooms, bar; garden, helipad, fishing
CREDIT CARDS DC, MC, V
CHILDREN babes-in-arms and children over 6 accepted
DISABLED access possible to restaurant **PETS** accepted in 1 room by arrangement
CLOSED 10 days in Jan
PROPRIETORS Mark Watson and Lorraine Fielding

WALES

PORTMEIRION, GWYNEDD

PORTMEIRION HOTEL

~ SEASIDE HOTEL ~

Portmeirion, Gwynedd LL48 6ET
TEL (01766) 770228 **FAX** (01766) 771331
E-MAIL hotel@portmeirion-village.com **WEBSITE** www.portmeirion-village.com

AT THE HEART OF Clough Williams-Ellis's delightful Italianate fantasy village is the Portmeirion Hotel, a magical white villa standing on a headland close to the seashore and surrounded by the 'Gwyllt', 70 acres of subtropical woodland gardens where camellias, rhododendrons and magnolias flourish. After it opened in 1926, the hotel became a magnet for the literati, attracting the likes of George Bernard Shaw, H. G. Wells and Noel Coward, who wrote *Blythe Spirit* while staying here in 1941.

Guests have the choice of staying in the hotel or in one of the paintbox-coloured cottages which are dotted around the village, but enjoy all the facilities of the hotel. These include the pretty, circular outdoor swimming pool (heated from May to September) and the glorious 'ocean liner' dining room, a 1930s addition, which at high tide really seems to be afloat, and whose reputation for modern Welsh cuisine is growing.

The interior of the hotel is decorated in vibrant colours: from the dramatic black and white marble floor in the hall to the icy-blue Mirror Room and exotic Jaipur Bar, a small slice of Rajasthan. The bedrooms in the main building are equally stylish, and more expensive than the less flamboyant cottage rooms.

~

NEARBY Ffestiniog Railway; Harlech Castle.
LOCATION in Portmeirion village; with ample car parking
FOOD breakfast, lunch, dinner
PRICE ££–£££
ROOMS 26 double and twin, 14 suites, all with bath; all rooms have phone, TV, hairdrier; some have minibar; 17 self-catering cottages available
FACILITIES 2 sitting rooms, library, conservatory, dining room; garden, swimming pool, tennis **CREDIT CARDS** AE, DC, MC, V **CHILDREN** welcome
DISABLED no special facilities
PETS accepted in 2 cottages
CLOSED first 2 weeks in Jan **PROPRIETOR** Robin Llywelyn

WALES

REYNOLDSTON, NR SWANSEA

FAIRYHILL
∽ COUNTRY HOUSE HOTEL ∽

Reynoldston, Gower, near Swansea, SA3 1BS
TEL (01792) 390139 **FAX** (01792) 391358
E-MAIL postbox@fairyhill.net **WEBSITE** www.fairyhill.net

O**UR LATEST INSPECTION** confirmed that standards were being well maintained in this quiet and utterly civilized retreat situated in the heart of the Gower Peninsula and only about 25 minutes from the M4, since the current owners took over in late 1993.

Set in 24 acres of grounds – with walled garden, orchard, trout stream and lake, and much of it still semi-wild – the three-storey Georgian building has a series of spacious, attractively furnished public rooms on the ground floor, leading to the dining room.

Paul Davies, one of the proprietors, is the chef, assisted by Adrian Coulthard. They enjoy producing seasonal menus and make excellent use of traditional local specialities such as Gower lobster and crab, Penclawdd cockles, Welsh lamb and laverbread. The extensive wine list, cellared in the old vaults of the house, includes five wines from Wales. Most bedrooms overlook the large park and woodland, and are comfortable and well-equipped – they even have CD players, on which to play your choices from the hotel's large and catholic collection of disks. More reports please.

NEARBY Weobley Castle; Gower Peninsula; Heritage Centre; Swansea.
LOCATION 12 miles (19 km) W of Swansea, 1 mile (1.5 km) NW of village; in 24-acre park and woodland, with ample car parking
FOOD breakfast, lunch, dinner
PRICE £££
ROOMS 8 double with bath and shower; all rooms have phone, TV, CD player
FACILITIES sitting room, bar, 2 dining rooms, conference room; croquet, garden with a trailer full of art
CREDIT CARDS AE, MC, V **CHILDREN** accepted over 8
DISABLED access possible to restaurant only
PETS not accepted
CLOSED 24 to 27 Dec
PROPRIETORS P. Davies and A. Hetherington

WALES

TALSARNAU, GWYNEDD

MAES-Y-NEUADD
~ COUNTRY HOTEL ~

Talsarnau, Gwynedd, Wales LL47 6YA
TEL (01766) 780200 **FAX** (01766) 780211
E-MAIL maes@neuadd.com **WEBSITE** www.neuadd.com

IF YOU HAVEN'T BEEN to Maes-y-Neuadd before, you run the risk of running out of confidence in your own map-reading skills as the little road from the coast winds up and up through woods. Fear not and press on, for the journey will be worth it. You will arrive outside a stone-built slate-roofed manor that is only a century or so younger than Harlech Castle, creeper-clad in parts, and if the time is right you can look back across the water to see the sun set behind the Lleyn peninsula. It may be Snowdonia outside, but inside it is definitely deep-pile all the way. Chintzes in the drawing room, leather in the bar and, in the pale and elegant dining room, masterpieces from the kitchen of Peter Jackson (chef and co-owner) all combine to make this a seriously comfortable hotel.

Much of the fresh produce comes from Maes-y-Neuadd's own garden (the gardeners get a credit). Menus are set, with choices for each of the possible five courses until pudding when you reach 'Diweddglo Mawreddog' (the grand finale), which means you get them all. When you are shown to your room, take note of how you got there as the upstairs corridors are all similar. The reverse is true of the smart, variously-sized bedrooms, which are individually decorated and furnished.

~

NEARBY Portmeirion; Ffestiniog Railway; Harlech Castle.
LOCATION 3 miles (5 km) NE of Harlech, up small road off B4573; ample car parking
FOOD breakfast, lunch, dinner; room service
PRICE £££
ROOMS 16; 15 double and twin, 1 single, all with bath or shower; all rooms have phone, TV, fax/modem point, hairdrier
FACILITIES sitting room, conservatory, dining room, bar; terrace, garden, helipad
CREDIT CARDS AE, DC, MC, V **CHILDREN** accepted
DISABLED 3 ground-floor rooms, lift/elevator
PETS accepted in bedrooms
CLOSED never **PROPRIETORS** Doreen and Peter Payne, Peter and Lynn Jackson

WALES

THREE COCKS, POWYS

THREE COCKS

~ VILLAGE INN ~

Three Cocks, near Brecon, Powys LD3 0SL
TEL (01497) 847215 **FAX** (01497) 847339
WEBSITE www.hay-on-wye.co.uk/3cocks

THE BUILDING IS A CHARMING ivy-covered 15thC coaching inn in the Welsh hills, constructed around a tree (still in evidence in the kitchen) and with its cobbled forecourt on the most direct route from Hereford to Brecon. Inside, carved wood and stone walls continue the natural look of the exterior, with beams and eccentrically angled doorways serving as proof positive of antiquity. The kitchen, presided over by Michael Winstone, is now its primary business, and draws people great distances to the warm welcome and roomy restaurant with its lace-covered tables. There are plenty of places where you can sit in peace, and residents now have a drawing room of their own, in keeping with its public oak-panelled counterpart but with more light, stone and fabric in evidence.

Bedrooms are modest but comfortable and well equipped, with dark oak furniture and pale fabrics. But what makes the Three Cocks stand out is the Belgian influence on both the food and atmosphere – Marie-Jeanne is from Belgium and she and Michael used to live and work there. The cuisine is deceptively simple, with great attention paid to the freshness and quality of its elements. Game and shellfish regularly feature on the menu, local lamb is given a continental spin, and a large selection of Belgian beers complements a well balanced and keenly priced wine-list.

~

NEARBY Brecon Beacons; Hay-on-Wye; Hereford Cathedral; Black Mountains.
LOCATION in village, 11 miles (18 km) NE of Brecon on A438; ample car parking
FOOD breakfast, lunch, dinner
PRICE ££
ROOMS 7 double and twin, 6 with bath, 1 with shower
FACILITIES 2 sitting rooms, TV room, dining room, breakfast room; garden
CREDIT CARDS MC, V **CHILDREN** welcome
DISABLED access difficult
PETS not accepted **CLOSED** Dec to mid-Feb; restaurant only, Sun lunch, Tue
PROPRIETORS Michael and Marie-Jeanne Winstone

MIDLANDS

ASHBOURNE, DERBYSHIRE

CALLOW HALL
~ COUNTRY HOUSE HOTEL ~

Mappleton, Ashbourne, Derbyshire DE6 2AA
TEL (01335) 300900 **FAX** (01335) 300512
E-MAIL reservations@callowhall.co.uk **WEBSITE** www.callowhall.co.uk

THE SPENCERS HAVE been 'foodies' for generations. They have been master bakers in Ashbourne since 1724, and one of the highlights of staying at this fine Victorian country house hotel is its excellent dining room. As well as growing many of their own ingredients, the Spencers also smoke and cure meat and fish themselves – arts that have been passed down through the family.

Set in extensive grounds at the entrance to the Peak National Park, the hotel overlooks the stunning landscape of the Dove valley. Public rooms and bedrooms are done out in an appropriate and not too flamboyant country-house style. The walls of the entrance are guarded by stags' heads and the flag-stoned floor is scattered with Persian rugs. In winter an open fire crackles, while guests dine in the glow of the deep-red dining room, and in the drawing room, comfy sofas and chairs provide plenty of space for relaxing. Carved antiques and family heirlooms mingle with period repro furniture. Ask for a decent-sized room when you book: one or two are on the small side for the price. Staff are helpful yet unobtrusive, and the Spencers are hands-on owners, with Dorothy front of house and David and Anthony in charge of the kitchen.
~

NEARBY Chatsworth House; Haddon Hall; Hardwick Hall.
LOCATION 0.75 mile (1 km) N of Ashbourne off A515; with ample car parking
FOOD breakfast, lunch Sun or on request, dinner
PRICE £££
ROOMS 16; 15 double and twin, 1 suite, all with bath or shower; all rooms have phone, TV, hairdrier
FACILITIES sitting room, dining rooms, bar; garden, fishing
CREDIT CARDS AE, DC, MC, V **CHILDREN** welcome
DISABLED 1 specially adapted room **PETS** accepted by arrangement
CLOSED Christmas Day, Boxing Day, New Year's Day
PROPRIETORS David, Dorothy, Emma and Anthony Spencer

MIDLANDS

ASHFORD-IN-THE-WATER, DERBYSHIRE

RIVERSIDE HOUSE
~ COUNTRY HOTEL ~

Fennel Street, Ashford-in-the-Water, Bakewell, Derbyshire, DE4 1QF
TEL (01629) 814275 **FAX** (01629) 812873
E-MAIL riversidehouse@enta.net **WEBSITE** www.riversidehousehotel.co.uk

NESTLING IN ONE of the Peak District's prettiest villages, this stone-built, ivy-clad house, has an idyllic setting in its own secluded grounds, bordered by the river Wye. The village is aptly named – on our inspector's visit during a spate of heavy rain, the river was threatening to encroach, and manager Sonia Banks was coping admirably, sandbags at the ready, with the possibility of a flood alert.

Penelope Thornton (of the Thornton chocolate family), who took over the hotel in 1997, has instituted a refreshingly plain style, entirely in keeping with the house's Georgian origins. A large plant-filled conservatory leads into a cosy snug with a recessed carved-oak mantelpiece and open fire. There is an elegant, comfortable sitting room and a variety of well-equipped bedrooms of different sizes. Rooms in the newer Garden wing overlook the river.

Crucial to Riverside is its reputation for fine food, which is served in two intimate dining rooms. Chef John Whelan creates imaginative dishes such as *mille-feuille* of marinated salmon with beetroot *confit*, and celery and wild mushroom *strüdel*; he also offers an intriguing selection of cheeses – Lincolnshire Poacher, Belineigh Blue and Gubbeen. Coffee is accompanied by a little box of locally made Thorntons chocolates.

~

NEARBY Chatsworth; Haddon Hall; Bakewell.
LOCATION 2 miles (3 km) NW of Bakewell off A6, at top of village, next to Sheepwash Bridge; with ample car parking
FOOD breakfast, lunch, dinner
PRICE £££
ROOMS 15; 1 executive suite, 6 doubles, 8 twin, 13 with bath, 2 with shower; all rooms have phone, TV, hairdrier **FACILITIES** 2 sitting rooms, conservatory, bar, 2 dining rooms; garden **CREDIT CARDS** AE, DC, MC, V
CHILDREN welcome over 10 **DISABLED** access possible to 4 rooms
PETS not accepted **CLOSED** never **PROPRIETOR** Penelope Thornton

MIDLANDS

ATHERSTONE, WARWICKSHIRE

CHAPEL HOUSE
~ TOWN HOTEL ~

Friar's Gate, Atherstone, Warwickshire CV9 1EY
TEL (01827) 718949 **FAX** (01827) 717702

FROM ATHERSTONE'S MARKET SQUARE, you get a tantalising glimpse of trees and flowers in the glorious, mature walled garden that envelopes this handsome 18thC town house, and once beyond the walls, it feels so secluded that, if it weren't for the church bells next door that ring hourly (day and night, be warned), you might be in the depths of the country. Built as Atherstone Hall's dower house, it shows some signs of its 18thC roots, especially in the fine porticoed entrance and flag-stoned hallway beyond. Both decoration and furnishings reinforce the style: pale rooms are filled with period furniture, gilt mirrors, swagged pelmets and anti-macassar-draped chairs. All the pretty, homely bedrooms are different. Some are small and some have shower rooms not bathrooms, but they compensate with their charm, particularly those under the eaves.

So far so good. It must also be said that the hotel is looking distinctly tired now, but the owner knows it, and a refurbishment is planned. More serious, an exceptionally negative reader's letter criticizes not only housekeeping but food and service. We hope that this was a one off experience. Bear in mind the relatively low prices and pretensions of this place -- but further reports will be especially welcome.

~

NEARBY Bosworth battlefield; Arbury Hall; Tamworth Castle; Coventry Cathedral; Lichfield Cathedral.
LOCATION beside church in NE corner of Market Square; with ample car parking, 18 miles from Birmingham airport.
FOOD breakfast, dinner; lunch by arrangement
PRICE ££
ROOMS 14; 9 double and twin, 5 single, 5 with bath, 9 with shower; all rooms have phone, TV **FACILITIES** sitting room, conservatory, dining room, garden
CREDIT CARDS MC, V **CHILDREN** welcome over 12 **DISABLED** access to public rooms only **PETS** Guide dogs only **CLOSED** Christmas Day, Boxing Day; restaurant only, Sun (open for lunch once a month) **PROPRIETOR** Keith Hawes

MIDLANDS

BASLOW, DERBYSHIRE

THE CAVENDISH

~ COUNTRY HOUSE HOTEL ~

Baslow, Derbyshire DE45 1SP
TEL (01246) 582311 **FAX** (01246) 582312
E-MAIL info@cavendish-hotel.net **WEBSITE** www.cavendish-hotel.net

THE CAVENDISH DOESN'T SOUND LIKE a personal small hotel. But the smart name is not mere snobbery – it is the family name of the Duke of Devonshire, on whose glorious Chatsworth estate the hotel sits (and over which the bedrooms look). And neither the hotel's size nor its equipment interferes with its essential appeal as a polished but informal and enthusiastically run hotel – strictly speaking an inn, as Eric Marsh is careful to point out, but for practical purposes a country house.

Outside, the solid stone building is plain and unassuming. Inside, all is grace and good taste: the welcoming entrance hall sets the tone – striped sofas before an open fire, elegant antique tables standing on a brick-tile floor, while the walls act as a gallery for Eric Marsh's eclectic collection of more than 300 pictures. The whole ground floor has recently been remodelled, and a café-style conservatory added. Bedrooms are consistently attractive and comfortable, but vary in size and character – older ones are more spacious.

The elegant restaurant claims to have a 'controversial' menu. It is certainly ambitious and highly priced, but it met the approval of recent guests who described the food as 'unsurpassed – we were spoilt to death!' The Garden Room is less formal.

~

NEARBY Chatsworth; Haddon Hall; Peak District.
LOCATION 10 miles (16 km) W of Chesterfield on A619; with ample car parking
FOOD breakfast, lunch, dinner
PRICE £££
ROOMS 23 double with bath; all rooms have phone, TV, minibar, hairdrier
FACILITIES sitting room, dining room, bar, garden room; garden, putting-green, fishing **CREDIT CARDS** AE, DC, MC, V **CHILDREN** welcome
DISABLED access difficult
PETS not accepted
CLOSED never **PROPRIETOR** Eric Marsh

MIDLANDS

THE OLD BAKERY
~ RESTAURANT-WITH-ROOMS ~

High Street, Blockley, Moreton-in-Marsh, Gloucestershire GL56 9EU
TEL (01386) 700408 **FAX** (01386) 700408

PART OF BLOCKLEY LOOKS as if it was built simply to prove that one *could* build on slopes that steep. Part of the way along the downhill side of Blockley High Street (a narrow road to nowhere), cling four rose-covered Victorian cottages now joined to form The Old Bakery. Linda Helme and John Benson are so enthusiastic about cookery and warm in their welcome that you feel they might even relish the challenge of a desert island. As it is, they scour the region for the best of the season and your route to one of their three splendid bedrooms is to visit their red and rose dining room and appreciate the four-course dinner that results from their careful and creative preparation of the fruits of their search. The wine list has been selected with care and the wines are offered at prices that can leave room only for very modest margins.

The bedrooms are unfussy but by no means austere: all are a good size and if you can remember a colour (green, yellow or blue), then you'll know which is yours. Each has the kind of bathroom you wish you could take home with you. There is no smoking anywhere in the hotel.

~

NEARBY Hidcote Manor Garden; Snowshill Manor; Broadway; Stratford-upon-Avon; Evesham; Cheltenham.
LOCATION in centre of village, 4 miles (6.5 km) NW of Moreton-in-Marsh; with limited car parking or on street
FOOD breakfast, dinner
PRICE £
ROOMS 2 doubles, 1 single with bath and shower; all rooms have TV
FACILITIES sitting room, dining room, bar; garden
CREDIT CARDS AE, MC, V
CHILDREN accepted over 14
DISABLED not suitable **PETS** not accepted
CLOSED mid-Dec to mid-Jan, 2 weeks Jun
PROPRIETORS Linda Helme and John Benson

MIDLANDS

BROAD CAMPDEN, GLOUCESTERSHIRE

MALT HOUSE

~ COUNTRY GUEST-HOUSE ~

Broad Campden, Chipping Campden, Gloucestershire GL55 6UU
TEL (01386) 840295 **FAX** (01386) 841334
E-MAIL info@malt-house.co.uk **WEBSITE** www.malt-house.co.uk

IT IS EASY TO MISS THIS 17thC Cotswold house (in fact a conversion of three cottages) in a tiny picture-postcard hamlet comprising little more than a cluster of thatched, wistaria-covered cottages, a church and a pub. Once found, the Malt House is delightful – with low beamed ceilings, antique furniture and leaded windows overlooking a dream garden, where the resident cat potters contentedly about. 'Beautifully done out and a peaceful, charming atmosphere,' comments our latest reporter.

Since Judi took the Malt House over she has decreased the number of bedrooms, most of which overlook the gardens and paddock and orchard beyond. They are individually decorated in tasteful neutral shades (some with *toille de jouie*) and furnished with antiques and collections from Judi's travels. The public rooms are immensely comfortable, with log fires in winter, but small, adorned with *objets d'art* from India and other exotic destinations. The accommodation includes a pleasantly laid out garden suite with a private sitting room and an entrance to the garden. Guests breakfast and dine in the beamed dining room, complete with inglenook fireplace.

Janice Rogers (the chef) cooks delicious evening meals using ingredients that are fresh locally or from the kitchen garden.

~

NEARBY Batsford Park Arboretum; Sezincote Garden; Snowshill Manor; Stratford-upon-Avon; Cotswold villages; Cheltenham.
LOCATION 1 mile (1.5 km) SE of Chipping Campden; with ample car parking
FOOD breakfast, dinner (except Tuesday)
PRICE ££
ROOMS 7; 6 doubles, 1 suite, all with bath and shower; all rooms have TV, hairdrier, tea and coffee making facilities
FACILITIES 2 sitting rooms, dining room; croquet **CREDIT CARDS** AE, DC, MC, V
CHILDREN welcome if well behaved
DISABLED access difficult **PETS** by arrangement **CLOSED** Christmas
PROPRIETORS Judi Wilkes

MIDLANDS

BURFORD, OXFORDSHIRE

BURFORD HOUSE
~ TOWN HOUSE HOTEL ~

99 High Street, Burford, Oxfordshire OX18 4QA
TEL (01993) 823151 **FAX** (01993) 823240
E-MAIL stay@burfordhouse.co.uk **WEBSITE** www.burfordhouse.co.uk

WITHOUT DISTURBING its historical integrity, Simon and Jane Henty have smuggled 21stC comforts into their 15thC Cotswold stone and black-and-white timbered house in the heart of Burford. The whole place positively gleams with personal care and attention, with fresh flowers, books and magazines in the smartly decorated, dark-beamed bedrooms, and their own belongings, including family photos, dotted amongst the public furniture. There are two comfortable and contrasting sitting rooms downstairs, one of which gives on to a walled and paved garden as does the ground-floor bedroom. There is also that welcome reviver of the thirsty traveller, an honesty bar, and the welcome reviver of the wet walker, a drying room.

Upstairs there are six more bedrooms, four with four-posters and one of these also has a huge free-standing bath in it. Each thoughtfully organized room is full of character, and each has an immaculate bathroom. Breakfast (included in the price of the room) is an excellent production, taken in the dining room looking out on to the High Street. Dinner is not available in the hotel, but there are plenty of restaurants and pubs within easy walking distance.

~

NEARBY Cotswold Wildlife Park; Blenheim Palace; Broadway.
LOCATION middle of Burford High Street; parking in street or free car park nearby
FOOD breakfast, light lunch
PRICE ££
ROOMS 8 doubles with bath and shower; all rooms have phone, TV, fax/modem point, hairdrier
FACILITIES sitting room, breakfast room, courtyard garden
CREDIT CARDS AE, MC, V **CHILDREN** welcome
DISABLED 1 ground-floor room
PETS not accepted
CLOSED Jan **PROPRIETORS** Jane and Simon Henty

MIDLANDS

THE LAMB
~ TOWN INN ~

Sheep Street, Burford, Oxfordshire OX18 4LR
TEL (01993) 823155 **FAX** (01993) 822228

IF YOU WANT SOME RESPITE from Burford's summer throng, you won't do better than The Lamb, only a few yards behind the High Street, but a veritable haven of tranquillity – particularly in the pretty walled garden, a view endorsed by a recent inspection. Not to be confused with the Lamb at Shipton-under-Wychwood, page 195.

Inside the creeper-clad stone cottages, you won't be surprised to find traditional pub trappings (after all, The Lamb has been an inn since the 15th century), but you may be surprised to discover 15 spacious beamed bedrooms decorated with floral fabrics and antiques. All are different – 'Shepherds', for example, has a vast antique four-poster bed and a little attic-like bathroom, 'Malt' (in what was once the neighbouring brewery) has a smart brass bed and large stone mullion windows.

The hotel is run by Caroline and Richard De Wolf, with the help of Caroline's mother Bunty. It's very much a family enterprise, although they employ four chefs (one French) to produce the impressive-sounding, daily-changing meals. These are served in the dining room, looking on to the geranium-filled patio. Coffee can be taken in here, or in the sitting room or TV room, both of which have comfortable chairs and sofas grouped around open fires. The Lamb manages to combine the convivial atmosphere of a pub with that of a comfortable hotel.

~

NEARBY Minster Lovell Hall; Cotswold villages; Blenheim Palace.
LOCATION in village; with car parking for 6 cars
FOOD breakfast, lunch, dinner
PRICE ££
ROOMS 15 double and twin with bath or shower; all have phone, TV, hairdrier
FACILITIES 3 sitting rooms, dining room, bar; garden **CREDIT CARDS** MC, V
CHILDREN welcome **DISABLED** 3 ground-floor bedrooms
PETS dogs in room by prior arrangement **CLOSED** Christmas Day, Boxing Day
PROPRIETORS Richard and Caroline De Wolf

MIDLANDS

CHIPPING CAMPDEN, GLOUCESTERSHIRE

COTSWOLD HOUSE
~ TOWN HOTEL ~

The Square, Chipping Campden, Gloucestershire GL55 6AN
TEL (01386) 840330 **FAX** (01386) 840310
E-MAIL reception@Cotswold-house.demon.co.uk **WEBSITE** www.cotswoldhouse.com

DESCRIBED BY ONE READER as 'the place to stay' in Chipping Campden, Cotswold House can claim to be a very popular hotel. Set in a fine street, the building, dating from 1650, was renovated in the late 1980s with great attention to detail; then, in 1999, it was brought by new owners Ian and Christa Taylor, realizing their ambition of owning (rather than being employed in) a hotel. They further upgraded the rooms and added the new coach house, where clean modern lines, gas log fireplaces and broad exposed beams definitely add to the place. Thoughtful touches include flat screen TVs that automatically swivel out over the bed, heated bathroom floors, chrome bookrests and small TVs in the bathroom. In the main hotel, an impressive spiral staircase leads to well-appointed rooms, which are a similar standard to those in the coach house.

You have the choice of two restaurants: the relaxed brasserie and the formal dining room. The dinner menu might offer warm salad of pigeon and wild mushroom with shallot dressing; pork belly with roasted scallops and pancetta crisps; toffee caramel mousse and vanilla roasted pineapple. Alongside the coach house, a Mediterranean-style garden, attractively lit in the evening, is perfect for an after-dinner stroll.

~

NEARBY Broadway; Stratford on Avon.
LOCATION in main street of town; parking for 12 cars
FOOD breakfast, lunch, dinner
PRICE £££
ROOMS 20; all doubles with bath; all rooms have phone, TV, hairdrier
FACILITIES 2 sitting rooms, bar; croquet
CREDIT CARDS AE, MC, V **CHILDREN** accepted over 6
DISABLED access difficult
PETS accepted
CLOSED never
PROPRIETORS Ian and Christa Taylor

MIDLANDS

CORSE LAWN, GLOUCESTERSHIRE

CORSE LAWN HOUSE
~ COUNTRY HOTEL ~

Corse Lawn, Gloucestershire GL19 4LZ
TEL (01452) 780771 **FAX** (01452) 780840
E-MAIL enquiries@corselawn.com **WEBSITE** www.corselawnhouse.com

THIS TALL, RED-BRICK Queen Anne house, set back across common land from what is now a minor road, must have been one of the most refined coaching inns of its day. Should you arrive in traditional style, you could still drive your coach-and-four down the slipway into the large pond in front of the house, to cool the horses and wash the carriage.

The Hines have been here since the late 1970s, first running the house purely as a restaurant, later opening up four rooms and in recent years adding various extensions (carefully designed to blend with the original building) to provide more and more bedrooms as well as more space for drinking, eating and sitting. The Falstaffian Denis Hine – a member of the famous French Cognac family – and son Giles extend a warm welcome to guests, while Baba Hine cooks. Her repertoire is an eclectic mix of English and French, modern and provincial dishes, all carefully prepared and served in substantial portions; there are fixed-price menus (with a vegetarian alternative) at both lunch and dinner as well as a *carte*, all notably good value.

Bedrooms are large, with a mixture of antique and modern furnishings and the atmosphere of the house is calm and relaxing. Breakfasts are a home-made feast. A recent visitor was enchanted.

~

NEARBY Tewkesbury Abbey; Malvern Hills.
LOCATION 5 miles (8 km) W of Tewkesbury on B4211; with ample car parking
FOOD breakfast, lunch, dinner
PRICE ££
ROOMS 18; 16 double and twin, 2 suites, all with bath; all rooms have phone, TV, hairdrier **FACILITIES** 3 sitting rooms, bar, restaurant, 2 meeting rooms; garden, croquet, tennis, indoor swimming pool **CREDIT CARDS** AE, DC, MC, V
CHILDREN accepted if well-behaved **DISABLED** 5 ground-floor bedrooms
PETS accepted in bedrooms **CLOSED** 24 to 26 Dec
PROPRIETORS Denis, Baba and Giles Hine

MIDLANDS

DIDDLEBURY, SHROPSHIRE

DELBURY HALL

~ COUNTRY GUEST-HOUSE ~

Diddlebury, Craven Arms, Shropshire SY7 9DH
TEL (01584) 841267 **FAX** (01584) 841441
E-MAIL wrigley@delbury.demon.co.uk **WEBSITE** www.delbury.com

THIS PART OF SHROPSHIRE used to be a dangerous place to live: Offa's Dyke serves as a reminder of how hard it was to keep the Welsh away, and a string of castles runs the length of the Marches. Luckily, things had settled down by the middle of the 18th century when Delbury was built in Corvedale, and this rural Georgian gem was quite obviously designed to let in the wonderful view rather than keep out projectiles. Once past the lodge, you've still got about a mile to go through an 80-acre park before you reach the satisfyingly crunchy gravel between the house and the first lake (of no less than three).

Lucinda and Patrick Wrigley have set this house to rights in every department, inside and out. Their walled garden produces vegetables for the kitchen, their hens lay eggs for breakfast, they cure their own ham, smoke salmon and even churn their own butter. Inside are a stunning double-height hall, with galleries on three sides, a grand drawing room, dining room, cosy morning room, pets and children. Antiques (and ancestors) abound, even in the bedrooms, and you'll get your own bathroom but it will *not* have been hacked out of a corner of your gracefully proportioned room. Patrick is cook and cellar master: he'll give you a chance to vote on what's for dinner and an excellent choice on what to drink with it. This year Patrick is scaling down his operation and space will be limited. Booking only for parties of four or more and we recommend contacting him well in advance to avoid disappointment.

~

NEARBY Ludlow; Stokesay Castle; Much Wenlock.
LOCATION in village 5 miles (8 km) NE of Craven Arms; with ample car parking
FOOD breakfast, dinner
PRICE ££
ROOMS 3 double and twin with bath; all rooms have phone, TV, hairdrier
FACILITIES 2 sitting rooms, games room, dining room; garden **CREDIT CARDS** MC, V
CHILDREN accepted **DISABLED** not suitable **PETS** not accepted **CLOSED** Christmas
PROPRIETORS Patrick and Lucinda Wrigley

MIDLANDS

GREAT RISSINGTON, GLOUCESTERSHIRE

LAMB INN

~ COUNTRY INN ~

Great Rissington, Gloucestershire GL54 2LP
TEL (01451) 820388 **FAX** (01451) 820724
WEBSITE www.thelamb-inn.com; www.thelambinn.co.uk

IF YOU FOLLOW THE RIVER WINDRUSH as it rises westwards from Burford, and then roughly follow its curve from the north (where it has given Bourton-on-the-Water its name), you will arrive in Great Rissington, deep in the Cotswolds. Overlooking gently rolling farmland and built from the local stone, the original elements of this inn are 300 years old. Taken over 3 years ago by Paul and Jackie Gabriel, The Lamb is still very much a pub, indeed it is enough of a pub to merit a recommendation in a national guide to good beer. But it also now has two elements that many other inns lack – good board and lodging. Board comes in the shape of a surprisingly large – and comfortingly busy – restaurant. In its smoking and non-smoking sections, it does a roaring trade in traditional dishes freshly prepared from the best of local produce, often with a modern twist: the most popular of these is a half shoulder of lamb.

The bedrooms are bright, fresh and individually designed, and more than half have space for sitting as well as sleeping.

~

NEARBY The Slaughters; Stow-on-the-Wold; Burford; Sudeley Castle.
LOCATION 4 miles (6 km) SE of Bourton-on-the-Water, 3 miles (5 km) N of A40; with ample car parking
FOOD breakfast, lunch, dinner
PRICE £
ROOMS 14; 7 double, 1 twin and 6 suites, all with bath or shower; all rooms have TV
FACILITIES sitting room, bar; garden
CREDIT CARDS AE, MC, V
CHILDREN welcome
DISABLED not suitable
PETS accepted in bedrooms by arrangement
CLOSED Christmas Day, Boxing Day
PROPRIETORS Paul and Jackie Gabriel

MIDLANDS

HAMBLETON, RUTLAND

HAMBLETON HALL

~ COUNTRY HOUSE HOTEL ~

Ketton Road, Hambleton, Oakham, Rutland LE15 8TH
TEL (01572) 756991 **FAX** (01572) 724721
E-MAIL hotel@hambletonhall.com **WEBSITE** www.hambletonhall.com

IF YOU'RE PLANNING a second honeymoon, a break from work or a weekend away from the kids, this Victorian former shooting lodge in the grand hotel tradition is a sybaritic paradise, from which only your wallet and your waistline will suffer. The location is unrivalled, standing in stately grandeur on a wooded hillock, surrounded by manicured lawns, surveying the expanse of Rutland Water. The interior is sumptuous. In her design of the rooms, Stefa Hart uses rich, heavy fabrics, combining stripes and chintzes in some of the bedrooms, and showing a preference for delicate colours. The rooms still have their original mouldings and fireplaces and are furnished with fine antiques and paintings. Bedrooms with a view over the water are the most sought-after and expensive, though one reporter was happy in her smaller, cheaper room overlooking lawns and cedars. A record is kept of the pet likes and hates of regular guests.

Many people are drawn here by the wizardry of Michelin-starred chef, Aaron Patterson. He works his magic on only the freshest of ingredients, whether Angus beef, sea bass or veal sweetbreads. One of the joys of staying here is that you can blow the cobwebs away with an exhilarating walk from the front door of the hotel as far as you want around Rutland Water, bird-watching as you go.

~

NEARBY Burghley House; Rockingham Castle; Stamford, Belvoir Castle.
LOCATION 2 miles (3 km) E of Oakham on peninsula jutting into Rutland Water; with ample car parking
FOOD breakfast, lunch, dinner
PRICE ££££
ROOMS 15 double and twin with bath; all rooms have phone, TV, hairdrier
FACILITIES sitting rooms, 3 dining rooms, bar; garden, swimming pool, tennis, fishing, helipad **CREDIT CARDS** AE, DC, MC, V **CHILDREN** accepted
DISABLED access possible, lift/elevator
PETS by arrangement **CLOSED** never **PROPRIETORS** Tim and Stefa Hart

Midlands

Hopesay, Shropshire

The Old Rectory

~ Country guest-house ~

Hopesay, Craven Arms, Shropshire SY7 8HD
Tel (01588) 660245 **Fax** (01588) 660502

IF YOU'D RATHER STAY with friends than go to a hotel, then this elegant 17thC rectory, home to Roma and Michael Villar, might well be the amiable compromise that you've always been looking for. In gentle hills, and surrounded by mature trees, the setting is English countryside at its best. Built when the vicar was second only to the squire in the local pecking-order (and lived in the sort of property that proved it), you can see before you even go in that this is not a house where any corners have been cut. Inside you have the run of the drawing room (which has an Adam fireplace) and the dining room with its large oak refectory table. In suitable weather you can step through a floor-level Georgian sash window in the drawing room to a raised terrace paved with York stone. The whole house has been decorated with a discerning eye, comfortably in keeping with the architecture, and setting off the many excellent pieces of furniture that you are trusted with. Unless it's late enough for a drink (help yourself), you'll be given tea when you arrive. Dinner is a treat. It is taken at eight at the single table, and comes with style but without fanfares from Roma's kitchen; breakfast, ditto, but with Michael in charge. The comfortable bedrooms (and the beds themselves) are good-sized, with bathrooms to match.

~

Nearby Ludlow; Offa's Dyke; Stokesay Castle; Stretton Hills; Stiperstones.
Location in village beside church, 3.5 miles (6 km) NE of Craven Arms; with car parking
Food breakfast, dinner
Price ££
Rooms 3 double and twin with bath; all rooms have TV, hairdrier
Facilities drawing room, dining room; terrace, garden
Credit cards not accepted **Children** accepted over 12
Disabled not suitable
Pets not accepted **Closed** Christmas to Mar **Proprietors** Mrs M Villar

MIDLANDS

KEMERTON, GLOUCESTERSHIRE

UPPER COURT
~ COUNTRY HOUSE HOTEL ~

Kemerton, near Tewkesbury, Gloucestershire GL20 7HY
TEL (01386) 725351 **FAX** (01386) 725472
E-MAIL diana@uppercourt.co.uk **WEBSITE** www.uppercourt.co.uk

KEMERTON IS A PRETTY VILLAGE on Bredon Hill, an outcrop of the Cotswolds, on the edge of the Vale of Evesham. Its stunning Georgian manor house acts as a home, a shop and a hotel for its friendly owners, Bill and Diane Herford, and their children. The interior is filled with fine furniture and *objets d'art*, some of it stock from their antiques business, and some of it for sale.

Bedrooms are in the grand country-house style, three with romantic four-posters. In the lovely, rather wild 15-acre grounds (open under the National Gardens Scheme) can be found the ruins of a thousand-year-old watermill and a huge lake (complete with two islands) on which guests may row. Upper Court is ideal for house parties taking a long weekend break or for the keen racer-goers coming for the famous Cheltenham Gold Cup. Dinner is by arrangement for house parties, but the Herfords much prefer their guests (who come in twos or threes) to frequent the Crown pub, which is a two-minute walk down the road.

As well as the bedrooms in the main house, more accommodation is available in the adjoining cottages and the coach-house in the courtyards, which are self-catering and can also have meals delivered to them. They are all exceedingly cosy and individual, with the possibilty of hiring a cook for the length of your stay to cater for the larger house parties.

~

NEARBY Cotswold villages; Malvern Hills; Tewkesbury Abbey.
LOCATION 4 miles (6.5 km) NE of M5, exit 9, 1 mile (2.5 km) E of Bredon; house is behind parish church; with ample car parking
FOOD breakfast, dinner by arrangement
PRICE ££
ROOMS 5; 3 double, 2 twin, all with bath; 4 cottages with bath; all rooms have TV, hairdrier, radio **FACILITIES** drawing room, smoking room, dining room, billiards room; garden, lake, swimming pool, tennis court, clay pigeon shooting, pottery lessons
CREDIT CARDS MC, V **CHILDREN** welcome **DISABLED** 1 ground-floor bedroom
PETS not accepted **CLOSED** Christmas **PROPRIETORS** Bill and Diana Herford

MIDLANDS

KINGTON, HEREFORDSHIRE

PENRHOS COURT

~ ORGANIC COUNTRY HOTEL ~

Kington, Herefordshire HR5 3LH
TEL (01544) 230720 **FAX** (01544) 230754
E-MAIL martin@penrhos.co.uk **WEBSITE** www.penrhos.co.uk

PENRHOS COURT IS MORE a way of life than a hotel. In 1971 it was in such a parlous state that it was due for demolition. Martin Griffiths and Daphne Lambert have spent the last 30 years rolling the clock back, but perhaps not as far as 1280, when it was probably built. Now, as well as being a faithfully restored example of medieval architecture, it is an organic farm and (unusually) a certified organic restaurant; Daphne, a professional nutritionist and chef of the restaurant for better than two decades, buys from other organic producers what she doesn't grow herself in her own kitchen garden, and runs organic cookery courses for those who want to become initiates. Menus change through the year to bring to the table the best of whatever is in season. It would be a misnomer to describe the place where you eat as 'the dining room', because it is self evidently a large beamed and galleried hall set with oak tables and lit through stained-glass windows.

The handsomely decorated and furnished bedrooms are all on the same scale, varying from the merely large to enormous. This is a relaxing, peaceful spot in unspoiled Border countryside and if you want to get back to nature without travelling too far, try the farm pond: there is a perpetual mini-wildlife programme running.

~

NEARBY Offa's Dyke Path; Hergest Croft Garden.
LOCATION 1 mile (2 km) E of Kington on A44; in 6-acre grounds with ample car parking
FOOD breakfast, dinner
PRICE ££
ROOMS 15; 2 4-posters, 2 suites, 11 double and twin, all with bath or shower; all rooms have phone, TV, hairdrier; fax/modem lead by arrangement
FACILITIES 2 sitting rooms, 2 dining rooms, bar; garden
CREDIT CARDS MC, V **CHILDREN** welcome
DISABLED access easy **PETS** not accepted **CLOSED** never
PROPRIETORS Martin Griffiths and Daphne Lambert

MIDLANDS

LANGAR, NOTTINGHAMSHIRE

LANGAR HALL
~ COUNTRY HOUSE HOTEL ~

Langar, Nottinghamshire NG13 9HG
Tel (01949) 860559 **Fax** (01949) 861045
E-MAIL langarhall-hotel@ndirect.co.uk **WEBSITE** www.langarhall.com

AFTER THE DEATH of Imogen Skirving's father, a pre-war captain of Nottinghamshire County Cricket Club and the last owner of Langar Hall, she couldn't bear the thought of losing the house, nor could she afford to keep it on, except on the basis of sharing it with guests. Thus was born the concept of Langar Hall as a hotel and, despite burgeoning success, people who stay here feel more like guests in a beautiful Georgian stuccoed country house rather than customers in a hotel. The library appears to be totally unchanged, with hundreds of books available to leaf through with a drink or two before dinner. The food is superb and the wine list well judged.

The best bedrooms are light and airy, with furniture appropriate to the house that Imogen wanted to save, and enjoy glorious views of the Vale of Belvoir. For exercise, you can play croquet or stroll round the village church just behind the house. Best of all is the friendliness of the hostess and her staff. Imogen wanders around the dining room, alighting at tables of single, bored businessmen and exchanging any sort of gossip, while nothing is too much trouble for the chef or staff. When our inspector realised, at 1 am, after an excellent dinner, that he had forgotten his sponge bag, an assortment of toothbrushes, toothpaste and razors was put at his disposal.

NEARBY Belton House; Chatsworth; Sherwood Forest; Lincoln Cathedral.
LOCATION in village behind church; with ample car parking
FOOD breakfast, lunch, dinner
PRICE ££
ROOMS 11 doubles, 1 single; 1 room has shower, all others have baths; all rooms have phone, TV, hairdrier
FACILITIES sitting rooms, dining rooms, bar; garden, croquet, fishing, helipad
CREDIT CARDS AE, DC, MC, V **CHILDREN** welcome **DISABLED** 1 ground-floor bedroom
PETS accepted by arrangement **CLOSED** never **PROPRIETOR** Imogen Skirving

MIDLANDS

LEAMINGTON SPA, WARWICKSHIRE

THE LANSDOWNE

~ TOWN HOTEL ~

Clarendon Street, Leamington Spa, Warwickshire CV32 4PF
TEL (01926) 450505 **FAX** (01926) 421313
E-MAIL thelansdowne@cwcom.net **WEBSITE** www.thelansdowne.co.uk

A CREEPER-COVERED Regency house in the heart of Leamington Spa – 'just as well there is double-glazing,' says our reporter, who liked it not for its location but its food. David Allen (a Swiss-trained chef) and his wife Gillian concentrate on quality and value

On a menu that changes each evening, dishes might include new season's Cornish lamb's kidneys, *lardons* of bacon and caramelised red onions in a red wine cream sauce, marinated herring fillets with apples, celery and walnuts in sour cream, and prime barbary duck breast, oven roasted and served with a blueberry and cassis *jus*.

The Allens have combined home with hotel. The public rooms are elegantly decorated in vibrant colours; the bedrooms, comfortable and cosy with pine furniture and pretty fabrics. Readers comment on the friendly, relaxed atmosphere, and our reporter thought the Allens charming hosts.

Leamington's heyday as a popular spa town might be over, but the Royal Pump Rooms were reopened to visitors in 1999 as a cultural complex, and there is still much to see in the neighbourhood. The Lansdowne makes an ideal base from which to explore.

~

NEARBY Warwick Castle; Upton House; Stratford-upon-Avon; Kenilworth Castle.
LOCATION in middle of town near A425 Warwick road; with car parking
FOOD breakfast, dinner (on demand when booking), snacks
PRICE ££
ROOMS 14; 7 doubles, 4 singles, 3 twin all with bath and shower; all rooms have phone, TV, hairdrier, tea and coffee making facilities
FACILITIES sitting room, dining room, bar; discount tickets for Warwick Castle
CREDIT CARDS MC, V
CHILDREN welcome over 5
DISABLED 2 ground-floor bedrooms
PETS not accepted **CLOSED** never
PROPRIETORS Mr Ross

MIDLANDS

LEONARD STANLEY, GLOUCESTERSHIRE

GREY COTTAGE
VILLAGE GUEST-HOUSE

Leonard Stanley, Stonehouse, Gloucestershire GL10 3LU
TEL (01453) 822515 **FAX** (01453) 822515

THIS STONE-BUILT COTTAGE, owned by Andrew and Rosemary Reeves, dates from 1824 and is spotless and pleasingly furnished. During renovation, original stonework and a tessellated hall floor were laid bare. The cottage is a very private guest-house with a cosy, cottagey atmosphere; there is no roadside advertisement and advance bookings only are accepted.

Generous home cooking includes such dishes as stewed *paupiettes* of plaice with smoked salmon and lime and cumin sauce followed by prune and coffee mousse. Rosemary often joins her guests for after-dinner coffee. An evidently discriminating New York couple give Grey Cottage a rave review: 'Even more than your guide promised. Beautiful garden with a 100-foot Wellingtonia, planted almost 150 years ago. The bedrooms and bathrooms are on the small side, but they are immensely cosy, with firm beds, reliable hot water, heated towel rails, trouser presses and fresh fruit. A thoughtful touch is the 'funny tales from Grey Cottage,' written by Rosemary, put by the bedside.

'The food is fresh, of high quality, and abundant. Rosemary is capable, charming and dedicated – but not intrusive. Unfortunately, most tourists are preoccupied with location, and end up paying more for accommodation nearer the principal sights hereabouts – but actually getting far less.'

NEARBY Cotswold villages; Owlpen Manor; Gloucester; Tetbury.
LOCATION 4 miles (6.5 km) SW of Stroud, 1 mile (2.5 km) off A419 between Leonard Stanley and King Stanley; with ample car parking
FOOD breakfast, dinner by prior arrangement
PRICE £
ROOMS 1 double, 1 twin, 1 single, all with bath or shower; all rooms have TV, hairdrier, trouser press **FACILITIES** sitting room, garden room, dining room; garden
CREDIT CARDS not accepted **CHILDREN** by arrangement
DISABLED not suitable **PETS** not accepted **CLOSED** occasional holidays
PROPRIETORS Andrew and Rosemary Reeves

MIDLANDS

LINCOLN, LINCOLNSHIRE

D'ISNEY PLACE

～ TOWN GUEST-HOUSE ～

Eastgate, Lincoln, Lincolnshire LN2 4AA
TEL (01522) 538881 **FAX** (01522) 511321
E-MAIL info@disneyplacehotel.co.uk **WEBSITE** www.disneyplacehotel.com

SINCE MOVING TO this delightful red-brick Georgian house, on a bustling street a few yards from Lincoln Cathedral, David and Judy Payne (he a property developer, she an ex-antique dealer) have been continually improving and adding to it. A few years ago they converted the former billiard room into a family suite; now they have a fully-equipped cottage for longer-staying guests.

For the purposes of this guide, D'Isney Place, named after its 15thC founder John D'Isney, is on the large side. And unfortunately it has no public rooms or restaurant – though there are plenty of respectable ones within walking distance. But we continue to recommend it because of the comfortable, stylish bedrooms, the well co-ordinated decorations and fabrics, the breakfast (cooked to order, served on bone china and delivered to the rooms along with the morning newspaper) and, last but certainly not least, the impressive walled garden which incorporates a 700-year-old tower from the old cathedral close wall.

～

NEARBY Cathedral; Bishop's Palace; Usher Gallery.
LOCATION in middle of city, just E of cathedral; with adequate car parking
FOOD breakfast, snacks at night; no licence
PRICE ££
ROOMS 17; 16 double and twin, 1 twin, all with bath or shower (3 with spa bath); family rooms available; all rooms have phone, TV; some rooms have hairdrier
FACILITIES walled garden
CREDIT CARDS AE, DC, MC, V
CHILDREN welcome
DISABLED ground-floor bedrooms
PETS welcome
CLOSED never
PROPRIETORS David and Judy Payne

MIDLANDS

HOLDFAST COTTAGE

~ COUNTRY HOTEL ~

Little Malvern, near Malvern, Worcestershire WR13 6NA
TEL (01684) 310288 **FAX** (01684) 311117
EMAIL enquiries@holdfast-cottage.co.uk **WEBSITE** www.holdfast-cottage.co.uk

'COTTAGE' SEEMS TO BE stretching things somewhat – and yet, despite its size, this Victorian farmhouse does have the cosy intimacy of a cottage, and Martin Bishop creates an atmosphere of friendly informality.

Inside, low oak beams and a polished flagstone floor in the hall conform to cottage requirement; beyond, headroom improves – though flowery decoration emphasizes the cottage status. Bedrooms are light and airy, with carefully co-ordinated fabrics and papers; some bathrooms are small. Outside, the veranda with its wistaria keeps the scale of the house relatively intimate. The garden – scarcely cottage-style – adds enormously to the overall appeal of the place, with its lawns, shrubberies, fruit trees and delightful 'wilderness'. Beyond is open farmland with spectacular views of the Malvern Hills.

The daily-changing *carte* is based on continental as well as traditional English dishes, employing the best local produce, and might feature chilled beetroot and apple soup, served with natural yoghurt and chives, monkfish in smoky bacon jackets with creamy parmesan dressing or salmon and thyme parcels with tomato butter.

~

NEARBY Eastnor Castle; Worcester; Hereford; Gloucester.
LOCATION 4 miles (6.5 km) S of Great Malvern on A4104; with ample car parking
FOOD breakfast, lunch, bar meals, dinner
PRICE ££
ROOMS 8; 5 doubles, 2 twins, 1 single all with bath or shower; all rooms have phone, TV, hairdrier
FACILITIES sitting room, bar, dining room, conservatory; croquet
CREDIT CARDS MC, V **CHILDREN** welcome
DISABLED access difficult
PETS accepted
CLOSED never
PROPRIETORS Mr Martin Bishop

MIDLANDS

LUDLOW, SHROPSHIRE

BROMLEY COURT
∽ TOWN BED-AND-BREAKFAST ∽

73-74 Lower Broad Street, Ludlow, Shropshire SY8 1PH
TEL (01584) 876996 **FAX** (01584) 876860
E-MAIL phil@ross-b-and-b-ludlow.co.uk **WEBSITE** www.ross-b-and-b-ludlow.co.uk

WHETHER IT'S HOUSES or horses that brought you to Ludlow, you'll find plenty of both – all thoroughbreds. The entire centre of Ludlow is listed Grade II (a bit too late for the castle, which is a ruin), and the racetrack brings people from far and wide. Another strong draw is the plethora of gourmet restaurants, several of them Michelin-starred, from which to choose.

In Lower Broad Street, Patricia and Philip Ross ran, for many years, a superb bed-and-breakfast establishment, Number 28, which featured in this guide. Now they have sold Number 28 and renovated instead three tiny Tudor cottages further along the road, Broadgate Mews, creating three suites, each on two levels and with a well-equipped breakfast bar. Each has its own front-down, with a delightful communal courtyard where guests can chat after afternoon tea or pre-dinner drinks if they feel so inclined. The suites are charming, cottagey, impeccable. The Ross's themselves live across the road, at Bromley Court. This is the real headquarters and this is where you will collect a warm welcome from Patricia and Phillip, and their black labrador will check you out as walking material. Here too is where you need to come if you want an (excellent) cooked breakfast rather than something simpler at your breakfast bar. For lunch or dinner, take advice from either Ross – they'll tell you which of the Michelin-starred restaurants is on song at the moment.

∽

NEARBY Ludlow Castle; Stokesay Castle; Berrington Hall; Ironbridge; Stiperstones; Stretton Hills.
LOCATION in town centre near River Teme; car parking in street
FOOD breakfast
PRICE ££ **ROOMS** 3 suites, all have sitting room and bath and shower; all rooms have phone, TV, hairdrier **FACILITIES** sitting rooms, breakfast room; gardens
CREDIT CARDS MC, V **CHILDREN** accepted **DISABLED** not suitable
PETS by arrangement **CLOSED** never **PROPRIETORS** Patricia and Philip Ross

MIDLANDS

MALVERN WELLS, WORCESTERSHIRE

THE COTTAGE IN THE WOOD
~ COUNTRY HOTEL ~

Holywell Road, Malvern Wells, Worcestershire WR14 4LG
TEL (01684) 575859 **FAX** (01684) 560662
E-MAIL manager@cottageinthewood.co.uk **WEBSITE** www.cottageinthewood.co.uk

THREE BUILDINGS AND a family form this glossy little hotel perched, very privately, in seven wooded acres, high above the Severn valley and with a superb vista across to the Cotswolds thirty-something miles away (binoculars provided). There are bedrooms in all three buildings, taking the hotel over our usual size for this guide; but the smartly furnished Georgian dower house at its heart is so intimate, calm and comfortable that we decided to relent.

A short stroll away is the soon-to-be-rebuilt Coach House, where rooms are smaller but have the best views, and Beech Cottage with four cottage-style bedrooms. The family consists of John and Sue Pattin, their daughters Maria and Rebecca, son Dominic (head chef) and his wife Romy. Apart from its food, the restaurant (modern English cuisine) has two other substantial qualities: windows that let you see the view and a wine list that lets you roam the world. Walkers can get straight out on to a good stretch of the Malvern Hills and for tourers the Pattins provide leaflets giving concise notes on everything that's worth visiting for 50 miles (80 km) around. For the rest of us, there's a very well stocked bar and a free video library.

NEARBY Malvern Hills; Eastnor Castle; Worcester Cathedral.
LOCATION 2 miles (3 km) S of Great Malvern off A449; with ample car parking
FOOD breakfast, lunch, dinner
PRICE £££
ROOMS 31 double and twin with bath or shower; all rooms have phone, TV, hairdrier; 1 has air-conditioning
FACILITIES sitting room, dining room, bar; garden
CREDIT CARDS AE, MC, V **CHILDREN** welcome
DISABLED ground-floor rooms in annexe
PETS accepted in ground-floor rooms and beach house
CLOSED never **PROPRIETORS** John and Sue Pattin

MIDLANDS

MATLOCK, DERBYSHIRE

RIBER HALL

~ MANOR HOUSE HOTEL ~

Matlock, Derbyshire, DE4 5JU
TEL (01629) 582795 **FAX** (01629) 580475
E-MAIL info@riber-hall.co.uk **WEBSITE** www.riber-hall.co.uk

NEARLY THREE DECADES AGO, Alex Biggin rescued this peaceful, sturdy Elizabethan manor from the verge of dereliction, furnished it sympathetically, and opened it as a restaurant to the applause of local gourmets, who are not spoilt for choice of ambitious and competent French cooking. The bedrooms came later – created in outbuildings across an open courtyard and ranging from the merely charming and comfortable to the huge and delightful, with deep armchairs. Exposed timbers, stone walling, and antique four-posters are the norm. All the thoughtful trimmings you could wish for are on hand. There are no twin beds; five rooms have exotic whirlpool baths.

The spacious, new main dining room, The Garden Room, has mullioned windows and is furnished with antiques. Wedgewood bone china, and exclusively designed cut glass adorn the dining table. Breakfast is taken in the traditional old dining room and the recent addition of a new sitting room has increased the area available for relaxation in the public rooms.

A romantic and cosy pastime at Riber is simply to sit by an open fire on a stormy winter evening – umbrellas are provided for crossing the courtyard. In the morning you can enjoy the delicious seclusion of the luxuriant walled garden and orchard.

~

NEARBY Chatsworth House; Haddon Hall; Calke Abbey; Carsington Water.
LOCATION 2 miles (3 km) SE of Matlock by A615 (20 minutes from exit 28, M1); take minor road S at Tansley; with car parking in courtyard
FOOD breakfast, lunch, dinner
PRICE £££
ROOMS 14; 12 doubles, 2 twins; all rooms have TV, minibar, hairdrier
FACILITIES sitting room with bar service, conservatory, dining room; tennis court, tennis trainer, ball machine **CREDIT CARDS** AE, DC, MC, V
CHILDREN accepted over 10 **DISABLED** not suitable **PETS** accepted
CLOSED never **PROPRIETOR** Alex Biggin

MIDLANDS

MOULSFORD-ON-THAMES, OXFORDSHIRE

BEETLE AND WEDGE
~ RIVERSIDE INN ~

Ferry Lane, Moulsford-on-Thames, Oxfordshire OX10 9JF
TEL (01491) 651381 **FAX** (01491) 651376
E-MAIL kate@beetleandwedge.co.uk **WEBSITE** www.beetleandwedge.co.uk

THE BEST THING ABOUT this large Victorian inn, where Jerome K. Jerome wrote his classic *Three Men in a Boat*, is its superb position on the banks of the Thames. Almost an entire wall of huge windows and glazed doors, overlooking a pretty garden and the river beyond with its colourful boats and barges, makes the most of the setting. For meals, guests can choose between the Dining Room, where Richard Smith's cuisine matches the sophistication of the decoration, and the Boathouse, a brasserie-style restaurant with exposed rafters and brickwork, a cosy feel and an à la carte menu, featuring delicious char-grilled dishes. But most delightful of all, on fine summer days lunch is served in the Watergarden.

The spacious bedrooms have been individually and tastefully decorated by Richard and Kate Smith; the bathrooms – some of which are large enough to contain a dressing table – have wonderful huge cast-iron baths. The best rooms have a river view.

The Beetle and Wedge has always been enthusiastically endorsed by our readers' letters, though recently there have been one or two dissenting voices, mainly expressing reservations about the 'sky-high prices'.

~

NEARBY Abingdon; Oxford; Thames valley.
LOCATION 2 miles (3 km) N of Goring on A329; with car parking
FOOD breakfast, lunch, dinner
PRICE £££
ROOMS 10; 9 double, 1 suite, all with bath; all rooms have phone, TV, hairdrier
FACILITIES 2 restaurants, sitting room; garden
CREDIT CARDS AE, DC, MC, V
CHILDREN accepted
DISABLED ground-floor rooms and adapted WC
PETS accepted by arrangement
CLOSED restaurant only, Sun eve, Mon
PROPRIETORS Richard and Kate Smith

MIDLANDS

NORBURY, SHROPSHIRE

THE SUN AT NORBURY
~ COUNTRY INN ~

Norbury, near Bishops Caslte, Shrophire SY9 5DX
TEL (01588) 650680
E-MAIL suninn.norbury@virgin.net **WEBSITE** freespace.virgin.net/suninn.norbury

WE ARE ALWAYS on the look-out for that rare thing, an atmospheric, genuine country pub away from the tourist trail, with above-average, if fittingly simple, rooms and food to match. The Sun offers all of these, and a strong farmyard smell in the car park, lost, of course, as you enter. Set in glorious Welsh marshes landscape, overlooked by Long Mynd, it's a low stone building with a traditional beamy interior and three neat, warm bedrooms. The furnishings are unremarkable, but in keeping, and the beds are comfortable, prettily presented with plump duvets and fat pillows. Small bathrooms with efficient showers are behind folding doors.

Everything is freshly painted and well maintained. The kindly couple who run the pub and restaurant and cook the food also serve you with a generous English breakfast. Come here for silence and a feeling of remoteness – but you won't be bored because nearby Ludlow is worth at least a day of your time and there's great walking all around, including the Mortimer Trail – enquire at the tourist office. Don't miss a sighting of the beautiful private house, Linley, a mile away.

~

NEARBY Bishops Castle; Ludlow Castle; Offas Dyke.
LOCATION in Norbury off B4383, ample car parking
FOOD breakfast, dinner, lunch at weekends
PRICE £–££
ROOMS 3 double, all with shower
FACILITIES restaurant, dining room, sitting room, bar; garden, fish ponds
CREDIT CARDS MC, V
CHILDREN accepted
DISABLED not suitable
PETS not accepted; kennels, paddocks can be arranged
CLOSED Christmas Day
PROPRIETORS Charles and Carol Cahan

MIDLANDS

NORTON, SHROPSHIRE

HUNDRED HOUSE HOTEL

～ COUNTRY HOTEL ～

Bridgenorth Road, Norton, Near Shifnal, Telford, Shropshire, TF11 9EE
TEL (01952) 730353 **FAX** (01952) 730 355
E-MAIL hundredhouse@lineone.net **WEBSITE** www.hundredhouse.co.uk

"QUITE EXTRAORDINARY, a pleasant surprise around every corner" says one recent reporter. From the moment you pull in to the car park you don't quite know what to expect next. The building itself dates back to the 1500's it was the local court house, the remains of the stocks and the whipping post can still be seen opposite. Push open the stained glass doors, and the atmosphere hits you, dim lighting, mellow wood floors, panelled walls, bouquets of dried herbs and flowers hanging from ceilings. The dining areas are spacious – the Hundred House caters for non-residential guests, but the tables are cosy and intimate, some in front of a large open fire, others tucked in various nooks. The menu is impressive and unusual, but cooked well with no corners cut. The bar is in the brasserie area and offers an impressive range of ales, with more little tables for a quick bite of lunch.

The bedrooms are, well, eccentric: swings in the 'superior' rooms; lively, floral decoration; and some very spacious bathrooms. The one single room in the house is a little cramped. The herb garden tended by Sylvia Phillips, is magical and is regularly used for marriage blessings. Elsewhere, you'll find relaxing sitting areas and a small pond. It is very much a family-run hotel, with parents and sons working together to create a memorable experience.

～

NEARBY Telford, Chester, Ironbridge Gorge Museum, Severn Valley steam way, The Long Mynd (walk).
LOCATION just off the M54 from junction 4, on the A442 between Telford and Bridgnorth, with car parking
FOOD breakfast, lunch, dinner
PRICE ££–£££ (min 2 night stay)
ROOMS 10 double and twin, 1 single, all with bath; all have TV, phone, tea and coffee making facilities, hairdrier **FACILITIES** dining room, sitting room, bar, brasserie; herb garden, beer garden **CREDIT CARDS** AE, MC, V **CHILDREN** welcome
DISABLED some access in public rooms **PETS** well behaved dogs (£10 charge)
CLOSED never **PROPRIETORS** Henry, Sylvia, Stuart and David Phillips

MIDLANDS

OXFORD

OLD BANK

~ TOWN HOTEL ~

92-94 High Street, Oxford OX1 4BN
TEL (01865) 799599 **FAX** (01865) 799598
E-MAIL info@oldbank-hotel.co.uk **WEBSITE** www.oxford-hotels-restaurants.co.uk

ALL CHANGE IN OXFORD: metropolitan chic has brazenly asserted itself amongst the dreaming spires with the opening, in December 1999, of the Old Bank Hotel. Hardly a quintessential charming small hotel, but we include it for the breath of fresh air it has created in central Oxford. What was, until recently, a venerable bank with a fine Georgian façade and an Elizabethan core, has become a cool, sophisticated hotel with a buzzing brasserie as its centrepiece.

The building has much to recommend it. The best bedrooms are graced with floor-length windows or, in the Tudor part, beams and deep window seats under lattice windows. All the rooms – and the bathrooms – are impeccably decorated in the understated chic-rustic style of the day (think taupe, think beige, think cream). They feel elegant and luxurious, and, because they are new, pristine and unsullied.

As well as a hotel, the Old Bank has become the 'in' place to eat in Oxford. The Quod Bar and Grill stretches across the former banking hall ("weird to think that I used to cash my cheques and see the bank manager here", says one guest, a touch wistfully), and while hotel guests may yearn for a relaxing sitting room of their own, most will enjoy the buzz and bonhomie that emanates from this always packed, Italian-influenced new meeting place.

~

NEARBY Oxford colleges; Botanical Gardens; Sheldonian Theatre.
LOCATION in city centre, with ample car parking
FOOD breakfast, lunch, dinner; room service
PRICE £££-££££
ROOMS 44; 42 double and twin, 2 suites; all rooms have phone, TV, CD player, fax/modem point, air-conditioning, safe, hairdrier
FACILITIES restaurant, bar, courtyard
CREDIT CARDS AE, DC, MC, V **CHILDREN** accepted
DISABLED 1 room is specially adapted, most other rooms have lift/elevator access
PETS not accepted **CLOSED** Christmas **PROPRIETOR** Jeremy Mogford

MIDLANDS

OXFORD

OLD PARSONAGE

~ TOWN HOTEL ~

1 Banbury Road, Oxford OX2 6NN
TEL (01865) 310210 **FAX** (01865) 311262
E-MAIL info@oldparsonage-hotel.co.uk **WEBSITE** www.oxford-hotels-restaurants.co.uk

TALK ABOUT CONTRAST. Jeremy Mogford now owns the two best hotels in Oxford, the recently opened Old Bank (see page 189), and this one, much more typical of our guide, occupying a characterful, wistaria-clad house that has been owned by University College since 1320. Compared to its sleek, hip younger sibling, it seems at first quaint and old-fashioned, yet there is no themed olde worlde charm here, despite the great age of the building. The place has panache: the staff are young and charming, the atmosphere informal, and the laid-back bar/brasserie (part sitting room, part dining room) has a clubby, cosmopolitan feel. Here drinks and a varied menu – salmon fish cakes, wild mushroom tart, *tarte tatin* – are served all day long. In fine weather, large white parasols adorn the front terrace (the heavy, studded front door, by the way, is three centuries old), making a delightful place to eat lunch, and there is a roof garden for residents' use in summer too.

Bedrooms – which tend to be on the small side – are pretty and traditional in feel, with pale panelling and unfussy chintz, and marble bathrooms (with telephone). However, changes may be afoot: we've heard that Gladys Wagner, the interior designer of the Old Bank, was set to begin work here too.

~

NEARBY Oxford colleges; Botanical Gardens; Sheldonian Theatre.
LOCATION 5 minutes' walk from city centre, at N end of St Giles, close to junction of Woodstock and Banbury Roads; limited car parking
FOOD breakfast, lunch, dinner; room service and afternoon tea
PRICE £££ **ROOMS** 30; 25 double and twin, 1 single, 4 suites, all with bath; all rooms have phone, TV, hairdrier **FACILITIES** sitting room, dining room, bar; terrace, roof garden **CREDIT CARDS** AE, DC, MC, V **CHILDREN** accepted
DISABLED access difficult **PETS** not accepted
CLOSED Christmas **PROPRIETOR** Jeremy Mogford

MIDLANDS

PAINSWICK, GLOUCESTERSHIRE

CARDYNHAM HOUSE
~ VILLAGE BED-AND-BREAKFAST ~

The Cross, Painswick, Gloucestershire GL6 6XX
TEL (01452) 814006 **FAX** (01452) 812321
E-MAIL info@cardynham.co.uk **WEBSITE** www.cardynham.co.uk

B UILT WITH MONEY FROM WOOL and from pale gold stone out of a local
quarry, Painswick is a classic Cotswold town perched rather
precariously on (and over the brink of) a steep hillside. If you're not
paying attention you might quite easily walk past Cardynham House – a
discreet sign above the venerable front door of this Grade II-listed
flower-hung building, right on the street, is hardly enough to focus your
attention when everything else around is so worth looking at. The real
fun starts once you get inside. A cavernous open fireplace, flanked by a
bread oven, warms a cosy drawing room which seems to metamorphose
at some point into a conservatory.

Somehow, nine totally unique bedrooms have been created in this
apparently modest-sized house, and each one is a triumphal exercise of
imagination. Dotted with antiques and murals, each is decorated to a
different theme and, even side by side in the same building, they all work
unusually well. The most eccentric of all, air-conditioned because it hasn't
a window to its name, has been got up like a desert pavilion. Another has
its own private patio largely taken up with a covered plunge pool (heated,
and with a powered current to swim against). Breakfast is taken in the
restaurant that, in the evenings that it's open, serves Thai food.
~

NEARBY Cheltenham; Chedworth Roman Villa; Cirencester, Gloucester, Sudeley.
LOCATION in village, 3 miles (5 km) N of Stroud; car parking on street
FOOD breakfast, Tues to Sat dinner and Sun lunch
PRICE ££
ROOMS 9; 6 double, 3 family, all with bath or shower; all rooms have phone, TV
FACILITIES sitting room, breakfast room
CREDIT CARDS AE, MC, V **CHILDREN** accepted
PETS not accepted
DISABLED not suitable **CLOSED** restaurant only, Sun eve, Mon eve
PROPRIETORS John and Sharon Paterson

MIDLANDS

PAINSWICK HOTEL
~ COUNTRY HOUSE HOTEL ~

Kemps Lane, Painswick, Gloucestershire GL6 6YB
TEL (01452) 812160 **FAX** (01452) 814059
E-MAIL reservations@painswickhotel.com **WEBSITE** www.painswickhotel.com

THIS DISTINCTLY UPMARKET Georgian rectory is tucked away in the back lanes of prosperous Painswick. The graceful proportions of the rooms 'beautifully and expensively furnished with an elegant mix of classy reproductions, antiques and well chosen objects', the serenity of the gardens, and the fine views of the westerly Cotswold scarp, all contribute to the effect.

Our latest inspection revealed that Painswick manages, despite its class, to retain the feel of a friendly, family-run establishment. It is in a beautiful Cotswold village, and some of the better rooms had the best views of any our inspector had experienced in several weeks on the road. The panelled dining room is 'elegant rather than cosy', and the food very acceptable, making good use of Gloucestershire produce, including locally reared lamb and home-smoked salmon. A sea water fish tank provides fresh seafood and the cheese board includes local farmhouse cheeses, some really unusual.

Painswick was taken over by new owners, Gareth and Helen Pugh, in 1998. We would welcome reports.

~

NEARBY Cotswold villages; Gloucester.
LOCATION near middle of village, 3 miles (5 km) N of Stroud on A46; with car parking in front of hotel
FOOD breakfast, dinner, lunch
PRICE £££
ROOMS 19; 14 double and twin, all with bath; 2 single, 1 with bath, 1 with shower; 3 family rooms, all with bath; all rooms have phone, TV
FACILITIES sitting room, 2 dining rooms, bar; croquet
CREDIT CARDS AE, MC, V
CHILDREN welcome
DISABLED access difficult **CLOSED** never
PETS by arrangement **PROPRIETORS** Gareth and Helen Pugh

MIDLANDS

PUDLESTON, HEREFORDSHIRE

FORD ABBEY

~ BED-AND-BREAKFAST ~

Pudleston, Leominster, Herefordshire HR6 0RZ
TEL (01568) 760700 **FAX** (01568) 760264
E-MAIL info@fordabbey.co.uk **WEBSITE** www.fordabbey.co.uk

I F THE COMBINATION of an 800-year-old farmhouse together with a large
dollop of luxury (and a security system designed to attract world
leaders) appeals to you, then Ford Abbey is perfect. The creation of
Albert and Monique, who live at nearby Pudleston Court, Ford Abbey (a
Benedictine abbey in medieval times) was almost derelict when they
bought and restored it, sparing no expense or attention to detail. It's a
beautiful – and now immaculate – half-timbered building, surrounded
by pretty landscaped grounds, including a stream, and rolling (organic)
farmland, complete with picturesque farm animals.

Bedrooms, some with four-posters, are traditional and extremely
comfortable, with 21stC facilities. Guests congregate in the sitting room for
pre-dinner drinks, then move to seperate tables in the beamed, low-ceilinged
former chapel where an exemplary dinner, cooked by a professional chef, is
served, along with a small but excellent choice of wines. Not bad for what
manager Michael Wildmoser calls 'a simple b&b'. Guests we met were
drooling with happiness, loving the sense of peace and security.

~

NEARBY Hereford 18 miles; Ludlow 16 miles.
LOCATION in middle of countryside, 18 miles NE of Hereford; with car parking
FOOD breakfast, dinner
PRICE £££
ROOMS 5 double, 1 single, all with bath; 4 self-catering apartments, 2 with 2
bedrooms, 2 with 1 bedroom; all rooms have phone, TV, modem point, hairdrier
FACILITIES sitting room, library, dining room, indoor swimming pool, sunbed;
terrace, hawking, riding, fishing
CREDIT CARDS AE, MC, V
CHILDREN accepted over 12
DISABLED 1 specially adapted suite **CLOSED** never
PETS accepted **MANAGER** Michael Wildmoser

MIDLANDS

RHYDYCROESAU, SHROPSHIRE

PEN-Y-DYFFRYN

∼ COUNTRY HOTEL ∼

Rhydycroesau, Near Oswestry, Shropshire, SY10 7JD
TEL (01691) 653700 **FAX** (01691) 650066
E-MAIL stay@peny.co.uk **WEBSITE** www.peny.co.uk

DRIVING THROUGH the windy lanes cutting through the Shropshire hills from Oswestry, you can easily miss this attractive Georgian House tucked away off the main road. It nestles serenely among trees and green fields and you will be taken aback by the views that stretch (on a clear day) to the Welsh mountains. The dining room and sitting areas are decorated in warm, rich colours open log fires for the chilly winter evenings and are perfect, in the summer, for a sun-downer while watching the spectacular sunsets. If you prefer to drink or dine outside, there's a delightful little patio stretching round the side of the hotel.

The bedrooms are large and spacious, decorated in relaxing pastel shades, with large fluffy towels provided in all the en suite bathrooms (some with spa baths and Jacuzzis) and fresh flowers on arrival. Four of the bedrooms are in the coach house, which is ideal for guests with animals. They each have spectacular views and their own private little patio. The food is as you would expect: hearty and fresh-cooked, mostly with organic and local produce, and vegetables from the hotel's own garden. The small bar by the entrance is staffed by helpful and friendly staff who can advise you on sightseeing, walking, or shopping in Wales or Shropshire.

∼

NEARBY Erdigg; Llanrhaedar waterfall; Powys Castle; Pistyll Rhaedar waterfall
LOCATION 3 miles (4.5 km) West of Oswestry on the B4580. Hotel is 3 miles (4.5 km) down on that road on the left
FOOD breakfast, dinner, light lunch on request **PRICE** £
ROOMS 12 double; all with bath and shower; all rooms have TV, hairdrier, modem point, tea and coffee making facilities, phone
FACILITIES dining room, sitting room, bar, reading room; garden
CREDIT CARDS AE, MC, V **CHILDREN** welcome **DISABLED** 1 ground-floor room
CLOSED 21st of Dec for 4 weeks **PETS** by arrangement
PROPRIETORS Mr and Mrs Hunter

MIDLANDS

SHIPTON-UNDER-WYCHWOOD, OXFORDSHIRE

LAMB INN
~ VILLAGE INN ~

Upper High Street, Shipton-under-Wychwood OX7 6DQ
TEL (01993) 830465 **FAX** (01993) 832025

NORTH OF BURFORD and skirted by the River Evenlode, Shipton-under-Wychwood is a Cotswold village built in the pale gold native stone. Safely off the main road up a quiet *cul-de-sac*, the early 17thC Lamb Inn was originally three houses, now combined to make a higgledy-piggledy interior full of nooks, crannies and steps. Run by Simon Clifton for The Old English Company, the beamed ceilings are hung with hops and punctuated with horse brasses, while the walls are bare stone and the floors are polished wood. As well as being a working pub, it has a large dining room where fresh and well-prepared dishes, with seafood and local game strongly represented, are on offer, together with a very reasonable range of wines. Lunchtime buffets in the bar are something of a speciality and a range of dishes (from which you can construct a very appetizing three-course meal) are also available in the evenings for those who prefer to eat where they drink rather than the other way round. Residents have the use of a cosy sitting room where a fire burns in winter. None of the bedrooms, reached by a steep and narrow staircase, are particularly large but they are thoughtfully equipped and well decorated – two have four-posters. Bathrooms are most definitely younger than the inn.

~

NEARBY Blenheim Palace; Oxford; Burford.
LOCATION at edge of village 4 miles (6.5 km) N of Burford; with car parking
FOOD breakfast, lunch, dinner
PRICE £££
ROOMS 5 double with bath; all rooms have, TV, hairdrier
FACILITIES bar, restaurant; garden
CREDIT CARDS AE, MC, V **CHILDREN** accepted
DISABLED not suitable
PETS dogs by arrangement
CLOSED restaurant only, Sun eve, Mon eve
PROPRIETOR Simon Clifton

MIDLANDS

THE SHAVEN CROWN
~ COUNTRY HOUSE HOTEL ~

Shipton-under-Wychwood, Oxfordshire OX7 6BA
TEL (01993) 830330 **FAX** (01993) 832136
WEBSITE www.shavencrown.co.uk

THE SHAVEN CROWN, as its name suggests, has monastic origins; it was built in 1384 as a hospice to nearby Bruern Abbey, and many of the original features remain intact – most impressively the medieval hall, with its beautiful double-collar braced roof and stone walls decorated with tapestries and wrought ironwork. The hall forms one side of the courtyard garden, which is decked with flowers and parasols, and on a sunny day is a lovely place in which to enjoy wholesome pub lunches. Some of the bedrooms overlook the courtyard, others are at the front of the house and suffer from road noise – though this is unlikely to be a problem at night.

Robert and Jane Burpitt, who moved south to take over The Shaven Crown after running a hotel in Dumfriesshire for ten years, have been refurbishing as they promised. Rooms are decorated sympathetically, leaving the low ceilings, uneven floorboards, exposed beams and open fireplaces intact, and are furnished with antiques and Jacobean furniture.

Dinner is taken in the oak-beamed dining room which leads off the hall. The menu offers plenty of choice and changes with the seasons – it is not elaborate, but the food is interesting and competently cooked. And if you still have the energy after four or five courses, you can join the locals in the narrow chapel-like bar, or adjourn to the hall, which doubles as a sitting room.

~

NEARBY North Leigh Roman Villa, Breurn Abbey; Blenheim Palace.
LOCATION in middle of village; with ample car parking
FOOD breakfast, lunch, dinner
PRICE ££
ROOMS 9; 7 double and twin, 1 single, 1 family, all with bath; all rooms have TV
FACILITIES restaurant, bar, medieval hall, courtyard garden; bowling green
CREDIT CARDS AE, MC, V **CHILDREN** welcome
DISABLED 1 ground-floor bedroom
PETS accepted in bedrooms only **CLOSED** never
PROPRIETORS Robert and Jane Burpitt

MIDLANDS

STADHAMPTON, OXFORDSHIRE

THE CRAZY BEAR
~ COUNTRY HOTEL ~

Bear Lane, Stadhampton, Oxfordshire OX44 7UR
TEL (01865) 890714 **FAX** (01865) 400481
WEBSITE www.crazybearhotel.co.uk

OUTSIDE, THE CRAZY BEAR looks like any other country pub/hotel but inside, it's far from predictable. The public rooms consist of a beautiful old beamed bar with open log fire; a bottle roofed dining room that serves traditional English food with a twist of French; and an atmospheric Thai restaurant downstairs. The bedrooms in the main building are only accessible by very steep stairs and are all named after makes of cigars, such as Monte Christo and Romeo Y Juliet. They are not particularly spacious, but are richly decorated with opulent fabrics giving a delightfully decadent feel. Most of the bathrooms are 'wet' (shower not enclosed) in order to achieve maximum space but this does mean everything gets a little soggy. There are more bedrooms in an outbuilding reached through the lush, Italianesque gardens. There are more spacious, and are themed (and named) by colour, beginning with the colour of the door and finishing with co-ordinating furniture and fabrics. An unusual touch is the deep, modern bath at the end of most of the beds: you can wallow while watching TV, or mellow out listening to music. A cottage down the road can also be used by guests and is similarly decorated in keeping with the other bedrooms.

In the summer, you can sit outside with your drinks in the beer garden by the pond, surrounded by somewhat out-of-context Greco statues. The new reception area is pure retro: a red London bus in the car park.

~

NEARBY Oxford City centre; Oxford University.
LOCATION leave the M40 at junction 7 onto the A329 at the petrol station turn left then left again into Bear Lane
FOOD breakfast, lunch, dinner
PRICE £££
ROOMS 12 doubles, 1 cottage, all with bath and shower apart from 1; all rooms have phone, TV, hairdrier, DVD, CD **FACILITIES** 2 dining rooms, bar; garden
CREDIT CARDS AE, MC, V **CHILDREN** welcome **DISABLED** 2 ground-floor rooms
PETS by arrangement **CLOSED** 1st week in Jan **PROPRIETOR** Jason Hunt

MIDLANDS

STOW-ON-THE-WOLD, GLOUCESTERSHIRE

THE ROYALIST HOTEL
~ TOWN HOUSE HOTEL ~

Digbeth Street, Stow-on-the-wold, Gloucester, GL54 1BN
TEL (01451) 830670 **FAX** (01451) 870048
E-MAIL info@theroyalisthotel.co.uk

LIKE SEVERAL other pubs we know, The Royalist claims to be the oldest inn in Englan, dating from 947 AD. It has three parts: the hotel itself, the 947AD restaurant and the Eagle and Child pub, which has been voted the eighth best pub in England.

The restaurant is just off the airy reception area. Many of the original beams are still in place, making it look suitably old and worn; but more modern furnishings keep it fresh and comfortable. Alan Thompson, chef, produces a good but not over ambitious menu of English/French food. The Thompsons owned 755 a London restaurant before moving to the Cotswolds.

The Eagle and Child pub is great for eating a deux, or for a larger group, serving traditional hearty pub food in a cosy, friendly atmosphere. However if you prefer to slump into an armchair to enjoy a quiet drink with a paper, the residents lounge complete with roaring log fire is perfect. The bedrooms are all decorated individually in rather pleasing, calming shades, fresh flowers greet you and you will not be disappointed at the size of the beds. By contrast the twin room is tiny, heavily beamed but all the same charming, perfect for children.

~

NEARBY Cotswold Villages,; Cheltenham.
LOCATION just off the A429, turn into Sheep street and you will find the hotel on the left hand corner of Digbeth street and Well Lane
FOOD breakfast, lunch, dinner
PRICE ££
ROOMS 7 double, 1 twin; 2 with shower only; all rooms have TV, phone, hairdrier, modem points
FACILITIES dining room, sitting room, bar, pub/brasserie; garden
CREDIT CARDS AE, MC, V
CHILDREN welcome **DISABLED** access difficult
PETS by arrangement **CLOSED** never
PROPRIETORS Alan and Georgina Thompson

MIDLANDS

CATERHAM HOUSE

~ TOWN BED-AND-BREAKFAST ~

58-59 Rother Street, Stratford-Upon-Avon, Warwickshire CV37 6LT
TEL (01789) 267309 **FAX** (01789) 414836

TWO GEORGIAN HOUSES have been knocked together to form this friendly B&B which, despite its central location – just a ten-minute walk from the Royal Shakespeare Theatre – has a surprisingly peaceful ambience. There is a small conservatory-style sitting room with an eclectic assortment of furniture, where generous teas are served each afternoon. Although there are no gardens, the sitting room opens out to a colourful terrace. You couldn't call the bedrooms huge, but all are spacious enough to accommodate a comfy chair. Each one is individually decorated with antique furniture (there are even antiques in the pristine, modern bathrooms). Beds are luxuriously downy and many are in French country style, revealing the roots of the owner Dominique Maury. This charming, chatty, Shakespeare-loving Frenchman has owned and run the hotel with his wife Olive since the late 1970s. Without being intrusive, he is always willing to talk, especially about the latest Shakespeare productions.

Apart from tea, breakfast is the only meal served, but guests rate it very highly. One writes, 'I would go back for the breakfasts if for no other reason.' He praised a dried fruit mixture in cinnamon-flavoured juice, the home-made jam, 'served in full jars, not little dishes', and the 'deliciously creamy' scrambled eggs. He also thought that his bill was 'a snip'.

~

NEARBY Royal Shakespeare Theatre; Shakespeare's Birthplace.
LOCATION in centre of town; with car parking
FOOD breakfast
PRICE ££
ROOMS 12 double and twin, all with bath or shower; all rooms have TV
FACILITIES sitting room, breakfast room, bar
CREDIT CARDS MC, V **CHILDREN** accepted
DISABLED not suitable
PETS accepted in bedrooms by arrangement
CLOSED Christmas Day **PROPRIETORS** Dominique and Olive Maury

MIDLANDS

CALCOT MANOR
~ COUNTRY HOUSE HOTEL ~

Near Tetbury, Gloucestershire GL8 8YJ
TEL (01666) 890391 **FAX** (01666) 890394
E-MAIL reception@calcotmanor.co.uk **WEBSITE** www.calcotmanor.co.uk

THIS 15THC COTSWOLD FARMHOUSE has been functioning as a hotel since 1984. Richard Ball took over Calcot Manor from his parents when they retired, and with a team of dedicated staff continues to provide the highest standards of comfort and service while preserving a calm and relaxed atmosphere. The lovely old house itself was a sound choice – its rooms are spacious and elegant without being grand – and the setting amid lawns and old barns, surrounded by rolling countryside, is all you could ask for.

Furnishings and decorations are carefully harmonious, with rich fabrics and pastel colours throughout. A converted cottage provides nine family suites, designed specifically for parents travelling with young children. For their entertainment, there's an indoor playroom.

Michael Croft is head chef of both the Conservatory Restaurant and the adjoining Gumstool Inn, which is more informal and moderately priced. In the restaurant, you might dine on asparagus, herb and lemon risotto, followed by seared sea bass served on parmesan mash with a spinach sauce, while in the inn, you could choose baked mature cheddar cheese soufflé and Gloucestershire Old Spot sausages with sage and red wine sauce.

NEARBY Chavenage; Owlpen Manor; Westonbirt Arboretum.
LOCATION 3 miles (5 km) W of Tetbury on A4135; with ample car parking
FOOD breakfast, lunch, dinner
PRICE £££
ROOMS 28, 18 double and twin, 4 family suites, 6 family rooms, all with bath or shower; all rooms have phone, TV, hairdrier **FACILITIES** 2 sitting rooms, dining room; garden, swimming pool, croquet, 2 all weather tennis courts; playroom, Spa
CREDIT CARDS AE, DC, MC, V
CHILDREN welcome
DISABLED 4 ground-floor bedrooms
PETS by arrangement **CLOSED** never **PROPRIETOR** Richard Ball

MIDLANDS

ULEY, GLOUCESTERSHIRE

OWLPEN MANOR

~ COUNTRY HOUSE COTTAGES ~

Owlpen, near Uley,Dursley, Gloucestershire GL11 5BZ
TEL (01453) 860261 **FAX** (01453) 860816/819
E-MAIL sales@owlpen.com **WEBSITE** www.owlpen.com

NICHOLAS AND KARIN MANDER have converted a clutch of cottages, barns, farmhouses and a mill to provide luxurious 'serviced' self-catering accommodation in their own idyllic Cotswold valley. At the heart of the enterprise is their Grade I listed Tudor manor, where huge bedrooms, some with four-posters, are also available to guests. The manor dates from the 15th and 16th centuries, when it was home to the de Olepenne family, but after standing empty for more than 100 years, it was restored in 1926 in Arts and Crafts style as many of the furnishings bear witness. Other material relics of the past include the magnificent Tudor Great Hall and a Jacobean wing; and then there is Margaret of Anjou's ghost, which has been glimpsed from time to time.

Owlpen has nine self-contained cottages, ranging in size from Tithe Barn, a split-level studio with massive oak beams and abundant rustic charm, to the 18thC Grist Mill, which sleeps nine and still sports its gigantic waterwheel and mill machinery. All are well-furnished and equipped, and have their own private terrace or garden. In the Cyder House Restaurant at the centre of the hamlet, Karin Mander's menu features seasonal produce from the estate: specialities are pheasant, venison and fish dishes from her native Sweden, seasoned with herbs from the Elizabethan herb garden.

~

NEARBY Cirencester; Bath; Cheltenham.
LOCATION 0.5 mile (1 km) E of Uley off B4066; with ample car parking
FOOD breakfast, lunch, dinner
PRICE ££
ROOMS 9 cottages sleeping 2-9 people; all cottages have phone, TV, hairdrier, kitchen **FACILITIES** restaurant; garden **CREDIT CARDS** AE, DC, MC, V
CHILDREN accepted **DISABLED** not suitable **PETS** by arrangement
CLOSED restaurant only, Mon and at other times, reservations essential
PROPRIETORS Nicholas and Karin Mander

MIDLANDS

WOODSTOCK, OXFORDSHIRE

FEATHERS

~ TOWN HOTEL ~

Market Street, Woodstock, Oxfordshire OX20 1SX
TEL (01993) 812291 **FAX** (01993) 813158
E-MAIL enquiries@feathers.co.uk **WEBSITE** www.feathers.co.uk

AN AMALGAM OF FOUR tall 17thC town houses of mellow red brick, now an exceptionally civilized town hotel. One visitor was full of praise for the way the staff managed to make a weekend 'entirely relaxing, without intruding in the way that hotel staff so often do'.

'The upstairs drawing room (with library and open fire) has the relaxed atmosphere of a well-kept English country home rather than a hotel, with antiques, fine fabrics, an abundance of fresh flowers and a refreshing absence of the ubiquitous Olde Worlde. There is also a cosy study for reading the papers or drinking tea. If you want fresh air, there is a pleasant courtyard garden and bar. Bedrooms are spacious (on the whole) and beautifully decorated, comfortable yet still with the understated elegance that pervades the whole hotel. Five further bedrooms are to be found in the building next door, renovated a few years ago. The elegant panelled dining room serves excellent food from Mark Treasure's interesting contemporary menu. Recent visitors have been impressed by both the food and service in the 'lively' restaurant.

Technically, this has all the trappings of a smart business hotel, but don't be put off by that because it has character and a very home-like atmosphere.

~

NEARBY Blenheim Palace; Oxford.
LOCATION in middle of town; with limited car parking
FOOD breakfast, lunch, dinner
PRICE £££
ROOMS 20; 17 double and twin, 3 suites all with bath or shower (some have steam showers); all rooms have phone, TV
FACILITIES 2 sitting rooms, conservatory, bar, dining room, restaurant
CREDIT CARDS AE, DC, V **CHILDREN** welcome
DISABLED access difficult
PETS accepted by arrangement **CLOSED** never
MANAGER Gavin Thomson

MIDLANDS

WORFIELD, SHROPSHIRE

OLD VICARAGE

⁓ COUNTRY HOUSE HOTEL ⁓

Worfield, near Bridgnorth, Shropshire WV15 5JZ
TEL (01746) 716497 **FAX** (01746) 716552
E-MAIL admin@the-old-vicarage.demon.co.uk **WEBSITE** www.oldvicarageworfield.com

WHEN this substantial red-brick vicarage was converted into a small hotel in 1981, every effort was made to retain the Edwardian character of the place – restoring original wood block floors, discreetly adding bathrooms to bedrooms, furnishing the rooms with handsome Victorian and Edwardian pieces, carefully converting the coach house to four 'luxury' bedrooms (one of which, 'Leighton', has been specially designed for disabled guests). Readers have praised the large, comfortable bedrooms, named after Shropshire villages and decorated in subtle colours, with matching bathrobes and soaps.

Attention to detail extends to the sitting rooms (one is the conservatory, with glorious views of the Worfe valley) and the three dining rooms. The award-winning food (a daily changing menu with several choices and impressive cheeseboard) is English-based, ambitious and not cheap, served at polished tables by cheerful staff. There is a reasonably extensive wine cellar. The dining room is strictly non-smoking, as are the bedrooms.

⁓

NEARBY Ludlow; Severn Valley Railway; Ironbridge Gorge Museum.
LOCATION in village, 8 miles (12 km) W of Wolverhampton, 1 mile off A454 , 8 miles (12 km) S of junction 4 of M54; in own grounds with ample car parking
FOOD breakfast, lunch, dinner
PRICE £££
ROOMS 14 double, 1 family, 2 rooms with shower, 1 room with bath only, all the rest have both; all rooms have phone, TV, minibar, hairdrier
FACILITIES 2 sitting rooms, 3 dining rooms, 1 with bar
CREDIT CARDS AE, DC, MC, V **CHILDREN** welcome
DISABLED 1 specially adapted bedroom
PETS accepted in bedrooms
CLOSED Christmas
PROPRIETORS David and Sarah Blakstad

EAST ANGLIA AND REGION

BEYTON, SUFFOLK

MANORHOUSE
~ COUNTRY BED-AND-BREAKFAST ~

The Green, Beyton, Bury St Edmunds, Suffolk IP30 9AF
TEL (01359) 270960

E-MAIL manorhouse@beyton1.freeserve.com **WEBSITE** www.beyton1.freeserve.co.uk

THIS B&B IN A BEAUTIFUL 15thC Suffolk longhouse is run full-time by husband and wife Mark and Kay Dewsbury and overlooks the village green. It's an elegant but down to earth place – the half-timbered rooms in the main house have been colourwashed and are filled with antiques, but outside, chickens have the run of the gravelled yard, garden and sometimes the vegetable garden too. All of them lay, and between them provide most of the eggs served for breakfast.

There's a great deal of space in which to spread out. The Yellow Room in the main house is suite-sized, with its own sitting area, and there are two more rooms – the Garden Room and the Dairy – in a converted barn at right angles to the house. The decoration is comfortably rustic: the Dairy has exposed brick and flint walls, the traditional building materials of the area, and bright and cheerful furnishings and a walk-in power shower in the large bathroom. French windows open from the Garden Room on to a tiny paved area for sitting out in summer and contemplating the venerable old lichen-covered trees. The Dewsburys are excellent hosts – laid back and unflummoxed. Their only rule is that it is a non-smoking house. For guests who fancy a stroll, there are a couple of pleasant pubs in the village.

~

NEARBY Bury St Edmunds; Lavenham.
LOCATION 4 miles (6 km) E of Bury St Edmunds, signposted off A14; with ample car parking
FOOD breakfast, dinner on request **PRICES** £
ROOMS 4 double with bath or shower; all rooms have TV, hairdrier
FACILITIES sitting room, dining room; garden
CREDIT CARDS not accepted
CHILDREN accepted over 5
DISABLED access possible to 2 ground-floor rooms **PETS** not accepted
CLOSED never **PROPRIETORS** Mark and Kay Dewsbury

EAST ANGLIA AND REGION

BURNHAM MARKET, NORFOLK

HOSTE ARMS
~ VILLAGE HOTEL ~

The Green, Burnham Market, North Norfolk
TEL (01328) 738777 **FAX** (01328) 730103
E-MAIL reception@hostearms.co.uk **WEBSITE** www.hostearms.co.uk

OVERLOOKING THE GREEN in a village whose main claim to fame is that it was Admiral Nelson's birthplace, this handsome yellow-and-white 17thC inn has won a clutch of awards for its bedrooms, bar and restaurant. Downstairs, it positively buzzes with life in the evenings, when locals come here to drink and eat – in that order. On Friday nights between October and March, a pianist plays jazz in the restaurant, where the brasserie-style menu includes British, European and Oriental-inspired dishes.

The man responsible for its lively reputation, Paul Whittome, bought the Hoste Arms in 1989. Despite being deaf, he is a chatty, affable proprietor, whose wife Jeanne is responsible for the rustic-chic decoration. She clearly has a penchant for dramatic colour schemes, painting walls downstairs deep red, and using colourful plaids and eye-catching striped fabrics in the bedrooms. These vary in style and size; some have been criticized for being poky, so book carefully. Several are on the ground floor, three with small patios that lead on to the pretty walled garden, which provides a welcome refuge when the bar becomes too crowded. Changing art exhibitions mean that the walls are always packed with pictures. There have been major changes with the addition of new bedrooms and an eccentric "African Wing". More reports please.

~

NEARBY Houghton Hall; Holkham Hall; Sandringham House; Titchwell, Holme, Holkham and Cley nature reserves.
LOCATION in centre of village; with ample car parking
FOOD breakfast, lunch, dinner
PRICE ££
ROOMS 44; 37 doubles in main house, 7 in Railway Inn, all with bath or shower; all rooms have phone, TV, hairdrier
FACILITIES sitting room, conservatory, dining room, bar; garden
CREDIT CARDS MC, V **CHILDREN** accepted **DISABLED** ground-floor bedrooms
PETS not accepted **CLOSED** never **PROPRIETORS** Paul and Jeanne Whittome

EAST ANGLIA AND REGION

BURY ST EDMUNDS, SUFFOLK

OUNCE HOUSE
~ TOWN HOTEL ~

Northgate Street, Bury St Edmunds, Suffolk IP33 1HP
TEL 01284 761779 **FAX** 01284 768315
E-MAIL pott@globalnet.co.uk **WEBSITE** www.ouncehouse.co.uk

OUNCE HOUSE IS A RED BRICK, gable-ended, three-storey house, set back from the road a five-minute walk from the abbey and pedestrianized shopping streets in the centre of Bury St Edmunds.

The interiors are formal but homely with drawing room and dining room decorated in calm colours; these are 'statement' swagged and draped curtains, plenty of lamps, *objets d'art* and interesting pictures. Most of the bedrooms are large and one of the most attractive has pale yellow walls, a crown arrangement over the bedhead, two chintzy armchairs and a decorative chimneypiece.

A set-menu is offered at dinner and everyone eats around the large, highly polished oval table – the owners, warm and open hosts, are good at putting people at their ease. If you don't want to eat in, there are several restaurants within walking distance. Guests also have the use of the library, which is more like a den, with a large leather wing armchair, smaller easy chairs, an upright piano, shelves packed with books and an honesty bar. It is somewhere to go with a friend for a long conversation, or watch TV, and is one of the few places in the house where you can smoke, though this is tolerated rather than encouraged (you have to burn a scented candle if you indulge).

~

NEARBY Cathedral; Abbey; Gershom-Parkington Collection.
LOCATION close to town centre; with ample car parking
FOOD breakfast
PRICE ££
ROOMS 3 double and twin with bath; all rooms have phone, TV, hairdrier
FACILITIES 2 sitting rooms, library/TV room, dining room; garden
CREDIT CARDS AE, DC, MC, V
CHILDREN welcome
DISABLED access difficult **PETS** not accepted
CLOSED never **PROPRIETORS** Simon and Jenny Pott

EAST ANGLIA AND REGION

BURY ST EDMUNDS, SUFFOLK

TWELVE ANGEL HILL
~ TOWN HOTEL ~

12 Angel Hill, Bury St Edmunds, Suffolk IP33 1UZ
TEL (01284) 704088 **FAX** (01284) 725549

'GETS AWAY WITH TROUSER-PRESSES without being boring,' says one of our highly satisfied inspectors. Twelve Angel Hill occupies a house in a mellow brick terrace, close to Bury's cathedral. It is Georgian to the front but Tudor behind, and opened as a hotel in 1988 after being thoroughly renovated. The large bedrooms are light, generously proportioned with a special sitting area, in superb condition and beautifully furnished with antiques and sympathetic reproductions, and have bold floral decoration and fabrics.

The Clarkes have made the most of the original features of the house, and have evidently thought carefully about the comfort of their guests: witness the charming window seat scattered with cushions overlooking the Italian walled garden; a fine four-poster bed with canopy; an intimate oak-panelled bar; and the light, pleasant drawing room overlooking Angel Hill (not noisy, since it's double-glazed). It all has the feel of a private house, yet manages to include all the bedroom comforts of a hotel. Breakfast is, by all accounts, well above the average.

Totally non-smoking. Dinner can be arranged at one of the many local restaurants. The Clarkes are charming hosts and our inspector saw plenty of evidence that guests are highly impressed.

~

NEARBY Cathedral; museums; Abbey gardens.
LOCATION on Angel Hill, 100 m from cathedral; with car parking
FOOD breakfast
PRICE ££
ROOMS 6; 5 double, 1 single, all with bath or shower; all rooms have phone, TV, hairdrier **FACILITIES** sitting room, dining room, bar, patio room, patio garden
CREDIT CARDS AE, DC, MC, V **CHILDREN** not accepted
DISABLED access difficult
PETS not accepted **CLOSED** Jan
PROPRIETORS Bernie and John Clarke

EAST ANGLIA AND REGION

CLEY-NEXT-THE-SEA, NORFOLK

CLEY MILL
~ CONVERTED WINDMILL ~

Cley-next-the-Sea, Holt, Norfolk NR25 7RP
TEL (01263) 740209 **FAX** (01263) 740209
WEBSITE www.cleymill.co.uk

IMAGINE STAYING IN A 'REAL' WINDMILL. That is the sense of adventure that Cley Mill can induce even in the most world-weary. Memories of *Swallows and Amazons* or the *Famous Five* crowd in as you climb higher and higher in the mill, finally mounting the ladder to the look-out room on the fourth floor. Superb views over the Cley Marshes, a Mecca for bird-watchers.

The sitting room on the ground floor of the Mill is exceptionally welcoming – it feels well used and lived-in, with plenty of books and magazines, comfortable sofas, TV and an open fire. Bedrooms in the Mill feel rather like log cabins – much wood in the furniture and fittings. They are pretty rooms, with white lace bedspreads, and bathrooms ingeniously fitted in to the most challenging nooks and crannies that the old building provides.

Jeremy Bolam took over the running of the Mill several years ago. He used to own a restaurant in Battersea, so greater emphasis is put on food and dining in now, but he won't mind a bit if you simply take B&B.

A recent reporter stayed in The Boathouse, which is usually self-catering, and which takes the overflow from the Mill. She found it 'basic and not very comfortable', so it's worth holding out for a room in the mill, even though they are sought-after. Try to book well in advance. See also our other windmill (page 38).

~

NEARBY Sheringham Hall; Cromer Lighthouse; Holkham Hall.
LOCATION 7 miles (11 km) W of Sheringham on A149, on N edge of village; with ample car parking
FOOD breakfast, dinner on request
PRICE ££
ROOMS 7 double, 1 single, 6 with bath, 1 with shower
FACILITIES sitting room, dining room, garden **CREDIT CARDS** MC, V
CHILDREN welcome **DISABLED** access difficult
PETS accepted **CLOSED** never **MANAGER** Jeremy Bolam

EAST ANGLIA AND REGION

HOLKHAM, NORFOLK

THE VICTORIA AT HOLKHAM
∾ COUNTRY HOTEL ∾

Park Road, Holkham, Norfolk NR23 1RG
TEL (01328) 711008 **FAX** (01328) 711009
E-MAIL victoria@holkham.co.uk **WEBSITE** www.victoriaatholkham.co.uk

PART OF THE HOLKHAM ESTATE owned by Lord and Lady Leicester, The Victoria (named after Queen Victoria, a year after she became queen) is an eclectic and stylish blend of colonial and local furniture and fabrics. Built in 1838 by Coke of Norfolk, the hotel is a ten-minute stroll from the beautiful white beach of Holkham where there's water sports and horse riding. Tom Coke, a descendent of the Coke of Norfolk, and his new wife Polly recently acquired the hotel and have undertaken a major project of refurbishment.

Everywhere you turn your attention is caught by some curious object or another, since most of the furnishings and ornaments have been flown in from Rajasthan there's a strong sense of the exotic. All of the bedrooms are decorated individually with flare and extremely good taste. Although the rooms may look old they have modern comforts such as seriously comfy beds, big warm duvets and deep baths for a serious soak.

The restaurant and bar area is very much in keeping with the colonial feel, slightly hard chairs, but beautiful wall hangings and views. The food is cooked and presented to a high standard (don't overlook the fish and chips); and there's a long wine list.

∾

NEARBY Holkham Hall, Holkham beach, Banham Zoo.
LOCATION just off the B1105 on th A149 near Wells; with ample car parking
FOOD breakfast, lunch, dinner
PRICE £££
ROOMS 11 double, 1 twin, 1 single, all en suite except 1, all have bath, some have hand-held showers; all rooms have satellite TV, phone, hairdrier
FACILITIES 2 dining rooms, 2 sitting rooms, 3 bars; garden, 2 helipads
CREDIT CARDS MC, V
CHILDREN welcome **DISABLED** 1 ground-floor room
PETS not accepted
CLOSED never **PROPRIETORS** Viscount and Viscountess Coke

EAST ANGLIA AND REGION

KING'S LYNN, NORFOLK

CONGHAM HALL
~ COUNTRY HOUSE HOTEL ~

Lynn Road, Grimston, King's Lynn, Norfolk PE32 1AH
TEL (01485) 600250 **FAX** (01485) 601191
E-MAIL reception@conghamhallhotel.demon.co.uk **WEBSITE** www.conghamhallhotel.co.uk

'QUINTESSENTIALLY ENGLISH' is how some guests describe their stay here. Practically everything about this white 18thC Georgian house, set in 40 acres of lawns, orchards and parkland, is impressive. The spacious bedrooms and public areas are luxuriously furnished and, despite a change of ownership in October 1999, our reporter found the service to be as solicitous and efficient and the staff as helpful and welcoming as ever. Cooking (in the modern British style) is adventurous and excellent, making much use of home-grown herbs. The restaurant is a spacious, airy delight, built to look like an orangerie, with full-length windows overlooking the wide lawns of the parkland, where the herb gardens are an attraction in their own right. Visitors stop to admire the array of 600 herb varieties and to buy samples, from angelica to sorrel. The restaurant doors open on to the terraces for pre-dinner drinks and herb garden strolls. Dressing for dinner is requested.

Personal attention is thoughtful. For walkers and cyclists, the hotel will arrange to collect luggage from guests' previous destinations and deliver it onwards too. It also keeps a book of special walks, devised by the previous owners, the Forecasts, and can arrange tuition at the Sandringham Shooting School.

~

NEARBY Sandringham; Ely; Norwich.
LOCATION 6 miles (10 km) NE of King's Lynn near A148; with parking for 50 cars
FOOD breakfast, lunch, dinner
PRICE £££
ROOMS 14; 11 double, 2 suites, all with bath, 1 single with shower; all rooms have phone, TV **FACILITIES** 2 sitting rooms, bar, dining room; garden, spa bath, swimming pool, tennis, croquet, putting
CREDIT CARDS AE, DC, MC, V
CHILDREN welcome over 12 **DISABLED** easy access to restaurant
PETS by arrangement **CLOSED** never **PROPRIETOR** Lord Andrew Davies

EAST ANGLIA AND REGION

LAVENHAM, SUFFOLK

THE GREAT HOUSE
~ RESTAURANT-WITH-ROOMS ~

Market Place, Lavenham, Suffolk CO10 9QZ
TEL (01787) 247431 **FAX** (01787) 248007
E-MAIL greathouse@clara.co.uk **WEBSITE** www.greathouse.co.uk

THE OLD TIMBER-FRAMED houses, the fine Perpendicular 'Wool Church' and the high street full of antiques and galleries make Lavenham a high point of any visitor's itinerary of the pretty villages of East Anglia.

The Great House in the market place was built in the heyday of the wool trade but was extensively renovated in the 18th century and looks more Georgian than Tudor – at least from the outside. It was a private house (lived in by Stephen Spender in the 1930s) until John Spice, a Texan with family roots in Suffolk, had the bright idea of turning it into a restaurant-with-rooms. It is now owned by chef Régis Crépy, and the food (predominantly French) is the best for miles – 'stunningly good', enthuses one visitor (a fellow hotelier). If you can secure one of its four bedrooms it is also a delightful place to stay. All are different, but they are all light, spacious and full of old-world charm, with beams and antiques. Each has its own fireplace and sitting area, with sofa or upholstered chairs. The dining room is dominated by an inglenook fireplace that formed part of the original house. In winter, log fires blaze; in summer, French doors open on to a pretty stone-paved courtyard for drinks, lunch or dinner.

NEARBY Little Hall, Guildhall Priory (Lavenham); Melford Hall; Gainsborough's House, Sudbury.
LOCATION 16 miles (26 km) NW of Colchester, in middle of village; with car parking
FOOD breakfast, lunch, dinner
PRICE £££
ROOMS 4 family-size suites with bath; all rooms have phone, TV
FACILITIES sitting room/bar; dining room; patio, garden
CREDIT CARDS AE, MC, V
CHILDREN welcome **DISABLED** access difficult
PETS welcome **CLOSED** Jan **PROPRIETOR** Régis Crépy

EAST ANGLIA AND REGION

LAVENHAM PRIORY

~ VILLAGE BED-AND-BREAKFAST ~

Water Street, Lavenham, Suffolk CO10 9RW
TEL (01787) 247404 **FAX** (01787) 248472
WEBSITE www.lavenhampriory.co.uk

GILLI PITT RUNS LAVENHAM PRIORY with great flair, and the term B&B doesn't do it justice. It is a very special place: the beautiful Grade I-listed house dates from the 13th century when it was home to Benedictine monks, and has been restored in keeping with its later life as home to an Elizabethan merchant, complete with original wallpaintings, huge Tudor fireplace and sofas covered in cushions and throws. More important, however, is the warmth of the welcome from Gilli and her husband Tim, which stems from an enjoyment of sharing the main part of their home.

This is a place to enjoy, whatever the season. In summer the courtyard garden is fragrant with herbs, but in winter it's just as appealing to drink a hot toddy by the fire. The house is large, and as well as the Great Hall sitting room there's a smaller room (where shelves are stacked with board games) so more than one party can use the public rooms without feeling crowded. Each of the bedrooms has a superb bed, including a four-poster in the Painted Chamber and a solid cherrywood sleigh in the Gallery Chamber – worth a journey in their own right. Breakfast in the Merchants Hall is a feast, with fresh stewed and candied fruits, as well as the full English fry up. There's a no-smoking rule.

~

NEARBY Guildhall; 'Wool Church' of SS Peter and Paul.
LOCATION in centre of village beside Swan; with ample parking
FOOD breakfast
PRICE ££
ROOMS 6 double, 5 with bath, 1 with shower; all rooms have TV, hairdrier
FACILITIES 2 sitting rooms, dining room; garden
CREDIT CARDS MC, V
CHILDREN accepted over 10
DISABLED not suitable
PETS not accepted **CLOSED** Christmas and New Year
PROPRIETORS Tim and Gilli Pitt

EAST ANGLIA AND REGION

THE BLACK LION
~ COUNTRY HOTEL ~

The Green, Long Melford, Suffolk CO10 9DN
TEL (01787) 312356 **FAX** (01787) 374557
E-MAIL enquiries@blacklion.net **WEBSITE** www.blacklionhotel.net

LONG MELFORD IS A FAMOUSLY attractive Suffolk village, and The Black Lion is at the heart of it, overlooking the green. It is an elegant early 19thC building, decorated and furnished with great sympathy, taste and lightness of touch. The hotel changed hands in December 1999, and the new owner, Craig Jarvis, has reinstated its original name (the previous owners, the Erringtons, had renamed it 'The Countrymen'). The two dining rooms, one principally for private functions, offer 'modern *cuisine* with a strong classical influence' and a wide-ranging wine list.

Our latest reporter was also delighted with the accommodation. Bedrooms are comfortable and 'non slick: nothing much matches in a charming sort of way'. She noticed the half-open trunk on a landing, spilling out hats and costumes; an antique typewriter on a desk; and bookcases groaning with old books, in the wine bar. Craig Jarvis plans to update the rooms – we hope that they lose none of their character in the process.

The Erringtons used to organize numerous events, from wine tastings or live jazz in the bar to murder dinners and midsummer balls. These will continue, though 'there may not be quite so many'. We hope that the lively atmosphere and sense of fun will survive the change of ownership. Reports please.

~

NEARBY Long Melford church; Melford Hall; Kentwell Hall.
LOCATION in village 3 miles (5 km) N of Sudbury, overlooking village green; with car parking
FOOD breakfast, lunch, dinner
PRICE ££
ROOMS 8 double, 1 suite, 1 twin; all have phone, TV **FACILITIES** sitting room, 2 dining rooms, bar, study
CREDIT CARDS AE, MC, V
CHILDREN welcome **DISABLED** no special facilities
PETS accepted in bedrooms **CLOSED** never **PROPRIETOR** Mr Craig Jarvis

EAST ANGLIA AND REGION

MELBOURN, HERTFORDSHIRE

MELBOURN BURY

~ COUNTRY GUEST-HOUSE ~

Melbourn, near Royston, Hertfordshire SG8 6DE
TEL (01763) 261151 **FAX** (01763) 262375
E-MAIL melbournbury@biztobiz.co.uk

THIS GRACIOUS MANOR HOUSE, dating mainly from Victorian times, although of much earlier origin, offers an intimate retreat only 20 minutes' drive from Cambridge. The whitewashed and crenellated house, with roses round the door, has a delightful setting in mature parkland, with its own lake and gardens.

All the public rooms are furnished with antiques, but have just the right degree of informality to make the house feel like a lived-in home and not a museum – not surprising, when you learn that Sylvia Hopkinson's family have been here for 150 years. As well as an elegant drawing room, there is a splendid Victorian billiards room (full-size table) incorporating a book-lined library, and a sun-trap conservatory. The three bedrooms are spacious and comfortably furnished in harmony with the house; particularly delightful is the 'pink room', which looks out over the lake and the garden; it is a profusion of Sanderson prints and antiques, and has a large bathroom.

The Hopkinsons' dinner-party food (by prior arrangement) is home-made, down to the ice-creams and sorbets and served dinner-party-style around a large mahogany table in the dining room.

~

NEARBY Cambridge colleges and Fitzwilliam Museum; Duxford Air Museum; Wimpole Hall; Audley End.
LOCATION 10 miles (16 km) SW of Cambridge, on S side of village off A10; with ample car parking
FOOD breakfast, dinner
PRICE ££
ROOMS 3; 2 double, 1 single, all with bath or shower; all rooms have TV
FACILITIES 2 sitting rooms, conservatory, dining room, billiards room; garden
CREDIT CARDS AE, MC, V **CHILDREN** welcome over 8
DISABLED not suitable **PETS** not accepted
CLOSED Christmas, New Year, Easter **PROPRIETORS** Anthony and Sylvia Hopkinson

EAST ANGLIA AND REGION

MORSTON, NORFOLK

MORSTON HALL

~ COUNTRY HOTEL ~

Morston, Holt, Norfolk NR25 7AA
TEL (01263) 741041 **FAX** (01263) 740419
E-MAIL reception@morstonhall.com **WEBSITE** www.morstonhall.com

DON'T BE PUT OFF BY the rather severe-looking flint exterior of this solid Jacobean house on the North Norfolk coast. Inside, the rooms are unexpectedly bright and airy, painted in summery colours and overlooking a sweet garden, where a fountain plays in a lily pond and roses flourish. The *raison d'être* of Morston Hall is its dining room, the responsibility of Galton Blackiston, who shot to fame as a finalist in ITV's 'Chef of the Year'. He has since won huge acclaim for his outstanding modern European cuisine and, the icing on the cake, a Michelin star in 1999. His set four-course menu changes daily and might feature: *confit* of leg of duck on sautéed Lyonnaise potatoes with thyme-infused *jus* or grilled fillet of sea bass served on fennel *duxelle* with *sauce vierge*. The carefully-stocked wine cellar offers a comprehensive selection of (not overpriced) wines from all over the world. Galton and his wife, Tracy, also organize wine-tasting dinners and cookery lessons. He gives a number of half-day cookery demonstrations and runs two three-day residential courses each year. Most of the large bedrooms are decked out in chintz fabrics, with armchairs and all the little extras, such as bottled water, bathrobes and large, warm, fluffy towels.

~

NEARBY Sandringham; Felbrigg Hall; Holkham Hall; Brickling.
LOCATION 2 miles (3 km) W of Blakeney on A149; with ample car parking
FOOD breakfast, Sun lunch, dinner
PRICE ££
ROOMS 7; 4 doubles, 1 suite, 2 twins; all rooms have phone, TV, video, CD player, hairdrier **FACILITIES** 2 sitting rooms, conservatory, dining room; garden, croquet
CREDIT CARDS AE, DC, MC, V
CHILDREN welcome
DISABLED 1 ground-floor bedroom
PETS accepted in bedrooms **CLOSED** Jan, Christmas, Boxing Day
PROPRIETORS Galton and Tracy Blackiston

EAST ANGLIA AND REGION

NAYLAND, SUFFOLK

WHITE HART INN
~ COUNTRY INN ~

High Street, Nayland, near Colchester, Suffolk CO6 4JF
TEL (01206) 263382 **FAX** (01206) 263638
E-MAIL nayhart@aol.com **WEBSITE** www.whitehart-nayland.co.uk

'A GREAT COMBINATION of old and new,' says a recent report. Set in a cobbled Suffolk village, the inn dates from the 15th century, and was a popular halt for coaches to refuel and water. Nowadays good food and comfortable rooms still draw people in. Frank Deletang and Karine Bordas took over managing the Inn in 1999 and since then there have been some notable improvements in the standard of the food and the bedrooms.

Breakfast, lunch and dinner are served in the restaurant, which is not as hushed as it first appears. The Head Chef, Karl Shillingford, has an impressive pedigree and it shows in the beautifully presented food created from local ingredients whenever possible.

The bedrooms epitomise the balance between old and new that Frank and Karine wanted: calm shades on the walls contrasting with the bright, chic furnishings, sitting comfortably with the antique elements, such as the old beams, which have been preserved in most of the rooms. The bathrooms are contemporary, adequately equipped with large, fluffy towels.

~

NEARBY Colchester; Ipswich.
LOCATION on the 314N of Colchester in the High Street
FOOD breakfast, lunch, dinner
PRICE ££
ROOMS 6 double with en suite bath and shower; all rooms have TV, phone, radio, hairdrier, modem point, trouser press **FACILITIES** dining room, small lounge, bar, private dining room; garden
CREDIT CARDS AE, DC, MC, V
CHILDREN welcome
DISABLED access difficult except in public rooms
PETS not accepted
CLOSED 26th December to 9th Jan; restaurant only, Mon
PROPRIETOR Michel Roux

East Anglia and Region

Needham Market, Suffolk

Pipps Ford

MANOR HOUSE HOTEL

Needham Market, near Ipswich, Suffolk IP6 8LJ
Tel (01449) 760208 **Fax** (01449) 760561
E-Mail b+b@pippsford.co.uk **Website** www.pippsford.co.uk

THIS BLACK AND WHITE, half-timbered manor house was built in 1540 for Richard Hakluyt, a commissioner of maps who opened up much of the globe to explorers. It's fitting that the tide has now turned and visitors come here from all over world for New Zealander Raewyn Hackett-Jones' relaxed, thoughtful hospitality. When Raewyn and her husband bought the house in 1974, the main water supply came from the well by the front door. Now, despite every up-to-date fitting and the fact that it's next to the A14, the house still feels slightly otherworldly, with the River Gipping meandering through the garden, where old-fashioned roses run rampant, and the rooms named after cottage garden plants. There are more rooms in a stable annexe and all guests have the run of the sitting rooms, the main one with grand piano and log fire.

There are no televisions in rooms, as Raewyn likes people to stay and chat after dinner. The atmosphere encourages sociability, with one large dining table if you want to eat with other guests, or smaller ones if you prefer to dine *à deux*. Food is excellent, with homemade bread, jams and honey from the hives in the garden, game and pork from nearby suppliers and locally smoked fish.

Nearby Blakenham Woodland gardens; Ipswich; Snape meetings
Location one mile (1.5 km) E of Needham Market, off roundabout where A140 meets A14; with car parking
Food breakfast, dinner Mon to Sat
Price £
Rooms 9; 5 double, 3 twin, 1 single, all with bath or shower; all rooms have hairdrier **Facilities** 3 sitting rooms, dining room, conservatory; garden, tennis court
Credit cards AE, MC, V
Children accepted over 5
Disabled not suitable **Pets** not accepted
Closed Christmas to mid-Jan **Proprietor** Raewyn Hackett-Jones

EAST ANGLIA AND REGION

NORWICH, NORFOLK

BY APPOINTMENT
~ RESTAURANT-WITH-ROOMS ~

25-29 St Georges Street, Norwich, Norfolk NR3 1AB
TEL (01603) 630730 **FAX** (01603) 630730

THERE IS SO MUCH to see in Norwich and if you want to be in the thick of things, then this quirky establishment, in a 15thC merchant's house owned by Timothy Brown and Robert Culyer, might be the place for you. It is in St Georges Street, which runs parallel to Elm Hill, gloriously cobbled and lined with historic houses, and is ideally placed for seeing the sights.

As you enter through the kitchen, you are struck by the friendly atmosphere, which also pervades the five rooms that comprise the restaurant. They have somewhat theatrical furnishings – heavy swagged curtains, rich night-time colours, crystal and silver glittering on impeccably laid tables. In this setting, you choose dishes from the large *carte*, such as fillet of beef, filled with a *duxelle* of tomatoes and mushrooms, wrapped in puff pastry, with a fresh garden mint and mustard sauce. Don't overdo it: otherwise you won't manage the magnificent cooked feast that goes by the name of breakfast the next morning.

The layout of the building seems more like a warren than a house. Appropriately, reception rooms and bedrooms, all with exotic and colourful decoration, are crammed with Victoriana and *objets trouvés*. It may not suit everybody, but it is thoroughly original and, as far as we're concerned, a breath of fresh air.

~

NEARBY Cathedral; Castle; Guildhall; Bridewell Museum.
LOCATION in city centre; with car parking
FOOD breakfast, dinner
PRICE ££
ROOMS 4; 2 double, 1 twin, 1 single, all with bath; all rooms have phone, TV, hairdrier **FACILITIES** sitting room, dining rooms
CREDIT CARDS MC, V **CHILDREN** accepted over 12
DISABLED access possible to public rooms **PETS** not accepted
CLOSED Christmas Day; restaurant Sun, Mon
PROPRIETORS Timothy Brown and Robert Culyer

EAST ANGLIA AND REGION

NORWICH, NORFOLK

OLD CATTON HALL
~ COUNTRY HOUSE HOTEL ~

Lodge Lane, Old Catton, Norwich, Norfolk NR6 7HG
TEL (01603) 419379 **FAX** (01603)400339
E-MAIL enquiries@catton-hall.co.uk **WEBSITE** www.catton-hall.co.uk

AN IMPRESSIVE 17THC gentleman's residence, built from reclaimed Caen stone, local flint and oak timbers, has been transformed with great success into this genteel family-run hotel. Though located in an unprepossessing suburb of Norwich, it has the twin advantages of being within easy reach of the city centre, yet away from the bustle. With its mullioned windows, beamed ceilings, inglenook fireplaces, polished antiques and warm colour schemes, the interior feels intimate and inviting. Owners Anthea and Roger Cawdron are on hand to welcome guests and pamper them during their stay, placing books and glossy magazines by their beds, and a tantalising array of soaps, bubble baths, lotions and potions in the bathrooms. Named after former inhabitants of the house, the bedrooms have been decorated boldly and with dash in country-house style by Anthea, and the beds, some of which are four-posters, are made up with delicious Egyptian cotton sheets.

Anthea's talents also extend to the kitchen, where she prepares interesting dishes, using local produce and herbs from the garden, according to – among others – old family recipes. There is a thoughtfully chosen and not-too-exorbitant wine list.

~

NEARBY Cathedral; Castle; The Broad; Norwich Castle.
LOCATION 2.5 miles (4 km) NE of Norwich, off B1150; with ample car parking
FOOD breakfast, dinner
PRICE ££
ROOMS 7 double, twin and family with bath; all rooms have phone, TV, hairdrier
FACILITIES sitting room, dining room; garden
CREDIT CARDS AE, DC, MC, V
CHILDREN accepted over 12
DISABLED not suitable
PETS not accepted **CLOSED** restaurant only, Sun eve
PROPRIETORS Roger and Anthea Cawdron

EAST ANGLIA AND REGION

SNAPE, SUFFOLK

CROWN INN
~ VILLAGE INN ~

Snape, Suffolk, IP17 1SL
TEL (01728) 688324

SNAPE IS THE TINY VILLAGE close to the estuary of the River Alde, a tidal river that meanders its way through salt marshes to the sea. In the centre of the village is the Crown Inn, boasting the menu and accomplished cooking of a restaurant combined with the liveliness of a local pub. The three small bedrooms are located up a steep spiral staircase off the lounge bar. They are simply decorated with half-timbered walls, sprigged-flower fabrics and stripped pine furniture. They have basic bathrooms and worn carpets, but are well heated and comfortable enough for a night or two's stay.

The heart of the inn is the bar and restaurant downstairs, where both do a brisk trade at weekends. Two polished-wood, high-backed Suffolk settles around the fire make a kind of seating well, or you can sit at tables in the brick-floored dining room. The wide choice of dishes often includes goose, quail, crayfish, sea bass and steak, with polenta, rocket and wild mushrooms also on the menu. Adnams beers and a 60-strong list of wines are reasons why you might choose to stay rather than drive home. But the Crown is also ideally located for the Aldeburgh Festival (which is not held in Aldeburgh, but just up the road at Snape Maltings). You can book for a pre- or a post-concert dinner and then stay the night.

~

NEARBY Aldeburgh; Orford; Dunwich; Minsmere RSPB Reserve.
LOCATION In village centre, on B1069; Snape is well signposted from A12
FOOD breakfast, lunch, dinner
PRICE £
ROOMS 3; 2 double, 1 twin, all with bath
FACILITIES dining room, bar; garden
CREDIT CARDS MC, V **CHILDREN** accepted over 14
DISABLED not suitable
PETS not accepted
CLOSED Christmas Day, Boxing Day **PROPRIETOR** Diane Maylott

EAST ANGLIA AND REGION

SOUTHWOLD, SUFFOLK

THE SWAN
~ TOWN HOTEL ~

High Street, Southwold, Suffolk IP18 6EG
TEL (01502) 722186 **FAX** (01502) 724800
E-MAIL hotels@adnams.co.uk **WEBSITE** www.adnams.co.uk

ONE OF THE MOST WELCOMING rooms in The Swan is the drawing room, with its carved wood chimneypieces and architraves, Murano glass chandeliers, chintzy sofas and armchairs and relaxed atmosphere. On Sunday mornings the place is full of newspapers and chat, with guests and non-residents ordering coffee and shortbread, and, on a fine day, the sun pours in through the windows from the market square. The Swan is ideal for a long stay – the bedrooms at the front are largest, though all, including the standard rooms, are inviting and well-decorated in smart, strong colours and with interesting prints on the walls. Many have a view of the sea, lighthouse or square. There are also modern garden rooms, grouped around a former bowling green, with large picture windows which mean that, though you can see out, everyone else can see in. As we went to press, bedrooms and bathrooms were being upgraded throughout in cool colours.

Staff are professional and helpful and ensure that the hotel operates on a human scale. It made us wish that there were more places like this. Adnams Brewery owns The Swan and its sister hotel, The Crown, down the road. If you eat at The Crown, a cross-billing system operates – just remember to tell reception before you go.

~

NEARBY 'Cathedral of the Marshes'; Dunwich Heath and Minsmere nature reserves.
LOCATION next to market square; with car parking
FOOD breakfast, lunch, dinner
PRICE ££-£££
ROOMS 43 double, 26 in main hotel and 17 garden rooms, 40 with bath and shower; all rooms have phone, TV, hairdrier
FACILITIES sitting rooms, dining room, bar; garden, croquet
CREDIT CARDS AE, DC, MC, V **CHILDREN** welcome **DISABLED** access possible, lift/elevator **PETS** accepted in garden rooms by arrangement
CLOSED never **MANAGER** Francis Guildea

EAST ANGLIA AND REGION

STOKE BY NAYLAND, SUFFOLK

ANGEL INN

~ VILLAGE INN ~

Stoke by Nayland, Suffolk, CO6 4SA
TEL (01206) 263245 **FAX** (01206) 263373
WEBSITE www.horizoninns.co.uk

A PROPER INN RATHER THAN A PUB, with spick-and-span bedrooms off a long gallery landing upstairs, the Angel Inn has been in business since the 16th century. There are plenty of nooks and crannies in the bar and a variety of seating in the series of interconnecting public rooms. You'll find sofas and chairs grouped together in a corner next to the fire and grandfather clock; and a dining room with its ceiling open to the rafters, rough brick-and-timber-studded walls and a fern-lined well-shaft 52 feet (16 m) deep. The bedrooms are a fair size, individually and unfussily decorated, and are ideal for a one- or two-night stop on a tour of Suffolk.

The public rooms downstairs have great character, with interesting pictures and low lighting, and are filled with the hum and buzz of contented lunch and dinner conversation. The food is excellent, with local produce used where possible, including fresh fish and shellfish from nearby ports, and game from local estates. Dishes might include griddled hake with red onion dressing, or stir-fried duckling with fine leaf salad, Cumberland sauce and new potatoes. Service is informal, friendly and helpful. Children are not allowed in the bar, and though flexible, there are rules about young children eating in the dining room – check when booking.

~

NEARBY Guildhall; Dedham Vale; Flatford Mill; East Bergholt.
LOCATION in village centre, on B1068 between Sudbury and Ipswich; small car park for 20 cars
FOOD breakfast, lunch, dinner
PRICE £
ROOMS 6 double, 1 twin, all with bath; all rooms have phone, TV, hairdrier
FACILITIES sitting room, dining rooms, bar; garden **CREDIT CARDS** MC, V
CHILDREN accepted in 1 room
DISABLED not suitable **PETS** not accepted
CLOSED Christmas Day, Boxing Day, New Year's Day **PROPRIETORS** Horizon Inns

EAST ANGLIA AND REGION

SWAFFHAM, NORFOLK

STRATTONS
~ COUNTRY HOTEL ~

Ash Close, Swaffham, Norfolk PE37 7NH
TEL (01760) 723845 **FAX** (01760) 720458
E-MAIL strattonshotel@btinternet.com **WEBSITE** www.strattonshotel.com

STRATTONS EPITOMIZES everything we are looking for in this guide. Perhaps it's because Les and Vanessa Scott are such natural hosts who love entertaining; perhaps it's because of their artistic flair (they met as art students) or perhaps it's because they had a very clear vision of what they wanted to create when they bought this elegant listed villa in 1990. A reader writes: '20 out of 20 for staff attitude, value for money, quality of accommodation… An absolute delight.'

Bedrooms, several of which are being upgraded, are positively luxurious. Plump cushions and pillows jostle for space on antique beds, books and magazines fill the shelves, and the same coordinated decoration continues into smart bathrooms – one resembling a bedouin's tent. The two beautifully furnished sitting rooms, *trompe l'oeil* hallway and murals painted recently by a local artist are equally impressive. Yet it is emphatically a family home and you share it with the Scott cats and children. The food is special, too. Vanessa, a cookery writer, continues to gain awards for her cooking. There are fresh eggs every day from their own chickens, and the daily changing menu is inventive and beautifully presented. It is cheerfully served by Les in the cosy basement restaurant. There is a no-smoking rule.

~

NEARBY Norwich; North Norfolk coast.
LOCATION down narrow lane between shops on main street; with ample car parking
FOOD breakfast, dinner
PRICE £££
ROOMS 7; 4 double, 3 suites, all with bath or shower; all rooms have phone, TV, hairdrier **FACILITIES** 2 sitting rooms, dining room, bar
CREDIT CARDS AE, MC, V **CHILDREN** welcome
DISABLED access difficult **PETS** welcome
CLOSED Christmas
PROPRIETORS Vanessa and Les Scott

EAST ANGLIA AND REGION

WOODBRIDGE, SUFFOLK

RAMSHOLT ARMS
~ COUNTRY PUB-WITH-ROOMS ~

Dock Road, Ramsholt, Woodbridge, Suffolk IP12 3AB
TEL (01394) 411229 **FAX** (01394) 41181
WEBSITE www.ramsholtarms.co.uk

THE RAMSHOLT ARMS is one of only a few buildings visible for miles around on the shores of the Deben estuary. It lies at the end of a long flat road that cuts through the Suffolk Breckland, a lonely expanse of heath. The pub is right on the water, and at low tide waders walk the silvery, mirror-like surface of the mud. The interior is decorated with artful simplicity, with brown sailcloth blinds lashed to a wooden mast curtain rail at the huge picture windows and seagrass on the floor. It's well kept and attractive, but the kind of place where nobody frowns at people wearing Wellington boots or sailing clothes, or bringing wet dogs into the bar.

Bedrooms have been refurbished in unfussy style in cool blue or white, with prints on the walls and country furniture. Although all have their own bathrooms, they are not en suite. Some will be made so this year, but meanwhile owner Patrick Levy promises plenty of hot water to compensate for having to cross the corridor. In the rooms with wide views of the river, guests wake up to the call of curlews or the slapping of halyards against masts.

The food is wonderful: glistening, fresh shell-on prawns; Orkney herrings; fishcakes; and main courses with chips – perfect for eating after sailing, birdwatching or riverside treks.

~

NEARBY Felixstowe; Orford; Aldeburgh.
LOCATION off B1083, follow signs for Bawdsey out of Woodbridge and take right turn to Ramsholt Dock; with ample car parking
FOOD breakfast, lunch, dinner
PRICE ££
ROOMS 4 double, all with bath; all rooms have TV; hairdrier on request.
FACILITIES dining room, bar; garden **CREDIT CARDS** MC, V
CHILDREN welcome
DISABLED not suitable **PETS** accepted
CLOSED never **PROPRIETOR** Patrick Levy

THE NORTH-WEST

BARNGATE, CUMBRIA

DRUNKEN DUCK INN
~ COUNTRY HOTEL ~

Barngate, Ambleside Cumbria, LA22 0NG
TEL (015394) 36347 **FAX** (015394) 36781
E-MAIL info@drunkenduckinn.co.uk **WEBSITE** www.drunkenduckinn.co.uk

SITUATED IN THE HEART OF LAKELAND amidst sprawling hills and dales lies the Drunken Duck, so named after a Victorian landlady who found her ducks lying on the nearby crossroads. Presuming them dead, she started to pluck them; but soon realized that they were actually blind drunk, and not dead in the slightest. This inn has real character and charm. The bar/pub is delightful and exactly as you would hope an old country inn should look and feel, with old pictures, prints and hunting memorabilia adorning the walls. The menu in the bar and the dining room is extensive, yet not over ambitious; don't miss their home-brewed ale produced at the back of the property; or choose from a fine selection of wines (around 20 of them come by the glass).

Ambling round the side of the inn you will come across the 'deluxe' and 'supreme' rooms that certainly live up to their titles. Each room is individually decorated with contemporary yet very comfortable furniture and fabrics and the added perk of private garden sitting areas and even a balcony in the ever popular-Garden Room. The standard bedrooms in the main house are equally tastefully done out, if a little cramped, but the friendliness of the staff and overall quality of the place itself makes up for this.

There are serious walks in the vicinity – not least on the 60 acres of land that the proprietors are hoping to develop into gardens for relaxing and short strolling areas. Book well in advance.

~

NEARBY Lake walks, Ambleside, Coniston.
LOCATION After Ambleside, just off the B5286 signposted to Hawkshead – on the right is a directional sign to the Duck, ample private car parking
FOOD breakfast, lunch, dinner **PRICE** ££–£££
ROOMS 16 double and twin, half with bath, half with shower; all rooms have TV, phone, modem point, hairdrier **FACILITIES** dining room, sitting room, bar; fly fishing
CREDIT CARDS AE, MC, V **CHILDREN** welcome **DISABLED** 2 rooms **PETS** not accepted
CLOSED Christmas Day **PROPRIETORS** Paul Spencer and Stephanie Barton

THE NORTH-WEST

BASSENTHWAITE LAKE, CUMBRIA

THE PHEASANT
~ COUNTRY INN ~

Bassenthwaite Lake, near Cockermouth, Cumbria CA13 9YE
TEL (017687) 76234 **FAX** (017687) 76002
E-MAIL info@the-pheasant.co.uk **WEBSITE** www.the-pheasant.co.uk

'STILL A VERY SPECIAL PLACE,' says our most recent inspector. Nestled away behind trees just off the A66, the Pheasant was originally an old coaching inn, and there are many reminders of this within, particularly in the little old oak bar, which is full of dark nooks and crannies – a real piece of history, little changed from its earliest days. The building is a long, low barn-like structure that has been exceptionally well maintained. There is a small but well-kept garden to the rear and grounds that extend to 60 acres.

The three sitting areas are one of the main attractions of the place. The two to the front are low-ceilinged, with small windows and plenty of prints on the walls. The third has an open log fire and a serving hatch to the bar.

The grand refurbishment scheme was undertaken in early 2000, and smaller, more recent ones have seen the conversion of 20 old bedrooms into 13 larger, lighter, more modern rooms. They are attractive and individually decorated, partnered by en suite bathrooms, and some have spectacular views of the fells. The dining room has been organized to make the best of its slightly uncomfortable shape. The menu changes daily and has won one Rosette and is close to achieving its second. The service is still outstandingly friendly.

NEARBY Bassenthwaite Lake; Keswick.
LOCATION 5 miles (8 km) E of Cockermouth, just off A66; with ample car parking
FOOD breakfast, lunch, dinner, bar snacks
PRICE ££
ROOMS 14; 10 double and twin, 3 suites and 1 single; all with bath and shower, hairdrier, phone; TV on request
FACILITIES sitting rooms, dining room, bar; garden **CREDIT CARDS** MC, V
CHILDREN accepted over 8, but not in the bar or dining room at night
DISABLED access possible to public rooms, Garden Lodge and 3 en suite rooms
PETS accepted in public rooms only
CLOSED Christmas Eve and Day **MANAGER** Matthew Wylie

THE NORTH-WEST

BORROWDALE, CUMBRIA

THE LEATHES HEAD
~ COUNTRY HOTEL ~

Borrowdale, Keswick, Cumbria CA12 5UY
TEL (017687) 77247 **FAX** (017687) 77363
E-MAIL enq@leatheshead.co.uk **WEBSITE** www.leatheshead.co.uk

ROY AND JANICE SMITH have recently taken over The Leathes Head in the beautiful Borrowdale valley. Originally built for a Liverpool ship owner, it is a Lakeland stone Edwardian house perched in its own wooded grounds near Derwent Water. Many of its period features, the plasterwork, the stained glass and a wood-panelled ceiling in the hall, are still there. It is informal enough to attract the walkers and climbers who return to the area year after year (even if it means carrying the newest additions to their families on their backs). Children of all sizes are welcome (the hotel has all the necessary cots and high chairs) and can have a high tea in the evenings to give their parents the chance of a quiet dinner by themselves.

All the rooms are comfortably furnished (the largest being at the front) and most can squeeze in an extra bed. The three-acre grounds include lawns big enough and level enough to play *boules* or croquet – and flat areas are few and far between in this region. The real challenges are, of course, the fells beyond the gate and the hotel can help here too, with its extensive collection of walking guides.

~

NEARBY Derwent Water; Buttermere; Castlerigg Stone Circle.
LOCATION 3.5 miles (5.5 km) S of Keswick, off B5289 to Borrowdale; in garden with ample car parking
FOOD breakfast, dinner; half-board obligatory at weekends
PRICE ££
ROOMS 11 double and twin, 6 with bath, 5 with shower; all rooms have phone, TV, hairdrier **FACILITIES** 3 sitting rooms, dining room, bar; garden, croquet, boules
CREDIT CARDS MC, V
CHILDREN accepted over 7
DISABLED 2 ground-floor rooms
PETS not accepted
CLOSED mid-Nov to mid-Feb; open Christmas and New Year
PROPRIETORS Roy and Janice Smith

THE NORTH-WEST

BOWNESS-ON-WINDERMERE, CUMBRIA

LINDETH FELL
~ COUNTRY HOUSE HOTEL ~

Bowness-on-Windermere, Cumbria LA23 3JP
TEL (015394) 43286 **FAX** (015394) 47455
E-MAIL kennedy@lindethfell.co.uk **WEBSITE** www.lindethfell.co.uk

To STAY AT LINDETH FELL is like visiting a well-heeled old friend who enjoys making his visitors as comfortable as possible, who enjoys his food (but likes to be able to identify what's put in front of him), is unreasonably fond of good puddings, has a rather fine wine cellar – and is justifiably proud of the view from his house. Pat and Diana Kennedy's establishment hits this mark (they are always there to see that it does), and, not unsurprisingly, their approach and warm courteous welcome have been duly rewarded with a faithful following.

Approached through trees, and set in large mature gardens glowing with azaleas and rhododendrons in spring, Lindeth Fell's wood-panelled hall leads to a pair of comfortable and attractive sitting rooms and a restaurant where large windows let in the tremendous view. Weather permitting, drinks and tea can be taken on the terrace, and the same warm weather might even allow for a game of tennis or croquet. Upstairs, the rooms vary in size and outlook. Both qualities are reflected in their price but, as a general rule, the further up the house you go, the smaller the room but the better the view. All the rooms are comfortably furnished and pleasingly decorated.

~

NEARBY Windermere Steamboat Museum; Lake Windermere.
LOCATION 1 mile (1.5km) S of Bowness on A5074; with ample car parking
FOOD breakfast, lunch, dinner
PRICE ££
ROOMS 14; 12 double and twin, 2 single, 12 with bath, 2 with shower; all rooms have phone, TV, hairdrier
FACILITIES sitting rooms, dining room, bar; garden, lake, croquet, bowling green
CREDIT CARDS MC, V **CHILDREN** accepted
DISABLED access possible to ground-floor bedroom
PETS not accepted **CLOSED** 3 weeks in Jan
PROPRIETORS Pat and Diana Kennedy

THE NORTH-WEST

BOWNESS-ON-WINDERMERE, CUMBRIA

LINTHWAITE HOUSE
～ COUNTRY HOUSE HOTEL ～

Crook Road, Bowness-on-Windermere, Cumbria LA23 3JA
TEL (015394) 88600 **FAX** (015394) 88601
E-MAIL admin@linthwaite.com **WEBSITE** www.linthwaite.com

YOU COULD SAY OF Mike Bevans that he liked the view so much that he bought the best place to see it from. It is our good luck that he and his wife have also created in this Edwardian country house a very professionally-run hotel with a unique style. The reception rooms are filled with palms, wicker furniture and old curios as well as antiques. Painted decoys, well-travelled cabin trunks and oriental vases help to evoke days of leisure and service in the far reaches of the Empire. Service here manages to be crisp and amiable at the same time: you are made to feel that you are on holiday and not on parade. Whether you eat in the richly coloured dining room or the new Mirror Room, the food has come from Ian Bravey's kitchen – well-thought-out menus, beautifully presented. Bad luck, though, if you're under seven: it's an early tea for you, without the option.

Of the bedrooms, the best look directly towards Windermere, some are in a modern annexe, and there is quite a variation in size. They all have style though, with thoughtful use of fabrics and furnishings and bathrooms that are attractive rather than utilitarian. Beyond the terraces outside are 14 acres of lawn, shrubs, woods and a small lake.

～

NEARBY Windermere Steamboat Museum; Lake Windermere.
LOCATION 1 mile (1.5km) S of Bowness off the A5074; with ample car parking
FOOD breakfast, lunch, dinner
PRICE ££-£££
ROOMS 26 double and twin with bath; all rooms have phone, TV, hairdrier; some have fax/modem points
FACILITIES sitting rooms, conservatory, dining rooms, bar; terrace, garden
CREDIT CARDS AE, MC, V
CHILDREN accepted
DISABLED one specially adapted room
PETS not accepted **CLOSED** never
PROPRIETOR Mike Bevans

THE NORTH-WEST

BRAMPTON, CUMBRIA

FARLAM HALL
~ COUNTRY HOUSE HOTEL ~

Brampton, Cumbria CA8 2NG
TEL (016977) 46234 **FAX** (016977) 46683
E-MAIL farlamhall@dial.pipex.com **WEBSITE** www.farlamhall.co.uk

'CHARMING FAMILY, quiet surroundings, excellent food,' are the phrases that encapsulate Farlam Hall. For over 20 years now the Quinion and Stevenson families have assiduously improved their solid but elegant Border country house. It has its roots in Elizabethan times, but what you see today is essentially a large Victorian family home, extended for a big family and frequent entertaining. No coincidence that it makes such a good hotel.

The dining room and public rooms are discreet and the atmosphere is one of traditional English service and comfort. The bedrooms vary widely, with some decidedly large and swish. Nevertheless, all are luxurious and charmingly done out, and some have beautiful views of the grounds that are home to a variety of llamas and sheep.

The chef, being one of the family, takes pride in his food and it shows. The menu changes daily (so guests staying for longer than one night don't get bored) and there is an impressive wine list that is overseen by Mr Quinion, not to mention the extensive English cheese board or a choice of deliciously unhealthy puddings.

Farlam Hall is well placed for the Lakes, Dales and Northumberland Coast as well as Hadrian's Wall.

~

NEARBY Naworth Castle; Hadrian's Wall; Lanercost Priory.
LOCATION 3 miles (5 km) SE of Brampton on A689, NE of (not in) Farlam village; with ample car parking
FOOD breakfast, dinner; light lunches on request
PRICE ££££
ROOMS 12 double with bath; all rooms have phone, TV, hairdrier
FACILITIES 2 sitting rooms, dining room; garden, croquet
CREDIT CARDS MC, V **CHILDREN** accepted over 5
DISABLED 2 ground-floor bedrooms **PETS** welcome in some rooms
CLOSED Christmas week
PROPRIETORS Quinion and Stevenson families

THE NORTH-WEST

CARLISLE, CUMBRIA

NUMBER THIRTY ONE

∼ TOWN GUEST-HOUSE ∼

31 Howard Place, Carlisle, Cumbria CA1 1HR
TEL (01228) 597080 **FAX** (01228) 597080
E-MAIL bestpep@aol.com **WEBSITE** www.numberthirtyone.freeservers.com

SINCE EXPERIENCED HOTELIERS Philip and Judith Parker opened their
Victorian town house in the mid '90s, they have scooped some
prestigious awards, including the English Tourism Council's Best B&B in
England in 1999. In fact it's not just a B&B, and Philip's superb dinners
(he produces a no-choice three-course menu every evening) might be one
of the reasons for the place's immediate popularity. The menu is based on
what is freshest and best that day, and emphasis is placed on as much as
possible being home-made. Philip bakes his own bread, makes jam and
marmalade, and even has a 'smokee' where he smokes the results of
successful fishing expeditions.

There are just three bedrooms, all decorated with flair and taste: Blue
is the largest, with a walk-in wardrobe; Yellow has a half-tester bed and a
Mediterranean bathroom; and the smallest, but most dramatic, Green, is
done out in Oriental style with a black-and-gold dragon breathing fire
behind the pillows. Downstairs, the sitting room is charmingly cluttered
with objects and mementoes, which lend it a suitably Victorian flavour,
and there's a pretty patio garden. With Number Thirty One, the Parkers
have achieved that rare thing – a winning combination of hospitality and
hands-on professionalism. They have a no-smoking policy.

∼

NEARBY Cathedral; Castle; Tullie House; Hadrian's Wall.
LOCATION in city centre; with free street car parking for guests
FOOD breakfast, dinner
PRICE ££
ROOMS 3 double and twin with bath; all rooms have TV, hairdrier
FACILITIES sitting room, dining room; patio garden
CREDIT CARDS AE, MC, V
CHILDREN accepted over 16
DISABLED not suitable **PETS** not accepted **CLOSED** Dec to Mar
PROPRIETORS Philip and Judith Parker

THE NORTH-WEST

CROSTHWAITE, CUMBRIA

CROSTHWAITE HOUSE
~ COUNTRY GUEST-HOUSE ~

Crosthwaite, near Kendal, Cumbria LA8 8BP
TEL (015395) 68264 **FAX** (015395) 68264
E-MAIL booking@crosthwaitehouse.co.uk **WEBSITE** www.crosthwaitehouse.co.uk

WHITE WITH DAMSON BLOSSOM in the spring, Lyth Valley is a gentle landscape with distant fells to remind you of where you are. Crosthwaite House is an attractive Georgian building with classic proportions and fine, tall rooms. Robin and Marnie Dawson are the relaxed owners who make their guests very welcome. There is an open fire in the comfortable sitting room, and a varied collection of books and games. You get the feeling that no-one would think you at all odd if, after a long walk and a hot shower, you just dozed off in front of the television until supper time.

Good hearty breakfasts are always there in the mornings in the wooden-floored dining room, but evening meals tend to be more movable feasts: if there aren't enough takers, you might be encouraged to take a short pre-dinner stroll to the Punch Bowl Inn and eat there. Luckily, it doesn't really matter where you eat – you'll get an excellent meal either way. There are six bright and simply furnished bedrooms, each with their own shower room (although these can be something of a snug fit). Side windows are being let into the rooms at the rear of the house so that they can share the view with those at the front.

~

NEARBY Lake Windermere; Hill Top; Sizergh Castle.
LOCATION in countryside just off A5074, 5 miles (8 km) W of Kendal; with ample car parking
FOOD breakfast, dinner
PRICE £
ROOMS 6; 5 double and twin, 1 single, all with shower; all rooms have TV
FACILITIES sitting room, dining room; garden
CREDIT CARDS not accepted
CHILDREN welcome
DISABLED access difficult
PETS accepted **CLOSED** late Nov to Feb
PROPRIETORS Robin and Marnie Dawson

THE NORTH-WEST

DIDSBURY VILLAGE, LANCASHIRE

ELEVEN DIDSBURY PARK
~ TOWN HOUSE HOTEL ~

11 Didsbury Park, Didsbury Village, Manchester, M20 5LH
TEL (0161) 4487711 **FAX** (0161) 4488282
E-MAIL enquiries@elevendidsbury park.com **WEBSITE** www.elevendidsburypark.com

SET IN THE LEAFY SUBURBS, 15 minutes from Manchester City centre, is Didsbury Park. This hotel seems to have the best of both worlds, being far enough outside the centre to be undisturbed by noise but within easy access of all its amenities, not to mention having great restaurants and a certain amount of shopping in Didsbury itself. A Victorian Town house from the outside but 'city chic' and luxurious on the inside, the hotel balances old and new, city and country.

Numerous reader's reports have focused primarily on the Irish charm of the proprietors, Eamonn and his wife Sally, who are exceedingly friendly and chatty without being interfering. All of the rooms in the hotel are simple and contemporary, with neutral restful shades in some and deep rich colours in others, but modernity has not come at the cost of comfort. Bathrooms have deep, free- standing baths and large, fluffy towels.

Dinner is not served at this hotel, so Eamonn and Sally put on a free car that chauffeurs guests to and from restaurants in nearby Didsbury. The breakfast room is interestingly decorated, with cutlery adorning the walls, and serves full English, Continental or Irish breakfasts. If you do get peckish in the evening, but don't fancy going out, you can order light meals / snacks from the 'deli menu'. Eat or drink outside on the Mediterranean style terrace amongst Sally's tomatoes, or wallow in the hot tub in the gazebo.

~

NEARBY Manchester city centre; Trafford Centre; The Lowry.
LOCATION from M56 at junction 1 take the A34 Kingsway to Manchester city centre, turn on to the A4145 Wilmslow Rd. The hotel is on the right in Didsbury Park
FOOD breakfast , Deli menu in evening
PRICE ££
ROOMS 14 doubles with bath; all rooms have phone, stereo, minibar, trouser press, TV, hairdrier **FACILITIES** sitting room, bar, breakfast room; garden, croquet, hot tub
CREDIT CARDS AE, DC, MC, V **CHILDREN** welcome **DISABLED** access difficult
PETS not accepted **CLOSED** never **PROPRIETORS** Eamonn and Sally O'Loughlin

THE NORTH-WEST

DINHAM, SHROPSHIRE

MR UNDERHILL'S AT DINHAM WEIR

~ RESTAURANT-WITH-ROOMS ~

Dinham, Ludlow, Shropshire, SY8 1EH
TEL(01584) 874431 **FAX** (01584) 874431
WEBSITE www.mr-underhills.co.uk

A S WE APPROACHED this Michelin-starred restaurant-with-rooms at the end of the walk to Ludlow on the Mortimer Trail, we could almost have been reminded of many a similar place on the Lot or Dordogne. The paved garden, with its Mediterranean plants, is a sun trap looking on to the weir that breaks the flow of the River Teme below Ludlow Castle's walls. Here you can have breakfast or tea, or a glass of wine before an impressive dinner. Ludlow is now well known as a centre of haute cuisine: this is not the only Michelin-starred restaurant in the vicinity. The restaurant is sunny too, with a picture window overlooking the river. The no-choice (until pudding) menu might include (to start) smoked haddock on spinach with a quail's egg in champagne *beurre blanc*; and local venison. The six bedrooms are contemporary and stylish, if mostly compact, all with river views and cleverly shaped bathrooms. A great place, run on a personal scale.

~

NEARBY Martinier Falls, Ludlow Castle, market in town, Shakespeare festival.
LOCATION at Market Square, turn left at Castle Walls, on a lane called Dinham Weir; limited off-road parking
FOOD breakfast, dinner
PRICE ££
ROOMS 7 doubles, 6 with bath, 1 with shower
FACILITIES dining room, small lounge; garden
CREDIT CARDS MC, V
CHILDREN welcome
DISABLED access difficult
PETS not accepted
CLOSED restaurant only, Tue
PROPRIETORS Chris and Judy Bradley

THE NORTH-WEST

GRASMERE, CUMBRIA

WHITE MOSS HOUSE
~ COUNTRY HOUSE HOTEL ~

Rydal Water, Grasmere, Cumbria LA22 9SE
TEL (015394) 35295 **FAX** (015394) 35516
E-MAIL dixon@whitemoss.com **WEBSITE** www.whitemoss.com

LIKE MANY MODERN PARENTS, Wordsworth probably had to resort to bribery to persuade his son to fly the nest. Whether that was the case or not, Wordsworth certainly bought him White Moss House and visited here often. Built of grey Lakeland stone, now creeper-clad, and set in a pretty, rose-rich garden above the road from Grasmere to Ambleside, Sue and Peter Dixon's small hotel has a disproportionately large (but richly deserved) reputation for the quality of its food and the scope of its cellar. There is a firm timetable for the superb five-course dinners (no choice until you reach dessert) that are served in the snug dining room and that always end with a selection of the best of British cheeses. Not surprisingly, the breakfasts are also masterpieces, so it's just as well that there are walks to suit all ages that start from the front door.

The whole house seems to have comfort as its watchword. None of the pretty bedrooms are vast, but all are filled with a host of little touches ranging from fresh flowers to bath salts. If taken together, the two largest bedrooms get exclusive use of a sitting room (bridge players take note), and there are two bedrooms removed from the main house in a cottage a little further up the hill, which have the best views.

~

NEARBY Rydal Mount; Dove Cottage.
LOCATION 1 mile (1.5 km) S of Grasmere on A591; with ample car parking
FOOD breakfast, dinner (half-board obligatory except Sun)
PRICE ££
ROOMS 5 doubles, all with bath; 2-bedroom cottage suite; all rooms have phone, TV, hairdrier **FACILITIES** sitting room, dining room, bar; garden, fishing, free use of local leisure club
CREDIT CARDS AE, MC, V **CHILDREN** older children welcome
DISABLED access difficult
PETS accepted in cottage suite only
CLOSED Dec to Jan **PROPRIETORS** Sue and Peter Dixon

THE NORTH-WEST

GREAT LANGDALE, CUMBRIA

OLD DUNGEON GHYLL
~ COUNTRY HOTEL ~

Great Langdale, Ambleside, Cumbria LA22 9JY
TEL (015394) 37272 **FAX** (015394) 37272
E-MAIL staff@oldhotel.fsnet.co.uk **WEBSITE** www.odg.co.uk

LANGDALE IS A MAGNIFICENT VALLEY in the centre of the Lake District, dominated by the Langdale Pikes. Walkers and climbers flock here to hike and scale some of the highest mountains in England (including the Scafell range). In 1885 the Old Dungeon Ghyll Hotel (then known as Middlefell) was run by John Bennett, a well-known guide for tourists. The historian G. M. Trevelyan bought it in the early 1900s and gave it to the National Trust. The horse-drawn 'charas' bringing visitors from Little Langdale over Blea Tarn Pass would stop at the top and blow their horn, a signal to get lunch or tea ready – the number of blasts matching the number of passengers. As an unofficial home for most of Britain's climbing clubs, the visitors' book was like a roll-call of the leading British climbers.

Neil and Jane Walmsley have been the proprietors since 1983 and have continued to improve and develop this popular family hotel retaining as many old features as possible. The climbers were a pretty uncritical bunch (any kind of a roof was a luxury), but there is now a comfortable residents' sitting room with an open fire, a warm busy bar (open to the public) and a snug dining room offering wholesome uncomplicated food. There are fewer bathrooms than bedrooms, although five of the rooms have their own showers.

~

NEARBY Lake Windermere; Grasmere; Kendal.
LOCATION 7 miles (11 km) NE of Ambleside off B5343; in countryside with ample car parking
FOOD breakfast, packed lunch, dinner, bar meals
PRICE ££
ROOMS 14; 11 double, 3 single, 5 with shower
FACILITIES sitting room, dining room, 2 bars; garden
CREDIT CARDS AE, MC, V
CHILDREN welcome **DISABLED** access difficult **PETS** welcome
CLOSED 24 to 26 Dec **PROPRIETORS** Neil and Jane Walmsley

THE NORTH-WEST

HAWKSHEAD, CUMBRIA

EES WYKE

~ COUNTRY HOUSE HOTEL ~

Near Sawrey, Ambleside, Cumbria LA22 0JZ
TEL (015394) 36393 **FAX** (015394) 36393
E-MAIL eeswyke@aol.com **WEBSITE** www.eeswyke.com

ESTHWAITE WATER, to the east of Windermere, has been kept safely in private hands, so has escaped the development that has ravaged some of the other Lakes. Ees Wyke, a gem of a white-painted Georgian mansion, is perched above park-like meadows that roll gently down to the reed banks on the shore, punctuated here and there by sheep and mature trees. As well as unmarred views, Richard and Margaret Lee have happily discovered the secret of making people feel instantly at home. No-one could be more relaxed than Ruff the dog, whose speciality is imitating the famous immovable object.

This is a well-kept house, with everything just so, even down to a plentiful supply of games and books for those inclement days. In the dining room are beautiful large windows to show off the view (these are new since Beatrix Potter stayed here for her holidays), Windsor chairs and crisp white tablecloths. The dinners (Richard's department) run to five generous and unhurried courses and the price/quality ratio of the wine list is definitely tipped in your favour. The bedrooms are attractive and generously proportioned, most with small but well-equipped bathrooms, and comfortable enough to allow you to build up the strength you need to tackle the truly heroic breakfast.

~

NEARBY Hill Top; Lake Windermere; Grasmere.
LOCATION in hamlet on B5285, 2 miles (3 km) SE of Hawkshead; with car parking
FOOD breakfast, dinner
PRICE ££
ROOMS 8 double and twin, 3 with bath, 5 with shower; all rooms have TV, hairdrier
FACILITIES 2 sitting rooms, dining room; garden
CREDIT CARDS AE, MC, V **CHILDREN** accepted over 8
DISABLED 1 ground-floor room
PETS accepted in bedrooms
CLOSED Jan to Feb **PROPRIETORS** Richard and Margaret Lee

THE NORTH-WEST

KIRKBY LONSDALE, CUMBRIA

HIPPING HALL
~ COUNTRY HOTEL ~

Cowan Bridge, Kirkby Lonsdale, Cumbria LA6 2JJ
TEL (015242) 71187 **FAX** (015242) 72452
E-MAIL hippinghal@aol.com **WEBSITE** www.dedicate.co.uk/hipping-hall

'MORE LIKE STAYING WITH FRIENDS than in a hotel', is the typical reaction to a weekend at Hipping Hall. When we last visited we were much impressed – it was fairly priced, too. But a change of ownership was announced as we went to press, so we wait to hear whether Ian and Jo Bryant's laid-back style has been adopted by the Skeltons.

The Bryants were very experienced, and knew exactly what they were doing. They adopted the house-party approach – you expected to make friends with strangers: helped yourself to drinks from the sideboard, and dinner was eaten at one table under the minstrel's gallery in the spectacular beamed Great Hall. Jo's daily five-course feast (no choice, but preferences taken account of) used home-grown and local produce. 'The food was excellent as was the way it was presented', is a recent commentator's verdict.

Parts of the Hall date back to the 15th century when a hamlet grew up around the 'hipping' or stepping stones across the beck. After a strenuous day on the fells, you can sink into sofas in front of a wood-burning stove at the other end of the Great Hall. Bedrooms (no smoking allowed) are spacious, comfortable and furnished with period pieces. More reports please.
~

NEARBY Yorkshire Dales; Lake District; Settle to Carlisle railway.
LOCATION on A65, 2.5 miles (4 km) SE of Kirkby Lonsdale; in 3-acre walled gardens with ample car parking
FOOD breakfast, dinner
PRICE ££
ROOMS 7; 5 double, 4 with bath; 1 with shower; 2 suites with bath; all rooms have phone, TV, hairdrier **FACILITIES** sitting room, dining room, breakfast room, conservatory with bar; garden, croquet, boules **CREDIT CARDS** AE, MC, V
CHILDREN welcome over 12 **DISABLED** not suitable
PETS accepted in bedrooms by arrangement
CLOSED never **PROPRIETORS** Mr and Mrs Skelton

THE NORTH-WEST

LOW LORTON, CUMBRIA

WINDER HALL
∼ COUNTRY GUEST-HOUSE ∼

Low Lorton, near Cockermouth, Cumbria CA13 9UP
TEL (01900) 77247 85107 **FAX** (01900) 77247 85107
E-MAIL winderhall@lowlorton.freeserve.co.uk **WEBSITE** www.winderhall.freeserve.co.uk

IF YOU TAKE THE BEAUTIFUL road from Keswick by the Whinlatter Pass, you will drop down towards Lorton into the prettiest countryside you could wish for. Winder Hall is a Grade II-listed Tudor manor, oozing character and charm. An inspector was recently greeted by the proprietors, Nick and Ann Lawler, plus young daughters spilling out of the door, and invited to enjoy some of the fantastic fell walks surrounding the property.

This is by no means a hotelly hotel: you get much more the feeling of being welcomed into the family home as a close friend. Dark oak panels cover the dining room walls, but light is abundant from the long low window overlooking the beautiful medieval herb garden and fells beyond. Nick is the chef and only uses local fresh produce in his Mediterranean/classic French dishes, and is looking to go completely organic in the next few years.

The drawing room and bedrooms are bright and airy, yet distinctly cosy. Of the six individually decorated bedrooms, only one has a vast fireplace and Priest's hole. But they all greet you with fresh flowers and home-made biscuits. Perfect for large parties wanting to take over the whole house or couples looking for a romantic weekend break to experience the beauty of the North.

∼

NEARBY Derwent Water; Keswick; Loweswater.
LOCATION 3 miles (5 km) S of Cockermouth, off B5289; with car parking
FOOD breakfast, dinner
PRICE ££
ROOMS 6; 5 double and 1 twin, 3 with bath; all rooms have TV, hairdrier
FACILITIES sitting room, dining room; garden
CREDIT CARDS MC, V **CHILDREN** welcome
DISABLED not suitable
PETS not accepted **CLOSED** Jan
PROPRIETORS Nick and Ann Lawler

THE NORTH-WEST

MUNGRISDALE, CUMBRIA

THE MILL
~ COUNTRY HOTEL ~

Mungrisdale, Penrith, Cumbria CA11 0XR
TEL (017687) 79659
E-MAIL themill@quinlan.evesham.net **WEBSITE** www.themillhotel.com

THIS FORMER 17THC mill cottage below Skiddaw still has the millrace running past it and is in very open, unspoilt countryside. Like Mungrisdale itself (which you can travel through in three minutes), it is by no means large, but manages to maintain a big reputation for its welcome, its food and its thoroughly professional management. High season must test its capacity a little, but it has a substantial fan club who come back year after year. The snug dining room, where crazy stacks of candle stubs and their accumulated drips, look like small-scale models of spectacular limestone caverns, and where strangers actually talk to one another, is the scene both for first-rate breakfasts and Eleanor Quinlan's excellent five-course dinners. How she manages to find time to bake the bread as well is a mystery to one and all.

Wall space everywhere is almost entirely given over to the results of 30 years' worth of oil and watercolour collecting by the Quinlans. Some bedrooms are quite small, but if you need more space there are two bedrooms in the picturesque old mill that share a sizeable sitting room. Popular with bridge players, says John Quinlan. All around are excellent walks for people of all ages and any abilities. Don't mistake this hotel for the neighbouring Mill Inn.

~

NEARBY Derwentwater; Ullswater; Hadrian's Wall.
LOCATION 9.5 miles (15 km) W of Penrith close to A66, in village; with parking for 15 cars
FOOD breakfast, dinner
PRICE ££
ROOMS 7 double and twin with bath; all rooms have TV
FACILITIES sitting room, TV room, games room, dining room; garden
CREDIT CARDS not accepted **CHILDREN** welcome
DISABLED access difficult **PETS** accepted in bedrooms by arrangement
CLOSED Nov to Mar **PROPRIETORS** Richard and Eleanor Quinlan

THE NORTH-WEST

NEWLANDS, CUMBRIA

SWINSIDE LODGE
~ COUNTRY HOTEL ~

Grange Road, Newlands, Keswick, Cumbria CA12 5UE
TEL (017687) 72948 **FAX** (017687) 72948
E-MAIL info@swinsidelodge-hotel.co.uk **WEBSITE** www.swinsidelodge-hotel.co.uk

THIS ATTRACTIVE VICTORIAN lakeland house occupies a picture-postcard setting by Derwent Water, far removed from the fleshpots of Keswick. There's no wine to be had and for dinner you eat what you're given (until pudding, anyway). So why do people queue up in droves to stay here? Visit it once and the answer becomes crystal clear: if you want wine, then take your own (as Kevin Kniveton does not even charge corkage, it will certainly be the best value you could find anywhere), and the excellent four-course dinners, with a choice of freshly-baked breads, are exactly what you'd cook for yourself if you had the imagination to think them up, knew how and had the time to do it.

As for the hotel itself, it is decorated with flair (*not* overdone) and you are trusted with good carpets and even better furniture. Everything that should be clean is clean, and everything else has been polished. The comfortable bedrooms are no different. The hotel's prime assets, though, are outside. Lying at the foot of Cat Bells as it does, there are walks of every description through genuinely unspoilt territory – and if you haven't the energy, you can always sit and look at it. All in all a relaxed, friendly, keenly priced (no-smoking) hotel.

~

NEARBY Derwent Water; Bassenthwaite Lake.
LOCATION 3 miles (5 km) SW of Keswick, 2 miles (3 km) S of A66; with garden and parking for 10 cars
FOOD breakfast, dinner
PRICE £
ROOMS 5 double, 3 with bath, 2 with shower; all have TV, hairdrier
FACILITIES 2 sitting rooms, dining room; garden
CREDIT CARDS MC, V
CHILDREN accepted over 10
DISABLED not suitable **PETS** not accepted
CLOSED never **PROPRIETORS** Susan and Kevin Kniveton

THE NORTH-WEST

SEATOLLER, CUMBRIA

SEATOLLER HOUSE
~ COUNTRY GUEST-HOUSE ~

Seatoller, Borrowdale, Keswick, Cumbria CA12 5XN
TEL (017687) 77218 **FAX** (017687) 77189
E-MAIL seatollerhouse@bt.connect.com **WEBSITE** www.seatollerhouse.com

IT SHOULD BE SAID at the outset that a stay at Seatoller House is something quite different from the run-of-the-mill hotel experience. You eat communally at set times, and to get the best out of the place you should take part in the social life of the house. If you do, the 'country house party' effect, much vaunted elsewhere, really does come about.

Seatoller House is over 300 years old and has been run as a guest-house for more than 100 years; the first entry in the visitors' book reads 23 April 1886. The long, low house, built in traditional Lakeland style and looking like a row of cottages, is in the tiny village of Seatoller, at the head of Borrowdale and the foot of Honister Pass. Bedrooms are simple and comfortable, and now all have their own bathrooms (although some are physically separate from the bedrooms). The dining room is in a country-kitchen style, with a delightfully informal atmosphere – one that spills over into the two sections of the low-ceilinged sitting room. Food is excellent; and if you are thirsty, just wander to the fridge, take what you like and sign for it in the book provided.

Several times a year the house is taken over by members of the Lakes Hunt, who enjoy running up and down the surrounding fells in pursuit, not of foxes (the traditional quarry) but of one another.

~

NEARBY Derwentwater; Buttermere; Keswick.
LOCATION 8 miles (13 km) S of Keswick on B5289; ample car parking
FOOD breakfast, packed lunch, dinner (not Tue)
PRICE £
ROOMS 10 double and twin, all with bath
FACILITIES sitting room, library, dining room, tea room, drying room; garden
CREDIT CARDS MC, V **CHILDREN** welcome
DISABLED 2 ground-floor bedrooms
PETS welcome in bedrooms
CLOSED Dec to Feb **PROPRIETORS** Morven and Jay Anson

THE NORTH-WEST

WASDALE HEAD, CUMBRIA

WASDALE HEAD
~ COUNTRY INN ~

Wasdale Head, Gosforth, Cumbria CA20 1EX
TEL (019467) 26229 **FAX** (019467) 26334
E-MAIL wasdaleheadinn@msn.com **WEBSITE** www.wasdale.com

THE WASDALE HEAD is in a site unrivalled even in the consistently spectacular Lake District. It stands on the flat valley bottom between three major peaks – Pillar, Great Gable and Scafell Pike (England's highest) – and only a little way above Wastwater, England's deepest and perhaps most dramatic lake.

Over the last decade and a half, the old inn has been carefully and thoughtfully modernized, adding facilities but retaining the characteristics of a traditional mountain inn. The main sitting room of the hotel is comfortable and welcoming, with plenty of personal touches. The pine-panelled bedrooms are not notably spacious but they are adequate, with fixtures and fittings all in good condition. There are also six self-catering apartments in a converted barn, and three hotel apartments. The dining room is heavily panelled, and decorated with willow pattern china and a pewter jug collection. Children under eight are not allowed in here after 8pm. Food is solid English fare, served by young, friendly staff. There are two bars. The one for residents has some magnificent wooden furniture, while tasty bar meals are served in the congenial surroundings of the public bar, much frequented by walkers and climbers.

~

NEARBY Hardknott Castle Roman Fort; Ravenglass and Eskdale Railway; Wastwater; Scafell.
LOCATION 9 miles (14.5 km) NE of Gosforth at head of Wasdale; with ample car parking
FOOD breakfast, bar and packed lunches, dinner
PRICE ££
ROOMS 13; 7 double and twin, 3 single, 3 suites, 11 with bath, 2 with shower; all rooms have phone; also 6 self-catering apartments and 3 hotel apartments
FACILITIES sitting room, dining room, 2 bars; garden **CREDIT CARDS** AE, MC, V
CHILDREN welcome **DISABLED** access possible to ground floor only
PETS not accepted in public areas **CLOSED** never **LANDLORD** Howard Christie

THE NORTH-WEST

WATERMILLOCK, CUMBRIA

OLD CHURCH
~ COUNTRY HOTEL ~

Watermillock, Penrith, Cumbria CA11 0JN
TEL (017684) 86204 **FAX** (017684) 86368
E-MAIL info@oldchurch.co.uk **WEBSITE** www.oldchurch.co.uk

THERE ARE MANY HOTELS with spectacular settings in the Lakes, but for our money there are few to match that of this whitewashed 18thC house on the very shore of Ullswater.

Since their arrival in the late 1970s, Kevin and Maureen Whitemore have developed the hotel carefully and stylishly. The three sitting rooms, one of which is formed by the entrance hall, are all very well furnished with clever touches in their decorations that give some hint of Maureen's interior design training. They also have the natural advantage of excellent views across the lake. The bedrooms are all different in decoration, but they too show a confident and a harmonious use of colour. Most have lake views and are pleasantly free of modern gadgetry.

Ex-accountant Kevin does more than keep the books in order: his daily changing dinners are both enterprising and expertly prepared, with a reasonable choice at each course.

'Everything one expects of a charming small hotel,' says one completely satisfied visitor, 'with not a single jarring note.'

~

NEARBY Dalemain; Penrith Castle; Brougham Castle; Ullswater.
LOCATION 5.5 miles (9 km) S of Penrith on A592; on lakeshore with ample car parking
FOOD breakfast, dinner
PRICE £££
ROOMS 10 double with bath; all rooms have phone, TV, hairdrier
FACILITIES 2 sitting rooms, dining room, bar; garden, boat, fishing
CREDIT CARDS AE, MC, V
CHILDREN by arrangement
DISABLED access difficult
PETS not accepted
CLOSED Nov to Mar; restaurant only, Sun eve
PROPRIETOR Kevin Whitemore

THE NORTH-WEST

WHITEWELL, LANCASHIRE

THE INN AT WHITEWELL
~ COUNTRY INN ~

Forest of Bowland, near Clitheroe, Lancashire BB7 3AT
TEL (01200) 448222 **FAX** (01200) 448298

PAST AND PRESENT COME TOGETHER with great effect at this welcoming inn with a glorious situation, on a riverbank plumb in the middle of the Forest of Bowland. In the 14th century it was a small manor house where the Keeper of the Forest lived. Today, some of the original architecture survives and rooms are furnished with antiques, but modern comfort is the order of the day, with, for example, videos and hi-tech stereo systems in all the bedrooms. Most of these are spacious and attractive, with warm lighting and prints clustered on the walls; many contain an extra sofa bed; a couple have four-posters. To keep romance alive, you can book one of the rooms with a fireplace and snuggle up to a cosy peat fire while your favourite CD plays on the Bang and Olufsen, or wallow in the deep vintage baths.

Food is an important consideration here. English dishes feature predominately on the menu – seasonal roast game or grilled fish, followed by wicked home-made puddings and a selection of farmhouse cheeses. Alternatively, bar meals are on offer at lunchtime and in the evening. Just past the bar is a small shop that sells a great selection of wines, books, cheeses and other bits and bobs. Be sure to check the terms and conditions of the inn before making a booking.

~

NEARBY Browsholme Hall; Clitheroe Castle; Blackpool. **LOCATION** 6 miles (9.5 km) NW of Clitheroe; with ample car parking **FOOD** breakfast, picnic lunch on request, dinner, bar meals
PRICE ££
ROOMS 15; 14 double and twin, 1 suite, all with bath; all rooms have phone, TV, CD; some have minibar, hairdrier, peat fire
FACILITIES dining rooms, bar; garden, fishing
CREDIT CARDS DC, MC, V
CHILDREN welcome **DISABLED** 2 ground-floor rooms
PETS welcome **CLOSED** never **PROPRIETOR** Richard Bowman

THE NORTH-WEST

WINDERMERE, CUMBRIA

GILPIN LODGE
~ COUNTRY HOUSE HOTEL ~

Crook Road, near Windermere, Cumbria LA23 3NE
TEL (015394) 88818 **FAX** (015394) 88058
WEBSITE www.gilpinlodge.com

JUST OCCASIONALLY, whether by luck or judgement, you can arrive somewhere that tells you to congratulate yourself on your choice of hotel before you even step through the door: Gilpin Lodge is one of these happy places. John Cunliffe's grandmother lived in this Edwardian house for 40 years, and when he and his wife Christine came 25 years later, it had become a rather ordinary B&B. Now, with manicured grounds and gleaming paint, quite substantially and wholly sympathetically enlarged and set on a peaceful hillside with moor beyond the boundary, you are to some extent prepared for the warm welcome and deep-pile comfort waiting for you inside. This is a highly professional and well-staffed operation, yet still driven by the enthusiasm of owners whose unmistakeable priority is the happiness of their guests.

If your tastes run to good pictures, fine furniture and immaculate service you will be happy; if they include excellent and imaginatively presented food with more than the occasional touch of outright luxury (when did you last have a strawberry sorbet with pink champagne for breakfast?) you will be happier still; and if you want a large, thoughtfully decorated room, probably with its own sitting area, and a bathroom to talk about when you get home, then you're in luck. If you have the energy, there is free access to the nearby country club.

~

NEARBY Windermere Steamboat Museum; Holker Hall; Sizergh Castle; Kendal; Grasmere.
LOCATION on B5284 Kendal to Bowness road, 2 miles (1 km) SE of Windermere; with ample car parking
FOOD breakfast, lunch, dinner
PRICE £££
ROOMS 14 double and twin with bath; all rooms have phone, TV, minibar, hairdrier
FACILITIES 2 sitting rooms, 4 dining rooms; garden **CREDIT CARDS** AE, DC, MC, V
CHILDREN accepted over 7 **DISABLED** access possible to ground-floor rooms
PETS not accepted **CLOSED** never **PROPRIETORS** John and Christine Cunliffe

The North-West

WINDERMERE, CUMBRIA

HOLBECK GHYLL
~ COUNTRY HOUSE HOTEL ~

Holbeck Lane, Windermere, Cumbria LA23 1LU
TEL (015394) 32375 **FAX** (015394) 34743
E-MAIL stay@holbeckghyll.com **WEBSITE** www.holbeckghyll.com

AN AWARD-WINNING HOTEL in a classic Victorian lakeland house, ivy-clad with steep slate roofs and mullioned windows – plus oak panelling and art noveau stained glass. Our latest reporter had a 'friendly welcome' and was impressed by its superb set-back position providing both privacy from the bustle of Windermere and grand lake views from the immaculate gardens; also indeed by the two comfortable sitting rooms, both homelike and beautifully furnished with plenty of contrasting harmonious fabrics.

The Nicholsons, professional hoteliers both, took over in 1988 and have refurbished to very high standards in a traditional, slightly formal style – though proprietors and staff alike are friendly and relaxed. Bedrooms and bathrooms are beautifully and individually decorated, very spacious, some with their own sitting room. At the top of the house is a 'very special' four-poster room. In the Lodge nearby are six further rooms (four are self-catering), with breathtaking views. The food is a clear attraction: pre-dinner canapés are served while you select from the inventive daily-changing menu designed by chef Stephen Smith, recent winner of a Michelin star. No smoking in the dining rooms. The grounds are being developed, and there is now a jogging trail from which you can spot deer and red squirrels, as well as a tennis court, croquet and putting.

~

NEARBY Lake Windermere.
LOCATION 3 miles (5 km) N of Windermere, E of A591; with ample car parking
FOOD breakfast, light lunch, dinner
PRICE ££££
ROOMS 21 double, all with bath; 4 suites; all have phone, TV, hairdrier
FACILITIES 2 sitting rooms, 2 dining rooms; garden, health spa, tennis, croquet, putting
CREDIT CARDS AE, DC, MC, V **CHILDREN** welcome
DISABLED 3 lodge rooms
PETS accepted in bedrooms only
CLOSED 3 weeks Jan **PROPRIETORS** David and Patricia Nicholson

THE NORTH-WEST

WINDERMERE, CUMBRIA

THE SAMLING

~ COUNTRY HOTEL ~

Ambleside road, Windermere, Cumbria, LA23 1LR
TEL (015394) 31922 **FAX** (015394) 30400
E-MAIL info@thesamling.com **WEBSITE** www.thesamling.com

Fʀᴏᴍ ᴏᴜᴛsɪᴅᴇ The Samling looks like an unpretentious country house in a wonderful position above Lake Windermere, with breathtaking Wordsworthian views of the Lake and the surrounding countryside. Built in 1780 by a Mr Edward Thorneycroft, it stands in a 67 acre estate, with a beautiful garden and was, in fact, a haunt of the Lakeland poet himself.

Inside, it's much smarter than you might expect, though still with a private home feel. As all of the bedrooms are suites, they are pricey; but for your money you get delightful, unusual and luxurious accommodation. Some beds are on the balcony; others that have been converted from bothys and stables. There are Turkish rugs, fat armchairs and fabulous views.

The food is good, but maybe a little fussy: portions are generous and fresh produce is used whenever possible in dishes such as red mullet escabeche, breast of duck, finishing with the hot chocolate fondant with pistachio ice cream. To enjoy the sunset, sit outside in the deep hot tub on the terrace. Perfect for large parties.

~

NEARBY Lake Windermere, Ambleside, Kendal.
LOCATION leave M6 at junction 36, take A591, 2 miles (3 km) after Windermere there is a sharp bend and Low Wood Hotel, hotel is on the right; with ample car parking
FOOD breakfast, dinner, Sun lunch
PRICE ££££
ROOMS 10 suites
FACILITIES drawing room, 2 dining rooms, small library; garden, helipad
CREDIT CARDS AE, MC, V
CHILDREN welcome
DISABLED not suitable
PETS by arrangement
CLOSED never
GENERAL MANAGER Nigel Parkin

THE NORTH-WEST

WINDERMERE, CUMBRIA

STORRS HALL
~ COUNTRY HOUSE HOTEL ~

Windermere, Cumbria LA23 3LG
TEL (015394) 47111 **FAX** (015394) 47555
E-MAIL reception@storrshall.co.uk **WEBSITE** www.storrshall.co.uk

A CHANGE OF OWNERSHIP at Storrs Hall has given a new and opulent lease of life to a hotel that had become sadly dilapidated. In 1997 Blackpool antiques dealer Richard Livstock, and Northern businessman Les Hindle, bought this Georgian pile, built to look like an Italian lakeside villa and spectacularly positioned on a promontory jutting out into Lake Windermere. They have given the place a no-expense-spared facelift, filling the beautifully proportioned rooms with superb pieces of antique furniture, statues, paintings, rare books, and Richard Livstock's own collection of model ships. The ships are particularly apposite since it was a maritime fortune that financed the building of the house. As well as the handsome drawing room with its 1910 Steinway grand, guests can retreat to the library or writing room or, if feeling more sociable, to the cheerful bar decorated with hunting and fishing trophies. On chilly days, log fires blaze in the reception rooms.

A recent report praises 'the large bedrooms', most of which have uninterrupted views of the glittering lake, and contains plaudits for the food: 'The cooking is sophisticated and assured, the service delightful – go before word gets round.'

~

NEARBY Windermere Steamboat Museum; Lake Windermere.
LOCATION 2 miles (3 km) S of Bowness off A592; with ample car parking
FOOD breakfast, lunch, dinner
PRICE ££££
ROOMS 24 doubles, all with bath; all rooms have phone, TV, hairdrier
FACILITIES sitting rooms, dining rooms, bar; garden, fishing
CREDIT CARDS AE, MC, V
CHILDREN accepted over 12
DISABLED no special facilities
PETS accepted in bedrooms by arrangement
CLOSED late Dec to early Feb **MANAGER** Nigel Lawrence

THE NORTH-WEST

WITHERSLACK, CUMBRIA

OLD VICARAGE
~ COUNTRY HOTEL ~

Church Road, Witherslack, near Grange-over-Sands, Cumbria LA11 6RS
TEL (015395) 52381 **FAX** (015395) 52373
E-MAIL hotel@old-vic.demon.co.uk **WEBSITE** www.oldvicarage.com

Revisiting a couple of years ago, our happy impressions of the Old Vicarage were reconfirmed. The key to the charm is its peace and seclusion, with large, mainly wooded grounds, at the edge of a tiny, half-asleep Lakes village – yet some of the area's major tourist sights and thoroughfares are only minutes away by car. There are views out to some low fells.

The building is no more, nor less, than a Georgian vicarage: some of the reception rooms are smallish, but it's all pleasantly but unexceptionally furnished, with some interesting touches here and there, to create a relaxing atmosphere. The bedrooms are not swanky, but comfortable, and usually prettily done; the priciest, especially in the annexe, are spacious and well-equipped with CD players and verandas. And here's more charm: the prices are certainly fair, if not good value.

The owners are relaxed and welcoming. The food is impressive, with the recent introduction of an *à la carte* menu, prepared on the premises using fresh ingredients: which is more than can be said of some reputable Lakes hotels, where dinner is delivered to the back door by caterer's van. The wine list is unusually well chosen and explained.

~

NEARBY Levens Hall and Topiary Garden; Sizergh Castle; Holker Hall.
LOCATION 5 miles (8 km) NE of Grange off A590; with ample car parking
FOOD breakfast, dinner, Sun lunch
PRICE £££
ROOMS 14 double and twin, 10 with bath, 4 with shower; all rooms have phone, TV, hairdrier
FACILITIES 2 sitting rooms, breakfast room, dining room; garden, tennis court
CREDIT CARDS AE, MC, V
CHILDREN welcome
DISABLED not suitable
PETS accepted by arrangement **CLOSED** never
PROPRIETORS Jill and Roger Burrington-Brown, Irene and Stanley Reeve

THE NORTH-EAST

ARNCLIFFE, NORTH YORKSHIRE

AMERDALE HOUSE

~ COUNTRY HOTEL ~

Arncliffe, Littondale, Skipton, North Yorkshire BD23 5QE
TEL (01756) 770250 **FAX** (01756) 770250
E-MAIL amerdalehouse@btopenworld.com **WEBSITE** www.amerdalehouse.co.uk

SINCE THEY TOOK IT OVER in 1987, the Crappers (ex-restaurateurs) have gradually transformed this hotel and the bedrooms have all been refurbished over the last few years. The setting is one of the most seductive in all the Dales: on the fringe of a pretty village in a lonely valley, wide meadows in front, high hills behind.

We visited a few years ago and were smitten with the location ('total peace and serenity'); the comfortable and beautifully decorated bedrooms and bathrooms – the top-floor four-poster bedroom is particularly charming and romantic with stunning views; and the exceptional welcome given by Nigel Crapper, who is also the chef. A more recent inspector endorsed this praise. Its food, in the modern English style, is, to quote a visitor, 'unbelievably good'. Dishes singled out by our inspector include local lamb with minted couscous and a port and redcurrant *jus*; pan-roast fillet of sea bass with baked cherry tomatoes and a warm pesto dressing; avocado pear salad with a lightly curried mayonnaise; and a terrine of oranges in Campari and orange jelly. Nigel's imaginative menus change frequently and the food often gets ecstatic press reviews. Amerdale House is usefully situated for a number of Dales sights – and is well priced, too.

NEARBY Wharfedale; Grassington; Pennine Way.
LOCATION in a rural setting, 7 miles (10 km) NW of Grassington, 3 miles (5 km) off B6160; with ample car parking
FOOD breakfast, dinner
PRICE ££
ROOMS 11; 8 double with bath, 3 twin with shower; all rooms have phone, TV, fax/modem point, hairdrier
FACILITIES sitting rooms, bar, dining room; garden **CREDIT CARDS** MC, V
CHILDREN welcome **DISABLED** 1 ground-floor room
PETS not accepted **CLOSED** Nov to mid-Mar
PROPRIETORS Nigel and Paula Crapper

THE NORTH-EAST

BOLTON ABBEY, NORTH YORKSHIRE

DEVONSHIRE ARMS
∼ COUNTRY HOUSE HOTEL ∼

Bolton Abbey, Skipton, North Yorkshire BD23 6AJ
TEL (01756) 710441 **FAX** (01756) 710564
E-MAIL reservations@devonshirearms.co.uk **WEBSITE** www.devonshirehotel.co.uk

As YOUR HELICOPTER WHIRLS towards its helipad, you can see that the moorland of the Dales proper comes to within a mile or so of the 17thC Devonshire Arms. Follow the path down the bank of the Wharfe, which gives the valley its name, for the half mile from Bolton Abbey village to the stone bridge and you're there. Owned by the Duke and Duchess of Devonshire, the hotel is doubly graced since it contains antiques and paintings from Chatsworth, the family seat; the Duchess has masterminded their placement and the design of the interior. This is a hotel in two parts, old and new. The elegant old wears its years well and has happily grown out of exact right angles. The new extension, which has brought with it an indoor swimming pool, gym and beauty salon, still has its sharp corners, but is settling in well.

The dining alternatives cover a similar spectrum. On the one hand is the quiet comfort of the classical Burlington Restaurant, which has been awarded a Michelin star, and on the other a buzzy blue and yellow brasserie with dishes to suit most moods and a snappy wine list to go with them. The bedrooms also come in old and new varieties: the older win on character and the newer score better with their views.

∼

NEARBY Castle Howard; Skipton Castle; Brontë Parsonage; Harewood House.
LOCATION on B6160 just N of junction with A59; in grounds with ample car parking
FOOD breakfast, lunch, dinner
PRICE £££–££££
ROOMS 41; 38 double and twin, 1 family, 2 suites, all with bath; all rooms have phone, TV, hairdrier; some have fax, video
FACILITIES 3 sitting rooms, conservatory, 2 dining rooms, 2 bars, gym, sauna, indoor swimming pool; garden, tennis, croquet, putting, helipad, fishing
CREDIT CARDS AE, DC, MC, V **CHILDREN** accepted
DISABLED 1 specially adapted room
PETS accepted **CLOSED** never **MANAGER** Jeremy Rata

THE NORTH-EAST

CROOKHAM, NORTHUMBERLAND

THE COACH HOUSE
~ COUNTRY GUEST-HOUSE ~

Crookham, Cornhill-on-Tweed, Northumberland TD12 4TD
TEL (01890) 820293 **FAX** (01890) 820284
E-MAIL stay@coachhousecrookham.com **WEBSITE** www.coachhousecrookham.com

LYNNE ANDERSON IS a charming hostess, whose energy and enthusiasm have not dimmed in more than 20 years of looking after guests in this group of converted 17thC farm buildings. Some bedrooms are grouped around a sunny courtyard, while others are in a separate stone house. They are generally large, furnished simply but attractively, with crisp white linen on the beds and cheered by vases of fresh flowers, an attention to detail that is typical of Lynne, whose devoted guests often return year after year.

There's an honesty bar in the pleasant beamed sitting room, where guests are served afternoon tea, with delicious home-baked cakes, and congregate for pre-dinner drinks. Great Gothic windows look out to a damson orchard, where sheep can often be spotted grazing under the trees – a perfect rural scene. The four-course dinners are wholesome affairs employing much local produce – border beef and lamb, Tweed salmon and vegetables from the garden. You may feel you should restrain yourself at breakfast: there's a choice of fresh fruit, home-made cereals and porridge, bacon and eggs, devilled kidneys and kedgeree.

~

NEARBY Northumberland National Park; Holy Island.
LOCATION 4 miles (6 km) E of Cornhill-on-Tweed on A697; with ample car parking
FOOD breakfast, dinner, afternoon tea
PRICE ££
ROOMS 9; 7 double and twin, 2 single, 7 with bath; all rooms have phone, TV, fridge
FACILITIES 2 sitting rooms, dining room; terrace, garden
CREDIT CARDS MC, V
CHILDREN welcome
DISABLED 3 specially adapted rooms
PETS accepted
CLOSED Nov to Easter
PROPRIETOR Lynne Anderson

THE NORTH-EAST

GOLCAR, HUDDERSFIELD

WEAVERS SHED
∽ RESTAURANT-WITH-ROOMS ∽

Knowl Road, Golcar, Huddersfield HD7 4AN
TEL (01484) 654284 **FAX** (01484) 650980
E-MAIL info@weavers-shed.demon.co.uk **WEBSITE** www.weavers-shed.demon.co.uk

A T FIRST ACQUAINTANCE GOLCAR would probably be dropped from just about anybody's list of places of outstanding natural beauty. But it has a fine secret – and the secret is the Weavers Shed. High on a hill, away from Huddersfield, in what started life in the 18th century as a cloth finishing mill and still has a fine flagged floor, is an excellent restaurant – and, what's more, you can sleep very comfortably indeed where you have just eaten.

Owner (and chef) Stephen Jackson and his collaborators in the kitchen are also keen market gardeners and have a plot which supplies many of their needs for fresh herbs, fruit and vegetables. Other elements of the menu are equally carefully chosen, with pork, for example, from traditional breeds and fish only featuring if the market is offering something worthwhile on the day. The style is modern British which, because of its simplicity, offers no hiding place for second-rate ingredients. Not surprisingly, the same sort of care has been taken with the wine list. The bedrooms are in the house next door. Built originally for the owner of the mill, it is a substantial building with light airy rooms, filled with a pleasing mixture of ancient and modern furniture and good-quality but unfussy fabrics. You won't forget breakfast.

∽

NEARBY Peak National Park; Pennine Way.
LOCATION 3 miles (5 km) W of Huddersfield on A62 and B6111; ample car parking
FOOD breakfast, lunch, dinner
PRICE ££
ROOMS 5 double and twin with bath and shower; all rooms have phone, TV, fax/modem point, hairdrier
FACILITIES 2 restaurants, bar; garden
CREDIT CARDS AE, DC, MC, V **CHILDREN** accepted
DISABLED access possible **PETS** not accepted
CLOSED Christmas Day, Boxing Day, New Year's Eve, New Year's Day; restaurant only, Sun, Mon, Sat lunch
PROPRIETORS Stephen and Tracy Jackson

THE NORTH-EAST

GRASSINGTON, NORTH YORKSHIRE

ASHFIELD HOUSE
~ COUNTRY GUEST-HOUSE ~

Summers Fold, Grassington, near Skipton, North Yorkshire BD23 5AE
TEL (01756) 752584 **FAX** (01756) 752584
E-MAIL info@ashfieldhouse.co.uk **WEBSITE** www.ashfieldhouse.co.uk

GRASSINGTON, AND WHARFEDALE in general, is a little-known Northern gem, especially for the keen walkers. Tucked away off the main street is Linda and Keith Harrison's small private stone and slate hotel, a peaceful sanctuary at the end of its own yard. What's more, and unlike anywhere else in Grassington, you can park your car there. Oak and pine furniture, bare beams and stone walls are combined with fresh flowers and neat new furnishings. An excellent dinner is served in the pretty dining room at seven each evening except Saturday, with a choice of starter and pudding. The menu does change daily but it is not extensive as all the cooking is done by the proprietors, however, they pride themselves on being able to cater for almost any tastes. Breakfast consists of a hearty full English or Continental. The bedrooms are modestly sized with fresh, clean decoration and their own shower rooms (one has its own bathroom just outside the door).

Beyond the house, insulated from the bustle of the town, is a quiet walled garden with a table and chairs where you can simply sit and enjoy the sunshine if the prospect of a walk along the river seems too testing. This is a non-smoking hotel.

~

NEARBY Skipton Castle, Gordale Scar, Janet's Foss, Ripon, Malham Cove, Bolton Abbey
LOCATION in Grassington, just NW of main square; with ample car parking
FOOD breakfast, dinner
PRICES ££
ROOMS 7 double and twin with bath or shower; all rooms have TV, hairdrier
FACILITIES 2 sitting rooms, 1 with bar, dining room; garden
CREDIT CARDS MC, V
CHILDREN welcome over 5
DISABLED not suitable **PETS** not accepted
CLOSED over Christmas, but open for New Year
PROPRIETORS Keith and Linda Harrison

THE NORTH-EAST

HAROME, NORTH YORKSHIRE

THE STAR INN
~ COUNTRY HOTEL ~

Harome, Nr Helmsley, North Yorkshire, YO62 5JE
TEL (01439) 770397
WEBSITE www.yorkshireholidays.com/thestarinn.htm

'ONE OF THE MOST comfortable, relaxing nights I have spent in a hotel' says a recent inspector. Wellies and umbrellas wait by the front door of Cross House (the Inns guest house) just in case you feel like having a stroll around the beautiful countryside. The large opulent sitting room is kept warm by the grand fire in the centre and once sat on the sofas with tea and seriously good cakes you can hardly make it to your bedroom. When you do, you'll discover that they are immaculate, balancing the contemporary and the rustic perfectly with fantastic en suite bathrooms (some with whirlpool baths) and music, DVD players and chocolates and crisps to tide you over until supper.

Supper and lunch can also be served in the Inn itself: just a stumble across the road. The pub and restaurant are bursting with charm and decorated in keeping with the 14thC thatched image, so expect old beams, dark nooks and crannies, and secret little loft spaces in which to enjoy coffee after the Michelin-starred food cooked by Andrew. Upstairs the fairytale private dining room has been decorated by local artists and the attention to detail is superb. The small but well stocked shop at the front of Cross House sells everything from beautiful silver jewellery or match holders to the finest hams, cheeses and wines. Hampers are frequently sent over to the 3 suites in Black Eagle cottages – they're behind Cross House Lodge and can accommodate small groups of friends or families.

~

NEARBY Helmsley market town, Castle Howard, Duncan Park.
LOCATION 2.5 miles SE of Helmsley off the A170, ample car parking
FOOD breakfast, lunch, dinner (restaurant in the Inn closed on Mon) **PRICE** £££
ROOMS 8 doubles, 3 suites, all with bath or shower; all rooms have TV, DVD, CD, radio, hairdrier, phone, tea and coffee making facilities **FACILITIES** dining rooms, breakfast room, bar, sitting room; heated swimming pool, garden **CREDIT CARDS** MC, V
CHILDREN welcome **DISABLED** a couple of ground-floor rooms **PETS** not accepted
CLOSED 1 week in winter, 1 week in summer **PROPRIETORS** Andrew and Jacquie Pern

THE NORTH-EAST

HAWES, NORTH YORKSHIRE

SIMONSTONE HALL

~ COUNTRY HOUSE HOTEL ~

Hawes, North Yorkshire DL8 3LY
TEL (01969) 667255 **FAX** (01969) 667741
E-MAIL simonstonehall@demon.co.uk **WEBSITE** www.simonstonehall.co.uk

A T THE TIME OF inspection Simonstone was in the throes of a major
refurbishment (the first in five years) but still had the air of
something special, exacerbated by the friendliness of the staff. Outside,
it is the same dignified, slightly forbidding, large Dales country house;
but as you enter you will probably hear the lively chatter coming from
the extensive bar area which is intended to re-create the hotel as a place
that will attract local non-residents as well as overnight guests. To have
this popular country pub within an essentially dignified old country
hotel is something of a novelty – and not unpleasant. The pub is
handsomely done out; bar meals and the range of wines by the glass are
imaginative; waiters in black tie and apron, French bistro-style, bustle
about. It gives the place an injection of life, but if you've come here for
peace, or a romantic twosome, just cross the hall and slump beside the
open fire in the stylish drawing room. Beyond is the panelled Game
Tavern, serving Sunday lunch and an excellent three-course dinner.

The recent refurbishment has meant that all bedrooms now have en
suite bathrooms with showers. The superior bedrooms are handsomely
done out in country house style, some with sleigh beds, others with four-
posters, many of them with fantastic views of the Dales. Prices have risen,
some say unjustifiably, so we would welcomer further reports.

~

NEARBY Pennine Way; Wharfedale; Ribblesdale.
LOCATION 1.5 miles (2.5 km) N of Hawes on Muker road; with ample car parking
FOOD breakfast, bar lunch, Sun lunch, dinner
PRICE £££
ROOMS 18 double and twin with bath and shower; all rooms have phone, TV
FACILITIES bar, 2 sitting rooms, garden room; garden
CREDIT CARDS AE, DC, MC, V **CHILDREN** welcome
DISABLED access possible to ground floor only
PETS welcome **CLOSED** never **MANAGER** Mrs Jill Stott

THE NORTH-EAST

HAWNBY, YORKSHIRE

THE HAWNBY HOTEL
~ COUNTRY HOTEL ~

Hill Top, Hawnby, near Helmsley, York YO6 5QS
TEL (01439) 798202 **FAX** (01439) 798344
E-MAIL info@hawnbyhotel.co.uk **WEBSITE** www.hawnbyhotel.co.uk

A FTER A SPECTACULAR DRIVE through rolling valleys and the unspoilt stone village of Hawnby, this hotel may come as something of a let-down. It is not until you are ushered into the elegant sitting room that you realize how deceptive first appearances can be.

The 'village pub' façade hides an exquisite small hotel which was decorated with obvious flair by the Countess of Mexborough. The hotel used to be part of the 13,000-acre Mexborough estate and Lady Mexborough gave it much personal attention, refurbishing the six bedrooms which are named after colour schemes (Cowslip, Coral, Jade and so on), choosing Laura Ashley wallpaper and fabrics throughout the cosy rooms and immaculate bathrooms.

The hotel does suffer slightly from a lack of space. The sitting room is at one end of the dining room, and although it does not feel cramped and can be curtained off at guests' request, it might be noisy and crowded at peak times. The hotel caters for shooting parties, and is popular with walkers. Reports continue to heap praise on the Hawnby: 'Having visited the hotel on three occasions, my wife and I have found the hotel's high standards ... remain consistent.' 'This charming country hotel ... is an ideal base for touring North Yorkshire; a 'gem' with 'fabulous views', 'home cooking' and 'friendly service'. Dave and Kathryn Young are the new owners.

~

NEARBY Rievaulx Abbey; Jervaulx Abbey; North York Moors.
LOCATION at top of hill in village 7 miles (11 km) NE of Helmsley; with car parking
FOOD breakfast, dinner, bar snacks
PRICE £
ROOMS 9 double and twin with bath; all rooms have phone, TV, hairdrier
FACILITIES sitting room/dining room, bar **CREDIT CARDS** MC, V
CHILDREN accepted
DISABLED access difficult **PETS** not accepted **CLOSED** never
PROPRIETORS Dave and Kathryn Young

THE NORTH-EAST

HUNMANBY, NORTH YORKSHIRE

WRANGHAM HOUSE
~ COUNTRY HOUSE HOTEL ~

Stonegate, Hunmanby, North Yorkshire YO14 0NS
TEL (01723) 891333 **FAX** (01723) 892973
E-MAIL wrangham@mywebpage.net **WEBSITE** www.mywebpage.net/wrangham

WRANGHAM HOUSE is a well-preserved and elegant Georgian former vicarage set in an acre of wooded garden. The main part of the house was built in the second half of the 18th century. The eponymous Francis Wrangham added a wing, now housing the dining room, in 1803. Mervyn Poulter and his wife Margaret, both recently returned from the British Virgin Islands, offer a warm reception and comfortable accommodation. Downstairs there is a light panelled sitting room with a handsome tiled fireplace, a snug and well-stocked bar and a fair-sized dining room looking out over the garden. Dinners here are a blend of contemporary and bourgeois (the latter signifying that the use of cream and the art of sauce-making is, thankfully, alive and well). Lunch is only served on Sundays, but Sunday lunch it *is,* with roast sirloin and all the trimmings.

The bedrooms are individually furnished and decorated. Four are in the Coach House and one of these (on the ground floor) is equipped for guests with disabilities. Parking is a little scarce in Hunmanby but Wrangham House has plenty of its own. Almost uniquely, Hunmanby has a railway station that survived the sweeping cuts in the 1960s – if you want to let the train take the strain you can arrange to be picked up at the station.
~

NEARBY Scarborough Castle; North York Moors National Park.
LOCATION behind church in village, 1 mile (1.5 km) SW of Filey; ample car parking
FOOD breakfast, dinner; lunch Sun by arrangement
PRICE ££
ROOMS 12; 11 double and twin, 1 single, 7 with bath, 5 with shower; all have phone, TV, hairdrier **FACILITIES** sitting room, dining room, bar; garden
CREDIT CARDS AE, MC, V
CHILDREN accepted over 12
DISABLED 1 specially adapted room
PETS by arrangement **CLOSED** never
PROPRIETORS Mervyn and Margaret Poulter and Diane Norvick

THE NORTH-EAST

LASTINGHAM, NORTH YORKSHIRE

LASTINGHAM GRANGE
~ COUNTRY HOUSE HOTEL ~

Lastingham, North Yorkshire YO6 26TH
TEL (01751) 417345/417402 **FAX** (01751) 417358
E-MAIL reservations@lastinghamgrange.com **WEBSITE** www.lastinghamgrange.com

LASTINGHAM GRANGE – a wistaria-clad former farmhouse – nestles peacefully in a delightful village on the edge of the North York Moors. Unlike many country house hotels, it manages to combine a certain sophistication – smartly decorated public rooms, friendly unobtrusive service, elegantly laid gardens – with a large dash of informality, which puts you immediately at ease. From the moment you enter, you feel as if you are staying with friends. Recently, we had this reaction from an inspector: 'Family feeling; very child friendly; charming rooms; however, dining room a little dour.'

The main attraction is the garden. You can enjoy it from a distance – from the windows of the large L-shaped sitting room (complete with carefully grouped sofas, antiques and a grand piano) – or, like most guests, by exploring. There is a beautifully laid rose garden, enticing bordered lawns and an extensive adventure playground for children.

In comparison, bedrooms are more ordinary. They are perfectly comfortable, with well-equipped bathrooms, but some people may find the decoration unsophisticated in places. Jane cooks straightforward English meals.

~

NEARBY North York Moors; Scarborough; Rievaulx Abbey.
LOCATION at top of village, 6 miles (10 km) NW of Pickering; ample car parking
FOOD breakfast, lunch on request, dinner
PRICE £££
ROOMS 12; 10 double, 2 single, all with bath; all rooms have phone, TV, hairdrier
FACILITIES sitting room, dining room; terrace, garden
CREDIT CARDS MC, V
CHILDREN welcome
DISABLED access difficult
PETS accepted in bedrooms by arrangement
CLOSED Dec to mid-Mar
PROPRIETORS Dennis and Jane Wood

THE NORTH-EAST

LEEDS, WEST YORKSHIRE

42 THE CALLS
~ TOWN HOUSE HOTEL ~

42 The Calls, Leeds, West Yorkshire LS2 7EW
TEL (0113) 244 0099 **FAX** (0113) 234 4100
E-MAIL hotel@42thecalls.co.uk **WEBSITE** www.42thecalls.co.uk

EXPECT THE UNEXPECTED at 42 The Calls. Through a small glass-porched entrance and revolving doors, the sight of massive beams, girders, ducts and grain chutes are, one supposes, in keeping for an old corn mill turned hotel. The real surprises are the airy split-level foyer with light wooden floors and mirrored doors, the ultra-modern bar with a stylish display of decanters, a cosy sitting area and a quirky collection of modern chairs and amusing glass and wood tables.

In the bedrooms, fabrics and furniture are traditional; some feature cleverly designed desk lamps that are black ceramic shelves in the shape of the number 42. A two-way serving hatch means that breakfast can be placed straight into the room, or shoes and laundry collected, without disturbance. Every comfort has been considered – a coffee machine, iron and ironing board, CD player and radio with a switchable extension to the bathroom; hot water bottles are available and some rooms overlooking the river have fishing rods. Suites are full of character, with vast sitting rooms.

Formal frockcoats belie the friendliness of the staff, and although somewhat larger than our usual choice of entry, its delightful idiosyncrasy makes 42 The Calls one of *the* places to stay in Leeds.
~

NEARBY Corn Exchange; Tetley's Brewery; museums, galleries, shops, West Yorkshire Playhouse.
LOCATION Exchange quarter, overlooking river Aire in central Leeds; with inexpensive valet parking
FOOD breakfast, snacks
PRICE £££
ROOMS 41; 31 double, 7 single, 3 suites, all with bath; all rooms have phone, TV, fax/modem point, CD player, minibar, hairdrier **FACILITIES** sitting room, breakfast room, bar **CREDIT CARDS** AE, DC, MC, V **CHILDREN** welcome
DISABLED one specially adapted room, lift/elevator **PETS** by arrangement
CLOSED Christmas **PROPRIETORS** The Scotsman Hotel Group

THE NORTH-EAST

NEWTON-LE-WILLOWS, NORTH YORKSHIRE

THE HALL

~ COUNTRY GUEST-HOUSE ~

Newton-le-Willows, Bedale, North Yorkshire DL8 1SW
TEL (01677) 450210 FAX (01677) 450014
WEBSITE www.yorkshirenet.co.uk

As well as being very beautiful, Bedale is in the heart of horse country. The Middleham Moors, where the racehorses are ridden out each morning, are only a few minutes' drive away.

Some of the places in this guide are only welcoming because of their hosts; and some can make you feel welcome all by themselves: The Hall belongs firmly in the latter category and, when Oriella Featherstone adds her hospitality, the two make an irresistible combination. The stable block and paddock beside the two-acre garden are not for show either – visiting horses can be put up as well. The Georgian house is filled with antiques and oddments from other places and other times, but is very much for living in rather than just admiring: the drawing room may be grand, but you also get the impression that you can put your feet up if you want. Tea, coffee and fruitcake are perpetually available in the kitchen as a virtuous alternative to the honesty bar. Dinner, if you ask for it, is home-cooked, traditional, and taken at the single table; breakfast is as generous as you could want. There are fresh flowers in the bedrooms which are large, light and well furnished and are not let down by their bathrooms.

Walkers will be pleased by what opens up for them right outside the front door; and there's a drying room.

~

NEARBY Middleham; Jervaulx Abbey; Bolton Castle; Thorp Perrow; Fountains Abbey; Newby Hall.
LOCATION 4 miles (6.5 km) W of Bedale; with ample car parking
FOOD breakfast, dinner by arrangement
PRICE ££
ROOMS 3; 2 double, 1 twin, all with bath or shower
FACILITIES 2 sitting rooms, breakfast room, dining room; garden
CREDIT CARDS not accepted **CHILDREN** accepted over 13
DISABLED not suitable **PETS** by arrangement **CLOSED** Christmas, New Year
PROPRIETOR Oriella Featherstone

THE NORTH-EAST

SPORTSMAN'S ARMS
~ COUNTRY HOTEL ~

Wath-in-Nidderdale, Pateley Bridge, near Harrogate, North Yorkshire HG3 5PP
TEL (01423) 711306 **FAX** (01423) 712524
WEBSITE www.nidderdalechambers.co.uk

OUR LATEST INSPECTION confirms that the Sportsman's Arms is going from strength to strength. The long, rather rambling building dates from the 17th century, and the setting is as enchanting as the village name sounds; the River Nidd flows across the field in front; Gouthwaite reservoir, a bird-watchers' haunt, is just behind; glorious dales country spreads all around.

Jane and Ray Carter have been running the Sportman's Arms, with the help of a young enthusiastic team, for over 20 years now, and continue to make improvements. Bedrooms (two with four-posters) have been redecorated and are light and fresh, with brand-new bathrooms. Six more rooms, four with views across open countryside, have been created in the barn and stable block. All the public rooms have recently been refurbished as well.

And then there is the food. The Sportsman's Arms is first and foremost a restaurant, and the large dining room is the inn's focal point, sparkling with silver cutlery and crystal table lights. The lively menu embraces sound, traditional local fare, as well as fresh fish and seafood brought in daily from Whitby. To back it up, there is a superb wine list – and an extremely reasonable bill.

~

NEARBY Wharfedale, Wensleydale; Fountains Abbey, Bolton Abbey.
LOCATION 2 miles (3 km) NW of Pateley Bridge, in hamlet; with ample car parking
FOOD breakfast, bar lunch, dinner
PRICE ££
ROOMS 11; 9 double, 2 twin with bath or shower; all rooms have TV
FACILITIES 3 sitting rooms, bar, dining room; fishing
CREDIT CARDS MC, V
CHILDREN welcome
DISABLED easy access to public rooms **PETS** welcome by arrangement
CLOSED Christmas Day, Boxing Day, New Year's Day
PROPRIETORS Jane and Ray Carter

THE NORTH-EAST

RAMSGILL-IN-NIDDERDALE, NORTH YORKSHIRE

YORKE ARMS
~ VILLAGE INN ~

Ramsgill-in-Nidderdale, near Harrogate, North Yorkshire HG3 5RL
TEL (01423) 755243 **FAX** (01423) 755330
E-MAIL enquiries@yorke-arms.co.uk **WEBSITE** www.yorke-arms.co.uk

ON THE GREEN IN A PRETTY Nidderdale village, the creeper-clad Yorke Arms has been a fully-functioning pub for the past 150 years. It's a traditional 'no-frills' village inn, the ideal setting for owners Frances and Gerald Atkins to accomplish their aim of providing good food and a warm welcome. You are greeted as you enter by flagged floors, beams and, in winter, open fires. There is also a reassuring feeling of order: what should have been polished *has* been polished, and what should have been swept has been.

In the restaurant, wooden tables and a wooden floor strewn with rugs keep the techno-age at bay and serve as a showcase for Frances Atkins' Michelin-starred daily changing menu: traditional and modern English dishes are her starting-point, but she also draws on other cuisines from all over the world. Old favourites such as Yorkshire hot pot and halibut cheesy mash usually make an appearance. The wine list is comprehensive and sympathetically priced. Simpler meals are available in the brasserie or the lounge.

The bedrooms are unpretentious, but freshly decorated and comfortably furnished and range in size (and price) from cosy to a modest suite, 'Gouthwaite', which boasts a sofa and armchairs. Bathrooms are outdated, but are gradually being renewed.

~

NEARBY Harewood House; Newby Hall; Fountains Abbey; Ripon Cathedral.
LOCATION in centre of village; take Low Wath Road from Pateley Bridge bordering Gouthwaite Reservoir; with car parking
FOOD breakfast, lunch, dinner; room service
PRICE ££££
ROOMS 13; 11 double and twin, 2 suites, all with bath; all rooms have phone, TV, hairdrier; some have minibar
FACILITIES sitting room, games room, dining rooms, bars; garden
CREDIT CARDS AE, DC, MC, V **DISABLED** not suitable **PETS** accepted in some public rooms **CLOSED** never **PROPRIETORS** Frances and Gerald Atkins

THE NORTH-EAST

BURGOYNE HOTEL

~ VILLAGE HOTEL ~

On the Green, Reeth, Richmond, North Yorkshire DL11 6SN
TEL (01748) 884292 **FAX** (01748) 884292
E-MAIL inquiries@theburgoyne.co.uk **WEBSITE** www.theburgoyne.co.uk

THE BURGOYNE HOTEL stretches its late-Georgian length along the top of the sloping green in Reeth. If you turn round and look the other way, you'll see why: the Swale valley is extremely pretty, and with only the green in front of it, the Burgoyne has an uninterrupted view. Inside, time, money and taste have conspired to produce something of a masterpiece to which has been added the magic ingredient of a warm welcome. There are two elegant and richly furnished sitting rooms on the ground floor with Medieval touches here and there: stone coats of arms on the fireplaces and 'Gothic' oak doors. The restaurant, where the snowy napkins, the crystal and the silver stand out against the cool blues of the decoration, is a kind of inner sanctum where Peter Carwardine's culinary art joins Derek Hickson's scientific (certainly encyclopaedic) understanding of wines.

The bedrooms, most of which face the valley, are beautifully appointed and deeply comfortable. Window seats offer pleasant perches for people who just want to sit and enjoy the view. Rather than hack space for bathrooms out of the well-proportioned rooms, one or two bathrooms are across the corridor – voluminous robes and slippers are provided for the short journey.

~

NEARBY Richmond Castle; Middleham Castle.
LOCATION 10 miles (16 km) W of Richmond on B6270; with car parking
FOOD breakfast, packed lunch on request, dinner; room service
PRICE ££
ROOMS 8 double and twin with bath; all rooms have phone, TV, hairdrier
FACILITIES sitting room, dining room; garden, fishing
CREDIT CARDS MC, V
CHILDREN accepted over 10
DISABLED access possible to ground-floor room
PETS accepted by arrangement **CLOSED** early Jan to mid-Feb
PROPRIETORS Derek Hickson and Peter Carwardine

THE NORTH-EAST

RIPLEY, NORTH YORKSHIRE

BOAR'S HEAD
~ COUNTRY HOUSE HOTEL ~

Ripley, Harrogate, North Yorkshire HG3 3AY
TEL (01423) 771888 **FAX** (01423) 771509
E-MAIL boarshead@ripleycastle.co.uk **WEBSITE** www.ripleycastle.co.uk

ANYONE WITH A SPARE INN and enough paintings and antique furniture to furnish it could do worse than emulate Sir Thomas and Lady Ingilby's successful renovation of the Boar's Head in Ripley. It is a thriving establishment with helpful, pleasant staff who do not leave your comfort to chance. There are bedrooms in the inn itself, lighter more contemporary ones in its cobbled courtyard, and across the road, in the peace and quiet of Birchwood House, are four of their six best rooms. All have fresh flowers, pristine modern bathrooms and thoughtful decoration.

The public rooms are warm and welcoming, filled with period furniture; seascapes and ancestors share the walls. There is a choice for dinner: you can either go to the relaxed bar/bistro (packed when we visited) or the richer candle-lit comfort of the restaurant to agonise over a choice that includes crisp seabass with squid ink noodles or supreme of guinea fowl on a sweet pea purée. Fresh vegetables and game make seasonal appearances from the Ingilby estate, presided over by their castle.

~

NEARBY York; Fountains Abbey and Studley Royal Water Gardens.
LOCATION in village centre, 3 miles (5 km) N of Harrogate on A61; with ample car parking
FOOD breakfast, lunch, dinner
PRICE ££
ROOMS 25 double and twin with bath; all rooms have phone, TV, fax/modem point, hairdrier; minibar on request
FACILITIES sitting room, dining rooms, 2 bars; garden, tennis, fishing
CREDIT CARDS AE, MC, DC, V
CHILDREN accepted
DISABLED 1 specially adapted room, 8 ground-floor rooms
PETS accepted in some rooms only
CLOSED never
PROPRIETORS Sir Thomas and Lady Ingilby

THE NORTH-EAST

ROMALDKIRK, COUNTY DURHAM

ROSE AND CROWN
~ COUNTRY INN ~

Romaldkirk, Barnard Castle, Co. Durham DL12 9EB
TEL (01833) 650213 **FAX** (01833) 650828
E-MAIL hotel@rose-and-crown.co.uk **WEBSITE** www.rose-and-crown.co.uk

THE ROSE AND CROWN was built in 1733 in this very pretty light stone village. It owes its original layout to the Saxons and its name to the patron saint of the church next door. Thoroughly renovated by Christopher and Alison Davy some ten years ago, the Rose and Crown has gone from strength to strength. It is set in the centre of the three-green village – (each green has its own set of stocks, and sometimes its own small group of cows). The bars are comfortingly traditional: real ales, natural stone walls, log fires, old photographs, copper and brass knick-knacks. Excellent pub food with 'blackboard specials' is served in the bistro-style 'Crown Room'. More traditional four-course dinners, English but imaginatively so, are served on white linen in the wood-panelled dining room and, when in season, often feature moorland game, fresh fish from the East Coast, and locally grown vegetables. Fresh bread is baked every day.

There are seven comfortable bedrooms, attractively decorated and furnished with antiques, in the main building. Five more have been added round the courtyard at the back, and open directly on to it. All come with fresh flowers.

~

NEARBY Barnard Castle; Egglestone Abbey; High Force.
LOCATION in centre of village, on B6277, 6 miles (9.6 km) NW of Barnard Castle; with ample car parking
FOOD breakfast, dinner, Sun lunch
PRICE ££
ROOMS 12; 11 double and twin, 1 family, 9 with bath, 3 with shower; all rooms have phone, TV, hairdrier
FACILITIES sitting room, dining room, bar, brasserie
CREDIT CARDS MC, V **CHILDREN** welcome
DISABLED 1 ground-floor bedroom **PETS** accepted in bedrooms
CLOSED Christmas Eve, Christmas Day, Boxing Day; restaurant only, Sun eve
PROPRIETORS Christopher and Alison Davy

THE NORTH-EAST

WINTERINGHAM FIELDS
~ MANOR HOUSE HOTEL ~

Winteringham, North Lincolnshire DN15 9PF
TEL (01724) 733096 **FAX** (01724) 733898
E-MAIL wintfields@aol.com **WEBSITE** www.winteringhamfields.com

HALFWAY BETWEEN SCUNTHORPE and the Humber bridge is one of Britain's gastronomic hotspots. Furthermore, you can sleep in great comfort no more than a few paces from the table. The hotel is in the middle of Winteringham, a quiet country village on the south bank of the Humber estuary. Swiss chef Germain Schwab and his wife Annie are crusaders for high standards in the preparation and, above all, appreciation of good food – witness their second Michelin star and numerous other awards.

The rambling 16thC house is full of nooks and crannies and still has many original features such as exposed timbers, period fireplaces and oak panelling. These are set off by the warm colours of walls and fabrics and the antique furniture.

The bedrooms are all uniquely decorated and sympathetically furnished. There are four in the main house (with not a single right-angle between them), three in the courtyard, which is the preserve of a large (friendly) boxer and an even larger (friendly) great dane, and one in a cottage round the corner. Two more rooms have just been made from a dovecote a couple of minutes away. All are named after former residents of the house or local dignitaries.

~

NEARBY Normanby Hall; Thornton Abbey; Lincoln.
LOCATION in centre of village on S bank of Humber, 4 miles (6 km) W from Humber bridge off A1077; with ample car parking
FOOD breakfast, lunch, dinner; room service
PRICE £££
ROOMS 10; 8 double, 2 suites, 7 with bath, 3 with shower; all rooms have phone, TV, hairdrier **FACILITIES** 2 sitting rooms, 1 dining room, conservatory; garden, helipad, boutique **CREDIT CARDS** AE, MC, V
CHILDREN babes-in-arms and children over 8 accepted
DISABLED access difficult **PETS** accepted by arrangement
CLOSED 1st week Aug, last week Oct **PROPRIETORS** Germain and Ann Schwab

SCOTLAND

From the fertile southern uplands bordering England, to the dramatic mountain ranges and barren coasts of the Highlands and Islands, Scotland is varied and often breathtakingly beautiful. Within a few hoursí drive, the scenery changes from gently rolling hills, purple in summer with flowering heather, to majestic, craggy peaks. Visitors come to hike, climb, ski, play golf, fish in the lochs and rivers, and to explore Scotland's fascinating historical heritage and lively cultural life. Featured here are many of the most remote hotels in Britain: some on the edges of lochs or by the sea, others on islands or deep in the countryside. Our selection includes converted castles, country manors, farmhouses, ferry inns and crofts as well as townhouses. Several are new to this edition of the guide. Visitors to the Scottish Borders might think of following the trail of Sir Walter Scott, staying at Hundalee House, a manor with exotic decoration (page 281); or the Arts and Crafts village hotel, Skirling House (page 284). In Dumfries and Galloway, where the land is rich and the sea warmed by the Gulf Stream, we recommend the friendly Riverside Inn (page 273) and Victorian Knockinaam Lodge (page 282). In Edinburgh, known for its historic buildings and annual Festival, we have two new hotels: Newington Cottage, a bed-and-breakfast just outside the centre (page 276) and The Witchery by the Castle in a wonderful 16thC building (page 277). In Glasgow, recent European Capital of Culture, we continue to recommend One Devonshire Gardens (page 279). Further north, in Argyll, where long fingers of sea and inland lochs probe the hills, you could spend a tranquil holiday at Ards House (page 274), Ballachulish House (page 272) or the ultimately secluded Isle of Eriska Hotel (page 291). There are two bed-and-breakfasts in the pretty Inverness-shire town of Fort William, Crolinnhe (page 278), new to the guide, and an old favourite, The Grange (page 289). To the east, Minmore House (page 290) is well placed for the Malt Whisky Trail, and solid Victorian Struan Hall is a recent discovery (page 271). If in search of true remoteness, you could choose relaxing Summer Isles (page 285), or one of the island hotels: Three Chimneys (page 287); or Kinloch Lodge on Skye (page 303); Scarista House on Harris (page 302) or Burrastow House on Shetland (page 307).

SOUTHERN SCOTLAND

ABERDOUR, N OF EDINBURGH

HAWKCRAIG HOUSE
∼ BED-AND-BREAKFAST ∼

Hawkcraig Point, Aberdour, Fife KY3 OTZ
TEL (01383) 860335 **FAX** (0131) 3131464

GETTING TO THIS former ferryman's cottage is a minor adventure, since the white-painted house is at the end of a narrow road, at the bottom of a steep cliff. The setting, however, makes the drive worthwhile. Right on the edge of the Firth of Forth, the view is due south across the water to Edinburgh and Inchcolm Island. A pair of binoculars stand ready in the sitting room, to use at the modern picture window. There is nothing fancy about the decorations, which include a wooden butter churn and a huge bell from a Second World War airfield. Elma and Dougal Barrie are down-to-earth hosts, with a fine sense of humour. Elma is also an excellent cook with room for a few non-residents to dine on traditional Scottish dishes, using fresh fish and local meat.

This may not appeal to those requiring space and luxury. Even though the bathrooms are modern, the bedrooms are rather small. However, it is a treat to walk along the shore to Aberdour's flower-decked railway station and catch a train across the famous Forth Bridge to Princes Street station in the heart of Edinburgh.

∼

NEARBY Edinburgh, St. Andrew's; golf, boat trips.
LOCATION on north shore of Firth of Forth; ample car parking
FOOD breakfast, evening meal by request
PRICE ££
ROOMS 2 double; all have TV, hairdrier
FACILITIES sitting room, dining room; garden
CREDIT CARDS no
CHILDREN over 12
DISABLED not suitable
PETS not accepted
CLOSED Nov to mid-Mar
PROPRIETORS Elma and Dougal Barrie

SOUTHERN SCOTLAND

ABOYNE, ABERDEENSHIRE

STRUAN HALL
~ BED-AND-BREAKFAST ~

Ballater Road, Aboyne, Aberdeenshire AB34 5HY
TEL (013398) 87241 **FAX** (013398) 87241
WEBSITE www.struanhall.co.uk

LOOKING AT THE SOLID mass of grey stone that is Struan Hall, we could hardly believe that its original site was five miles away. The house dates back to the 1800s, but in 1904 it was dismantled, moved stone by stone and rebuilt here, across the street from Arbor Lodge (see page 131). Set in 2 acres of grounds, with lawns and an Indian-style pavilion, a rockery and carp pool, Struan Hall makes a restful, comfortable base, whether guests are sightseeing, fishing, walking or playing golf.

Phyllis and Michael Ingham are accomplished hosts who have decorated their home to suit the Victorian atmosphere. Tartan carpets harmonize with the pine staircase, while the dining-room, where a communal breakfast is served, has a massive Victorian sideboard. Tiffany-style lamps light the hall.

Upstairs, the Scottish theme continues. The bedrooms are named after castles and have pine bedheads carved with Scottish motifs. Bathrooms, however, are right up-to-date. The Inghams do not serve dinner but are happy to recommend several pubs and restaurants in the town.

~

NEARBY castle, distilleries, the Grampians; fishing, golf.
LOCATION in village; ample car parking
FOOD breakfast
PRICE £
ROOMS 3 double; 1 single; all have TV, radio, hairdrier, tea/coffee kit
FACILITIES sitting room, dining room; garden
CREDIT CARDS MC, V
CHILDREN over 7
DISABLED not suitable
PETS not accepted
CLOSED Nov to Dec
PROPRIETORS Phyllis and Michael Ingham

SOUTHERN SCOTLAND

BALLACHULISH, ARGYLL

BALLACHULISH HOUSE

~ BED-AND-BREAKFAST ~

Ballachulish, Argyll PA39 4JX
TEL (01855) 811266 **FAX** (01855) 811498
E-MAIL mclaughalins@btconnect.com **WEBSITE** www.ballachulishhouse.com

ANYONE WANTING to immerse themselves in Scottish history should head straight for this 250-year-old country house, set in a valley with stunning views of Loch Linnhe and the nearby Morvern Hills. The present owner, Marie Mclaughalin, can tell you all about the chilling connections with the Glencoe Massacre (1692), as well as the Appin Murder (1752) that inspired Robert Louis Stevenson's novel, Kidnapped.

Despite its bloodthirsty past, however, Ballachulish House is a peaceful spot where good food, good wine and good company are the order of the day. Local lamb and venison, vegetables from the garden and shellfish from the loch are the basis for Liz's gourmet dinners. Since portions are ample, it is advisable to build up an appetite by walking, fishing or perhaps enjoying a game of badminton or croquet in the garden. After dinner, guests may retire to play billiards and smoke, "just like the good old days," according to one contented visitor. The bedrooms are vast, with space for chairs as well as large beds.

~

NEARBY Glencoe, Ben Nevis, West Highland Way; fishing, golf.
LOCATION on hillside in own grounds; ample car parking
FOOD breakfast; dinner on request
PRICE ££
ROOMS 8 double; all have phone, radio, hairdrier, tea/coffee kit
FACILITIES sitting room, dining room; garden, croquet, badminton
CREDIT CARDS MC, V
CHILDREN over 3
DISABLED unsuitable
PETS accepted by arrangement
CLOSED never
PROPRIETORS Marie Mclaughalin

SOUTHERN SCOTLAND

CANONBIE, DUNFRIES AND GALLOWAY

RIVERSIDE INN
VILLAGE INN

Canonbie, Dumfries and Galloway DG14 0UX
TEL (013873) 71512 **FAX** (013873) 71866
E-MAIL riverside@langholm.org **WEBSITE** www.langholm.org/riverside

FOR MORE THAN 25 years the Phillipses have been at the helm of this country-house-turned-inn, which you could view as a pub, a restaurant or a hotel. We guess that motorists travelling between England and Scotland remain the mainstay of trade, despite the fact that the A7 from Carlisle to Edinburgh has been shifted westwards to by-pass Canonbie. For those who do pause there, Canonbie and the Riverside are, not surprisingly, more attractive now that little traffic separates the hotel from the public park it faces, and from the River Esk, which it overlooks 50 yards away.

Inside, the atmosphere is warm and friendly. The comfortable bar and the cosy sitting rooms have the occasional beam and are furnished in traditional, chintzy style, while the dining room is brighter, with candlelit wooden tables. You can eat either in the bar or in the restaurant; wherever, the food is good, using fresh local produce, such as salmon from the Esk, and home-grown vegetables.

Bedrooms at the Riverside are comfortable but worn at the edges; bathrooms definitely need updating. Thoughtful extras include electric blankets and a basket of fruit in each.

As we went to press, Riverside Inn was for sale and, sadly, we don't know anything about the new proprietors. Reports welcome.

NEARBY Hadrian's Wall and the Borders.
LOCATION 11 miles (18 km) N of M6 on A7, in village by river; with garden and ample car parking
FOOD breakfast, lunch, dinner
PRICE ££
ROOMS 4 double, 1 with bath, 3 with shower, 3 twin with bath; all have TV, hairdrier
FACILITIES 2 sitting rooms, bar, dining room; fishing, tennis, bowls, will arrange shooting breaks **CREDIT CARDS** MC, V **CHILDREN** welcome **DISABLED** 1 ground-floor room
PETS accepted by arrangement **CLOSED** Christmas, New Year, 2 weeks Feb and Nov
PROPRIETORS Ed Baxter and Jane Buckley

SOUTHERN SCOTLAND

CONNEL, ARGYLL

ARDS HOUSE
~ BED-AND-BREAKFAST ~

Connel, by Oban, Argyll PA37 1PT
TEL (01631) 710857
WEBSITE www.ardshouse.com

THIS PRETTY VICTORIAN villa has uninterrupted views westward over the Firth of Lorn to the Morvern Hills. Sunsets are truly spectacular.

The house itself tends to ramble, as additions have been made over the years to the original cottage - the sitting room is conventional but comfortable with an log burning stove and a grand piano. The most recent owner, Margaret Kennedy, has retained the snug atmosphere, but no longer serves dinner (however there is a choice of restaurants nearby). Breakfasts are especially generous. You could choose not only the usual fresh fruit salad, muesli and yoghurt but also kippers, smoked salmon and scamble eggs, pancakes and bacon with maple syrup, haggis on toast (with whisky if you want). All this is in addition to the full Scottish breakfast accompanied by potatoe scone.

Although the Oban to Tyndrum road runs right in front of the house, traffic is rarely heavy enough to disturb the peace. Strictly non-smoking. Special terms are available for short breaks.

~

NEARBY Falls of Lora, ferries to the Hebrides, the Highlands.
LOCATION overlooking water; ample car parking
FOOD breakfast; dinner on request
PRICE £
ROOMS 7 double; all have radio, tea/coffee kit
FACILITIES sitting room, dining room; garden
CREDIT CARDS MC, V
CHILDREN not suitable
DISABLED not suitable
PETS not accepted
CLOSED Christmas and New Year
PROPRIETOR Margaret Kennedy

SOUTHERN SCOTLAND

EDINBURGH

THE HOWARD
~ TOWN HOUSE HOTEL ~

34 Great King Street, Edinburgh EH3 6QH
TEL (0131) 557 3500 **FAX** (0131) 557 6515
E-MAIL reserve@thehoward.com **WEBSITE** www.thehoward.com

THE ONLY INDICATION that 34 Great King Street is a hotel is the simple brass plate to the right of the front door. The location, a cobbled street in Edinburgh's New Town (new in the early 1800s, that is), could hardly be bettered, within walking distance of Princes Street and the Castle, but almost free of traffic noise.

The 1820s building, comprising three terraced town houses, displays all the elegance and sense of proportion one associates with the Georgian era. Push open the door, and willing service is immediately on hand, including directions to the hotel's own private car park. After checking in, the charming reception staff will ask if you'd like some tea and shortbread, thus reinforcing the sense of being a guest in a friend's house.

Public rooms are elegant and captivating, although the drawing room could do with better lighting. The breakfast room is graced by delightful Italianate murals, uncovered during restoration. Bedrooms are supremely comfortable.

~

NEARBY Edinburgh Castle; Holyrood Palace; Princes Street.
LOCATION in New Town, E of Dundas St; private car parking
FOOD breakfast, lunch, dinner; room service
PRICE ££££
ROOMS 18; 11 double and twin, 2 single, 5 suites; all rooms have phone, TV, fax/modem point, hairdrier
FACILITIES drawing room, bar, breakfast room, restaurant, dining room, drink service
CREDIT CARDS AE, DC, MC, V
CHILDREN welcome
DISABLED access possible, lift/elevator
PETS not accepted
CLOSED Christmas
MANAGER Johanne Falconer

SOUTHERN SCOTLAND

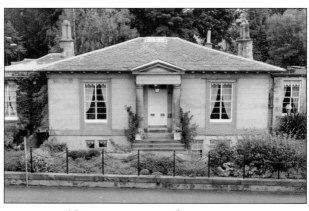

NEWINGTON COTTAGE
~ BED-AND-BREAKFAST ~

15 Blacket Place, Edinburgh EH9 1RG
TEL (0131) 6681935 **FAX** (0131) 6674644
E-MAIL fmickel@newcot.demon.co.uk **WEBSITE** www.newcot.demon.co.uk

SOME VISITORS to Edinburgh insist on staying right in the heart of the city, but we would be happy to stay in Newington Cottage, despite the 10-minute bus ride. Freda Mickel and her husband opened in 1996 and quickly established themselves among Edinburgh's upmarket bed-and-breakfasts. Their Regency villa was built in 1832 by Thomas Hamilton, who also designed the old Royal High School which has been earmarked as the new Scottish parliament building.

The house was derelict when the Mickels took over and they admit that the renovation was 'a labour of love'. They restored the elaborate mouldings and chose antiques and reproduction furniture to suit the period. The result is delightfully light and airy. Bedrooms are 'more like bed-sitting rooms, they are so spacious,' one guest told us, 'and the bathrooms are equally generous.' The garden and quiet setting are added advantages. Freda Mickel does not offer dinner, since most guests prefer to eat in the city. Although guests have to park their cars on the street, the meters are inexpensive.

~

NEARBY Edinburgh and its castle, museums, galleries.
LOCATION on quiet residential street; public street car parking
FOOD breakfast
PRICE ££££
ROOMS 3 double; all have TV, radio, hairdrier, tea/coffee kit, CD player
FACILITIES sitting room, dining room; terrace, garden
CREDIT CARDS MC, V
CHILDREN not suitable
DISABLED not suitable
PETS not accepted
CLOSED Christmas
PROPRIETOR Freda Mickel

SOUTHERN SCOTLAND

EDINBURGH

THE WITCHERY BY THE CASTLE
~ RESTAURANT-WITH-ROOMS ~

Castlehill, The Royal Mile, Edinburgh EH1 2NF
TEL (0131) 225 5613 **FAX** (0131) 220 4392
E-MAIL mail@thewitchery.com **WEBSITE** www.thewitchery.com

IT TAKES ITS NAME from the hundreds of witches burned at the stake nearby, but The Witchery is, thankfully, not macabre. However, it is gothic and, above all, luxurious. Started 23 years ago by James Thomson, it occupies a 16thC building at the gates of Edinburgh Castle and was previously used as committee rooms for the General Assembly of the Church of Scotland. Entering from a close off the Royal Mall, you pass through a doorway still marked with the original merchant's initials and motto. Inside, candlelight reveals painted and gilded ceilings and walls covered in tapestries and 17thC oak paneling rescued from a fire at St Giles Cathedral. Gilded leather screens, red leather upholstery and antique church candlesticks complete the feeling of mystery and intimacy.

Suites, either above the restaurant or in an adjacent building, are plush and opulent, with open fires, antiques, historic paintings and dramatic colour schemes, and have views towards the Old Town or over the Royal Mile. Previous guests have included Vivienne Westwood, Jack Nicholson, Michael Douglas and Catherine Zeta-Jones.

You can eat in either the award-winning restaurant of the same name, in the Secret Garden, a terrace garden restaurant built behind the Witchery on an abandoned schoolyard or in the sister restaurant, The Tower, on the fifth floor of the Museum of Scotland.

~

NEARBY Edinburgh Castle, the Royal Mile, Holyrood House.
LOCATION at the gates of Edinburgh Castle, public car park nearby
FOOD breakfast, lunch, dinner
PRICE ££££
ROOMS 6 suites, all with bath; all have TV, DVD, CD player, phone, hairdrier
FACILITIES 2 restaurants, sister restaurant at Museum of Scotland
CREDIT CARDS AE, DC, MC, V **CHILDREN** accepted
DISABLED access difficult **PETS** accepted by arrangement
CLOSED never **PROPRIETOR** James Thomson

SOUTHERN SCOTLAND

FORT WILLIAM, INVERNESS-SHIRE

CROLINNHE
~ BED-AND-BREAKFAST ~

Grange Road, Fort William, Inverness-shire PH33 6JF
TEL (01397) 702709
E-MAIL crolinnhe@yahoo.com **WEBSITE** www.crolinnhe.co.uk

FORT WILLIAM has long been the jumping-off point for visitors to the Western Highlands. Active types come to climb Ben Nevis, Britain's highest peak, though the Nevis Range Gondola is an easier way to the top. The Great Glen, with its chain of narrow lochs along a valley, cuts away to the northeast. A short walk from the middle of Fort William, Crolinnhe has been the home of Flora MacKenzie since 1982. After having restored the Victorian house she is constantly redecorating in what is a 'smart', though perhaps slightly old-fashioned, style. This obviously suits the regulars who come here for the outdoor activities such as fishing, golf and hiking.

No doubt the 'breakfast at 8.30 am' rule also suits them. Guests decide the night before what they want, which helps the hosts, since 'the full works' can be a feast of porridge, followed by fresh Mallaig kippers or even haggis. More modest eaters can opt for fresh fruit or scrambled eggs.

Set on a hillside, Crolinnhe has truly spectacular views over Loch Linnhe. We would stay here for that reason alone.

~

NEARBY Ben Nevis, West Highland Museum; fishing, golf.
LOCATION overlooking Loch Linnhe; ample car parking
FOOD breakfast
PRICE ££
ROOMS 3 double; all have TV, hairdrier, tea/coffee kit
FACILITIES sitting room, dining room; terrace, garden
CREDIT CARDS not accepted
CHILDREN over 12
DISABLED not suitable
PETS not accepted
CLOSED Nov to Mar
PROPRIETORS Flora MacKenzie

SOUTHERN SCOTLAND

GLASGOW

ONE DEVONSHIRE GARDENS

~ TOWN HOUSE HOTEL ~

1 Devonshire Gardens, Glasgow G12 0UX
TEL (0141) 339 2001 **FAX** (0141) 337 1663
E-MAIL devonshir5@aol.com **WEBSITE** www.onedevonshiregardens.com

THERE ARE a fair number of apparently unselfish people who, without a qualm, and certainly not for reasons of economy, would postpone their plans to visit Glasgow if they discovered that there was not a room to be had at One Devonshire Gardens. Ken McCulloch's hotel (actually three terraced houses in a row on the western side of the city) has that effect on many of its habitués. Where else would a baker get up at four every morning to make sure your shortbread was fresh? The entire hotel has an air of restrained luxury: in the public rooms ancestors gaze down from richly covered walls towards good antiques and plump upholstery. A pre-dinner drink by the drawing room fire should already have put you in a good mood before choosing between the House 5 restaurant or Amaryllis, a Gordon Ramsey restaurant. It is almost superfluous to add that the wine list – and the advice if you want it – are of matching quality.

The bedrooms are opulent: soft lighting, deep colours and heavyweight fabrics in some, pale and light-handed in others; all with fine furniture and sumptuous bathrooms. Fresh fruit and flowers, your own CD-player and up-to-date magazines complete the picture. Staff are polite, discreet and attentive.

~

NEARBY Cathedral, Hunterian Musueum and other sights.
LOCATION 2 miles (3 km) from centre at junction of Great Western and Hyndland roads; ample free street parking
FOOD breakfast, lunch, dinner
PRICE ££££
ROOMS 38 double and twin, most with bath; all rooms have phone, TV, minibar, hairdrier; some have DVD, fireplace
FACILITIES 3 drawing rooms, 2 restaurants, study, dining room, bar; patio garden
CREDIT CARDS AE, DC, MC, V **CHILDREN** welcome
DISABLED not suitable **PETS** accepted by arrangement
CLOSED Christmas (call to check) **MANAGER** Stephen McCorkell

SOUTHERN SCOTLAND

GREYWALLS
~ COUNTRY HOUSE HOTEL ~

Muirfield, Gullane, East Lothian EH31 2EG
TEL (01620) 842144 **FAX** (01620) 842241
E-MAIL hotel@greywalls.co.uk **WEBSITE** www.greywalls.co.uk

GREYWALLS IS A SLICK, expensive country house hotel, with - by our standards - quite a large number of bedrooms, but despite this we cannot resist including such a distinctive place. It is a classic turn-of-the-century house by Sir Edwin Lutyens, with gardens laid out by Gertrude Jekyll, and - more to the point for golf enthusiasts - it overlooks the tenth green of the famous Muirfield championship course.

The feel of Greywalls is very much one of a gracious private house, little changed in atmosphere since the days when King Edward V11 was a guest. Furnished largely with period pieces, public rooms include an Edwardian tea room, a little bar well stocked with whiskies, and a particularly appealing panelled library. This is a delightful room - with no sense of a hotel about it - in which to curl up on one of the sofas either side of the fire, and leaf through one of the many books from the shelves. Dinner, served in a room overlooking the golf course, is elegantly presented and imaginative. Bedrooms are attractive, comfortable and well-equipped, particularly those in the original house rather than the new wing.

~

NEARBY golf courses; beaches; castles; Edinburgh.
LOCATION in village, 17 miles (27 km) E of Edinburgh off A198 to North Berwick; ample car parking
FOOD breakfast, lunch, dinner; room service
PRICE ££££
ROOMS 23; 19 double and twin, 4 single, all with bath; all rooms have phone, TV, hairdrier **FACILITIES** two sitting rooms, library, bar, dining room, conservatory; garden, grass and hard surface tennis courts, croquet
CREDIT CARDS AE, DC, MC, V
CHILDREN welcome
DISABLED bedrooms on ground floor
PETS accepted, but not in public rooms
CLOSED mid-Oct to mid-Apr **MANAGER** Sue Prime

SOUTHERN SCOTLAND

JEDBURGH, ROXBURGHSHIRE

HUNDALEE HOUSE
~ BED-AND-BREAKFAST ~

Jedburgh, Roxburghshire TD8 6PA
TEL (01835) 863011 **FAX** (01835) 863011
E-MAIL sheila.whittaker@btinternet.com **WEBSITE** www.accommodation-scotland.org

SEEING THE PEACEFUL COUNTRYSIDE around Jedburgh today, it is difficult to believe that this land has a history of violent confrontations between the Scots and English. Among the attractions are the Mary, Queen of Scots House, a ruined abbey, a museum dedicated to Victorian prison life and Ferniehirst Castle, the ancient seat of the Kerr family.

Not far away is Hundalee House. Set back in the hills, this 18thC limestone manor house has been home to the Whittakers for a decade. They created the fine large garden, putting in flowering shrubs, adding peacocks and digging a pond for koi carp. Inside, the taste is even more exotic, reflecting their time in Egypt. Egyptian motifs hang on the walls and Egyptian hounds guard the fireplace in the sitting room, which has fine views of the Cheviot Hills to the south. Bedrooms may not be luxurious but one has a four-poster bed. Two others share a bathroom; these offer notable value and are useful for a family. Sheila Whittaker does not serve dinner, but her breakfasts are 'cooked and copious,' according to one teenage visitor.

~

NEARBY Kelso, Dryburgh Abbey, Abbotsford; golf, fishing.
LOCATION set in own grounds; ample car parking
FOOD breakfast
PRICE £
ROOMS 5 double; all have TV, radio, hairdrier, tea/coffee kit
FACILITIES sitting room, dining room; garden
CREDIT CARDS not accepted
CHILDREN over 10
DISABLED not suitable
PETS not accepted
CLOSED Nov to Mar
PROPRIETORS Mr and Mrs Whittaker

SOUTHERN SCOTLAND

PORTPATRICK, DUMFRIES & GALLOWAY

KNOCKINAAM LODGE

～ COUNTRY HOTEL ～

Portpatrick, Dumfries & Galloway DG9 9AD
TEL (01776) 810471 **FAX** (01776) 810435
E-MAIL reservations@knockinaamlodge.com

GALLOWAY IS VERY much an area for escaping the hurly-burly, and Knockinaam Lodge complements it perfectly (as well as being the ideal staging post for anyone bound for the ferry at Stranraer to Northern Ireland). Succeeding proprietors of the Lodge have had a reputation for fine food and warm hospitality, and the tradition is still maintained with the help of an enthusiastic staff and the present owners, Michael Bricker and Pauline Ashworth.

The house, a low Victorian villa, was built as a hunting lodge in 1869 and extended at the turn of the century. It was used by Sir Winston Churchill as a secret location in which to meet General Eisenhower during the Second World War. The rooms are cosy in scale and furnishings, the bedrooms varying from the stylishly simple to the quietly elegant. A key part of the appeal of the place is its complete seclusion – down a wooded glen, with lawned garden running down to a sandy beach. Children are welcome, and well catered for, with special high teas.

We would welcome reports on whether the prices here still represent value for money. Dinner, on our last inspection, was adventurous and competently cooked, but there were a few frayed edges about the place. It is currently quiet in the market.

～

NEARBY Logan, Ardwell and Glenwhan Gardens, Castle Kennedy.
LOCATION 3 miles (5 km) SE of Portpatrick, off A77; in grounds; ample car parking
FOOD breakfast, lunch, dinner
PRICE ££££
ROOMS 10; 9 double with bath, one single with shower; all rooms have phone, TV, video, hairdrier **FACILITIES** 2 sitting rooms, bar, dining room, garden; croquet, helipad
CREDIT CARDS AE, DC, MC, V **CHILDREN** welcome
DISABLED access easy, but no ground-floor bedrooms
PETS accepted, but not in public rooms **CLOSED** never
PROPRIETORS Michael Bricker and Pauline Ashworth

SOUTHERN SCOTLAND

ST ANDREWS, FIFE

KINKELL
BED-AND-BREAKFAST

St Andrews, Fife KY16 8PN
TEL (01334) 472003 **FAX** (01344) 475248
E-MAIL info@kinkell.com **WEBSITE** www.kinkell.com

QUALITY ACCOMMODATION is hard to find in or near the golfing paradise that is St Andrews. Close to the Old Course of the Royal and Ancient Golf Club, many bed-and-breakfasts do plenty of business with little or no effort, so it comes as a relief to find a comfortable home where the owners still take pride in offering traditional Scottish hospitality.

Part-Georgian and part-Victorian, Kinkell is a rambling house in a quiet setting of trees and fields running down to the shore. We like the cheerful informality of Sandy and Frippy Fyfe, frustrated restauranteurs who decided to offer bed-and-breakfast because they enjoy meeting guests from all over the world. In contrast to the rather grand dining room, bedrooms here are somewhat conservative, with the subdued colours of many family houses. The light twin-bedded room facing south still displays china models and porcelain painted by the owners' daughter. It is a pity that the only views of the gusty North Sea are from the small double room facing east. The tennis court and croquet lawn are an enjoyable bonus in fine weather.

NEARBY St Andrews and its golf, university, cathedral.
LOCATION in country, outside town; ample car parking
FOOD breakfast; dinner by request
PRICE £
ROOMS 3 double
FACILITIES sitting room, dining room; garden, tennis court, croquet lawn
CREDIT CARDS MC, V
CHILDREN welcome
DISABLED not suitable
PETS by arrangement
CLOSED never
PROPRIETORS Sandy and Frippy Fyfe

SOUTHERN SCOTLAND

SKIRLING BY BIGGAR, LANARKSHIRE

SKIRLING HOUSE
~ GUEST-HOUSE ~

Skirling by Biggar, Lanarkshire ML12 6HD
TEL (01899) 860274 **FAX** (01899) 860255
E-MAIL enquiry@skirlinghouse.com **WEBSITE** www.skirlinghouse.com

Set in the centre of a peaceful Borders village, Skirling House was designed in 1908 by the Arts and Crafts architect Ramsay Traquir. We are delighted to report that owners Bob and Isobel are well aware of the architectural gem they have on their hands and, from the ornate wrought ironwork and decorative carvings to period antiques, the Arts and Craft movement is evident throughout. Lord Carmichael commissioned the house and, left over from his family's art collection, is an impressive 16thC Florentine carved ceiling in the drawing room. In keeping with the relaxed atmosphere, you can sit back in one of the comfy sofas or armchairs and admire the ceiling, or simply cuddle up with a good book beside the log fire.

Bedrooms, although still very much in the style of the place, have lovely views over the three-acre garden. The grounds cover 155 cares and, with the surrounding rolling hills, provide ample chance for a light stroll or a more ambitious ramble. The menu, modern and reasonably light in style, changes daily and the Hunters use local produce as well as vegetables and herbs from the house gardens.

Located on one of the main routes to Edinburgh, Skirling House makes a convenient stop-over, but we think with its interesting design and tranquil setting, it makes a worthwhile stopover.

~

NEARBY Peebles, New Lanark, Edinburgh, Glasgow
LOCATION off A702 to Edinburgh, on A72 on the village green, private car parking
FOOD breakfast and dinner
PRICE ££
ROOMS 4; 3 double, 1 twin, all with bath; all rooms have TV, phone, radio, stereo, hairdrier **FACILITIES** library, drawing room, dining room, conservatory; garden, tennis court, croquet **CREDIT CARDS** MC, V **CHILDREN** welcome **DISABLED** access possible
PETS by arrangement **CLOSED** Jan and Feb
PROPRIETORS Bob and Isobel Hunter

HIGHLANDS AND ISLANDS

ACHILTIBUE, ROSS-SHIRE

SUMMER ISLES
~ COUNTRY HOTEL ~

Achiltibuie, by Ullapool, Ross-shire IV26 2YG
TEL (0185482) 622282 **FAX** (01854) 622251
WEBSITE www.summerisleshotel.co.uk

'THERE IS A MARVELLOUS amount of nothing to do' at Summer Isles. The emphasis is on eating well, sleeping well and relaxing in beautiful surroundings. 'Take your Wellingtons, your sunglasses, your dog, walking shoes, insect repellant, camera, paint boxes, binoculars and comfy clothes,' advise Mark and Geraldine Irvine, whose family have owned this remote, cottagey, civilized hotel since the late 1960s.

The views across Loch Broom and the Summer Isles are riveting, and the hotel's public rooms make the most of them with large picture windows. The decorations and furnishings are simple and cosy, with a touch of sophistication. There is a wood-burning stove in the sitting room to keep you warm, and modern art and photographs on the walls in the dining room. The food is a major attraction – the Irvines must be the holders of one of the furthest-flung Michelin stars in the British Isles, gained for the delicious and health-conscious cooking of Chris Firth-Bernard, featuring freshly-caught fish and shellfish and home-grown fruit and vegetables. Bedrooms are comfortable; best is the galleried Boathouse suite, which is stylish and spacious, with a spiral staircase up to the bedroom.

NEARBY Ullapool; Inverewe Gardens; beaches.
LOCATION 10 miles (16 km) N of Ullapool, turn left on to single track road for 15 miles (24 km) to Achiltibuie; hotel is close to village post office; with ample car parking
FOOD breakfast, lunch, dinner
PRICE ££-£££
ROOMS 13; 11 double and twin, 2 suites, all with bath; all rooms have phone, hairdrier; suites have TV
FACILITIES dining room, sitting room, 2 bars, sun room; fishing
CREDIT CARDS MC, V **CHILDREN** welcome over 6
DISABLED access difficult
PETS dogs allowed in bedrooms but not public rooms
CLOSED mid-Oct to Easter **PROPRIETORS** Mark and Geraldine Irvine

HIGHLANDS AND ISLANDS

MONACHYLE MHOR

~ FARMHOUSE HOTEL ~

Balquhidder, Lochearnhead, Perthshire FK19 8PQ
TEL (01877) 384622 **FAX** (01877) 384305
E-MAIL info@monachylemhor.com **WEBSITE** www.monachylemhor.com

A SMALL, FAMILY-RUN FARMHOUSE with a charm all its own. The setting is both serene and romantic – as well it might be: this was the family home of Rob Roy MacGregor, approached along the Braes of Balquhidder (described in *Kidnapped*) and set beside Lochs Doine and Voil.

Jean Lewis came here 16 years ago from her native Monmouth and, together with her two sons Tom and Rob, first farmed the 2,000-acre estate and then opened the building as a hotel as well. Tom Lewis is the highly-praised chef, and the hotel's restaurant - situated in a light and airy conservatory overlooking the two lochs – is popular with locals and guests alike. Much of the produce comes from the farm, including lamb, beef and organic vegetables.

Bedrooms are simple and homely. Some have loch views and those converted from the old farmstead across a courtyard are particularly spacious and furnished in a suitably rustic style.

For a relaxing, inexpensive country break in magnificent scenery and with memorable food, Monachyle Mhor would be hard to beat.

~

NEARBY in the heart of Rob Roy country.
LOCATION on private estate; turn off A84, 11 miles (17.5 km) N of Callander at Kingshouse Hotel, then follow single-track lane for 6 miles (9.5 km); well-signposted; ample car parking
FOOD breakfast, lunch, dinner
PRICE ££
ROOMS 10; 8 double, 2 twin, all with bath or shower; all rooms have phone, TV, hairdrier **FACILITIES** sitting room, bar, restaurant; terrace, garden, fishing, stalking
CREDIT CARDS MC, V
CHILDREN accepted over 12
DISABLED access difficult at present - plans afoot
PETS not accepted
CLOSED never **PROPRIETORS** Jean, Tom and Rob Lewis

HIGHLANDS AND ISLANDS

COLBOST, ISLE OF SKYE

THREE CHIMNEYS
~ SEASIDE RESTAURANT-WITH-ROOMS ~

Colbost, Dunvegan, Isle of Skye IV55 8ZT
TEL (01470) 511258 **FAX** (01470) 511358
E-MAIL eatandstay@threechimneys.co.uk **WEBSITE** www.threechimneys.co.uk

FOR MANY YEARS chef Shirley Spear and her husband Eddie have run Three Chimneys as an award-winning seafood restaurant in an idyllic seaside location in the far north-west corner of Skye. The good news is that you can now, having enjoyed yourself at dinner, stay the night - in style. The six suites created in a new building called the House Over-By, are luxurious, highly original – if understated – rooms designed to blend with the seascape and the changing light. Each contemporary, spacious and high-ceilinged room (some are on two levels) has direct access to the beach; bathrooms are heavenly. The view looks west to the Minch and sometimes to the misty islands of the Outer Hebrides on the horizon. Breakfast is served in a room overlooking the seashore and the islands in Loch Dunvegan.

Three Chimneys itself is a simple former crofter's cottage in which stone walls and exposed beams are mixed with modern furniture and fittings. As you would expect, the menu is a mainly fishy one – in the mornings you can watch the fishing boats set off to catch your dinner – but Highland beef, lamb and game are also a feature, and the puddings are just as good.

~

NEARBY Dunvegan Castle; the Cuillins.
LOCATION from Dunvegan take the single-track B884 toward Glendale for 5 miles (8 km); car parking
FOOD breakfast, lunch, dinner
PRICE £££
ROOMS 6 suites, all with bath; all rooms have phone, TV, video, CD player, minibar, hairdrier **FACILITIES** breakfast room; 2 dining rooms, bar, children's play area, yacht mooring
CREDIT CARDS AE, MC, V **CHILDREN** welcome
DISABLED 1 room specially adapted **PETS** not accepted
CLOSED never **PROPRIETORS** Shirley and Eddie Spear

HIGHLANDS AND ISLANDS

COMRIE, PERTHSHIRE

ROYAL HOTEL

~ TOWN INN ~

Melville Square, Comrie, Perthshire PH6 2DN
TEL (01764) 679200 **FAX** (01764) 679219
E-MAIL reception@royalhotel.co.uk **WEBSITE** www.royalhotel.co.uk

ALL TOO OFTEN, town hotels, surviving on a diet of passing trade, show a distinct lack of enthusiasm and a rather blank face to the world; it's only occasionally that we find a new one that excites our interest. Comrie's Royal Hotel is such a one: from the moment you step inside, it feels right. Situated in the centre of this attractive little Highland town, and dating from 1765, it began life as a coaching inn, and earned its grand title after a visit by - who else?- Queen Victoria, accompanied by her servant, John Brown.

The atmosphere is homely, yet at the same time elegant and stylish, with log fires in the public rooms as well as squashy sofas, comfortable armchairs, antiques and oil paintings. There is a Brasserie for informal dining, as well as the main restaurant.

Recent visitors were delighted by their stay, and enthused about the freshness and prettyness of their rooms. All eleven have been individually planned and furnished with a cool eye for detail and design, and a touch of luxury (bathrobes and soaps). The hotel's modish makeover was the brainchild of owner Edward Gibbons, but it is managed by hands-on couple Jerry and Teresa Milson.

~

NEARBY Loch Earn; Glenturret Distillery; Drummond Castle.
LOCATION in centre of Comrie, on A85, about 25 miles (40 km)W of Perth; limited car parking
FOOD breakfast, lunch, dinner; room service
PRICE £££
ROOMS 11; 10 double and twin, 1 suite, all with bath; all rooms have phone, TV, fax/modem point, hairdrier, safe
FACILITIES sitting room, library, 2 dining rooms
CREDIT CARDS AE, MC, V **CHILDREN** accepted
DISABLED access difficult **PETS** accepted
CLOSED never **MANAGERS** Jeremy and Teresa Milson

HIGHLANDS AND ISLANDS

FORT WILLIAM, INVERNESS-SHIRE

THE GRANGE
~ EDGE-OF-TOWN BED-AND-BREAKFAST ~

Grange Road, Fort William, Inverness-shire PH33 6JF
TEL (01397) 705516 **FAX** (01397) 701595
E-MAIL jcampbell@grangefortwilliam.com **WEBSITE** www.thegrange-scotland.co.uk

WE WERE DELIGHTED to discover this outstanding bed-and-breakfast establishment on the outskirts of Fort William, run with great flair by Joan and John Campbell. A ten-minute walk from the fairly charmless town centre brings you to this late Victorian house, set in pretty terraced grounds overlooking Loch Linnhe.

A feminine touch is distinctly in evidence in the immaculate interior, which is decorated with admirable taste and a flair for matching fabrics with furnishings and fittings. First glimpsed, you might expect a stand-offish 'don't touch' approach from the owners, but nothing could be further from the truth at the Grange. Joan Campbell, responsible for the decoration, is naturally easy-going, with a great sense of hospitality.

All four bedrooms are superbly, and individually, decorated and furnished, their bathrooms lavish and luxurious - it all comes as rather a surprise. The Rob Roy room was the one chosen by Jessica Lange, who stayed here during the filming of Rob Roy, while the Terrace Room has, as its name suggests, its own terrace leading on to the gardens. Two of the bedrooms have Louis XV-style king-size beds; all four overlook the garden and Loch Linnhe. A delightful place.

~

NEARBY Ben Nevis; 'Road to the Isles'; Loch Ness.
LOCATION on outskirts; from town centre take A82 direction Glasgow, then turn left into Ashburn Lane; hotel is at top on left; ample car parking
FOOD breakfast
PRICE ££
ROOMS 4 double and twin, 2 with bath and shower, 2 with shower; all rooms have TV, hairdrier **FACILITIES** breakfast room, sitting room; garden, sea loch close by
CREDIT CARDS by arrangement **CHILDREN** not accepted
DISABLED access difficult
PETS not accepted **CLOSED** mid-Nov to Easter
PROPRIETOR Joan and John Campbell

HIGHLANDS AND ISLANDS

GLENLIVET, BANFFSHIRE

MINMORE HOUSE

~ COUNTRY HOUSE HOTEL ~

Glenlivet, Banffshire AB37 9DB
TEL (01807) 590378 **FAX** (01807) 590472
E-MAIL minmorehousehotel@utonline.co.uk **WEBSITE** www.minmorehousehotel.com

WE HAVE ALWAYS been impressed by the friendly, relaxed atmosphere at Minmore House, which continues to be generated by Lynne and Victor Janssen.

It is a solid mid-Victorian family home set in four-and-a-half acres of landscaped gardens. It stands adjacent to the famous Glenlivet whisky distillery, and was the home of George Smith, the distillery's founder. Not surprisingly, whiskey plays its part in the hotel, and the fine oak-panelled bar displays an impressive range of single malts. From the hotel, enthusiasts can follow the signposted Whisky Trail, visiting renowned Speyside whiskey distilleries.

'Proper' Scottish breakfasts, with kippers and smoked haddock, are on offer, as well as complimentary afternoon tea. In the award-winning restaurant, the four-course set dinners (with vegetarian options) have a Scottish bias. The hotel has a tranquil, relaxed atmosphere, with open fires in all the public rooms. With the exception of the two single rooms, the bedrooms and bathrooms are spacious. The Janssens are happy to arrange all manner of activities – golf, shooting, stalking, salmon and trout fishing, walking, and castle and distillery visits.

~

NEARBY Glenlivet Distillery; Ballindalloch Castle.
LOCATION on the B9008, next to the Glenlivet Distillery; in 4.5 acres garden with ample car parking
FOOD breakfast, picnic lunch on request, dinner
PRICE ££
ROOMS 10; 8 double and twin, 2 single, all with bath; all rooms have phone, hairdrier **FACILITIES** 2 sitting rooms, bar, dining room; garden, croquet lawn, tennis court, outdoor heated swimming pool
CREDIT CARDS MC, V **CHILDREN** over 10
DISABLED access difficult **PETS** by arrangement
CLOSED Feb **MANAGERS** Lynne and Victor Janssen

HIGHLANDS AND ISLANDS

ISLE OF ERISKA, ARGYLL

ISLE OF ERISKA HOTEL
~ ISLAND MANSION ~

Isle of Eriska, Ledaig, Oban, Argyll PA37 1SD
TEL (01631) 720371 **FAX** (01631) 720531
E-MAIL office@eriska-hotel.co.uk **WEBSITE** www.eriska-hotel.co.uk

A SPLENDID HOTEL that has the twin advantages of seclusion, since it is set on its own remote island, and accessibility: it is connected to the mainland by a short road bridge. And for those who like to keep themselves occupied during their stay, its leisure centre, which includes a magnificent 17-metre heated swimming pool, and its sporting opportunities, will appeal.

Built in 1884 in grey granite and warmer red sandstone, in Scottish Baronial style, the Buchanan-Smith's hotel is a reminder of a more expansive and confident era. If it reminds you in feel, if not in appearance, of Balmoral, you will not be surprised to learn that the original wallpaper on the first-floor landing is also found in the royal castle. In fact the experience of staying here is very much like being in an old-fashioned grand private house, comfortable rather than stylish, with a panelled great hall, and roaring log fires and chintz fabrics much in evidence. In the library-cum-bar you can browse through the books with a malt whisky in hand, while excellent six-course dinners are served in the stately dining room. The handsome bedrooms vary in size and outlook.

NEARBY Oban; Isle of Mull; Inverary Castle; Glencoe.
LOCATION on private island connected by road bridge; from Connel take A828 toward Fort William for 4 miles (6 km) to N of Benderloch village, then follow signs; ample car parking
FOOD breakfast, dinner
PRICE ££££
ROOMS 17; 12 double and twin, 2 single, 3 family rooms, all with bath; all rooms have phone, hairdrier **FACILITIES** 3 drawing rooms, bar/library, dining room, indoor swimming pool, gym, sauna, garden; 6-hole golf course, driving range, tennis court, croquet, clay-pigeon shooting, watersports
CREDIT CARDS AE, MC, V **CHILDREN** welcome **DISABLED** access possible
PETS accepted **CLOSED** Jan **PROPRIETORS** Buchanan-Smith family

HIGHLANDS AND ISLANDS

ISLE ORNSAY, ISLE OF SKYE

EILEAN IARMAIN

∾ SEAFRONT HOTEL ∾

Isle Ornsay, Sleat, Isle of Skye IV43 8QR
TEL (01471) 833332 **FAX** (01471) 833275
E-MAIL hotel@eileaniarmain.co.uk

HEARING THE SOFT LILT of the voices of the staff is one of the pleasures of a stay at this traditional Skye hotel, and a sure sign that you are in the Western Isles. This is a bi-lingual establishment, and the friendly and welcoming staff are fluent in both Gaelic and English; they wear tags that give their names in both languages.

The hotel is part of an estate belonging to Sir Iain and Lady Noble. Its three buildings are beautifully situated right on the water's edge, on the small rocky bay of Isle Ornsay, looking across the Sound of Sleat to the mainland Knoydart Hills beyond. If you are lucky, you may see otters on the shore.

The hotel's core is a white-painted Victorian inn, which comprises the reception area, two appealing dining rooms and six bedrooms. A further six bedrooms are in a building opposite, while the latest addition, opened in 1999, houses four split-level suites. All the rooms are traditional in character, hospitable and homely, with modern fittings and smart bathrooms. In each is a complimentary miniature bottle of whisky supplied from Sir Iain's distillery. The restaurant specializes in local fish, shellfish and game, and enjoys a local reputation.

∾

NEARBY Clan Donald Centre; Aros Heritage Centre; Dunvegan Castle.
LOCATION on water's edge, on estate between Broadford and Armadale in the S of the island, 20 mins drive from Skye Bridge or Mallaig ferry point; ample car parking
FOOD breakfast, lunch, dinner
PRICE £££
ROOMS 16;12 double, twin or triple, 4 suites; all with bath; all rooms have phone, hairdrier **FACILITIES** sitting room, 2 dining rooms; anchorage for yachts
CREDIT CARDS AE, MC, V **CHILDREN** welcome
DISABLED access possible to suites
PETS accepted **CLOSED** never **PROPRIETOR** Sir Iain Noble

HIGHLANDS AND ISLANDS

KENTALLEN, ARGYLL

ARDSHEAL HOUSE
~ COUNTRY HOUSE ~

Kentallen of Appin, Argyll PA38 4BX
TEL (01631)740227 **FAX** (01631)740342
E-MAIL info@ardsheal.co.uk **WEBSITE** www.ardsheal.co.uk

A RDSHEAL HOUSE is the family home of Neil and Philippa Sutherland, charming hosts who succeed in making their guests entirely at home.

The feeling of well-being begins as soon as you turn off the main road and take a two mile (3 km) single-track private lane that leads to the house on the banks of Loch Linnhe. It was originally built in the early 16th century, but, having been destroyed by fire in the 1745 uprising, was rebuilt in 1760 and extended over the intervening years. The natural woodland, one of the oldest in Scotland, and lovely garden that surrounds it provide a wonderful setting, with many mature trees, shrubs, lawns and flower gardens.

Public rooms are elegant, with antique furniture, paintings, comfortable chairs and sofas, and log fires in the public rooms. The dining room is a light, sunny conservatory and, in Scottish country house tradition, there is a billiard room with full-size table. Bedrooms, full of family antiques and pictures, do not disappoint. Phillippa is an excellent cook, and prepares a daily-changing no-choice menu. In all, a lovely, relaxing place to stay, with superlative views.

~

NEARBY Glencoe; Ben Nevis; Oban; Isle of Mull; Isle of Skye.
LOCATION 17 miles (27 km) SW of Fort William off the A828, in private estate; ample car parking
FOOD breakfast
PRICE ££
ROOMS 3 double and twin, all with bath; all rooms have phone, hairdrier
FACILITIES 2 sitting rooms, billiards room; garden, pebble beach
CREDIT CARDS AE, MC, V
CHILDREN not accepted
DISABLED not accessible **PETS** accepted
CLOSED mid-Dec to mid-Jan
PROPRIETORS Neil and Philippa Sutherland

HIGHLANDS AND ISLANDS

KILCHRENAN, ARGYLL

TAYCHREGGAN

~ LOCHSIDE INN ~

Kilchrenan, by Taynuilt, Argyll PA35 1HQ
TEL (01866) 833211 **FAX** (01866) 833244
E-MAIL info@taychregganhotel.co.uk **WEBSITE** www.taychregganhotel.co.uk

APPROACHED BY a six mile (9.5 km) single-track road, this former drovers' inn, much modernized, is an isolated, utterly peaceful haven, surrounded by 25 acres of garden and natural woodland and lapped by the waters of Loch Awe, with spectacular views. A great place in which to unwind, especially for fishermen: the hotel has its own fishing rights, boats and ghillie and a well-equipped rod room. Riding, deer stalking, rough shooting, watersports and golf can also be arranged.

The core of the hotel is the old stone house, with exposed stone walls inside, and its pretty cobbled courtyard where, on sunny days, you can relax with a drink (an impressive range of malt whiskies is available). The fairly formal, two-part dining room is distinguished by huge arched picture windows that unite the room with the lovely view beyond and makes a memorable setting for dinner. Food is taken seriously, and is very good: inventive and sophisticated, using fresh local produce, with a fine wine list to match.

Bedrooms are all different, contemporary in feel, with some antique pieces. Ask for a loch view, even though you will pay more. The staff here are exemplary.

~

NEARBY Inverary; Loch Lomond; Kilchurn Castle; Western Isles.
LOCATION one mile (2.5 km) E of Taynuilt on A85, take the B845 and follow signs; ample car parking
FOOD breakfast, lunch, dinner
PRICE £££
ROOMS 19; 18 double and twin, 1 suite, all with bath; all rooms have phone, hairdrier **FACILITIES** 2 sitting rooms, TV room, bar, restaurant, conservatory, snooker room; garden, fishing, watersports
CREDIT CARDS AE, MC, V **CHILDREN** accepted over 12
DISABLED access difficult **PETS** accepted by arrangement
CLOSED never **MANAGER** Alastair Stevenson

HIGHLANDS AND ISLANDS

KILLIECRANKIE, PERTHSHIRE

KILLIECRANKIE HOTEL
~ COUNTRY HOUSE HOTEL ~

Killiecrankie, By Pitlochry, Perthshire PH16 5LG
TEL (01796)473220 **FAX** (01796) 472451
E-MAIL enquiries@killiecrankiehotel.co.uk **WEBSITE** www.killiecrankiehotel.co.uk

A SENSIBLE, REASSURING sort of establishment in a delightful setting that somehow encapsulates the modest Scottish country hotel. Built as a manse for a local clergyman in 1840, it stands at the foot of the Pass of Killiecrankie, formed by the River Garry slicing through the surrounding granite hills, and it has its own attractive grounds - a lovely place in which to relax and watch out for wildlife, including red squirrels and roe deer.

The ten straightforward yet comfortable bedrooms are done out in country house fabrics and custom-made furniture and fittings finished in natural pine, lending them a somewhat Scandinavian air. An unexpected touch: beds are turned down each evening. The mahogany-panelled bar is a cosy, convivial place in which to gather for drinks, and a bright conservatory section is set for light lunches and imaginative bar snacks, including a selection of tapas. This is also where guests eat breakfast, overlooking the garden. In the main restaurant, chef Mark Easton, shortlisted for the Chef of Scotland award, prepares a large, mainly vegetarian menu. Special diets are also catered for.

~

NEARBY Pitlochry; Pass of Killiecrankie; Blair Atholl; Glamis.
LOCATION in 4 acres, 3 miles (4.5 km) N of Pitlochry, just off A9 on the B8079; ample car parking
FOOD breakfast, lunch, dinner
PRICE ££
ROOMS 10; 8 double and twin, 2 single, 1 suite, 8 with bath, 2 with shower; all rooms have phone, TV, hairdrier
FACILITIES sitting room, 2 dining rooms, bar, conservatory, garden
CREDIT CARDS MC, V
CHILDREN accepted
DISABLED access possible
PETS not accepted **CLOSED** 3 Jan to 14 Feb
PROPRIETORS Tim and Maillie Waters

HIGHLANDS AND ISLANDS

KINGUSSIE, INVERNESS-SHIRE

THE CROSS
~ RESTAURANT-WITH-ROOMS ~

Tweed Mill Brae, Kingussie, Inverness-shire PH21 1TC
TEL (01540) 661166 **FAX** (01540) 661080
E-MAIL relax@thecross.co.uk **WEBSITE** www.thecross.co.uk

RUTH HADLEY'S inspired cooking had long made her and husband Tony's well-established, award-winning restaurant-with-rooms a must for gourmets. David and Katie Young took over in early 2003 and, in their own words, believe "if it ain't broke, don't fix it." And David should know – he was a chief inspector for the AA. In a secluded four-acre waterside setting, down a private drive, the Cross is a modest former 19thC tweed mill, which houses nine fresh and simple bedrooms as well as the restaurant and a residents' sitting room. A strict no-smoking policy operates in the dining room and bedrooms.

Bedrooms are individually furnished, and include canopied, twin and king-size beds. One has a balcony overlooking the Gynack, which flows alongside the mill, and where you may sometimes see salmon swimming and herons fishing.

The Youngs have also kept chef Becca Henderson on in the kitchen, so the food should continue to be good. We would welcome comments.

~

NEARBY Aviemore; Loch Insh; Highland Folk Museum.
LOCATION from the traffic lights in Kingussie town centre, take Ardbroilach Rd for 300 m, then turn left down Tweed Mill Brae; ample car parking
FOOD breakfast, dinner; room service
PRICE ££
ROOMS 9 double and twin, all with bath; all rooms have phone; hairdrier, TV on request **FACILITIES** sitting room, restaurant; garden
CREDIT CARDS MC, V
CHILDREN not accepted
DISABLED no special facilities
PETS not accepted
CLOSED Dec to Mar
PROPRIETORS David and Katie Young

HIGHLANDS AND ISLANDS

MUIR OF ORD, ROSS-SHIRE

THE DOWER HOUSE

~ COUNTRY HOUSE HOTEL ~

Highfield, Muir of Ord, Ross-shire IV6 7XN
TEL (01463)870090 **FAX** (01463)870090
E-MAIL cshgb@thedowerhouse.co.uk **WEBSITE** www.thedowerhouse.co.uk

THIS FORMER DOWER HOUSE of a baronial home, which burnt down in the 1940s, was converted from thatched farmhouse to charming residence in the Georgian cottage ornée style in about 1800. It became a hotel, run by Robyn and Mena Aitchison as if it were a private house receiving paying guests, in 1989. Something of an oasis in the rugged landscape between the rivers Beauly and Conon, it is set in beautifully maintained mature gardens and grounds.

The elegant, red-walled dining room, with its highly polished mahogany tables, makes a stunning setting for evening meals, and Robyn's self-taught cooking, does not disappoint. Herbs and vegetables are from the garden, eggs from their hens, and meat, game and seafood are all local. The menu offers no choice, though it changes every day. The sitting room has comfortable chairs, flowery fabrics, plenty of books, an open fire and a bar concealed in a cupboard.

The five bedrooms vary in size and furnishings and are fairly simple. The largest is the most luxurious, with an enormous bed and spacious bathroom, while the suite looks on to the pretty garden. All the baths are traditional cast iron, with period fittings.

~

NEARBY Inverness; Culloden; beaches.
LOCATION 1 mile (2.5 km) N of Muir of Ord, 14 miles (22 km) NW of Inverness on the A862 to Dingwall; ample car parking
FOOD breakfast, dinner
PRICE £££
ROOMS 5; 4 double and twin, 3 with bath, 1 with shower, 1 suite with bath; all rooms have phone, TV **FACILITIES** sitting room, dining room; garden
CREDIT CARDS MC, V
CHILDREN accepted by arrangement **DISABLED** 1 room
PETS accepted by arrangement **CLOSED** never
PROPRIETORS Robyn and Mena Aitchison

HIGHLANDS AND ISLANDS

NAIRN, NAIRNSHIRE

CLIFTON HOUSE
~ TOWN HOTEL ~

Viewfield Street, Nairn, Nairnshire IV12 4HW
TEL (01667) 453119 **FAX** (01667) 52836
E-MAIL macintyre@clifton-hotel.co.uk **WEBSITE** www.clifton-hotel.co.uk

ALTHOUGH CLIFTON HOUSE has downgraded considerably (from twelve to four rooms) and no longer stages plays and recitals, fans will be happy to know it hasn't lost its theatrical touch.

The Victorian house is richly furnished to ensure not only the comfort, but also the amusement of guests; paintings fill the walls, flowers fill antique vases, books fill shelves, knick-knacks fill every other nook and cranny. Whatever your mood, one of the public rooms should suit – the drawing room has stunning red, gold and black wallpaper with pomegranite motif, originally designed by Pugin for the Robing Room in the Palace of Westminster. Bedrooms are individually decorated and furnished in what Gordon (with characteristic modesty and humour) calls 'a mixture of good antiques and painted junk'. The bathrooms, however, need upgrading.

Clifton House no longer has a license, so rates include dinner, wine and drinks. Guests sit at one large table, dinner-party style. Dinner starts promptly at 7.30. The cooking imposes French provincial techniques on the best local produce – particularly seafood, upon which lunch in the smaller Green Room is largely based. Typically, breakfast is served without time limit.

Booking is essential.

~

NEARBY Cawdor Castle; Brodie Castle; Culloden.
LOCATION on the sea-front in middle of town, close to A96; ample car parking
FOOD breakfast, dinner
PRICE ££
ROOMS 4 double, all with bath
FACILITIES sitting room, dining room
CREDIT CARDS AE, DC, MC, V
CHILDREN welcome
DISABLED no special facilities **PETS** accepted
CLOSED mid-Dec to late Jan **PROPRIETOR** J Gordon Macintyre

HIGHLANDS AND ISLANDS

PITLOCHRY, PERTHSHIRE

KNOCKENDARROCH
~ TOWN MANSION ~

Higher Oakfield, Pitlochry, Perthshire PH16 5HT
TEL (01796) 473473 **FAX** (01796) 474068
E-MAIL info@knockendarroch.co.uk **WEBSITE** www.knockendarroch.co.uk

PITLOCHRY IS A particularly agreeable Highland town, and Knockendarroch House is the place to stay. Built in 1880 for an Aberdeen advocate, it displays more château-esque elegance than Scottish Baronial pomp. It stands on a plateau above the town, surrounded by mature oaks (its Gaelic name means Hill of Oaks).

Furnished in careful good taste, the house feels gracious and welcoming. There are two interconnecting sitting rooms in which to relax, with green ceilings, white cornices and pastel green curtains and carpets – all very soothing. The dining room is light and spacious, with many windows and some attractive furniture. The cooking draws praise, but we would like reports, please. Hosts Tony and Jane Ross, who are professional hoteliers, offer a glass of complimentary sherry to guests as they choose their evening meal.

All the bedrooms have views; those from the second floor are spectacular. They are all well furnished and two have small balconies.

Guests attending the famous Pitlochry Festival Theatre (which began here at Knockendarroch) are served an early dinner, and a courtesy bus is laid on to take them to and from the town. Non-smoking throughout.

~

NEARBY Blair Castle; Killiecrankie Pass; Loch Tummel.
LOCATION close to town centre, 26 miles (41 km) N of Perth on A9; ample car parking
FOOD breakfast, dinner
PRICE ££
ROOMS 12 double and twin, all with bath; all rooms have phone, TV, hairdrier, radio
FACILITIES 2 sitting rooms, dining room; garden
CREDIT CARDS MC, V
CHILDREN accepted over 12
DISABLED access limited
PETS not accepted
CLOSED mid-Nov to 1 Mar **PROPRIETORS** Tony and Jane Ross

HIGHLANDS AND ISLANDS

PORT APPIN, ARGYLL

AIRDS HOTEL
~ FERRY INN ~

Port Appin, Argyll PA38 4DF
TEL (01631) 730236 **FAX** (01631) 730535
E-MAIL airds@airds-hotel.com **WEBSITE** www.airds-hotel.com

THE OWNERS of this old ferry inn on the shores of Loch Linnhe have very sensibly taken every advantage of its superb location: the dining room, the conservatory and many bedrooms face the loch. To capitalize further, they have also created, across the road, an attractive lawn and rose garden in which guests can sit and admire the view across the loch to the island of Lismore. The sunsets here are stunning.

Despite its fairly ordinary exterior, Airds Hotel is a smart and decorous establishment, impeccably run and maintained. The interior is elegant, with two sitting rooms prettily furnished with comfortable chairs, deep-pile carpets and open fires. Rooms are full of flowers and books, and paintings are in abundance. Each of the bedrooms is individually decorated and carefully furnished, with very comfortable bathrooms. Each day the dinner menu and wine list is left in your room, so that you can consult it at leisure, give your orders by late afternoon, and relax before dinner with an aperitif, confident that there will be no unnecessary delays. The dining room is somewhat formal and hushed, but the food, cooked by chef Paul Burns, is highly praised and often features such local delicacies as Lismore oysters, smoked salmon or venison.

~

NEARBY Oban; Glencoe; 'Road to the Isles'; Ben Nevis.
LOCATION between Ballachulish and Connel, 2 miles (3 km) off A828; ample car parking
FOOD breakfast, light lunch, dinner; room service
PRICE ££££
ROOMS 12; 11double and twin, one suite, all with bath; all rooms have phone, TV, hairdrier **FACILITIES** 2 sitting rooms, conservatory, dining room, garden, shingle beach
CREDIT CARDS MC, V **CHILDREN** accepted
DISABLED no special facilities **PETS** accepted by arrangement
CLOSED mid to end-Dec; last three weeks Jan
PROPRIETORS Jenny and Shaun Mc Kivragan

HIGHLANDS AND ISLANDS

PORTREE, ISLE OF SKYE

VIEWFIELD HOUSE

~ COUNTRY GUESTHOUSE ~

Portree, Isle of Skye, IV51 9EU
TEL (01478) 612217 **FAX** (01478) 613517
E-MAIL info@viewfieldhouse.com **WEBSITE** www.viewfieldhouse.com

'IT WON'T SUIT EVERYONE,' writes our reporter about Viewfield House, 'but for those seeking an age gone by, the experience would be memorable.'

This is an imposing Victorian country mansion, which, as the name suggests, has some fine views from its elevated position. The need for costly repairs to the roof prompted Evelyn Macdonald, Hugh's grandmother, to open Viewfield House to guests. The delight of it is that the distinctive character of the house was preserved; and though you will not lack for comfort or service, a stay here is likely to be a novel experience. The house is full of colonial memorabilia: stuffed animals, and birds; priceless museum relics; and a magnificent collection of oil paintings and prints.

The rooms are original, right down to the wallpaper in one instance (though all but a couple now have en suite bathrooms in the former dressing-rooms); there is a classic Victorian parlour and a grand dining room with two huge wooden tables. Guests are entertained house-party style, although separate tables can be arranged if they prefer not to dine communally – we admire this flexibility. There is a five-course fixed menu, but individual needs can be met. The food, cooked by Linda and Hugh Macdonald, is hearty, traditional and plentiful.

~

NEARBY Trotternish peninsula.
LOCATION on outskirts of town, 10 minutes walk S of centre; from A87 towards Broadford, turn right just after BP garage on left; with ample car parking
FOOD breakfast, packed lunch, dinner
PRICE ££
ROOMS 12 double and twin, 10 with bath; all rooms have phone, radio, hairdrier
FACILITIES sitting room, dining room, TV room, washer and tumble drier for guests
CREDIT CARDS MC, V **CHILDREN** welcome **DISABLED** one specially adapted room on ground floor **PETS** accepted, but not in public rooms
CLOSED mid-Oct to mid-Apr **PROPRIETORS** Hugh and Linda Macdonald

HIGHLANDS AND ISLANDS

SCARISTA, HARRIS, WESTERN ISLES

SCARISTA HOUSE
~ ISLAND GUESTHOUSE ~

Isle of Harris, Western Isles HS3 3HX
TEL (01859) 550238 **FAX** (01859)550277
E-MAIL timandpatricia@scaristahouse.com **WEBSITE** www.scaristahouse.com

HARRIS HAS LITTLE in the way of hotels, but Scarista would stand out even among the country houses of the Cotswolds.

The converted Georgian manse stands alone on a windswept slope overlooking a wide stretch of tidal sands on the island's western shore. The decoration is elegant and quite formal, with many antiques, but the atmosphere is relaxed and, by the open peat fires, conversation replaces television. The bedrooms, all with private bathrooms, have selected teas and fresh coffee, as well as home-made biscuits. Most of them are in a new single-storey building; the one in the house itself is non-smoking.

Tim and Patricia Martin have taken over from the previous owners and continue to maintain a high standard. They aim to be welcoming and efficient, but never intrusive, and to preserve that precious private home atmosphere.

One of Scarista's greatest attractions, particularly rewarding after a long walk over the sands, is the meals. The imaginatively prepared fresh local and garden produce and an impressive wine list ensure a memorable dinner in the candle-lit dining room.

~

NEARBY beaches; golf; boat trips.
LOCATION 15 miles (24 km) SW of Tarbert on A859, over-looking sea; in 2-acre garden, with ample private car parking
FOOD breakfast, packed/snack lunch, dinner
PRICE £££
ROOMS 3 double, 2 twin, all with bath; all rooms have phone, hairdrier
FACILITIES library, 2 sitting rooms, dining room
CREDIT CARDS MC, V
CHILDREN welcome over 8
DISABLED no special facilities
PETS by arrangement **CLOSED** Christmas
PROPRIETORS Tim and Patricia Martin

HIGHLANDS AND ISLANDS

SLEAT, ISLE OF SKYE

KINLOCH LODGE

~ COUNTRY HOTEL ~

Sleat, Isle of Skye, Highland IV43 8QY
TEL (01471) 833214 **FAX** (01471) 833277
E-MAIL kinloch@dial.pipex.com **WEBSITE** www.kinloch-lodge.co.uk

THIS WHITE-PAINTED stone house, in an isolated position with uninterrupted sea views, at the southern extremity of the Isle of Skye, was built as a farmhouse around 1700 and later became a shooting lodge. But it escaped the baronial treatment handed out to many such houses – 'thank goodness,' says Lady Macdonald, whose style is modern interior-designer rather than dark panelling and tartan. The house has that easy-going private-house air. The guests' sitting rooms are comfortably done out in stylishly muted colours; there are open fires, and family oil paintings grace the walls. The dining room is more formal, with sparkling crystal and silver on polished tables. All but three of the bedrooms are undeniably on the small side. Since our last visit, the Macdonalds have built the New House with accommodation for themselves and five more double rooms for guests . New House is quite remarkable as it looks, both inside and out, as old as the Lodge, and includes a magnificent stone spiral staircase, as wells as a wealth of books, portraits and *objets d'art*.

The food at Kinloch Lodge is renowned – Lady Macdonald has written cookery books and gives cookery demonstrations. We would welcome reports on the food.

~

NEARBY Clan Donald Centre.
LOCATION in 60-acre grounds, 6 miles (9.5 km) S of Broadford, one mile (1.5 km) off A851; ample car parking
FOOD breakfast, lunch by arrangement, dinner
PRICE ££
ROOMS 15 double, all with bath; all rooms have TV, radio, hairdrier
FACILITIES 3 sitting rooms, bar, dining room; fishing
CREDIT CARDS AE, MC, V
CHILDREN accepted **DISABLED** access reasonable – one ground-floor bedroom
PETS accepted by arrangement but not in public rooms
CLOSED Christmas **PROPRIETORS** Lord & Lady Macdonald

HIGHLANDS AND ISLANDS

CORRIEGOUR LODGE
~ LOCHSIDE HOTEL ~

Loch Lochy, by Spean Bridge, Inverness-shire PH34 4EB
TEL (01397) 712685 **FAX** (01397) 712696
E-MAIL info@corriegour-lodge-hotel.com **WEBSITE** www.corriegour-lodge-hotel.com

A FORMER VICTORIAN hunting lodge commanding outstanding views over Loch Lochy and set in six acres of mature woodland and garden within the 'Great Glen'. With its own attractive private beach and jetty on the loch, as well as a fishing boat and the services of a private fishing school at its disposal, this is an obvious choice for keen anglers, as well walkers and climbers, pony trekkers and sailors.

The reception hall at Corriegour Lodge is somewhat gloomy, but negative first impressions are quickly dispelled when the proprietor, Christian Drew, comes on the scene. Her friendliness and enthusiasm for the hotel she runs with her son, Ian, are infectious. The decoration throughout the rest of the hotel is cosy and pleasant, with a log fire in the sitting room and magical views over the loch from the large picture windows in the restaurant. Many of the comfortable bedrooms have the same view.

Food is an important element here, using local meat, fish and game. For pudding you could have cloutie dumpling with rum custard. The staff are genuinely friendly and willing to help.

More reports please.

~

NEARBY Cawdor Castle; Urquhart Castle; Loch Ness; Glencoe.
LOCATION on the road to Skye, between Spean Bridge and Invergarry, in own grounds, 17 miles (27 km) N of Fort William on A82; ample car parking
FOOD breakfast, dinner
PRICE ££
ROOMS 9; 7 double and twin, 2 single, all with bath; all rooms have TV, hairdrier on request **FACILITIES** sitting room, bar, dining room, terrace, private beach and jetty, fishing, waterfall
CREDIT CARDS AE, DC, MC, V **CHILDREN** accepted over 8
DISABLED access possible **PETS** not accepted
CLOSED Dec and Jan, weekdays Feb and Nov, open for New Year
PROPRIETORS Ian and Christian Drew

HIGHLANDS AND ISLANDS

STRACHUR, ARGYLL

CREGGANS INN
~ LOCHSIDE INN ~

Strachur, Argyll PA27 8BX
TEL (01369) 860279 **FAX** (01369) 860637
E-MAIL info@creggans-inn.co.uk **WEBSITE** www.creggans-inn.co.uk

OVERLOOKING LOCH FYNE, this former hunting lodge of the 3000-acre Strachur Estate was first opened as an inn some 40 years ago by Sir Fitzroy Maclean. His son, Sir Charles Maclean, set out to transform a fairly simple establishment into something rather more sophisticated, with high standards of modern comfort. The Robertson family, from a small hotel on the isle of Mull, have taken over and done refurbishment that included knocking out some walls to create larger (and fewer) rooms.

A major natural advantage is the position of the inn. The views over Loch Fyne and across the Mull of Kintyre to the Western Isles are breathtaking. Many parts of the Strachur Estate, including the private flower garden, are open to guests and a wealth of country activities is available.

The comfortable bedrooms are best described as homely rather than elegant and finding your way around the maze of corridors can be tricky after a glass or two. Reports on chef Alex Dickson's cooking are excellent: drawing heavily on local products such as scallops and langoustines from Loch Fyne, it is light, inventive and delicious. The wine list is unusually good and well priced.

~

NEARBY Inverary town and castle; Loch Fyne; Loch Lomond.
LOCATION on E shore of Loch Fyne; from Glasgow via Loch Lomond and the A83, or from Gourock by car ferry across the Clyde to Dunoon and the A815; ample car parking
FOOD breakfast, lunch, dinner
PRICE ££
ROOMS 14; 13 double and twin, one suite, all with bath; all rooms have phone, TV, hairdrier **FACILITIES** 2 sitting rooms, bar, restaurant, garden, country sports
CREDIT CARDS MC, V
CHILDREN welcome
DISABLED access difficult **PETS** not accepted **CLOSED** never
PROPRIETORS The Robertson family

HIGHLANDS AND ISLANDS

STRONTIAN, ARGYLL

KILCAMBE LODGE

~ LOCHSIDE HOTEL ~

Strontian, Argyll PH36 4HY
TEL (01967) 402257 **FAX** (01967) 402041
E-MAIL enquiries@kilcambelodge.com **WEBSITE** www.kilcambelodge.com

THERE IS A SENSE of adventure in travelling to a hotel by ferry, particularly when it then involves a ten-mile journey, first alongside a loch and then over a pass through a steep-sided glen. Drop down through the glen, pass through the small village of Strontian, and there, in a romantic setting on the shores of Loch Sunart, is Kilcambe Lodge.

Originally built in the early 18thC, with Victorian additions, Kilcambe is a beautifully restored country house with ten bedrooms, each with a loch view. Set amidst lawns and woodland, filled in spring with the colours of rhododendrons, azaleas and many wild flowers, it is a romantic and calming bolthole, the perfect choice for nature lovers: sea otters, seals, pine martens, red and roe deer and golden eagles can all be seen.

The ground floor public rooms are pleasantly furnished with light and attractive pastel fabrics. There is a wonderful Victorian wrought-iron staircase and a large stained glass window. All the bedrooms are individually decorated and have triple-lined curtains (it stays light very late in summer). To cap it all, chef Neil Mellis has won awards for his admirable cooking. Non smoking throughout.

~

NEARBY ferry to Isle of Mull and Skye; Castle Tioram; Glencoe.
LOCATION Corran ferry to Ardgour from the A82 near Ballachulish, then follow A861 to Strontian; in 19 acres with ample car parking
FOOD breakfast, light lunch, dinner
PRICE ££
ROOMS 11; 10 double and twin, all with bath, one single with shower; all rooms have TV, hairdrier, phone **FACILITIES** 2 sitting rooms, bar, restaurant, garden, private beach, fishing, mountain bikes
CREDIT CARDS MC, V
CHILDREN welcome
DISABLED no special facilities **CLOSED** never
PETS accepted by arrangement **PROPRIETORS** Ian and Jenny

HIGHLANDS AND ISLANDS

WALLS, SHETLAND ISLANDS

BURRASTOW HOUSE
~ SEAFRONT GUESTHOUSE ~

Walls, Shetland Islands, ZE2 9PD
TEL (01595) 809307 **FAX** (01595) 809213
E-MAIL burr.hs@zetnet.co.uk **WEBSITE** www.users.zetnet.co.uk/burrastow-house

O**N THE REMOTE WEST** side of Shetland, at the end of the single track road, on a rocky promontory overlooking Vaila Sound and the Island of Vaila, stands this calm, solid 18thC stone house. It has been a guest-house since 1980, and for the last 12 years has been run with enthusiasm by Bo Simmons, along with her husband, Henry Anderton. In 1995 an extension was built to accommodate three more en-suite bedrooms. Peace, quiet, a love of nature and total informality are the keynotes here.

The original bedrooms in the compact main house are the ones to go for if you can. Both are large, and one has a second bedroom which is perfect for children. There are splendid beds in each: a four-poster in one and a half-tester, draped in blue silk, in the other. The newer bedrooms have less character, but they're comfortable. In the public rooms there are peat fires, books, an eclectic mix of furnishings and wonderful views from the windows; you may spy seals and otters. Bo has made her mark with her natural, homely cooking, and has written a cook book, *A Taste of Burrastow*. Dinners, which feature four courses with a choice of dishes, are served in the cosy panelled dining room. Burrastow House is quietly on the market, but it is business as usual until it sells.

~

NEARBY Vaila Sound; Walls.
LOCATION on sea, 2 miles (3 km) W of Walls; ample car parking
FOOD breakfast, light/packed lunch, dinner
PRICE ££
ROOMS 5; 4 double and twin, one family suite, 4 with bath, 1 with shower; TV, hairdrier on request **FACILITIES** dining room, 2 sitting rooms; boat for exploring area, civil wedding license
CREDIT CARDS AE, MC, V **CHILDREN** welcome
DISABLED access possible; one room specially adapted
PETS accepted by arrangement **CLOSED** Jan, Feb
PROPRIETOR Bo Simmons

IRELAND

AREA INTRODUCTION

With a temperate climate and a famously leisurely way of life, Ireland (also known in tourist literature as the Emerald Isle) is a place of contrasts and changing light, of mountains, lakes and rivers, lush pastures, bog and wild moorland, and 2,000 miles of coastline with small rocky coves, long sandy beaches, and some of the highest cliffs in Europe. In the most remote parts of the country, you can drive for miles without seeing anything but sheep. But if you want bright lights, music and good food, Ireland has any number of pubs that nightly celebrate the traditional Irish love of music and conversation, and excellent chefs to cook the abundant produce of their native land. Ireland also has a wealth of charming places to stay, and for this new edition of the guide, we have much expanded the section to include many more than previously: hotels, castles, great houses, country houses, converted cottages and stables, farmhouses, town houses, guest-houses and restaurants-with-rooms. Northern Ireland, shunned for years by travellers because of the troubles, may now develop into a popular holiday destination: as we went to press, the political situation looked calmer, but the future was by no means certain. Our recommendations here include The Bushmill Inn (page 312), just a mile from the famous Giant's Causeway; the serene island hotel, St Ernan's House (page 314) on the rugged Donegal coast; Dean's Hill, a delightful guest-house in the ecclesiastical city of Armagh (page 309); and homely and welcoming Ash-Rowan Lodge, in the Victorian boom town, Belfast (page 310). The spectacular natural beauty of the Irish Republic is legendary, from the rich farmlands, woodlands, fertile valleys and golden beaches of Counties Wicklow and Wexford in the east to the unspoilt coastlines of West Cork and Kerry, the romantic Lakes of Killarney, and the hills and lakes of County Sligo in the west. For a treat, try Marlfield House (page 354), in County Wexford; the romantic lakeside Ard-na-Sidhe (page 331) or Temple House (page 328). Brownes Brasserie and Townhouse stands out (page 345) among a surge of new hotels in the flourishing Georgian city of Dublin.

NORTHERN IRELAND

ARMAGH, CO ARMAGH

DEAN'S HILL

~ TOWN GUEST-HOUSE ~

College Hill, Armagh, Co Armagh BT61 9DF
TEL (028) 3752 4923 **FAX** (028) 3752 4923

THERE HAVE BEEN Armstrongs in this lovely Georgian house in the ecclesiastical city of Armagh since 1870. It was built for the cathedral's dean in 1760 and, although the setting is rural, is only ten minutes walk from the historical centre of Armagh. A stone gatehouse on the road draws visitors up the long, gently curving driveway leading through green, daffodil-strewn fields, with mature trees and a large Cedar of Lebanon in the rambling garden. Inside, the welcoming, easy-going house attractively wears its patina of age, with what our inspector (most enthusiastically) describes as 'gorgeous' antique furniture, paintings and prints. Some of the tall, sash windows still carry their original glass, there are long white shutters and old floorboards covered with slightly worn carpets. Rugs are thrown over the easy chairs in the comfortable, relaxed sitting room and the huge bedrooms are wonderfully old-fashioned and elegant. One has a single brass bedstead, and plenty of pictures hung, slightly crookedly, on the walls; another has dusky pink curtains and a wallpaper of climbing roses. The bathrooms, again, are old-fashioned, with pretty papers, prints and washstands. For breakfast, there is home-made jam and fresh eggs from the Armstrong farm.

~

NEARBY Armagh Planetarium; cathedral, museums.
LOCATION half a mile (0.8 km) from the town centre on A3 towards Craigavon – turn left at stone gate lodge; parking
FOOD breakfast
PRICE €
ROOMS 3; 1 four-poster with bath, 1 twin with bath, 1 single with private bath
FACILITIES gardens, tennis court, boules
CREDIT CARDS none
CHILDREN welcome
DISABLED not suitable **PETS** with advance warning
CLOSED Christmas and New Year **PROPRIETORS** Jill and Edward Armstrong

NORTHERN IRELAND

BELFAST

ASH-ROWAN LODGE
～ TOWN GUEST-HOUSE ～

b12 Windsor Avenue, Belfast BT9 6EE
TEL (028) 90661758 **FAX** (028) 9066 3227
E-MAIL ashrowan@hotmail.com

SAM AND EVELYN HAZLETT were restaurateurs and love good food and feeding people. The generous breakfasts at this comfortable, friendly, informal place keep you going throughout the day. We noted nine solid dishes on the menu, including mushrooms on toast, flambéed in sherry and with cream, kedgeree in ramekin dishes with cream and a 'hint of cumin', and variations on the Ulster Fry theme, depending on how faint-hearted you are feeling. The Hazletts' attractive Victorian family house stands in a tree-lined residential road and the welcoming hosts are especially popular with classical musicians making guest appearances with the Ulster Orchestra, most probably because of the homely atmosphere.

Each bedroom is decorated in an individual style: they are all comfortable and full of bits and pieces, as is the entire house. All have dressing gowns, and crisp Irish linens on beds. Some have antiques, some newer wicker furniture. Prettier, quite spacious rooms at the top of the house have sloping attic ceilings, old white crocheted bedspreads, armchairs, plants, mixed colours. There are plenty of family 'things' in corridors and on landings: books, ornaments, a bird cage, old mirrors and porcelain, and dried flowers. A conservatory extension was being planned when we visited; it may now already be built and nicely filling up with 'things'.

～

NEARBY Ulster Museum; Botanic Gardens; Queen's University.
LOCATION in residential street between the Malone and Lisburn roads; 1 mile (1.6 km) S of the city centre; private car parking available
FOOD breakfast, dinner on request
PRICE €€
ROOMS 5; 3 double/twin, 2 single, 3 with bath, 2 with shower; all with phone, TV, hairdrier, trouser press; safe on request **FACILITIES** sitting room
CREDIT CARDS AE, MC, V **CHILDREN** over 12
DISABLED not suitable **PETS** not accepted
CLOSED 22 Dec to 6 Jan **PROPRIETORS** Sam and Evelyn Hazlett

NORTHERN IRELAND

BELFAST

THE McCAUSLAND HOTEL
~ CITY HOTEL ~

34-38 Victoria Street, Belfast, BT1 3GH
TEL (028) 9022 0200 **FAX** (028) 9022 0220
E-MAIL info@mccauslandhotel.com **WEBSITE** www.mccauslandhotel.com

ALTHOUHGH MUCH LARGER than any of our other recommendations, we have made an exception for this stylish, interesting new hotel in the central Laganside quarter of Belfast, which opened in December 1998. Once two Victorian seed warehouses belonging to rival firms, the listed Italianate building with ornate carved stonework on the facade has been rescued from dereliction and given a smart, sophisticated, contemporary interior. Ground floor public rooms have the original columns and high beamed ceilings; the reception area positively glows, with light wood, pale, honey coloured stone floors and subtle lighting. Lofty palm trees decorate the hotel's attractive Marco Polo café bar and the restaurant has light parquet flooring, tall black columns and arched windows. The spaces and the architectural features of these handsome old commercial buildings lend themselves pleasingly and naturally to a new use. Warm, muted colours are used for the business like, comfortable bedrooms; larger rooms have sofas and armchairs; top rooms have city skyline views. All have CD players. Our inspector was very taken with the brightly-lit, black an white tiled bathrooms; shiny chrome fixtures and fluffy apricot coloured towels. There are special rooms for women.

~

NEARBY major galleries, theatres, shopping; Waterfront Hall.
LOCATION in centre, NE of City Hall and on west bank of river; street car parking and private car parking available.
FOOD breakfast, lunch, dinner
PRICE €€€
ROOMS 61; 31 double/twin, 15 singles; all with bath, 5 with shower; all rooms with phone, TV, radio, hairdrier, trouser press, safe; 15 suites, all with bath and shower
FACILITIES restaurant, bar, conference facilities, sitting room.
CREDIT CARDS AE, DC, MC, V
CHILDREN accepted **DISABLED** 3 rooms with bath **PETS** small **CLOSED** 24 to 28 Dec
PROPRIETORS Michelle Hislop

NORTHERN IRELAND

THE BUSHMILLS INN
~ CONVERTED COACHING INN ~

25 Main Street, Bushmills, Co Antrim BT57 8QA
TEL (028) 2073 2339 **FAX** (028) 2073 2048
E-MAIL mail@bushmillsinn.com **E-MAIL** www.bushmillsinn.com

IT IS DIFFICULT to believe that chickens once lived on the first floor when this charming little inn, only a mile from the Giant's Causeway, was going through hard times. All that changed in 1987 when the present owners spotted the potential of the building. The oldest part – now the restaurant – dates back to the early 17th century when the nearby Old Bushmills Distillery was granted the world's first licence to distil whiskey. The entrance, through an archway from the street into the courtyard, leads to the front door in a little whitewashed round tower. Almost the first thing to be seen, once inside, is a glowing turf fire, which is always lit. A series of attractive ground-floor rooms includes a small 'snug' – the original kitchen – with a roaring fire and old flagstones; the Victorian-style bar has gas lighting, leather chairs, dark wood panelling and a wooden floor. Bedrooms come in two varieties: older ones, furnished in comfortable cottage style are in the inn itself; newer ones in the Mill House extension – with river views – are larger, with natural wood panelling, rough white walls and their own sitting area. There are plenty of strategically-placed rocking chairs in which to savour a bedtime slug of one of the classic malts from up the road.

~

NEARBY Giant's Causeway; Glens of Antrim; golf at Royal Portrush.
LOCATION in main street of village on A2, 5 miles (8 km) E of Portrush; parking
FOOD breakfast, lunch, dinner
PRICE €€
ROOMS 32; 28 double (22 twin); 24 with bath, 26 with shower; 4 singles with shower; all with phone, TV; 22 with hairdrier, trouser press, computer socket
FACILITIES bar, restaurant, sitting rooms; terrace, garden
CREDIT CARDS AE, MC
CHILDREN welcome **DISABLED** adapted bedroom
PETS accepted; not in restaurant
CLOSED never **PROPRIETORS** Roy Bolton

NORTHERN IRELAND

CLONES, CO MONAGHAN

HILTON PARK
~ COUNTRY HOUSE ~

Clones, Co Monaghan
TEL (047) 56007 **FAX** (047) 56033
E-MAIL mail@hiltonpark.ie **WEBSITE** www.hiltonpark.ie

IN THE HIDDEN IRELAND group of country houses taking paying guests is Hilton Park – home of the Madden family since 1734 and remodelled in the Italianate manner in the 1870s. It is grand, beautiful, and most evocative of the great days of the Irish country house. Johnny Madden emerges out of his huge front door under the portico to greet guests and carries baggage into the hall and up the panelled staircase. A wizard with bacon, he prepares breakfast, which is served in the old servants' hall below stairs. He and his wife Lucy, a food writer and accomplished cook, are memorably delightful hosts. Many family stories are to be told about the guest bedrooms: one was Johnny's when he was a child.

Little seems to have changed over the years. The wallpaper in the Blue Room, with a four-poster bed and stunning view down to the lake, was put up in 1830. On our visit, the lace curtains had just come out of a box opened for the first time since 1927. Next door, a roll-top bath, marble washstand, print of Landseer's *Hunters at Grass*, and the scent of jasmine from plants in pots arranged at the foot of the tall window, all add to the grace and charm. Lucy's dinner is by candlelight, with fresh produce from her organic garden.

~

NEARBY Castle Coole and Florence Court (National Trust); Armagh. **LOCATION** 3 miles (5 km) S of Clones, near Clones Golf Club; in 500 acres of parkland, woods, lakes; car parking
FOOD breakfast, dinner
PRICE €€€
ROOMS 6; 5 double, 1 twin; all with bath; all rooms have hairdrier, electric blankets and hot water bottles. **FACILITIES** gardens; games room; grand piano; pike and brown trout fishing; rods; boating on lake **CREDIT CARDS** AE, MC, V
CHILDREN over 7 by arrangement **DISABLED** not possible **PETS** by arrangement
CLOSED end Sept to end Mar except weekends
PROPRIETORS Johnny and Lucy Madden

NORTHERN IRELAND

DONEGAL, CO DONEGAL

ST ERNAN'S HOUSE HOTEL

~ ISLAND HOTEL ~

St Ernan's Island, Donegal, Co Donegal
TEL (07497) 21065 **FAX** (07497) 22098
E-MAIL info@sainternans.com **WEBSITE** www.sainternans.com

T HIS SMALL SUGAR-PINK hotel on a wooded island caters for those who want peace and quiet and is tireless in striving for perfection. On a part of the Donegal coastline that has a natural serenity, the house was built in the 1820s by a nephew of the Duke of Wellington for his sick wife, who needed sea air to cure her of a debilitating cough. More recently a retirement home for clergy and a restaurant-with-rooms, it was bought in 1987 by banker Brian O'Dowd and his wife, Carmel, a teacher, who have gradually been restoring it to the country house it once was. The pursuit – and entrapment – of peace and quiet has produced a most pleasing and civilized result. And four-star comfort. From almost every window there is a view of mesmerising, still water, and Carmel has filled the house with antiques, pictures and pretty fabrics. The most coveted bedroom is the cosy attic, with views down over water and trees. The tone of the place is immediately set by the fact that there are no tables or chairs for sitting outside. The dress code prohibits sandals and shorts; there's no TV downstairs, either. A leisurely five-course meal in the evening rounds off the day. "A strange little breed" says Mrs O'Dowd, affectionately, of the peace and quiet *aficionados*. Wise, too.

~

NEARBY Donegal Town, 2 miles (3 km); Sligo, 42 miles (67.5 km).
LOCATION 2 miles out of Donegal on the N15; follow signposts; parking
FOOD breakfast, dinner
PRICE €€
ROOMS 12; all double/twin; all with bath/shower, 3 with full shower; all with phone, TV, radio, hairdrier
FACILITIES gardens, woodland and shore walks
CREDIT CARDS MC, V
CHILDREN not under 6
DISABLED not possible **PETS** not accepted **CLOSED** end Oct to mid-Apr
PROPRIETORS Brian and Carmel O'Dowd

NORTHERN IRELAND

DUNGANNON, CO TYRONE

GRANGE LODGE
~ COUNTRY HOUSE ~

Grange Road, Dungannon, Co Tyrone BT71 7EJ
TEL (028) 87784212 **FAX** (028) 87784313
E-MAIL grangelodge@nierland.com

OUR REPORTER was enchanted by the setting – on a little hill in large and lovely gardens – of this rambling, ivy clad, Georgian house with later additions. But it is the Grange Lodge table that has won distinction and found it so many friends. Norah Brown, who is self-taught, has several awards for her outstandingly good cooking and she and her husband, Ralph, are relaxed, easy-going, welcoming hosts. Much of the fruit, vegetables and herbs she uses are homegrown and sometimes a second dining room is opened up to outside groups looking for her special talent and dishes from her "best friend", the Aga. Admirers praise the ageless quality of her food and her sure touch; she says people have just forgotten what real home cooking is. Her husband has the happy task of bringing breakfast out from the kitchen: try Mrs Brown's porridge with brown sugar, cream and Bushmills whiskey, rhubarb compote, soda bread and Ulster grill with potato cake. The sitting room – there's a 'den' with TV, too – is immaculate, in elegant dark colours; most surfaces are crammed with ornaments, family photos, pewter and plates. Upstairs, ivy pushes at the window panes of the bedrooms. Some of Mrs Brown's biscuits are always to be found on the hospitality tray.

NEARBY Tyrone; Ulster American Folk Park
LOCATION in countryside 3 miles (5 km) S of Dungannon off the A 29 to Armagh; parking available
FOOD breakfast, dinner
PRICE €
ROOMS 5; 3 doubles, 1 twin, 1 single; 1 with bath, 1 with hip-bath, 3 with shower; all with phone, TV, hairdrier, tea/coffee making facilities
FACILITIES sitting rooms; gardens
CREDIT CARDS MC, V
CHILDREN over 12 **DISABLED** not possible **PETS** welcome outside
CLOSED 20 Dec to 1 Feb **PROPRIETORS** Norah and Ralph Brown

NORTHERN IRELAND

DUNKINEELY, CO DONEGAL

CASTLE MURRAY HOUSE
~ COUNTRY RESTAURANT-WITH-ROOMS ~

St John's Point, Dunkineely, Co Donegal
TEL (07497) 37022 **FAX** (07497) 37330
E-MAIL castlemurray@eircom.net WEBSITE www.castlemurray.com

ON OUR VISIT, this, despite all the accolades, was up for sale. The dynamic, gifted young couple, Claire Delcros and her chef husband, Thierry, who turned a small farmhouse into a thriving business with a considerable reputation, were planning to return to France. The longer it takes, the better it will be for anyone who has not yet enjoyed this charming little place. The setting could be called magical. In front of the hotel, bright green fields with low, drystone walls run down to the sea and a small ruined castle on the point is illuminated as night falls. Across the bay, the sun goes down over the Slieve League, the highest sea cliffs in Europe. Thierry's very French restaurant has the best food in the area, beams, flagged floor, exposed stone walls, lobsters pottering about in a tank by the raised, open fire, and – a typical Mme Delcros touch – Donegal tweed curtains. Up a pine staircase, bedrooms are basic, and remind one of any small French hotel. Our inspector noted matching curtains, bedspread and window seat cushions in *eau-de-nil* checks, a print of a Normandy seaside resort, and one rough wall and another in a rose-strewn paper. Verdant foliage rampages through the small enclosed terrace downstairs; game birds adorn the bar.

~

NEARBY Donegal.
LOCATION a mile (1.6 km) off the main N56 from Donegal to Killybegs, signposted in Dunkineely; parking
FOOD breakfast, dinner
PRICE €€
ROOMS 10 (9 with sea view); 5 double, 5 twin; 2 with bath, 2 with shower; all with phone, TV, hairdrier, tea/coffee making facilities
FACILITIES bar; garden, terrace
CREDIT CARDS MC, V
CHILDREN welcome **DISABLED** not possible **PETS** small dogs in rooms
CLOSED end Jan to beginning Feb **PROPRIETORS** Martin and Marguerite Howley

NORTHERN IRELAND

ARDNAMONA
~ COUNTRY HOUSE ~

Lough Eske, Co Donegal
TEL (07497) 22650 **FAX** (07497) 22819
E-MAIL info@ardnamona.com **WEBSITE** www.ardnamona.com

HALF-HIDDEN on a jungly hillside of rhododendrons and azaleas – planted in the 1880s and now a 40-acre National Heritage Garden – and on the shores of Lough Eske, with the Blue Stack mountains in the distance, this is a hauntingly romantic, beautiful place. Amabel Clarke, who worked as a Russian interpreter in London, and her husband, Kieran, a piano tuner, welcome guests to their gabled Victorian house, filled with charming rooms and the aroma of delicious home cooking wafting from the kitchen. The interiors are a pleasure: a leafy conservatory with bamboo furniture looks over the lake; green sofas, velvet curtains, tartan *chaise longue* and a wood fire in the sitting-room; upstairs, painted floorboards, faded pinks and mauves, patchwork quilts, white curtains and architectural prints. There are Sotheby's Reviews to read; walks through the restored gardens, once overgrown and neglected, and rescued by the Clarkes – best in April and May; fresh eggs from the free-range chickens for breakfast; leisurely evenings, talking, in front of the fire. Amabel has recently discovered an Italian delicatessen in Belfast that delivers. And, sometimes, across the stable yard, comes the sound of Kieran playing his piano that once belonged to Padarewski.

~

NEARBY Donegal, 6 miles (10 km).
LOCATION in own extensive lakeside grounds off the N15 from Donegal to Letterkenny; car parking
FOOD breakfast, dinner (Fri, Sat, light supper other evenings)
PRICE €€
ROOMS 6; 4 double, 2 twin; 3 with bathroom attached, 3 with bathroom next door; all with hairdrier
FACILITIES sitting room; gardens
CREDIT CARDS AE, MC, V
CHILDREN welcome **DISABLED** not possible **PETS** allowed outside
CLOSED 22nd to 30th Dec **PROPRIETORS** Kieran and Amabel Clarke

NORTHERN IRELAND

THE NARROWS
~ SEASIDE GUEST-HOUSE ~

8 Shore Road, Portaferry, Co Down BT22 1JY
TEL (028) 4272 8148 **FAX** (028) 4272 8105
E-MAIL reservations@narrows.co.uk **WEBSITE** www.narrows.co.uk

THIS IS AN ARCHITECTURAL treat. Not only that: its seafront position in a pretty fishing village on the tip of the beautiful Ards peninsula; its sunny, bright rooms with views over the water; and its prices, which take some beating, all make this a gem. Around an 18thC courtyard, owner-brothers Will and James Brown have restored and extended their father's family house with the help of architect, Rachel Bevan. The result is an exciting, airy, pleasing combination of old and new. The 13 bedrooms, all named after islands in Strangford Lough, have windows looking over boats and the new yacht pontoon. Decoration is simple, with white walls, coconut matting, natural wood floors, pine furniture and white-tiled bathrooms. Rooms in the older building have aged timber beams; all have good beds and power showers. The ground-floor restaurant is a bright, functional room, with wood floors, sponged terracotta-coloured walls and bare wood tables, serving delicious Modern Irish food, with local seafood, such as Portaferry mussels, smoked salmon, and sea bass. Organic vegetables and herbs come from the garden. The odd well-placed colourful piece of hand-weaving, painting or photograph hangs on the walls. Moorings available.

~

NEARBY Exploris Aquarium; Mount Stewart (National Trust); golf.
LOCATION on seafront in centre of town; with parking for 4-5 cars
FOOD breakfast, lunch, dinner
PRICE €€
ROOMS 13; 12 double and twin, 1 single, 3 with bath, 10 with shower; all rooms have phone, TV
FACILITIES sitting room, restaurant, sauna, lift, garden, terrace
CREDIT CARDS AE, MC, V
CHILDREN welcome
DISABLED 8 accessible rooms **PETS** accepted with own bedding
CLOSED never **PROPRIETORS** Will and James Brown

IRISH REPUBLIC

AGHADOE, CO KERRY

KILLEEN HOUSE HOTEL
~ COUNTRY HOTEL ~

Aghadoe, Lakes of Killarney, Co Kerry
TEL (064) 31711 **FAX** (064) 31811
E-MAIL charming@indigo.ie **WEBSITE** www.killeenhousehotel.com

W E HAD TO VISIT A HOTEL with 'charming' as its e-mail address. And there
it was: a charming small hotel, a rectory built in 1838 and given a
bright new white front and architectural twiddly bits painted in red by
Michael and Geraldine Rosney, who took it over in 1992. Michael is a jolly,
amusing – and kind – person who used to manage the Great Southern
Hotel in Killarney. He has created not so much a quiet retreat from
crowded Killarney (a short taxi drive away), but a warm, cosy,
entertaining and lively little place, where he spoils his golfing clients and
indulges their every whim. He sees them off in the morning and waits for
their return in the evening, like an anxious parent. Then he is to be found
in The Pub, 'possibly the only place in the universe that accepts golf balls
as legal tender', where he dispenses Guinness and sympathy. Nothing is
too much trouble for him: he puts phone messages in envelopes and
distributes them himself. All this activity provides loads of fun for
everyone, especially Michael, and you don't have to be a golfer to benefit
from his generous spirit. Comfortable, spacious bedrooms are often
decorated in checks and plaids; he has got a special one with a spa bath
that he gives to regular guests as a 'thank you' for coming back again and
again. Good showers; excellent food.

~

NEARBY Killarney, 4 miles (6 km); Muckross House; Gap of Dunloe; lakes.
LOCATION in countryside, 4 miles (6 km) from Killarney; parking available
FOOD breakfast, dinner
PRICE €
ROOMS 23; 8 championship, 15 standard; 8 with king-size double and single;
2 double, 5 twin, 2 single, 6 double and single; 22 with bath, 1 with shower;
all with phone, TV, radio, hairdrier **FACILITIES** bar, sitting room; garden, terrace,
tennis court **CREDIT CARDS** AE, DC, MC,V
CHILDREN welcome if well-behaved **DISABLED** not possible **PETS** welcome
CLOSED 1 Nov to 1 Apr **PROPRIETORS** Michael and Geraldine Rosney

IRISH REPUBLIC

AGLISH, CO TIPPERARY

BALLYCORMAC HOUSE

~ CONVERTED FARMHOUSE ~

Aglish, Borrisokane, Co Tipperary
TEL (067) 21129 **FAX** (067) 21200
E-MAIL bally@indigo.ie **WEBSITE** www.ballyc.com

SET AMID NORTH TIPPERARY FARMLAND, almost exactly in the middle of Ireland, this is a 300-year-old-farmhouse which has long been well known as a guest house, but which was taken over from the previous occupants in 1994 by an energetic American couple, Herbert and Christine Quigley. It's ideal for guests who simply wish to relax, or small groups who want to take advantage of their specialist holidays based on riding, fox-hunting, golfing, fishing and shooting. We learned, on going to press, that the Quigleys have left, so readers' reports would be especially welcome.

The Quigleys upgraded the pretty but compact house, creating a warm and cosy retreat. There are log fires in winter, and in summer guests can see the organic herb, fruit and vegetable gardens which provide produce for meals. And this is where the Quigleys' real prowess lay. Herb was a superb baker, and so breakfast might feature traditional Irish soda bread, or his own version of pain au chocolat, chocolate cherry soda bread, while dinner at the communal table might be accompanied by anything from home-made Swedish limpa to Indian naan. Let's hope that the new owners can maintain this quality and individuality.

~

NEARBY Terryglass; Birr.
LOCATION in 2 acres of garden, 0.5 mile (1 km) N of Borrisokane, signposted on right; with ample car parking
FOOD breakfast, picnic lunch on request, dinner
PRICE €
ROOMS 5; 3 double, 1 suite, 1 single, all with bath
FACILITIES sitting room, dining room; garden
CREDIT CARDS MC, V
CHILDREN welcome over 6
DISABLED access difficult **PETS** lodging available
CLOSED never **PROPRIETOR** John Lang

IRISH REPUBLIC

ARDARA, CO. DONEGAL

THE GREEN GATE

~ COTTAGE BED-AND-BREAKFAST ~

The Green Gate, Ardvally, Ardara, Co Donegal
TEL (07495) 41546

THIS LITTLE PLACE, a tiny farmhouse with stone outbuildings, owned and converted by a Frenchman who came to Donegal 11 years ago to write about "life, love and death", is bursting with charm. The book never got finished, but Paul Chatenoud, who left behind his musical bookshop and flat in Paris for a wilder existence on the top of a hill overlooking the Atlantic, has created what must be the most beautiful small B&B in Ireland. So much love and care has gone into this enterprise; he's done most of it with his own hands, from thatching the cottage roof to plumbing and whitewashing the four guest rooms. Simple they may be, but he thinks of everything: hot water bottles, a map in each room, and a bath in which you can rest your head back and gaze out of the window at the sky and the sea. His garden is filled with primroses, fuchsia and small birds, and he has planted hundreds, if not thousands, of orange montbretia up the lane. Breakfast is taken chez lui; in his own cosy kitchen he serves coffee/tea, cornflakes, bacon, eggs, sausage, toast and home-made jam – any time before 2 pm. And you get his delightful company. An English composer came for a night and was still there a week later. 'A treasure' says an entry in the visitor's book.

~

NEARBY Ardara (for tweed); Glenveagh National Park.
LOCATION 1 mile (1.6 km) from Ardara, up a hill; with car parking
FOOD breakfast
PRICE €
ROOMS 4; 2 double, 2 triple; all with bath and shower
FACILITIES garden, terrace
CREDIT CARDS not accepted
CHILDREN welcome
DISABLED access possible
PETS welcome in room
CLOSED never **PROPRIETOR** Paul Chatenoud

IRISH REPUBLIC

BALLINGARRY, CO LIMERICK

THE MUSTARD SEED AT ECHO LODGE

~ COUNTRY HOUSE AND RESTAURANT ~

Ballingarry, Co Limerick
TEL (069) 68508 **FAX** (069) 68511
E-MAIL mustard@indigo.ie **WEBSITE** www.mustardseed.ie

DAN MULLANE WON HIS SPURS with a restaurant in a tiny thatched cottage in Adare, often called the prettiest village in Ireland. Now he's moved his chefs to a shiny new kitchen in a former convent a few miles away, where he's blissfully happy gathering herbs in the vegetable garden and master of a much larger domaine. Echo Lodge is painted yellow, and has blue pots on the doorstep; he's filled the niches left empty when the nuns moved out with figures of Buddha, to whose calming powers he lights candles in the evenings. His regulars are as happy as he is. 'Foodies' flock to his blue-walled dining room with the yellow laburnum outside the window. In season, you may well find a big dark pink peony on the table. Service is smooth, professional and busy. Mullane is very 'hands on'. It takes a brave man to keep the green baize door to the kitchen propped open: he does. Breakfast could be stewed prunes with an Earl Grey and lemon syrup, or porridge with cream and Irish whiskey. Among his many gifts, Dan can design a pretty bedroom, too. He likes French toiles, wallpaper striped like a Jermyn Street shirt, and fresh, gleaming white bathrooms; two of his most successful rooms are all in black and white. 'Is this paradise?' asks an Argentinian in the visitors' book.

~

NEARBY Adare; Limerick, 18 miles (29 km); Shannon airport, 33 miles (53 km).
LOCATION in 7 acres of gardens and orchard on edge of village; car parking available
FOOD breakfast, snack lunch, dinner
PRICE €
ROOMS 11; 8 double, 2 twin, 1 single; 7 with bath; 5 with shower; all with phone, TV, hairdrier; 8 with trouser press; safe at reception
FACILITIES gardens, terraces
CREDIT CARDS AE, MC, V **CHILDREN** by arrangement **DISABLED** possible
PETS by arrangement **CLOSED** Feb **PROPRIETOR** Dan Mullane

IRISH REPUBLIC

BALLSBRIDGE, CO DUBLIN

ANGLESEA TOWN HOUSE

~ TOWN HOUSE ~

63 Anglesea Road, Ballsbridge, Dublin 4
TEL (01) 668 3877 **FAX** (01) 668 3461

BALLSBRIDGE – A LEAFY SUBURB across the Grand Canal from the city centre – is where many of Dublin's best hotels and restaurants are to be found. Helen Kirrane's large Edwardian house near Herbert Park is in a grand terrace and the minute you step into the hall, with its Tiffany lamps and watered silk curtains, you return to unhurried, gracious times. This house operates at its own stately pace, gently sweeping you along. The famed, prize-winning breakfasts are almost ceremonial: served at a Chippendale table on Wedgwood; accompanied by fresh flowers and white napkins folded into roses. One food critic describes them as 'orchestrated and meticulous' – 'gorgeous'. Mrs Kirrane, an ex-teacher, has been welcoming guests for 15 years and finds baking and house-keeping a perfect outlet for her creative talent. One element of the mighty Anglesea breakfast is her baked cereal – a secret recipe – with fruit, apples and nuts, fresh cream and Irish Mist liquor. Those on diets who bewail the numerous courses should, she says, just try to admire how "pretty" the whole show is. Guests are free to wander at will in the house – into the kitchen, too. There's a garden to sit in and an elegant drawing room with Edwardian fireplace, maple floor, books and magazines. Enduring friendships have been made here. Afternoon tea.

~

NEARBY city centre, 4 miles (6 km); rugby at Landsdowne Road.
LOCATION close to Lansdowne Road rugby ground and short walk from Sandymount Rd DART station; with parking
FOOD breakfast
PRICE €€
ROOMS 7; 2 with bath; 5 with shower; all with phone, TV, radio, hairdrier, dressing gown **FACILITIES** drawing room; garden; ironing service in basement
CREDIT CARDS AE, MC, V
CHILDREN welcome; baby-sitting **DISABLED** not possible **PETS** not accepted
CLOSED 22 Dec to 6 Jan **PROPRIETORS** Helen Kirrane and family

I R I S H   R E P U B L I C

BALLYCONNEELY, CO GALWAY

E R R I S E A S K   H O U S E   H O T E L
~ COUNTRY HOTEL ~

Ballyconneely, Co Galway
TEL (095) 23553 **FAX** (095) 23639
E-MAIL info@erriseask.com **WEBSITE** www.erriseask.com

WITH ITS OWN BEACH and surrounded by the windswept, wild beauty of the Connemara countryside, this is the perfect place for those who want to get away. And eat well while on the run. Because of the isolated position – we spent some time trying to find it – it is very much a sand-in-your-shoes summer place, with lazy days and easy living laid on. The kitchen here is busy, serious, and professional; the formal restaurant is open to non-residents. The 'foodies' come from far and wide; there is a *Menu Degustation*. The hotel itself is pretty basic and functional, with much pine furniture. There are five stunning split-level rooms, with spiral staircases leading up to a platform and views of the sea. Nothing fancy. Practical and minimal, they make you want to unpack swiftly, dig in, and take advantage of all the good, simple, unpretentious treats offered here: white coral beaches; glorious West Coast sunsets; moonlight over Mannin Bay.

~

NEARBY Connemara National Park; Kylemore Abbey; Clifden, 6 miles (10 km).
LOCATION in own gardens and grounds by seashore; parking available
FOOD breakfast, dinner
PRICE €
ROOMS 12; 6 doubles, 4 twins, 1 single, 1 family with double bed and 2 singles;
5 with bath and shower, 7 with shower; all with phone, hairdrier; TV on request
FACILITIES dining room; garden, terraces
CREDIT CARDS AE, DC, MC, V
CHILDREN not in dining room
DISABLED not possible
PETS not accepted
CLOSED end Oct to April
PROPRIETORS Peader Nevern and Fabrice Galand

IRISH REPUBLIC

BALLYLICKEY, CO CORK

BALLYLICKEY MANOR HOUSE

~ COUNTRY HOUSE HOTEL ~

Ballylickey, Batry Bay, Co Cork
TEL (027) 50071 **FAX** (027) 50124
EMAIL ballymh@eircom **WEBSITE** www.ballylickeymanorhouse.com

THIS FORMER SHOOTING LODGE, with romantic view of the sea from the front door, is a grande dame of the Irish country house hotel scene – the first to be accepted by the Relais and Chateaux group in 1967. So it has all the requisite comfort and style – and some extra very French touches added by Christiane Graves' talent with colours, fabrics and antiques. As a private family house, it was visited many times by the writer and poet, Robert Graves, uncle of owner George Graves, whose mother, Kitty, laid out the lovely gardens. Some rooms are in the main house; one has doors opening on to a little sheltered patio with table and chairs for sitting out; or you may choose simply to let in the sound of birdsong and the wonderful damp smell of the plants and foliage. You are even closer to nature in the blue-grey wooden cottages in the trees and shrubs by the swimming-pool. With the sound of French staff chattering away in the kitchen of the poolside Le Rendez-Vous restaurant - covered in May with clouds of pink clematis – it is not hard to imagine oneself in a Relais and Chateaux in the South of France. Full marks should go to Mr Graves for his decision – possibly an unpopular one with some guests – not to allow parking in front of the house, which wrecks the sea view, by placing obstacles on the gravel driveway.

~

NEARBY Ring of Kerry; Killarney; Bantry.
LOCATION in gardens and grounds, on N17 between Bantry and Glengariff; car parking available
FOOD breakfast, lunch, dinner
PRICE €€€
ROOMS 11; 7 suites, 4 double; all with bath and shower, phone, TV, hairdrier
FACILITIES 3 sitting rooms, restaurant; garden, terraces, swimming pool
CREDIT CARDS AE, DC, MC, V **CHILDREN** welcome
DISABLED poolside cottage **PETS** not accepted **CLOSED** end Oct to beginning Apr
PROPRIETORS George and Christiane Graves

I R I S H R E P U B L I C

BALLYLICKEY, CO CORK

S E A V I E W H O U S E
~ COUNTRY HOTEL ~

Ballylickey, Bantry, Co Cork
TEL(027) 50462 **FAX** (027) 51555
EMAIL info@seaviewhousehotel.com **WEBSITE** www.seaviewhousehotel.com

KATHLEEN O'SULLIVAN GREW UP in this white Victorian house, a stone's throw from Ballylickey Bay. In 1978 she turned it into a successful small hotel. Her plan for an extension, to give double the number of rooms, was finally realized in 1990. 'Kathleen is a delightful hostess,' writes a recent reporter, and Sea View really is a 'very nice, quiet comfortable hotel'.

The new bedrooms are all similar in style, beautifully decorated in pastel colours and floral fabrics with stunning antique furniture – especially the bedheads and wardrobes, and matching three-piece suites, collected or inherited from around the Cork area. The rooms in the old part of the house are more irregular and individual. All front rooms have large bay windows and views of the garden and sea (through the trees). The 'Garden Suite' downstairs is especially adapted for wheelchairs.

There are two sitting-rooms – a cosy front room adjoining the bar and a large family room at the back. The dining-room has also been extended (though many regular guests do not believe it). Our reporter thought the food 'excellent and generous'; breakfast was 'wonderful' with a big choice and traditional Irish dishes, such as potato cakes. The menu changes daily, and Kathleen is forever experimenting with new dishes – roast smoked pheasant on the day we visited.
~

NEARBY Bantry; Beira Peninsula; Ring of Kerry.
LOCATION in countryside, just off N71, 3 miles (5 km) N of Bantry; in large grounds with ample car parking
FOOD breakfast, lunch (Sun only), dinner
PRICE €€€
ROOMS 17; 14 double, 13 with bath, 1 with shower, 3 family with bath; all rooms have phone, TV, hairdrier **FACILITIES** 2 dining rooms, 2 sitting rooms, TV room, bar; garden
CREDIT CARDS AE, MC, V **CHILDREN** welcome
DISABLED one specially adapted room **PETS** accepted in bedrooms only
CLOSED Nov-Mar **PROPRIETOR** Kathleen O'Sullivan

I R I S H   R E P U B L I C

BALLYMACARBRY, CO WATERFORD

H A N O R A ' S   C O T T A G E
RIVERSIDE GUEST-HOUSE

Glenanore, Ballymacarbry, Co Waterford
TEL (052) 36134 **FAX** (052) 36540
E-MAIL hanorascottage@eircom.net **WEBSITE** www.hanorascottage.com

CHANGES HAVE TAKEN PLACE at award-winning Hanora's Cottage, built by a
little bridge over the river in the beautiful Nire Valley for owner
Seamus Wall's great-grandmother. With the village school and church next
door, the picturesque group of buildings and their setting made our
inspector think of somewhere in the Pyrenees. The guest-house is a
favourite with walkers, who come for the Comeragh Mountains and nearby
forests and lakes. Mary Wall puts comfort high on her list and pampers her
guests. She has added five new rooms and a spa tub in a conservatory-
with-views, where guests may rest aching limbs and emerge refreshed for
a candlelit dinner in the new dining room. Food is prepared by the Walls'
talented Ballymaloe-trained son, Eoin. In the new extension, brilliantly
designed to fit with the rest of the building, Mary has put in a drying and
boot room. Bedrooms are large, calm and peaceful, with thick carpets, and
most have spa baths (superiors have double Jacuzzis). There are books by
the beds, some Tiffany lamps, and quality bedlinen. The breakfast room
looks out on to the little stone bridge and Seamus's home-baked gluten-
free brown bread has an international reputation. Plenty of fruit and
freshly-squeezed juices, too. Ask for a front room if you want to fall asleep
to the sound of the river.

NEARBY Dungarvan, 18 miles (29 km); Clonmel, 15 miles (24 km); Blackwater Valley.
LOCATION in Nire Valley, 4 miles (6 km) out of Ballymacarbry; parking available
FOOD breakfast, packed lunch, dinner
PRICE €€
ROOMS 10; all double/twin; all with Jacuzzi; all rooms with phone, TV, hairdrier;
tea/coffee making facilities
FACILITIES garden, terrace, spa tub
CREDIT CARDS MC, V
CHILDREN not accepted **DISABLED** not possible **PETS** not accepted
CLOSED Christmas week **PROPRIETORS** the Wall family

I R I S H   R E P U B L I C

BALLYMOTE, Co SLIGO

T E M P L E   H O U S E
~ COUNTRY HOUSE ~

Mallymote, Co Sligo
TEL (07191) 83329 **FAX** (07191) 83808
E-MAIL guests@templehouse.ie **WEBSITE** www.templehouse.ie

Is THIS A DREAM? It begins as you enter the gates of what is a gentle, gracious world of its own. In parkland filled with fat sheep, this is a whopper of a Georgian mansion, the home of the Percevals since 1665. Much of what you see was refurbished in 1864; electricity was not put in until 1962. To be overcome by awe and wonder would be easy were it not for the charm and kindness of Sandy Perceval (he is allergic to perfumed products and sprays, so please avoid use) and his wife, Debonnaure (or Deb). They want the house to be enjoyed. The two-storey vestibule is so enormous that Deb waits until guests have absorbed it before she speaks: 'There's no conversation when they arrive, they are usually speechless,' she says. Bedrooms, with marble fireplaces and much of their original Victorian furniture, seem to be the size of football pitches – one is called the 'half-acre'. Bathrooms have been put into what used to be dressing rooms. As shadows fall, you can take a walk to the ruins of a 13thC Knights Templar castle and a Tudor house down by the lake. The family silver comes out for dinner; delicious dishes and freshly-baked bread emerge from Deb's all-electric kitchen, which, of course, is vast. Big breakfasts.

~

NEARBY Sligo, 12 miles (19 km); Yeats Country; Lissadell House.
LOCATION on 1,000-acre estate, 4 miles (6 km) from Ballymote; parking available
FOOD breakfast, dinner
PRICE €
ROOMS 5; 2 double, 2 twin (1 double and 1 single bed), 1 single; 2 with bath, 3 with shower; all rooms have hairdrier
FACILITIES garden, woodland, lake fishing, boat
CREDIT CARDS AE, MC, V
CHILDREN welcome, high tea in kitchen for under-5s
DISABLED access difficult
PETS dogs on leads (sheep); sleep in car
CLOSED 30 Nov to 1 Apr **PROPRIETORS** Sandy and Deb Perceval

IRISH REPUBLIC

BUTLERSTOWN, CO CORK

BUTLERSTOWN HOUSE
~ COUNTRY HOUSE ~

Butlerstown, Bandon, Co Cork
TEL (023) 40137 **FAX** (023) 40137

L IS JONES AND ROGER OWEN are an obviously happy couple who appear to be over the moon with their escape from South Wales to the lovely light and landscape of West Cork and the elegant spaces of this delightful Georgian house. Their pleasure is infectious and gives the place a special warmth. The airy rooms are filled with fine antiques – Roger is, usefully, a furniture restorer as well as 'butler' – and classic colours enhance the simple lines and architectural details of the house. A smart navy blue front door leads into the hall with bifurcated staircase; ornate plasterwork in the house takes the shape of scallop shells, flowers, grapes, vine leaves and ribbon tied into bows. Lis's bathrooms are a treat: she likes brass taps, heated towel rails, blue-and-white striped tiles. There's a four-poster in one room and twin French mahogany beds in another. The sitting room has a view of the bluebell wood where badgers roam at night; the dining room has a long, polished table and Spode on a Monmouth dresser; and there's an aga in the huge kitchen. Some of the best things about living in Butlerstown House, say Roger and Lis, are the fresh air and the stars in the West Cork night sky. The house is now self-catering, accommodating one group of up to ten adults.

~

NEARBY Kinsale; Clonakilty; Bandon; Cork.
LOCATION in 10-acre grounds; with car parking
FOOD self-catering
PRICE 1750 euros for 3 nights, 3995 euros for 1 week, 3-day minimum stay
ROOMS 1 self-catering apartment with 5 double and twin rooms, all with bath or shower **FACILITIES** sitting room, dining room, kitchen, communications room, games room; garden, terrace, croquet lawn
CREDIT CARDS MC, V **CHILDREN** accepted
DISABLED not possible **PETS** accepted by arrangement
CLOSED Christmas to early Feb
PROPRIETORS Elisabeth Jones and Roger Owen

IRISH REPUBLIC

LISDONAGH HOUSE
〜 COUNTRY HOUSE 〜

Caherlistrane, Co Galway
TEL (093) 31163 **FAX** (093) 31528
E-MAIL cooke@lisdonagh.com **WEBSITE** www.lisdonagh.com

HORSES GRAZE BY THE LAKE in front of this early Georgian house in the heart of the famous Galway hunting country – flat with drystone walls. Indeed, it used to belong to a maiden lady of the kind described as a 'colourful character', who rode to hounds and chased off intruders with a shotgun. Her antics may be read about in the enticing, cosy, basement 'den', where glowing fire, books and music are thoughtfully provided for guests, along with a help-yourself tray of various tipples and an Honesty Book. Extensively refurbished by current owners, John and Finola Cooke, over the last few years, the house has been refloored and filled with antiques, mainly found in England. Bedrooms are named after Irish writers; each one is different. Our inspector's room – with original shutters to fit the curved windows – had cream paintwork, a pretty French bed and chairs and a small bathroom with shower. The oval hallway – entered through the fanlighted front door – is quite remarkable, with frescoes of Ionic pillars and figures in grisaille of the Four Virtues – Valour, Justice, Chastity and Beauty – painted in 1790. A South African chef was cooking when we visited; delectable fresh breads come from the Aga. The kitchen garden is next for restoration.

〜

NEARBY Galway; Sligo; Yeats Country; Kylemore Abbey.
LOCATION in countryside, 1 mile (1.5 km) from village of Caherlistrane; parking available
FOOD breakfast, lunch
PRICE €€€
ROOMS 10; 5 double, 5 twin; 7 with bath, 3 with shower; all with phone, TV, video, radio, hairdrier; tea/coffee making facilities
FACILITIES lake fishing, boat, riding, woodland walks
CREDIT CARDS AE, MC, V
CHILDREN welcome **DISABLED** downstairs room
PETS not in house; kennel
CLOSED Oct to beginning of May **PROPRIETORS** John and Finola Cooke

IRISH REPUBLIC

CARAGH LAKE, CO KERRY

ARD-NA-SIDHE

~ LAKESIDE HOTEL ~

Caragh Lake, Killorglin, Co Kerry
TEL (066) 9769105 **FAX** (066) 9769282
E-MAIL khl@iol.ie **WEBSITE** www.killarneyhotels.ie

WHEN WE VISITED ARD-NA-SIDHE (Gaelic for Hill of the Fairies) there appeared to be no-one about. The lovely wooded prize-winning gardens, with paths leading down to little grassy areas by the lake where there are benches to sit on and dream, were deserted. Most of the guests, we told, were out playing golf. These golfing hotels are left like the *Marie Celeste* during the day, and lucky non-golfers may have the place to themselves. This handsome Victorian stone house, festooned with creeper, was built by a Lady Gordon and is so romantic that you can be as fanciful as you like. It certainly feels as if there are fairies about; indeed, behind the house is a fairy hill, with passages said to lead to a large cave. But these little creatures do not like to be seen. All credit must be given to Killarney Hotels for keeping the house quite uncommercialized and unspoiled, and bringing in Roy Lancaster to advise them on the gardens. There are no facilities here, except natural ones. But guests are given complimentary use of the 25-metre pool and sauna at the group's nearby sister hotels. Bedrooms (spacious) are in the main house or in the converted stables (very quiet and tranquil); all have impressive antiques and fabrics Lady Gordon might well have chosen herself; excellent bathrooms. Staff wear charming spotted frocks.

~

NEARBY Killorglin, 4 miles (7 km); Killarney, 21 miles (34 km); Dingle peninsula; golf.
LOCATION in lakeside gardens, $4\frac{1}{2}$ miles (7 km) from Killorglin; parking available
FOOD breakfast, dinner
PRICE ⓔⓔⓔ
ROOMS 20; 18 double/twin, 2 single; 18 with bath, 2 with shower; all with phone, hairdrier; reception safe; kettle on request; ironing room
FACILITIES gardens, terraces, boating, swimming pool nearby
CREDIT CARDS AE, DC, MC, V **CHILDREN** not suitable **DISABLED** downstairs room
PETS not accepted **CLOSED** 1 Oct to 1 May
PROPRIETOR Killarney Hotels **MANAGER** Adrian O'Sullivan

IRISH REPUBLIC

CARAGH LODGE

~ COUNTRY HOTEL ~

Caragh Lake, Co Kerry
TEL (066) 9769115 FAX (066) 9769316
E-MAIL caraghl@iol.ie WEBSITE www.caraghlodge.com

AN EXCELLENT RESPONSE to this comfortable house from a recent visitor: 'Full of warmth, and a marvellously peaceful setting' on the edge of Caragh Lake. The 100-year-old house is furnished with antiques and log fires, it has a 300-yard lake frontage, and there are nine acres of parkland with a fine planting of rare and sub-tropical shrubs. You get views of some of Ireland's highest mountains, abundant facilities for relaxation, quick access to the sea and glorious sandy beaches: a heady combination attractive to a great many holidaymakers (including golfers) – so much so that seven new rooms have been built to satisfy demand.

Mary Gaunt, described by our reporter as 'lively and fun', took over in 1989. She thoroughly redecorated the public rooms, bedrooms and the previously rather drab annexe rooms, and has achieved some impressive results. As a consequence the hotel is now a happy combination of elegance and informality. Mary's excellent cooking – featuring seafood, wild salmon and local lamb – has earned high praise from recent visitors.

~

NEARBY Killarney, 15 miles (24 km); Ring of Kerry.
LOCATION 22 miles (35 km) NW of Killarney, 1 mile (1.5 km) off Ring of Kerry road, W of Killorglin; in 9-acre gardens and parkland, with ample car parking
FOOD full breakfast, dinner; restaurant licence
PRICE €€€
ROOMS 15; 13 double, 1 single, 1 suite; all with bath
FACILITIES 2 sitting rooms, dining room; swimming in lake, fishing, boating, sauna, bicycles
CREDIT CARDS AE, MC, V
CHILDREN welcome over 7
DISABLED access easy – some ground-floor bedrooms
PETS not accepted
CLOSED mid-Oct to April
PROPRIETOR Mary and Graham Gaunt

IRISH REPUBLIC

CASHEL, CO TIPPERARY

CASHEL PALACE HOTEL
~ CONVERTED BISHOP'S PALACE ~

Main Street, Cashel, Co Tipperary
TEL (062) 62707 **FAX** (062) 61521
E-MAIL reception@cashel-palace.ie **WEBSITE** www.cashel-palace.ie

CHARM AND GRACE oozes out of every pore of this exquisite 18thC former archbishop's palace in the historic market town of Cashel, with its famous and dramatic Rock, one of Ireland's most visited sites. The story is that the Devil, in a hurry to fly on his way, bit a chunk out of the Slieve Bloom Mountains and dropped it here. From right outside the hotel drawing room you may follow the Bishop's Walk, which leads you through the delightful garden and a grassy meadow to the Rock and its cluster of grey ruins. In the garden are two mulberry trees planted in 1702 for the coronation of Queen Anne, and the descendents of the original hops planted by one of the Guinness family in the mid-18thC (there's plenty of the 'black', velvety stuff in the Guinness Bar, with flagged cellar floor and terracotta walls). We don't have enough room to sing all the praises of this jewel in the heart of racing country that used to be owned by trainer Vincent O'Brien; breakfast is served in the pine-panelled room named after him. There are four-poster beds, fine antiques and pictures, and spacious bathrooms – with towelling gowns – and a magnificent early-Georgian red pine staircase in the entrance hall with 'barley sugar' banisters. You have the choice of two restaurants and there are ten new bedrooms in the old mews and stables. Book early.

~

NEARBY Rock of Cashel; Holycross Abbey; Clonmel.
LOCATION in gardens, set back off road in town centre; with car parking
FOOD breakfast, lunch, dinner
PRICE €€€€
ROOMS 23 (13 in house, 10 in mews); 12 double, 7 twin, 4 single, all with bath; all rooms have phone, TV, hairdrier
FACILITIES sitting room, 2 dining rooms, lift, garden, terrace
CREDIT CARDS AE, DC, MC, V **CHILDREN** welcome
DISABLED access possible **PETS** not accepted
CLOSED 24 to 30 Dec **PROPRIETORS** Pat and Susan Murphy

I R I S H   R E P U B L I C

CASHEL BAY, CO GALWAY

ZETLAND HOUSE HOTEL

~ COUNTRY HOUSE HOTEL ~

Cashel Bay, Co Galway
TEL (095) 31111 **FAX** (095) 31117
E-MAIL zetland@iol.ie

T HE BROCHURE HAS PRETTY PICTURES of a little table laid with a pink cloth and sunlight slanting through windows into antique-filled rooms. But we think it is the charming Prendergast family that brings regualrs back again and again for more of the Zetland House experience. The setting happens to be spectacualr, in an area of outstanding beauty, with views over Cashel Bay. built in the early 19thC as a shooting lodge, the hotel is named after the Earl of Zetland, who was a frequent visitor. Mona Prendergast and her husband, John, who trained at the Ritz in Paris, have been joined by their children: son Ruaidhri has come home after working in Lille in France; daughter Cliodhna is in the kitchen. No wonder they've won an AA Care and Courtesy Award. Nothing is too much trouble. Ask Mona about the area, and she hurries off to find for you a copy of a map she has printed up, so she can show you the best route to take or where to shop in Galway. Bedrooms are delightful. the green Room has its own door to the garden, fresh, green trellis wallpaper, a marble washstand, and Edward Lear's Book of Nonsense on the bedside table. A fire is lit every morning in one of the sitting rooms; there's an eye-catching collection of china plates.

~

NEARBY Aran Islands; Connemara Natioanl Park; Clifden, 14 miles (22.5 km).
LOCATION in gardens overlooking Cashel Bay, on N340 to Roundstone from Galway; car parking
FOOD breakfast, lunch, dinner
PRICE €€€
ROOMS 20; 10 double; 10 twin; 9 with bath, 1 with shower; all with phone, TV, radio, hairdrier
FACILITIES snooker room; tenniscourt; garden; shooting, fishing
CREDIT CARDS AE, DC, MC, V **CHILDREN** welcome
DISABLED ground-floor room **PETS** dogs with baskets permitted in bedrooms
CLOSED Dec to Feb **PROPRIETORS** John and Mona Prendergast

IRISH REPUBLIC

CASTLEBALDWIN, CO SLIGO

CROMLEACH LODGE

~ RESTAURANT-WITH-ROOMS ~

Castlebaldwin, Boyle, Co Sligo
TEL (07191) 65155 **FAX** (07191) 65455
E-MAIL info@cromleach.com **WEBSITE** www.cromleach.com

A SMALL MIRACLE: from modest beginnings as a bungalow with B & B for fishermen on Christy Tighe's family farm overlooking Lough Arrow, this unique little place has a string of coveted awards to its name. The modern design may not suit all tastes, but the Tighes were determined it should not be a blot on the green and beautiful landscape. So the building is long and low, under a slate roof, and looks as if it has grown out of the hillside. Ever-changing skies, still waters of the lake, cattle in the fields and blue-grey hills in the distance have a strangely calming effect. But the 'lodge' is no country bumpkin; the Tighes' renowned professionalism and standards of excellence are everywhere. Every room has the gorgeous view. Bedrooms are sophisticated and Moira Tighe's thoughtful touch much in evidence. The hairdrier is where it should be: on the dressing table. There are flowers and fruit; fresh milk for tea; chairs enticingly placed by the picture windows; every toilet requisite imaginable in the gleaming bathrooms. In the evenings, beds are turned down and curtains drawn. Christy knows about walks, archaeological sites and Yeats Country; Moira presides over her all-female classy kitchen. A special place, worth a special journey.

NEARBY Yeats Country; Lissadell House; Carrowkeel Cairns; Sligo.
LOCATION in own farmland, near village of Ballindoon; car parking
FOOD breakfast, dinner
PRICE €€€
ROOMS 10; all double/twin; all with bath and shower; all rooms with phone, TV, minibar, hairdrier, safe
FACILITIES sitting room, bar; garden, terrace, fishing, helipad
CREDIT CARDS AE, DC, MC, V
CHILDREN welcome; cot; private family dining room
DISABLED not possible **PETS** not accepted
CLOSED Nov to Jan **PROPRIETORS** Christy and Moira Tighe

IRISH REPUBLIC

CASTLEGREGORY, CO KERRY

THE SHORES COUNTRY HOUSE

~ COUNTRY GUEST-HOUSE ~

Cappatigue, Castlegregory, Co Kerry
TEL (066) 7139196 **FAX** (066) 7139196
E-MAIL theshores@eircom.net **WEBSITE** www.shores.main-page.com

W E HEARD GLOWING REPORTS of The Shores – on the north side of the Dingle peninsula – on our travels, and of farmer's wife Annette O'Mahony's passion for looking after guests. She has recently more or less rebuilt her house to add on three extra rooms so that she can get her hands on some more people to cosset. The setting for the house is fabulous: just over the road in front is the 26-mile long sandy Brandon Bay beach; in five minutes, you can be in the sea. Towering up behind is Mount Brandon, the second highest mountain in Ireland. All rooms have sea views. One has its own balcony; there's a long balcony, too, for general use. And there's a library. Annette takes, as she says, "exceptional pride" in the interior decorating of the house, and there are all kinds of charming details in her rooms, such as writing desks, porcelain dolls, Laura Ashley papers and fabrics, cream and white bedlinen. Her style could loosely be described as Victorian. In her new cherry-wood kitchen she makes porter cake to accompany a welcome cup of tea on arrival, scrambles eggs and pours maple syrup over waffles for breakfast. Milk is from the farm. For dinner, there might well be beef raised on O'Mahony pastures, fresh salmon, prawns in garlic butter. Flasks of coffee and packed lunches hold you over through the day.

~

NEARBY Tralee; Dingle; Killarney; golf at Ballybunion.
LOCATION 1 mile (1.6 km) W of Stradbally on Connor Pass; with car parking
FOOD breakfast, packed lunch, dinner
PRICE €
ROOMS 6; 3 double, 2 twin, 1 triple, 3 with bath, 3 with shower; all rooms have phone, TV, hairdrier
FACILITIES sitting room; garden
CREDIT CARDS AE, DC, MC, V **CHILDREN** welcome
DISABLED ground-floor room available **PETS** not accepted
CLOSED 15 Nov 15 Feb **PROPRIETOR** Annette O'Mahony

IRISH REPUBLIC

CLIFDEN, CO GALWAY

THE ARDAGH HOTEL
~ COAST HOTEL AND RESTAURANT ~

Ballyconneely Road, Clifden, Co Galway
TEL (095) 21384 **FAX** (095) 21314
E-MAIL ardaghhotel@eircom.net **WEBSITE** www.ardaghhotel.com

THIS IS SO CLOSE TO THE SEA you feel you could reach out and dip your toe in the water. The view from the restaurant over Ardbear Bay is fabulous: light and colours constantly change; sunsets are memorable. This small family hotel has a continental flavour that gives it considerable charm. Monique Bauvet's Dutch father bought the site and blasted a hole out of the limestone hillside for the blue and yellow, gabled, chalet-style building. She's the chef, housekeeper and gardener; her seafood chowder is a treat; her rooms are pristine (she's phasing out the flowery look for something more bright and contemporary); she made the garden among the rocks. Her husband, Stephane, can be found behind the front desk, or serving wine, and is always ready to help. They met in Switzerland and their hotel has a satisfying combination of friendliness and reliable, discreet efficiency. Locals frequent the downstairs bar lounge; Billie Holliday plays in the dining room; the son of the house plays football in the car park with the receptionist. Not all the well-equipped rooms have sea views; ask when booking. Tucked under the eaves, a sunny sitting room for residents has piles of magazines and a profusion of greenery. (In high season the coast road in front of the hotel could be busy.)

~

NEARBY Kylemore Abbey; Connemara National Park.
LOCATION on coast road S of Clifden; car parking
FOOD breakfast, bar lunch, dinner
PRICE ©©©
ROOMS 21; 16 double/twin, 3 suites, 2 family; 19 with bath, 4 with shower only; all rooms with phone, TV, radio, hairdrier; tea/coffee making facilities; safe at reception
FACILITIES bar lounge, restaurant, sun room; garden, terrace
CREDIT CARDS AE, DC, MC, V
CHILDREN welcome **DISABLED** not possible **PETS** accepted
CLOSED Nov to Easter or Apr 1
PROPRIETORS Monique and Stephane Bauvet

IRISH REPUBLIC

CLIFDEN, CO GALWAY

MALLMORE HOUSE
~ COUNTRY BED-AND-BREAKFAST ~

Ballyconneely Road, Clifden, Co Galway
TEL (095) 21460
E-MAIL mallmore@indigo.ie **WEBSITE** www.mallmorecountryhouse.com

THE HARDMANS BREED CONNEMARA PONIES, for showing and dressage; these
hardy little natives are often kept beside the drive to the family's
lovingly restored house with a cheery red front door and late Georgian
porch. The place is stiff with historical interest: Baden Powell, founder of
the Boy Scouts, used to spend his holidays here. Alan and Kathleen
Hardman came from The New Inn at Tresco on the Isles of Scilly to work
for themselves and found the house in a derelict state: only one room had
been used since the 1920s. From the back of the house there is a lovely
view through trees over the bay to Clifden and out to the Atlantic. You can
walk down to the sea through the orchard and past the old cottage. Rooms
in this unusual and intriguing, mainly single-storey house, with original
pitch pine floors, have a variety of views; for water ask for Room 4. One
room has the original washbasin, and wallpaper with a pattern of birds;
another original wide shutters, yellow paper, a Bonnard print and spotless
bathroom. Award-winning breakfasts are served in the dining room, which
also has its original shutters; tables have pink cloths. On the menu:
smoked salmon pancakes; smoked mackerel; Irish bacon. Very much a
family affair; a daughter bakes brown bread each evening.

~

NEARBY Clifden; Connemara National Park; Kylemore Abbey.
LOCATION a mile out of Clifden town centre; in own 35-acre grounds on Ardbear
peninsula; car parking
FOOD breakfast
PRICE €
ROOMS 6; 3 double, 1 twin, 1 family room with 1 double and 2 singles, 1 with 1
double and 1 single; all with showers and spring water; hairdriers in most rooms
FACILITIES gardens and woodland **CREDIT CARDS** not accepted
CHILDREN welcome; 20% discount
DISABLED possible **PETS** not permitted in rooms **CLOSED** 1 Nov to 1 Mar
PROPRIETORS Alan and Kathleen Hardman

IRISH REPUBLIC

CLIFDEN, CO GALWAY

THE QUAY HOUSE
~ TOWNHOUSE ~

Beach Road, Clifden, Co Galway
TEL (095) 21369 **FAX** (095) 21608
E-MAIL thequay@iol.ie **WEBSITE** www.thequayhouse.com

PADDY FOYLE IS A CELEBRATED mover and shaker in this rapidly getting very hip little seaside town, where he was born in room 12 of Foyle's Hotel. He has a little blue-and-white restaurant called Destry's in Main Street and stylish Quay House, down on the harbour wall where the fishing boats tie up. A natural interior decorator, he has the boldness and panache of a set designer: the house, built in 1820 for the harbourmaster, is a stage for his fanciful ideas and outbursts of colour. You have the distinct sense you are in a producion of some kind – is it an opera? a film? – as you pass through the wondrous rooms. A favourite theme is Scandinavian: washed-out, distressed paintwork; plenty of grey and Nordic blue; wooden pannelling; striped fabrics. One room is a riot of blue tiole de Jouy; there's a Napolean Room at the top of the house; another has a frieze of scallop sea shells. It's pretty; it's fun. But Paddy is a restless pacer, always moving on, so expect changes. He's already stuck a bay on to the old flat-fronted house, brought the place next door and turned it into studios. On our visit, he had his eye on the conservatory, which was doing very nicely as a breakfast room, where you may start the day with fresh white table cloths and china among green plants. For now.

~

NEARBY Connemara National Park; Galway, 50 miles (80 km).
LOCATION on quay, 3 minutes by car from Clifden town centre; car parking in road
FOOD breakfast
PRICE €€
ROOMS 14; 5 superkings, 9 double (4 twin); all with bath and shower; all rooms with phone, TV, radio, hairdrier; 6 with balcony
FACILITIES sitting room; garden, terrace
CREDIT CARDS AE, MC, V
CHILDREN welcome **DISABLED** ground-floor rooms **PETS** not accepted
CLOSED mid-Nov to mid-Mar but open by arrangement
PROPRIETORS Paddy and Julia Foyle

IRISH REPUBLIC

CLIFDEN, CO GALWAY

ROCK GLEN COUNTRY HOUSE HOTEL
~ COUNTRY HOTEL ~

Clifden, Co Galway
TEL (095) 21035 **FAX** (095) 21737
E-MAIL rockglen@iol.ie

WITH CLEMATIS AND VIRGINIA CREEPER around the front door, Rock Glen is a proud winner of an award for the Most Romantic Hotel in Ireland and what we found was full of charm. The setting of this former shooting lodge, built in 1815, is glorious: in front of the hotel, a path through a meadow of long grass, wild flowers and yellow iris, leads to the shoreline. A yacht bobs about at anchor in the little bay. In the evenings, Connemara ponies and cattle come down to the water's edge. Rising up behind the hotel are the Twelve Pins mountains. With miles of sandy beaches nearby and rugged countryside criss-crossed with drystone walls, it's a lovely place to walk, or simply to sit and quietly enjoy watching the ebb and flow of the tide. Hosts John and Evangeline Roche (who was born in Clifden) are veterans who have thought of everything: a glassed-in extension to the bar has sofas in which to install yourself comfortably for the long view; turf fires; soft candlelight in the dining-room. They have taken the unusual step of reducing the number of bedrooms, to improve space and comfort for guests. Some rooms have balconies. The Roches' daughter, Siobhan, has come home to take over the management of this inviting, cosy place.
~

NEARBY Clifden; Connemara National Park; Kylemore Abbey.
LOCATION in own grounds by the sea, 1.5 miles (2 km) S of Clifden on the N59 to Galway; with car parking
FOOD breakfast, bar lunch, dinner
PRICE €€€
ROOMS 26; 23 double and twin, 3 family, all with bath or shower; all rooms have phone, TV, hairdrier **FACILITIES** dining room, sitting room, TV room, snooker; garden, croquet, putting, tennis
CREDIT CARDS AE, DC, MC, V
DISABLED ground-floor rooms available
PETS not accepted **CLOSED** mid-Jan to mid-Mar
PROPRIETORS John and Evangeline Roche

IRISH REPUBLIC

CLOYNE, Co CORK

BARNABROW HOUSE
~ COUNTRY HOUSE AND RESTAURANT ~

Cloyne, Middleton, Co Cork
TEL (021) 4652534 **FAX** (021) 4652534
E-MAIL barnabrow@eircom.net **WEBSITE** www.barnabrowhouse.ie

OPENED TWO YEARS AGO at the back gate, as it were, of nearby Ballymaloe, this could be called a 'cutting edge' country house. No faded chintzes or family portraits here. Semi-minimalist interiors, with bold, bright colours, moden design and vast expanses of gleaming wood floors look as if they have come out of glossy magazines. So many guests ask how they can achieve the Barnabrow look that owner/chef Geraldine O'Brien has a list of suppliers ready. The flooring, one learns, is teak from environmentally managed forests in Zimbabwe and the pointed, cone-shaped lamps in the restaurant can be brought from Cork. Behind the rejuvenated 17thC main house is a coach house with floors painted white and elsewhere much orange, pink and yellow; a rustic stone cottage; and restaurant with an outdoor timber terrace. It all looks rather new and waiting to be weathered, but already, according to John O'Brien, who makes furniture, it has been voted one of the best B & Bs in the world by a TV holiday programme, and attracts an ever-growing band of discerning regulars, among them academics from Trinity College, Dublin. Hens that are very free-range provide fresh eggs; organic produce for the table comes from the kitchen garden; Barnabrow even has its own spring for lashings of crystal-clear water.

~

NEARBY Youghal; Cork.
LOCATION in 40 acres of gardens and woodland; car parking
FOOD breakfast, lunch, dinner
PRICE €
ROOMS 19; 11 double, 4 twin, 4 family rooms; 2 with bath 17 with shower; all with phone, hairdrier **FACILITIES** garden, terraces, children's playground
CREDIT CARDS MC, V **CHILDREN** welcome
DISABLED ground-floor rooms
PETS accepted if well-behaved
CLOSED Christmas week **PROPRIETOR** Geraldine O'Brien

I R I S H   R E P U B L I C

COROFIN, CO CLARE

CLIFDEN HOUSE
~ COUNTRY HOUSE ~

Corofin, Co Clare
TEL (065) 6837692 **FAX** (065) 6837692

ONE OF the Hidden Ireland 'heritage' houses taking guests, this is listed, early Georgian, and stands on the wooded shore of Lake Inchiquin. When the Robsons found it, it had been abandoned for about 30 years: trees grew out of the roof; there were cows in the basement. Little by little, and most lovingly, they have brought it back to life. Guests will feel quite close to the work in hand, as in several places there are exposed bits of the innards of the lathe and plaster walls. There's quite a bit that Jim Robson hasn't got round to yet. It's a mammoth task, but herein lies the stuff of many of his amusing and entertaining stories. Ask Jim (who in his previous existence sold books in Hay-on-Wye) about the crooked mirrors. He is also something of an expert on the limestone Burren. When we visited, he was working on a new breakfast room and a fern garden in a corner of dappled shade by the ruined mill and the little bridge over the River Fergus. Entered through handsome Georgian doorways, the smart bedrooms have virtually been hand-made by him. Colours are bold: green, yellow, red, blue. One has an old roll-top bath actually *in* the room. There's a tree house, a boat on the lake, an old walled kitchen garden. Prepare for a bit of an adventure, with good food, too.

~

NEARBY The Burren National Park; Ennis, 9 miles (14 km); Shannon, 26 miles (42 km).
LOCATION in lakeside grounds and woodland, 1 mile from Corofin; car parking
FOOD breakfast; dinner
PRICE €
ROOMS 5 double and twin with bath or shower; all have hairdrier and books
FACILITIES garden, boat, bicycles, fishing rods
CREDIT CARDS AE, DC, MC, V
CHILDREN welcome **DISABLED** no facilities
PETS not accepted
CLOSED mid-Dec to mid-Mar
PROPRIETORS Jim and Bernadette Robson

IRISH REPUBLIC

DINGLE, CO CORK

PAX HOUSE
~ GUEST-HOUSE ~

Upper John Street, Dingle, Co Kerry
TEL (066) 9151518 **FAX** (066) 9152461
E-MAIL paxhouse@iol.ie **WEBSITE** www.pax-house.com

THERE IS AN ABUNDANCE of wild fuchsia in the hedgerows of the little lanes around Pax House, high on a green hill looking down over Dingle Bay. Before breakfast, you can take an early walk down to the shore, or, from the terrace, count the cows coming out of the milking parlour of the farm below this rather odd building that was once a retirement home. Joan Brosnan-Wright, a former Stoke Mandeville nurse, and her husband, Ron, who was a BBC engineer, have transformed the place to provide a series of comfortable bedrooms decorated with an early Celtic theme. Joan has used letters from the Ogham alphabet – the earliest form of written Irish used around the 4th century AD and found on standing stones – to decorate curtains, monastic parchment shades on bedside lamps and Donegal woollen blankets on beds. Most rooms have showers; cold taps produce water from the Wrights' own spring well. From the dining room, where Joan serves her delicious home-made breads (try the white almond or the brown fruit for breakfast) you can see the field on SleaHead that starred in a film with Tom Cruise, and over to the Ring of Kerry. The silence on the green hill is blissful, but Dingle, a swinging little town, with its full share of traditional music, pubs and restaurants, much frequented by celebs, is only a short walk away.

~

NEARBY Killarney, 42 miles (68 km); Mount Brandon; Tralee, 30 miles (48 km).
LOCATION in countryside, half a mile (0.8 km) out of Dingle town; signposted on N86; car parking
FOOD breakfast
PRICE €€
ROOMS 13; 8 double, 4 double and single, 1 single; 5 with bath, 8 with shower; all with phone, TV, radio, hairdrier, trouser press, tea/coffee making facilities
FACILITIES terraces **CREDIT CARDS** AE, MC, V
CHILDREN 1 family at a time **DISABLED** not possible **PETS** if well-behaved
CLOSED never **PROPRIETORS** Joan and Ron Brosnan-Wright

IRISH REPUBLIC

DRINAGH, CO WEXFORD

KILLIANE CASTLE
～ FARMHOUSE ～

Drinagh, Wexford, Co Wexford
TEL (053) 58885/58898 FAX (053) 58885
E-MAIL killianecastle@yahoo.com WEBSITE www.killianecastle.com

THOSE WHO HAVE ALREADY found Killiane Castle tend to have that special expression worn by people who have a secret they want to keep to themselves. For this is a remarkable place and farmer's wife, Kathleen Mernagh, a most charming and thoughtful hostess. The Mernaghs' early 18thC house was built inside the walls of a largely intact Norman castle, complete with tower (now listed) and dungeon. From the back rooms, you see the ruins of a small chapel in a field and the marshes running down to the sea. Down a leafy lane, miles from the main road, it seems centuries away from everywhere else. Twice a day, you can hear the hum of machines as the cows file in and out of the milking parlour. Kathleen Mernagh, mother of five boys, loves what she does and she does it extremely well. Long before she married a farmer she worked in hotel management. Our reporter heard one guest say to another at breakfast (Jack Mernagh serves his wife's dishes): "It's just like a small hotel." Some bedrooms overlook the weeping ash at the front of the house; more interesting ones overlook the courtyard and over the castle walls to green countryside beyond. All are spacious, well-equipped and comfortable. Happy birds twitter and swoop over the rooftops of this historic place, only a short drive from Rosslare.

～

NEARBY Wexford; Rosslare; Waterford Harbour; Kilmore Quay.
LOCATION in farmland, 3 miles (5 km) from Wexford; car parking
FOOD breakfast
PRICE €
ROOMS 8; 3 double, 3 twin, 2 family; 6 with bath; 2 with shower; all rooms with TV, hairdrier; iron in corridor; tea/coffee making facilities under stairs
FACILITIES garden, terrace; tennis court; public telephone
CREDIT CARDS MC, V **CHILDREN** welcome
DISABLED not suitable **PETS** not in house **CLOSED** 1 Dec to 1 Mar
PROPRIETORS Jack and Kathleen Mernagh

IRISH REPUBLIC

BROWNES BRASSERIE AND TOWNHOUSE

~ RESTAURANT-WITH-ROOMS ~

22 St Stephen's Green, Dublin 2
TEL (01) 638 3939 **FAX** (01) 638 3900
E-MAIL info@brownesdublin.com **WEBSITE** www.brownesdublin.com

THIS CLASSY NEW B&B is decidedly not in the minimalist mode of the smart new Fitzwilliam (located nearby), more an ode to Georgian Dublin: an elegant, listed townhouse on St Stephen's Green, only a few doors down from the Shelbourne. Owner Barry Canny spent more than I£1m on refurbishing what used to be the clubhouse of The Order of Friendly Brothers of St Patrick, founded in the 18thC to stop duelling. It is sumptuous. Mr Canny sees it as a "country house in the heart of the city"; he and his wife, Dee, shipped in antiques from Paris, London and Barcelona and used some top names in interior design and fabrics. Bathrooms have pink Alicante marble counter tops; bedrooms have fax and ISDN lines and 'laptop capability'. Some are on the smallish side. The classic Georgian exterior is untouched; inside great care has gone into keeping to the style of the building. The drawing-room has an Adam fireplace moved from a floor above and the room's mahogany door has been copied for all the bedrooms. The lift has been discreetly hidden away. An ingenious front suite doubles as an office, with a bed that folds away in the wall to become bookshelves, and a boardroom table that breaks up into smaller tables. The 'brasserie' at street level has been described as a bit 'fin-de-siècle Paris'; house guests have it to themselves for breakfast.

~

NEARBY Grafton Street; Trinity College; Temple Bar.
LOCATION overlooking St Stephen's Green; car parking
FOOD breakfast, lunch, dinner
PRICE €€€€
ROOMS 12; 8 double, 2 twin/double, 1 twin, 1 single; all with bath; all rooms with phone, TV, radio, hairdrier, a/c, ISDN and fax lines; trouser press by request; safe in office **FACILITIES** drawing room **CREDIT CARDS** all major
CHILDREN welcome **DISABLED** possible **PETS** by arrangement **CLOSED** Christmas Day
PROPRIETOR Barry Canny **PROPRIETOR** Stein Group

IRISH REPUBLIC

KILRONAN HOUSE
~ TOWN GUEST-HOUSE ~

70 Adelaide Road, Dublin 2
TEL (01) 475 5266 **FAX** (01) 478 2841
E-MAIL info@dublinn.com **WEBSITE** www.dublinn.com

THIS VETERAN, reasonably-priced Georgian guest-house in a quiet, leafy, residential street near St Stephen's Green has been in business for more than 30 years and is perfectly situated for walking to some of the city's most famous landmarks and shops. A new owner has just taken over and may carry out improvements, though there had been overhauls under the previous proprietors. Our reporter felt the exterior could do with a lick of paint but, once inside, was impressed with the warm, yellow walls and parquet floor of the entrance hall and the welcoming reception area tucked under the stairs. Bedrooms are on four 'creaking' floors, and it is a long climb to the top. Some are on the small side. Colours tend to be yellow again, with elegant fabrics and pretty, white-painted wrought-iron bedheads, some pine furniture, heavy off-white curtains and the odd print on the walls. We were told of one room – below ground level – that was described as 'tiny', so it is clearly advisable to check in advance which rooms are available. The yellow sitting room has a big, gilt-edged mirror over the fireplace, antique furniture and a chandelier. The yellow extends to the breakfast room, with shining silver and crisp white linens on the tables. The overall feel of the place is old-fashioned, comfortable and relaxed. Reports, please.

~

NEARBY Grafton Street; National Gallery; Trinity College.
LOCATION 5 minutes walk S of St Stephen's Green; private, secure car parking
FOOD breakfast
PRICE €
ROOMS 15; 11 double (8 twin), 2 single, 2 family; all with shower; all with phone, TV, hairdrier; safe in reception
FACILITIES sitting room **CREDIT CARDS** AE, DC, MC, V
CHILDREN over 10
DISABLED no special facilities **PETS** not accepted
CLOSED never **PROPRIETOR** Terry Masterson

IRISH REPUBLIC

DUBLIN

NUMBER 31

~ TOWN GUEST-HOUSE ~

31 Leeson Close, Dublin 2
TEL (01) 676 5011 **FAX** (01) 676 2929
E-MAIL number31@iol.ie **WEBSITE** www.number31.ie

HOMER, THE YELLOW LABRADOR who was very much part of the household at Kilronan House (page 122), has settled well into his new home at Number 31, which has been taken over by his owners, delightful hosts Noel and Deirdre Comer. This is a very special and visually pleasing place: a mews house designed in the mid-1960s by controversial Dublin architect, Sam Stephenson, and the Georgian house across the garden that was acquired three years ago giving much more space. The Comers loved the originality from the outset and do not plan to make major changes. Only a plate on the wall with '31' on it indicates this is somewhere you may stay. The Stephenson building is modern and open-plan, with painted white brickwork and much glass, wood and stone; kilims hang on the wall. There's a little sunken sitting area, with a black leather sofa custom-built around the fire. French windows and wooden decking lead to the garden and the back of the Georgian house. Deirdre's generous and delicious breakfasts (home-made breads, jams, potato cakes, granola) are served in a white upstairs room on long tables with fresh flowers, sparkling silver, and white linen napkins. Five stylish bedrooms are in the mews house (two have patios). Fifteen more are in the Georgian house, with moulded ceilings and painted in National Trust colours.

~

NEARBY St Stephen's Green; National Gallery; Grafton Street.
LOCATION just off Lower Leeson Street; 5 minutes walk from St Stephen's Green; car parking
FOOD breakfast
PRICE €€€€-€€€€
ROOMS 20; 15 double (12 twin), 5 family; 17 with bath, 3 with shower; all with phone, TV, hairdrier; safe at reception **FACILITIES** sitting room, breakfast room, conservatory; garden **CREDIT CARDS** all major **CHILDREN** over 10
DISABLED 2 ground-floor rooms **PETS** small dogs accepted; not in breakfast room
CLOSED never **PROPRIETORS** Noel and Deirdre Comer

IRISH REPUBLIC

DUBLIN

TRINITY LODGE

~ TOWN GUEST-HOUSE ~

12 South Frederick Street, Dublin 2
TEL (01) 679 5044/5184 **FAX** (01) 6795223
E-MAIL trinitylodge@eircom.net **WEBSITE** www.trinitylodge.com

OWNER PETER MURPHY OPENED this three-storey Georgian house in the heart of Dublin just off Nassau Street opposite Trinity College – in 1997 as an elegant, little guest-house that would not have any of the things he hates about hotels. So, guests are given individual attention from the moment they step in through the blue front door and he places a candle in each room to give a special romantic glow to evenings. This is a handsome, listed building and in order to keep its character and symmetry, Peter chose not to put in a lift, or carve chunks out of rooms for bathrooms. But, he's got almost everything else in the way of comfort and convenience, such as air-conditioning, trouser presses and personal safes. Colours are appropriately Georgian, green, deep red, yellow. There's a little sitting area in the entrance hall, with a window looking on to the street and some comfortable armchairs. Pictures in the house are by the Dublin artist, Graham Knuttel, who lives next door and whose work is very popular with Hollywood stars (he has a commission to paint a portrait for Robert de Niro). They are in bold bright colours and, as one of the staff observes, "have very suspicious-looking people in them, who don't want to look directly at you". You can walk easily to all the local sights from here

~

NEARBY National Art Gallery; Temple Bar; Dublin Castle; the Liffey.
LOCATION a short walk from Trinity College; with limited car parking (with charge; booking essential)
FOOD breakfast
PRICE €€
ROOMS 13; 2 double, 2 single, 6 family (with twin beds), 3 suites with sitting and kitchen area, all with shower; all rooms have phone, TV, air-conditioning, hairdrier, safe **FACILITIES** sitting room
CREDIT CARDS AE, MC, V **CHILDREN** welcome
DISABLED not possible **PETS** not accepted **CLOSED** 23 to 26 Dec
PROPRIETOR Peter Murphy

IRISH REPUBLIC

KILLEEN HOUSE
~ GUEST-HOUSE ~

Killeen, Bushypark, Galway, Co Galway
TEL (091) 524179 **FAX** (091) 528065
WEBSITE www.killeenhousehotel.com

WHAT ORIGINALITY AND IMAGINATION Catherine Doyle has shown in creating such charming quarters for guests in her fascinating early Victorian house. While the approach is somewhat dispiriting, through the outer suburbs of Galway and past new housing developments, once you get beyond the castellated gateway into the 25-acre garden and grounds, all that is forgotten in a trice. The interiors, packed with unusual antiques and bric-a-brac, are a feast for the eyes. The idea behind the bedrooms, Catherine explains, was 'to give everyone something different'. So, she has taken historical periods as themes: Regency; Victorian; Edwardian; Art Nouveau. But these are not artificial pastiches: they are comfortable, welcoming rooms that reflect the care Catherine puts into every aspect of running the house. (She writes the breakfast menu out by hand.) The detail goes right down to the sheets and hand towels. Each room has a reproduction radio, to fit in with the general style; each room even has its own pair of 'period' binoculars, for looking at birds when you take the path leading through the garden, past an old cottage, down to the shores of Lough Corrib. There is also the new Garden Suite; modern, for a change, with bright blue and yellow carpet and painted chairs.

~

NEARBY Galway city centre, 4 miles (6 km); Connemara; the Burren.
LOCATION in grounds, 4 miles (6 km) from centre of Galway; car parking
FOOD breakfast
PRICE €
ROOMS 5; 4 double/1 twin; 4 with bath; 1 with shower; all with phone, TV, radio, hairdrier, tea/coffee making facilities
FACILITIES drawing room, dining room; garden
CREDIT CARDS AE, DC, MC, V
CHILDREN not suitable for children under 12
DISABLED not suitable **PETS** kennel for dogs
CLOSED Christmas **PROPRIETOR** Catherine Doyle

IRISH REPUBLIC

GALWAY, CO GALWAY

NORMAN VILLA
~ TOWNHOUSE ~

86 Lower Salthill, Galway, Co Galway
TEL (091) 521131 **FAX** (091) 521131
E-MAIL info@normanvilla.com **WEBSITE** www.normanvilla.com

DEE KEOGH THINKS that the term 'bed-and-breakfast' has had its day, conjuring up, as it does, images of an impersonal place where you arrive, are given a bed, some breakfast, and leave, with 'no chat, no conversation, no cups of tea'. How very unlike Norman Villa, tall, of grey stone, mid-19thC; a little haven of friendliness and appreciation of the good things in life. The entire house is beautiful: the black and white tiled floor in the hall; gleaming brass beds; varnished wood floors; original shutters, pine furniture. Always buyers of pictures, the Keoghs' collection of modern art hangs on the walls, along with prints of classical remains. There's something pleasing everywhere. A balloon-back chair. A combination of colours. Or Dee's brilliant showers disguised as cupboards. Her husband, Mark, cooks breakfast, served in the old kitchen, with its slate floor and yellow walls. These two have reached a kind of perfection; it is as much a pleasure watching them at work as enjoying their house. Dee dispenses tea, plenty of chat, and her home-made Porter cake; Mark, a former gunnery captain, gives helpful directions with military precision. Thoughtfully, they have printed little maps for guests; the best shows you how to get back to Norman Villa.

~

NEARBY city centre; the Burren; Connemara; Yeats' Tower; Coole Park.
LOCATION 15 minutes walk from city centre; car parking
FOOD breakfast
PRICE €€
ROOMS 5; 4 double, 1 family with 2 double and 1 pull-out bed; all with shower; all with hairdrier
FACILITIES sitting room, dining room; garden
CREDIT CARDS MC, V
CHILDREN welcome
DISABLED not possible **PETS** no dogs
CLOSED Nov to Mar **PROPRIETORS** Dee and Mark Keogh

IRISH REPUBLIC

GLIN, CO LIMERICK

GLIN CASTLE
~ HERITAGE HOUSE ~

Glin, Co Limerick
TEL (068) 34173/34112 **FAX** (068) 34364
E-MAIL knight@iol.ie **WEBSITE** www.glincastle.com

ONE OF THE OUTSTANDING private houses of the world, this is the home of the 29th Knight of Glin, who represents Christie's in Ireland, and his wife who bears the charming title of Madam FitzGerald. On the banks of the Shannon, it is dreamy and beautiful, in pale stone and with castellations. As might be imagined with a title that goes back to the 14th century, it is filled with family history and lovely family things. Even when the Knight is at the castle, guests have the run of the house and garden. Friendly young staff are endlessly attentive. Glin exudes grace, and manages to be both grand and intimate at the same time. The entrance hall, which may have been used as a ballroom in the past, has Corinthian pillars and a plaster ceiling apparently untouched since the1780s. In the reception rooms is a unique collection of Irish 18thC mahogany furniture. To go to bed, you take the flying staircase – the only one of its kind in Ireland – to the first floor. Some rooms here have four-poster beds, and all have fabulous bathrooms.

You may tag along behind one of the guided parties to learn all about the place. A cosy little private sitting-room for guests has deep pink sofas round the fire, family photographs and after-dinner coffee. Be sure to make time for a walk to the walled garden.

~

NEARBY Limerick; golf at Ballybunion; Ring of Kerry.
LOCATION on 400-acre estate, on river's edge; with car parking
FOOD breakfast, dinner; room service
PRICE €€€€
ROOMS 15; 14 double, 1 twin, 2 with dressing rooms, all with bath; all rooms have phone, TV, hairdrier
FACILITIES sitting room, dining room; garden, tennis
CREDIT CARDS AE, DC, MC, V **CHILDREN** accepted
DISABLED not suitable **PETS** kennels provided **CLOSED** end Nov to Feb
PROPRIETORS Desmond and Olda FitzGerald **MANAGER** Bob Duff

IRISH REPUBLIC

GOLEEN, CO CORK

FORTVIEW HOUSE
～ FARMHOUSE BED-AND-BREAKFAST ～

Gurtyowen, Toormore, Goleen, Co Cork
TEL (028) 35324 **FAX** (028) 35324
E-MAIL fortviewhousegoleen@eircom.net WEBSITE www.westcorkweb.ie/fortview

THIS PLACE IS A LABOUR OF LOVE, and it radiates an appropriately warm glow. Richard Connell built the newer part of this house on the West Cork family dairy farm himself, out of stone, and roofed it in slate. The interior is the inspired work of his delightful wife, Violet. With her own ideas, and pictures from magazines, she has created something so fresh, welcoming and comfortable that it is hard to tear oneself away. You can tell what's in store by the two small bears in the retro pram in the hall and the boxy blue-and-red chairs in the sitting room. Violet's bedrooms are named after wild flowers: periwinkle; lavender; daffodil; fuchsia. In one, she has hung straw hats on the wall. She has made curtains out of striped mattress ticking and stencilled a bathroom with sea shells. In a family room with two single beds and pretty patchwork quilts, she props teddy bears up on the pillows as if they are waiting for new, young friends to come. The beamed dining room has a long table, terracotta tiles, wood-burning stove, and old pine furniture. Violet's breakfasts reflect the same attention and care: eggs from the Connell's own hens; freshly squeezed juices; hot potato cakes, salmon and crème fraîche. She already has many admirers. Be sure to book early.

～

NEARBY Goleen; Mizen Head; Schull peninsula; Skibbereen; Bantry.
LOCATION in countryside, 6 miles (10 km) from Goleen; car parking
FOOD breakfast
PRICE €
ROOMS 5; 2 with 2 double, 2 with double and single, 1 with double and 2 single; 1 with bath, 4 with shower; all rooms with hairdrier
FACILITIES sitting room; garden, terrace
CREDIT CARDS not accepted
CHILDREN over 6 welcome
DISABLED not possible **PETS** not accepted
CLOSED 1 Nov to 1 Mar **PROPRIETOR** Violet Connell

IRISH REPUBLIC

GOLEEN, CO CORK

THE HERON'S COVE
RESTAURANT-WITH-ROOMS

Goleen, Co Cork
TEL (028) 35225 **FAX** (028) 35422
E-MAIL suehill@eir.com.net **WEBSITE** www.heronscove.com

A FISHERMAN IN A TRAWLER brings Sue Hill's order to the door of her white-painted, waterside restaurant, which offers 'fresh fish and wine on the harbour' and, most likely, a view of a heron. It is an idyllic spot, on this rugged stretch of the West Cork coastline. It is not surprising to hear from Sue that some of her guests do not want to do anything but simply sit and watch the tide come in and go out again. Three of the bedrooms in this modern house open on to balconies overlooking the little sheltered cove, and from the terrace of the restaurant on the ground floor – which is open from May to October – there are steps down to the beach. Guests are clearly those who relish the peace and quiet. Along the upstairs landing runs a long shelf with a row of books. Bedrooms are well-equipped – some of the pillowcases may not match, but this might not be too important. There are posters of Aix-en-Provence on the walls and Sue has turned the staircase into a gallery for local artists. She is also very switched on to IT and offers guests e-mail and fax facilities. It's only a short walk to the village of Goleen and Sue sends all visitors off on the spectacular drive to Mizen Head, which is Ireland's most southwesterly point.

NEARBY Mizen Head; Cork, 75 miles (120 km); Bantry, 25 miles (40 km); Skibbereen, 24 miles (39 km).
LOCATION on Goleen Harbour; car parking
FOOD breakfast, lunch, dinner
PRICE €
ROOMS 5; 1 double, 2 twin, 2 double with a single bed; 1 with bath, 4 with shower; all with phone, TV, hairdrier, electric blanket, tea/coffee making facilities
FACILITIES terraces, garden
CREDIT CARDS AE, MC, V **CHILDREN** by arrangement
DISABLED not suitable
PETS not accepted
CLOSED Christmas and New Yead **PROPRIETOR** Sue Hill

IRISH REPUBLIC

GOREY, CO WEXFORD

MARLFIELD HOUSE
~ COUNTRY HOUSE HOTEL ~

Gorey, Co. Wexford
TEL (055) 21124 **FAX** (055) 21572
E-MAIL info@marlfieldhouse.ie **WEB SITE** www.marlfieldhouse.ie

A SIGN IN THE DRIVE of this stunning Regency house once owned by the Earls of Courtown and now a Relais and Chateaux hotel (one of the best in Ireland), reads: 'Drive carefully, pheasants crossing'. Not only is this a preserve of all good things for people, but it is pretty comfortable for animals, too. There's a little dog basket for a terrier beside the 18thC marble fireplace in the semi-circular architect-designed hall. Mary Bowe's peacocks, bantams, ducks and geese are cherished and indulged almost as much as her guests. This is a gorgeous, overblown place, a feast for the eyes because of Mary's passion for interior decoration. Her taste is reflected in Waterford crystal chandeliers, little French chairs, gilded taps and a domed conservatory dining room, with trompe l'oeil and trellis. Garlanded with awards – Hostess of the Year, Wine List of the Year, Best Breakfast, One of the World's Most Enchanting Hideaways – the hotel has a tradition of warm hospitality and the Bowes' daughter, Margaret, is now very much at the helm. Bedrooms are sumptuous and charming. Jewels in the crown are the State Rooms, decorated with rich fabrics and fine antique furniture: the French Room, with marble bathroom, overlooks the lake; the Print Room has views of the rose garden. Outstanding food.

~

NEARBY Waterford; Kilkenny; Wexford; Rosslare; beaches.
LOCATION in 35-acre gardens and woodland, 1 mile (1.6 km) out of Gorey on Wexford road; with car parking
FOOD breakfast, lunch, dinner
PRICE €€€-€€€€
ROOMS 20; 18 double and twin, 2 single, all with bath, phone, TV, hairdrier
FACILITIES sitting room, bar, dining room, sauna; garden, terraces, tennis, croquet
CREDIT CARDS AE, DC, MC, V
CHILDREN welcome; no under-10s in dining room **DISABLED** access possible
PETS welcome **CLOSED** mid-Dec to mid-Jan
PROPRIETORS Ray and Mary Bowe; Margaret Bowe

IRISH REPUBLIC

CULLINTRA HOUSE
~ COUNTRY HOUSE ~

The Rower, Inistioge, Co Kilkenny
TEL 051 423614
WEBSITE http.//indigo.ie/cullhse

PATRICIA CANTLON IS KNOWN FOR HER LONG, leisurely, candlelit dinner parties at the 200-year-old ivy-clad farmhouse where she was born. This is not for those with rigid eating habits. When our inspector called, Patricia had several important jobs to do before getting under way in the kitchen: station herself outside the front door with palette and brushes to finish off a painting; race off to the vet with one of her many cats. The day begins when a guest knocks on her door to alert her that people are up and about and waiting for breakfast (could be noon). Her informality and originality have won friends and admirers all over the world. They leave messages in the visitors' book such as 'Great fun'; 'The house, the surroundings, the food, and most of all Patricia, were a magnificent find'.

She has, indeed, created a bewitching retreat. The low-ceilinged house abounds in artistic extras such as the imaginatively-designed rooms in the green-roofed barn, and the conservatory, where Patricia lights banks of candles for pre-dinner drinks. There are log fires, long walks, conversations with cats and foxes, swimming with Patricia in the river. She's a natural hostess, with persuasive powers to make her guests feel they have entered a place that is not quite of this world. It works. (Maeve Binchy's *Circle of Friends* was filmed in Inistioge.)

NEARBY Kilkenny, 19 miles (31 km); New Ross, 6 miles (10 km); Jerpoint Abbey; Waterford.
LOCATION in wooded countryside, 6 miles (10 km) from New Ross; car parking
FOOD breakfast, dinner
PRICE € - €€ (minimum stay 2 nights)
ROOMS 6; 5 double/twin, 1 family; 2 with bath, 4 with shower; hairdrier available; all rooms equipped with hot water bottle
FACILITIES courtyard; gardens, terrace **CREDIT CARDS** extra charge of 3 per cent
CHILDREN welcome **DISABLED** not possible
PETS by prior arrangement **CLOSED** never **PROPRIETOR** Patricia Cantlon

IRISH REPUBLIC

INNISHANNON, CO CORK

INNISHANNON HOUSE
~ COUNTRY HOTEL ~

Innishannon, Co Cork
TEL (021) 4775121 FAX (021) 4775609
EMAIL info@innishannon-hotel.ie WEBSITE www.innishannon-hotel.ie

THIS ATTRACTIVE, IMPOSING 18thC house on the banks of the Brandon River has been delighting guests since seasoned hoteliers Conal and Vera O'Sullivan bought the place in 1989. However, it has recently been taken over by new proprietors Breda Keane and Neil Cumming, who have refurbished the interior and given the walls an apparently much needed lick of paint. While maintaining the rustic country house style, the new owners have thrown out furniture that has had its day, replacing it with smart but functional antique pieces, and fitted new carpets throughout. No. 16 is a cosy attic room with an antique bedspread, No. 14 a fascinating circular room with small round windows and a huge curtained bed. The enormous suite has a Victorian bathroom.

Jean-Marc does the cooking – duck confit, fillet steak, smoked salmon, – earning the place two rossettes. Dinner is served in the lovely pink dining room. Pre-dinner drinks are served outside in summer, or in the airy lounge or cosy bar. Innishannon is not the last word in seclusion or intimacy; there are facilities for conferences and wedding receptions. We would welcome reports on how the new owners are doing.

~

NEARBY Kinsale; Cork.
LOCATION on banks of river, near village; with car parking
FOOD breakfast, lunch, dinner
PRICE €€€–€€€€
ROOMS 13; 7double, 6 twin, all with bath and shower; all rooms have phone, TV, hairdrier **FACILITIES** dining room, sitting room, bar; garden, terrace, fishing, boating
CREDIT CARDS AE, DC, MC, V
CHILDREN welcome
DISABLED ground-floor suite available
PETS accepted in bedrooms
CLOSED mid-Jan to mid-Mar
PROPRIETORS Breda Keane and Neil Cumming

IRISH REPUBLIC

KANTURK, CO CORK

ASSOLAS COUNTRY HOUSE

~ COUNTRY HOUSE ~

Kanturk, Co Cork
TEL (029) 50015 **FAX** (029) 50795
E-MAIL assolas@eircom.net **WEBITE** www.assolas.com

THIS HISTORIC, mellow country house, in a fairy-tale setting of award-winning gardens beside a slow-flowing river, has been in the Bourke family since the early years of this century. The familiar story of escalating maintenance costs and dwindling bank balances led to their taking in guests in 1966, and since then they have never looked back. Assolas is still their family home, and the business of sharing it has obviously turned out to be a pleasure. One recent visitor described her stay there as 'stunning, with wonderful, beautifully served food'.

The house was built around 1590, and had unusual circular extensions added at two corners in Queen Anne's time; beyond the expanses of lawn are mature woods, and then hills and farmland. Inside, the public rooms are richly decorated and elegantly furnished, almost entirely with antiques, and immaculately kept. The bedrooms are notably spacious and many have large luxury bathrooms – the 'circular' rooms at the corners of the house are particularly impressive. Three of the rooms are in a renovated stone building in the courtyard. The food, prepared by Hazel Bourke, is in what might be called modern Irish style – country cooking of fresh ingredients (many home-grown).

~

NEARBY Killarney (Ring of Kerry); Limerick; Blarney.
LOCATION 12 miles (19 km) W of Mallow, NE of Kanturk, signposted from N72; with ample car parking
FOOD breakfast, light or packed lunch, dinner
PRICE €€€–€€€€
ROOMS 9 double/family rooms with bath; all rooms have phone
FACILITIES sitting room, dining room; garden, tennis, croquet, fishing, boating
CREDIT CARDS AE, DC, MC, V **CHILDREN** welcome
DISABLED access fair **PETS** welcome in stables
CLOSED Nov to mid March (except by prior arrangement)
PROPRIETORS Bourke family

Irish Republic

KENMARE, CO KERRY

MUXNAW LODGE

~ BED-AND-BREAKFAST ~

Castletownbere Road, Kenmare, Co Kerry
TEL (064) 41252
E-MAIL muxnawlodge@eircom.net

KENMARE IS A MARKET TOWN at the head of the sheltered Kenmare River estuary, with some handsome 19thC buildings. A popular tourist centre, it has two busy main streets with plenty of shops with painted fronts selling woollen goods, and two of the best hotels in Ireland. It is a perfect kicking-off point for the road around the gorgeous Ring of Kerry, which, in the summer, can become a long traffic jam, with nose-to-tail coaches. Allow a day for it, and set up base camp at charming, gabled Muxnaw Lodge, built in 1801, one of the oldest houses in the town, set on a hillside overlooking the suspension bridge. Hannah Boland has created an attractive period style for her lovely old house, with dark Laura Ashley wallpapers with little prints, brass beds and lovingly-polished antique furniture. In the bedrooms, she hides the modern electric kettles away in wooden boxes so they don't spoil the general look. In a bathroom at the back of the house, you may sit in the corner bath and look at the sea. Breakfasts include yoghurt with honey; fresh eggs from the butcher are cooked on Mrs Boland's big red Aga in the kitchen. Her apple tart is a resounding success at dinner. She is such a delightful hostess that guests may find themselves getting away rather later than planned on that trip around the Ring of Kerry.

~

NEARBY Ring of Kerry; Beara peninsula; Killarney; Bantry Bay.
LOCATION overlooking bay and suspension bridge; 10 minutes walk to town centre; car parking
FOOD breakfast; dinner on request
PRICE €
ROOMS 5; 3 double, 2 twin; 2 with bath, 3 with shower; all rooms with TV, radio, hairdrier, tea/coffee making facilities; trouser press available
FACILITIES garden, terrace, all-weather tennis court
CREDIT CARDS not accepted **CHILDREN** welcome **DISABLED** not suitable
PETS welcome outside **CLOSED** Christmas **PROPRIETOR** Hannah Boland

IRISH REPUBLIC

BUTLER HOUSE
~ TOWNHOUSE ~

16 Patrick Street, Kilkenny, Co Kilkenny
TEL (056) 7765707 **FAX** (056) 7765626
E-MAIL res@butler.ie

THIS TALL, GRAND GEORGIAN HOUSE was once the dower house to Kilkenny Castle, family seat of the Earls of Ormonde. It has beautiful sweeping staircases, plastered ceilings and marble fireplaces. In the 1970s, the house was refurbished in contemporary style by Kilkenny Design, and the result is stunning. The lovely lines and spaces of the Georgian interior have been enhanced by square, modern furniture and neutral colours in carpets and fabrics in the airy, uncluttered rooms. The designers chose black oak furniture, oatmeal carpets, cream curtains, tweed chair covers and the effect, with acres of white walls, is ordered, quiet and restful. Safely lodged at Butler House, you are right in the middle of Kilkenny, a busy tourist centre, and you have your own path to the castle that leads from the back of the house through the formal walled garden, and former stableyards, now converted to crafts workshops. In the cellar is The Basement Restaurant, (where guests go for breakfast), decorated with black and white photographs, black chairs, and all-white china. Morning coffee, biscuits and cake (all very BH colours) are served on a pale oak table in the entrance hall, which has white columns and heavy cream curtains. Superior bedrooms have bay windows and garden and castle views. Butler House is now run by the Kilkenny Civic Trust.

~

NEARBY Kilkenny Castle; cathedral; Kilkenny Design Centre.
LOCATION in gardens, in centre of town; car parking
FOOD breakfast, lunch, dinner
PRICE €€€
ROOMS 13; 11 double, 2 twin; 1 with bath, 12 with shower; all with phone, TV, radio, hairdrier, trouser press; some rooms have desks
FACILITIES garden, terrace
CREDIT CARDS all major **CHILDREN** welcome
DISABLED not possible **PETS** not accepted **CLOSED** 24 to 29 Dec
PROPRIETORS Kilkenny Civic Trust **ACTING MANAGER** Gabrielle Hickey

I RISH R EPUBLIC

KYLEMORE, CO GALWAY

KYLEMORE HOUSE
∽ GUEST-HOUSE ∽

Kylemore, Co Galway
TEL (095) 41143 **FAX** (095) 41143

O NCE THE HOME of the poet Oliver St John Gogarty – who features in James Joyce's *Ulysses* – there's still a strong artistic flavour about this white house on the edge of Kylemore Lough, built for Lord Ardilaun in 1785. Owner Nancy Naughton says her regulars – mostly fishermen – don't want any changes; so the somewhat off-beat charm of the house seems to be unchanging. Something of a character herself, she has a strong aversion to TV in bedrooms: "What will they be wanting with television?" she asks. Quite so: the pictures alone would keep anyone engrossed for hours. She has a portrait of Queen Henrietta Maria, said to be school of Vandyke (maybe he did the face himself?), some fine sporting prints and many more. In St John Gogarty's former library, with its unusual ceiling, is a suite of French painted furniture she bought in an auction in England. She says her fishermen don't care much where they sleep, but the bedrooms are spacious and filled with interesting pieces. Downstairs rooms have welcoming peat fires in beautiful fireplaces. The kitchen is always busy: breakfast includes black and white pudding, and Mrs Naughton's home-made marmalade and brown bread; packed lunches; fishermen's teas; dinner is often, not surprisingly, salmon.
∽

NEARBY Kylemore Abbey; Connemara National Park; Clifden.
LOCATION in garden and grounds, on the N59 to Clifden; car parking
FOOD breakfast, packed lunches, dinner
PRICE €
ROOMS 7; 4 double, 2 twin, 1 single, 2 with bath, 5 with shower; hairdrier on request
FACILITIES sitting rooms; garden; 3 private fishing lakes
CREDIT CARDS not accepted
CHILDREN not accepted
DISABLED 1 downstairs room
PETS dogs sleep in car
CLOSED Oct to Easter **PROPRIETOR** Mrs Nancy Naughton

IRISH REPUBLIC

LEENANE, CO GALWAY

DELPHI LODGE
~ FISHING LODGE ~

Leenane, Co Galway
TEL (095) 42222 **FAX** (095) 42296
E-MAIL delfish@iol.ie **WEBSITE** www.delphilodge.ie

THE 2ND MARQUESS OF SLIGO – who had been with Byron in Greece – thought this wild place as beautiful as Delphi, and built himself a fishing lodge here in the mid-1830s. When Peter Mantle, a former financial journalist, came across the house, it was semi-derelict. Falling under the same spell, he restored it with great care and vision, and Delphi is one of the finest and foremost sporting lodges in Ireland. Fishing is its main business, but everyone is made welcome here. Peter, a lively host and raconteur, runs it like a friendly country house. On our visit, on a misty April evening, wood smoke was rising from the chimney, a new delivery of Crozes Hermitage was stacked up in the hall and Mozart was playing in the snug little library overlooking the lake. Among the guests were a couple of bankers in their Jeremy Fisher waterproofs, a novelist finishing a book, and some Americans from Philadelphia. Salmon are weighed and measured in the Rod Room, creating frissons of excitement and stories for the communal dinner table; the ghillies come in during breakfast to discuss prospects for the day ahead. Bedrooms are unfussy but pretty, with pine furniture; larger ones have lake views; bathrooms have piles of fluffy, white towels. Book well ahead. Heaven for walkers.

~

NEARBY Westport; Kylemore Abbey; Clifden; golf.
LOCATION by the lake in wooded grounds on private estate; with car parking
FOOD breakfast, lunch, dinner
PRICE €€€€
ROOMS 12; 8 double, 4 twin, all with bath; all rooms have phone; hairdrier on request **FACILITIES** drawing room, billiard room, library, dining room; garden, lake
CREDIT CARDS AE, MC, V
CHILDREN welcome
DISABLED 2 ground-floor rooms
PETS not accepted **CLOSED** mid-Dec to mid-Jan
PROPRIETORS Peter and Jane Mantle

IRISH REPUBLIC

LEENANE, CO GALWAY

KILLARY LODGE

~ COUNTRY ACCOMMODATION ~

Leenane, Co Galway
TEL (095) 42276/42245/42302 **FAX** (095) 42314
E-MAIL adventure@killary.com **WEBSITE** www.killary.com

A LONG, ROUGH TRACK through rhododendrons leads to this remote, former 19thC hunting and fishing lodge on the edge of Killary Harbour and looking towards Mweelrea, the great 'grey, bald mountain', the highest in Connacht. Aptly, what began life as a gentleman's sporting residence is now an activities centre run by Jamie Young, voyager and adventurer – who has followed in the steps of Shackleton, the Irish Atlantic explorer – and his wife, Mary. Here, you might well wake up to find that, during the night, some trans-Atlantic yachtsmen have arrived and moored at the jetty on the deep, tidal inlet. You can also spot sea otters, seals and dolphin. Everything is simple, basic and practical, with the home fires kept burning for guests who have been out cycling, walking, fishing, water-skiing, boating. There are plenty of drying facilities and a Drip Room. It's not all outward bound; you can curl up with a book if you don't wish to be energetic. Rooms – in the house or the converted stabling and cottage – are comfortable and well-equipped. Laundry can be done for you. There is no TV; the Youngs consider it a conversation-killer. The young, enthusiastic staff are much involved in the social side of things, that's the spirit of this friendly place.

~

NEARBY Leenane; Letterfrack; Clifden; Westport.
LOCATION in own grounds; 4 miles (6 km) from Leenane; car parking
FOOD breakfast, lunch, dinner
PRICE €
ROOMS 21; 2 double, 5 twin, 2 with 3 beds, 7 family, 5 single, 9 with bath, 12 shower only; all rooms with phone; hairdrier on request; safe at reception
FACILITIES gardens, tennis, table-tennis, sauna, beach
CREDIT CARDS MC, V
CHILDREN welcome
DISABLED 3 ground-floor rooms **PETS** dogs in cars only; take care with sheep
CLOSED Christmas, 1 week Jan **PROPRIETORS** Jamie and Mary Young

IRISH REPUBLIC

LISDOONVARNA, CO CLARE

BALLINALACKEN CASTLE HOTEL
~ COUNTRY HOTEL ~

Lisdoonvarna, Co Clare
TEL (065) 7074025 **FAX** (065) 7074025
E-MAIL ballinalackencastle@eircom.net **WEBSITE** www.ballinalackencastle.com

THIS FASCINATING HOUSE, high on a green hillside with uninterrupted Atlantic views, was built as a 'villa' in the 1840s for John O'Brien, MP for Limerick. Not only does it have its own ruins of a 15thC O'Brien stronghold, but the entrance hall with cupola and green Connemara marble fireplace remains more or less unaltered. There is a newish, discreetish extension, but main house bedrooms have large, dark, old-fashioned pieces of antique furniture, huge wardrobes, and original shutters. From the bed in Room 4, you can see the Aran islands; and Room 7 has a view of the Cliffs of Moher. The lay-out is intriguing – mostly on one floor. The air of faded grandeur is enlivened by the youthful enthusiasm of Marian O'Callaghan – her grandfather bought the castle ruins 50 years ago – and her husband, Frankie Sheedy, a chef of the 'Modern Irish' school. He puts Connemara lamb with courgettes, tomatoes and polenta, and local seafood with saffron cream. The dining room has another cracker of a fireplace, turf fire, original wood floor, pink tablecloths. Nightcaps are served in the lounge bar, and you can steep yourself in the history of the place with locals and join in sing-alongs on weekend evenings, when live entertainment is laid on.

~

NEARBY The Burren; Ballyvaughan; Doolin Crafts Gallery.
LOCATION in 100-acre grounds, 3 miles (5 km) S of Lisdoonvarna on R477; car parking
FOOD breakfast, bar lunch, dinner
PRICE €
ROOMS 13; 2 king-size double, 4 standard double, 7 with double and single bed; 10 with bath, all with shower; all with phone, TV, radio, hairdrier
FACILITIES sitting room, bar; garden
CREDIT CARDS MC, V **CHILDREN** welcome **DISABLED** not suitable
PETS well-behaved dogs in room; not in public areas **CLOSED** mid-Oct to mid-Apr
PROPRIETORS Denis and Mary O'Callaghan

IRISH REPUBLIC

LISDOONVARNA, CO CLARE

SHEEDY'S RESTAURANT AND HOTEL

∼ RESTAURANT-WITH-ROOMS ∼

Lisdoonvarna, Co Clare
TEL (065) 7074026 **FAX** (065) 7074555
E-MAIL info@sheedys.com **WEBSITE** www.sheedys.com

THIS SMALL HOTEL was originally a farmhouse where the Sheedy family began looking after visitors to this little spa town (it has sulphurous springs) in 1855. Recently, however, some bright new changes have taken place: John Sheedy, ex-Ashford Castle head chef, has come home to cook; his delightful wife, Martina, looks after front of house and the wine list and adds her taste for contemporary design. John Sheedy's food is highly acclaimed and the restaurant has been given a completely new look to complement his celebrated 'Modern Irish' cooking. Walls are painted in a moody grey colour called 'Muddy River'. Martina, who used to work at Mount Juliet, has also begun her transformation of the hotel, bringing in help from the nearby Doolin Craft Gallery, renowned for sharp, simple design in wool, crystal, linen and tweed. The lobby already heralds the exciting shape of things to come, with shiny wood floor, little curved reception desk, a bit of exposed natural stone, paintwork in gentian blue and terracotta red. She can't wait to get upstairs, where bedrooms are to be upgraded; the priority is to be comfort, she says, but some modern design "will be in there somewhere". A place to watch; reports, please.

∼

NEARBY The Burren; Ballyvaughan; Doolin Craft Gallery.
LOCATION in centre of Lisdoonvarna, on edge of the Burren; car parking
FOOD breakfast, lunch, dinner
PRICE €
ROOMS 11; 5 double, 6 twin; 9 with bath, 2 with shower; all with phone, TV, hairdrier; ironing board available
FACILITIES south-facing sun lounge, seafood bar, sitting room, restaurant
CREDIT CARDS AE, MC, V
CHILDREN welcome **DISABLED** not possible
PETS not accepted
CLOSED end Sept to Easter
PROPRIETORS the Sheedy family

IRISH REPUBLIC

LONGUEVILLE HOUSE

～ COUNTRY HOUSE HOTEL ～

Mallow, Co Cork
TEL (022) 47156/47306 **FAX** (022) 47459
E-MAIL info@longuevillehouse.ie **WEBSITE** www.longuevillehouse.ie

ONE OF THE FINEST COUNTRY HOUSE hotels in Ireland: this elegant and imposing pink listed Georgian house on a 500-acre wooded estate on the Blackwater River has a three-storey block in the centre built in the 1720's, later wings, and a pretty Victorian conservatory. Inside, it is full of ornate Italian plasterwork, elaborately framed ancestral oils and graceful period furniture. The drawing room overlooks lawns and rows of oaks in the parkland; in the distance are the ruins of the O'Callaghans' Dromineen Castle, demolished under Cromwell, who dispossessed the family. But, after 300 years, they are back. Longueville House has everything, including internationally-recognised chef William O'Callaghan, who, according to one leading food critic, cooks 'some of the finest food in Europe'. Many of his ingredients come from the estate farm, and he also produces a white wine from his own vineyard. Bedrooms are comfortable and filled with antiques. The ones at the front of the house have the best views. A recent vistor says the O'Callaghans are 'charming and informal', and it is very easy to feel relaxed in their beautiful house. The Presidents' Restaurant is named after the portraits of Irish presidents that hang on the walls. The wine list is superb, as is William's seven-course Surprise Tasting Menu.

～

NEARBY Mallow Castle; Anne's Grove Gardens at Castletownroche.
LOCATION on wooded estate, 3 miles (5km) W of Mallow on Kilarney road; ample free car parking
FOOD breakfast, dinner
PRICE €€€
ROOMS 20; 13 double/twin with bath; 7 suites; all with central heating, TV, radio, phone, hairdrier **FACILITIES** sitting room, drawing room, bar, 2 dining-rooms; billiards, table-tennis; fishing **CREDIT CARDS** AE, DC, MC, V
CHILDREN welcome **DISABLED** easy access to public rooms only
PETS not accepted **CLOSED** Christmas
PROPIETORS the O'Callaghan family

IRISH REPUBLIC

MAYNOOTH, CO KILDARE

MOYGLARE MANOR

~ COUNTRY HOUSE ~

Moyglare, Maynooth, Co Kildare
TEL (01) 6286351 **FAX** (01) 6285405
E-MAIL info@moryglaremanor.ie **WEBSITE** www.moryglaremanor.ie

THIS LOVELY 18THC STONE COUNTRY house in the middle of the stud farm belt is so opulent as to seem fabulously decadent. When we visited, people were having lunch by candlelight in the gorgeous deep pink, chandeliered dining room, with draped curtains as thick as blankets, blazing fires and potted palms. A sweet aroma of roses comes in from the garden, filled with tall, dignified trees, and clouds of clematis cover the back of the house. Our inspector had never seen quite so many varieties of decorated lampshade: pleated, tasselled, fringed; or so many fabulous arrangements of flowers. It is all very Naughty Nineties, with lashings of Regency stripes, alabaster vases, and rooms crammed with ornate antique furniture, square chairs, round chairs, stuffed and buttoned chairs, and heavy gilt mirrors, put together so artfully by owner Nora Devlin to make a world of its own. It is meant to be fun – and it is. Bedrooms are large and comfortable, some with love seats, four-posters, and lashings of pink, ribbons and bows, drapes and frills. The history of the house is long and fascinating: Bridget, Countess of Tyrconnell, heard of the Flight of the Earls while walking in the garden here in 1607. The award-winning 16-page wine list is also long and fascinating; in the cellar is almost every Chateau Yquem since 1945.

~

NEARBY Maynooth; horses; Castletown House; National Stud.
LOCATION in countryside, 3 miles (5 km) from Maynooth; with car parking
FOOD breakfast, lunch, dinner
PRICE €€€
ROOMS 16; 14 double and twin, 2 triple; all with bath; all rooms have phone, hairdrier; TV on request
FACILITIES sitting room/bars, dining rooms; garden, terraces
CREDIT CARDS AE, DC, MC, V **CHILDREN** accepted over 12
DISABLED possible **PETS** not accepted **CLOSED** 24 to 26 Dec
PROPRIETOR Norah Devlin **MANAGER** Shay Curran

IRISH REPUBLIC

MILLSTREET, CO WATERFORD

THE CASTLE FARM

FARM GUEST-HOUSE

Millstreet, Cappagh, Dungarvan, Co Waterford
TEL (058) 68049 **FAX** (058) 68099
E-MAIL castlefm@iol.ie **WEBSITE** www.castlecountryhouse.com

REGULARS AT THIS CONVERTED FARMHOUSE, within the keep of a small 15thC castle on a rock among the lush green fields of the Blackwater Valley, know what they like: the Nugents have an 80 per cent repeat business. There is the walk down the drive that was once an avenue of elms, through the imposing front gates and along the lane to the little stone bridge over the River Finisk. The air is heavy with the scent of water and grass, and you may be joined by Bob, the house dog. You might have the bedroom in the original tower known as Miss O'Keeffe's Ballroom (in the 1700s the house belonged to her family). Meals come from Joan Nugent's farmhouse kitchen and are served in the yellow dining room, with walls more than five-and-half-feet thick and an original 15thC stone archway. Emmett Nugent can nearly always be distracted from his tasks to relate the history of his fascinating edifice. He has made a path around the base of the rocky mound, so visitors may make a circular tour; and he has also restored a clammy dungeon where, he explains, guests like to gather on warm evenings to enjoy a glass or two and get up to some 'medieval' fun and games. Joan also likes to hang her washing there. You feel that somehow you are the first to discover the comforting peace and quiet of Castle Farm. The Nugents are delightful, welcoming and thoughtful hosts.

NEARBY Cappoquin, 5 miles (8 km); Dungarvan; Waterford; Youghal.
LOCATION in countryside, on a 120-acre dairy farm, 9 miles (14 km) from Dungarvon; car parking
FOOD breakfast, lunch
PRICE €
ROOMS 4; double and single in each room; 1 with bath, 3 with shower; all with TV, hairdrier; tea/coffee making facilities **FACILITIES** gardens, terraces
CREDIT CARDS AE, MC, V **CHILDREN** welcome
DISABLED no downstairs rooms **PETS** small dogs, with baskets, accepted
CLOSED 1 Nov to 14 Mar **PROPRIETORS** Joan and Emmett Nugent

Irish Republic

Roundwood House

~ COUNTRY HOUSE ~

Mountrath, Co Laois
TEL (0502) 32120 **FAX** (0502) 32711
E-MAIL roundwood@eircom.net

A RECENT REPORTER REACTED very well to the Kennans' operation. The house is 'not in perfect repair, but for the type of place they run, this didn't seem to matter': it's a 'wonderful place, and the Kennans really are charming and informal hosts'. The perfectly proportioned Palladian mansion is set in acres of lime, beech and chestnut woodland. The Kennans have wholeheartedly continued the work of the Irish Georgian Society, who rescued the house from near-ruin in the 1970s. All the Georgian trappings remain – bold paintwork, shutters instead of curtains, rugs instead of fitted carpets, and emphatically no TV. Despite this, the house is decidedly lived in, certainly not a museum.

For Rosemarie's plentiful meals, non-residents sit at separate tables; residents must sit together – you don't have a choice – fine if you like to chat to strangers, not ideal for romantic twosomes. After-dinner conversation is also encouraged over coffee and drinks by the open fire in the drawing-room. You may well find the Kennans joining in.

Four pleasant extra bedrooms in a recently converted stable block are perhaps cosier and of a better standard than those in the main house. It's very child-friendly (the Kennans have six), with a lovely big playroom at the top of the house, full of toys.

~

NEARBY walking, horse-riding, fishing; Slieve Bloom mountains.
LOCATION in countryside, 3 miles (5 km) N of Mountrath on Kinnitty road; with gardens and ample car parking
FOOD full breakfast, lunch on Sunday only, dinner; wine licence
PRICE €€€
ROOMS 9; 7 double (3 twin), 2 family rooms; all with bath; all rooms have central heating **FACILITIES** sitting room, study, dining room, hall; croquet
CREDIT CARDS AE, DC, MC, V **CHILDREN** very welcome **DISABLED** not suitable
PETS accepted by arrangement **CLOSED** 3 weeks Jan and Christmas
PROPRIETORS Frank and Rosemarie Kennan

IRISH REPUBLIC

MULRANNY, CO MAYO

ROSTURK WOODS

~ COUNTRY GUEST-HOUSE ~

Rosturk, Mulranny, Co Mayo
TEL (098) 36264 **FAX** (098) 36264
E-MAIL stoney@iol.ie **WEBSITE** www.rosturk-woods.com

IT IS NO SURPRISE that word of Alan and Louisa Stoney's charming little complex among trees on the tidal, sandy shore of Clew Bay has spread so far. First of all it's a paradise for children – with the doorstep on the beach, so to speak. When the tide is out, you can walk across to an island and there is plenty to see in the way of wildlife. The Stoneys' adaptable newly-built family house was completed in 1991; an even newer self-catering cottage opened for business in 1999 and was booked – immediately – for the summer. But the buildings blend nicely into the leafy background, and with wood fires, wooden floors and lots of painted furniture, the house has an open, airy, seaside feel about it, which is instantly relaxing. Rooms are comfortable; some are up under the eaves. Louisa is a reflexologist when she is not looking after guests. Her ops centre is her enormous kitchen, with dogs, pots and pans, children's paintings on the wall, and windows facing south to the water. From here comes the freshly squeezed orange juice and smoked salmon and scrambled egg for breakfast; dinner could be organic spinach soup, fresh black sole from Achill Island (the fish man delivers daily), and home-made ice cream. The house has two boats; Alan is a sailing instructor.

NEARBY Westport, 18 miles (29 km); Achill Island, 11 miles (18 km); Newport, 7 miles (11 km).
LOCATION 3 miles before Mulranny on the Newport/Achill road; in 5-acre grounds with car parking
FOOD breakfast, dinner
PRICE €
ROOMS 4; 2 double, 2 twin; 2 with bath and shower, 2 with shower; radio on request; all with hairdrier
FACILITIES snooker room; tennis court, garden, woodland, beach
CREDIT CARDS not accepted **CHILDREN** welcome **DISABLED** not possible
PETS welcome **CLOSED** 1 Dec to 1 Mar **PROPRIETORS** Alan and Louisa Stoney

I R I S H   R E P U B L I C

NENAGH, CO TIPPERARY

ASHLEY PARK HOUSE
∼ COUNTRY HOUSE BED-AND-BREAKFAST ∼

Ardcrony, Nenagh, Co Tipperary
TEL (067) 38223 **FAX** (067) 38013
E-MAIL magaret@ashleypark.com **WEBSITE** www.ashleypark.com

A PEACOCK WAS SITTING, wailing, on the rail of the green veranda when we visited Ashley Park: one of the owner's beloved birds that are fed every morning in a ritual of the household. Mr Mounsey, who has a grocery store in Nenagh, is insistent that nothing here should be like a hotel. He need have no fears on that front. This wildly atmospheric early 18thC house comes complete with ballroom, ruined chapel on an island on the lake, original stabling and farmyard in a more-or-less untouched state, and a scheduled Neolithic ring fort in the woods. The whole place is a nature reserve, too. Mr Mounsey likes every guest to be given an electric blanket; Mozart is played at breakfast and Frank Sinatra at dinner. We were unable to see any bedrooms, as they were occupied by a sleeping film crew, but, like all the other rooms in the house, they are huge, as are the bathrooms with their Victorian fittings. The Irish President, Mary McAleese, has stayed in Room 2. Roses trail along the veranda that runs the length of the house and, to relax, you can sit and read in the octagonal Chinese Room. There are turf fires; Mr Mounsy's daughter, Magaret, bakes a delicious scone; fresh eggs can be ordered straight from the hen. Hotels just don't come like this.

∼

NEARBY Lough Derg; Limerick, 27 miles (43 km); Shannon.
LOCATION on private estate, with lake, 3.5 miles (6 km) out of Nenagh on Borrisokane road; car parking
FOOD breakfast, dinner
PRICE €
ROOMS 6; 3 double, 2 twin, 1 family; 3 with bath and shower, 3 with shower; TV and hairdrier on request
FACILITIES garden; lake, boat, fishing rods, riding; public telephone
CREDIT CARDS not accepted **CHILDREN** welcome
DISABLED not possible **PETS** accepted **CLOSED** never
PROPRIETOR Sean Mounsey

IRISH REPUBLIC

NEWMARKET-ON-FERGUS, CO CLARE

CARRYGERRY COUNTRY HOUSE

~ COUNTRY HOUSE HOTEL ~

Newmarket-on-Fergus, Co Clare
TEL (061) 363739 **FAX** (061) 363823
E-MAIL info@carrygerryhouse.com **WEBSITE** www.carrygerryhouse.com

BEING SO CONVENIENTLY close to Shannon airport – a ten-minute drive away – this could have settled for being a commercial hotel. But the kindness and warm hospitality of Niel Emerson and his wife, Gillian, have made this old manor house into a place to remember for those staying for either their first or last night in Ireland. In gardens, woodland, and pasture – now home to two donkeys – Carrygerry, built in the 18th century with a gable end and a remarkable courtyard entered through an archway, was a private house until as recently as the 1980s. Gillian is passionate about her house and she has filled it with antiques and pretty things. The two cosy sitting rooms, either side of the front door, are delightful places to pass away the time, with blazing fires, deep sofas, striped cushions, oriental carpets, and rich, dark colours. The house really seems to come alive in the evenings, when it positively glows in candlelight. In the former coach house in the courtyard is a bar; some bedrooms are there, too. At the end of a flight or a long drive, this is a comfortable, welcoming traveller's rest.

~

NEARBY Shannon airport, 8 miles (13 km); Limerick, 20 miles (32 km); Ennis (32 km).
LOCATION in gardens and grounds; car parking
FOOD breakfast, lunch, dinner
PRICE €€€–€€€€
ROOMS 12; 7 double, 3 twin, 2 single; 6 in courtyard; 10 with bath, 2 with shower; all with phone, TV, radio; hairdrier on request
FACILITIES restaurant, bar, courtyard
CREDIT CARDS AE, DC, MC, V
CHILDREN over 12
DISABLED access possible
PETS accepted
CLOSED 1 week Mar
PROPRIETORS Niel and Gillian Emerson

IRISH REPUBLIC

RATHNEW, CO WICKLOW

HUNTER'S HOTEL
~ COACHING INN ~

Newrath Bridge, Rathnew, Co Wicklow
TEL (0404) 40106 **FAX** (0404) 40338
E-MAIL reception@hunters.ie **WEBSITE** www.hunters.ie

THE AREA AROUND IT is fast becoming part of Dublin commuterland, but not many changes here in this little island of constancy. In 1840, some Victorian travellers touring Ireland reported: 'We strongly recommend Mr Hunter's Inn at Newrath Bridge, which is, according to our experience, the most comfortable in the county.' The same applies today. This is a delightful, proudly old-fashioned place, built as a coaching inn for several big houses in the vicinity. You would not be surprised if you were to hear the sound of horses' hooves and carriage wheels clattering into the enormous stable yard, or trunks being carried into the beamed front hall, which still has the tiled floor laid in 1720. Nothing clashes, nothing jars, to spoil the old world charm that brings people from far and wide. Present owner Maureen Gelletlie (a great great granddaughter of the original Mr Hunter) is renowned for her individual style of looking after guests. In a trice she manages to get complete strangers talking in the small bar, with bare, wide wooden floorboards, beams, and a print of the 1900 Grand National winner, Ambush 11, on the wall, where she serves drinks. There is good, plain cooking; a lovely garden by the river; courtesy; glowing fires; charming bedrooms (ask for garden view); tea on the lawn; billowing wisteria.

~

NEARBY Powerscourt Gardens; Russborough House; Glendalough; golf.
LOCATION in gardens on River Varty, in countryside half a mile from Rathnew; car parking
FOOD breakfast, lunch, dinner
PRICE €€€
ROOMS 16; 15 double/twin, 1 single, 15 with bath, 1 with shower; all rooms with phone, TV, hairdrier; hot water bottle
FACILITIES gardens, terrace
CREDIT CARDS all major **CHILDREN** welcome **DISABLED** ground-floor room
PETS accepted **CLOSED** 24 to 26 Dec **PROPRIETORS** the Gelletlie family

IRISH REPUBLIC

RECESS, CO GALWAY

LOUGH INAGH LODGE HOTEL

~ COUNTRY HOTEL ~

Inagh Valley, Recess, Co Galway
TEL (095) 34706 **FAX** (095) 34708
E-MAIL inagh@iol.ie **WEBSITE** www.loughinaghlodgehotel.ie

THIS SOLID, WELL-PROPORTIONED Victorian shooting lodge, romantically placed on one of the most beautiful lakes in Connemara, was boarded up when Maire O'Connor and her late husband, John, came across it looking for somewhere suitable to run as a small hotel. Remarkably, some of the old sporting record books survive and may be read by guests. Little has been overlooked in the way of comfort. Each bedroom, named after an Irish writer, has a dressing room with trouser press (not that we rate these very highly as creature comforts, but they're useful for damp Connemara days). Views are of water and The Twelve Bens mountains. Maire has kept to rich dark Victorian colours and polished wood; her careful attention to detail and service is reflected throughout the comfortable, cosy house. She arranges the fresh flowers, which are sent from Clifden. Rooms downstairs have inviting log fires and warm lighting. The green dining room with yellow curtains and gleaming, dark wood floor is delightful. Seafood and traditional wild game dishes are specialities of the kitchen. Loughs Inagh and Derryclare are on the doorstep; for walkers, there are miles of tracks through the wild and rugged landscape. The hotel also has a stable of bicycles.

~

NEARBY Recess; Oughterard; Clifden; Galway.
LOCATION in open country on shores of Lough Inagh; car parking
FOOD breakfast, lunch, dinner
PRICE €
ROOMS 12; 8 double; 4 twin; all with bath and shower; all rooms have phone, TV, radio, hairdrier, trouser press; ironing board on request
FACILITIES garden, lake, fishing, bicycles
CREDIT CARDS AE, DC, MC, V
CHILDREN welcome **DISABLED** ground-floor room
PETS acccepted
CLOSED mid-Dec to mid-Mar **PROPRIETOR** Maire O'Connor

I R I S H   R E P U B L I C

R I V E R S T O W N ,   C O   S L I G O

C O O P E R S H I L L
⌁ C O U N T R Y   H O U S E   H O T E L ⌁

Riverstown, Co Sligo
TEL (071) 9165466 **FAX** (071) 9165108
E-MAIL ohara@coopershill.com **WEBSITE** www.coopershill.com

B RIAN O'HARA HAS BEEN RUNNING this delightful country house with his wife, Lindy, for the past twelve years now, and has subtly improved the style of the place without interfering with its essential appeal.

It is a fine house – though some may not think it elegant by Georgian standards – with splendidly large rooms (including the bedrooms, most of which have four-poster or canopy beds). It is furnished virtually throughout with antiques; but remains emphatically a home, with no hotel-like formality – and there is the unusual bonus of a table-tennis room to keep children amused.

The grounds are extensive enough not only to afford complete seclusion, but also to accommodate a river on which there is boating and fishing for pike and trout. Lindy cooks honest country dinners based on English and Irish dishes, which are entirely in harmony with the nature of the place, while Brian knowledgeably organizes the cellar.

⌁

NEARBY Sligo, 12 miles (20 km); Lough Arrow; Lough Gara.
LOCATION 1 mile (1.5 km) W of Riverstown, off N4 Dublin-Sligo road; in large garden on 500-acre estate, with ample car parking
FOOD full breakfast, light or packed lunch, dinner; restaurant licence
PRICE €€
ROOMS 9; 8 double, 6 with bath, 1 with separate bath, 1 with shower; 1 family room with bath; all rooms have tea/coffee kit
FACILITIES sitting room, dining room; fishing, tennis
CREDIT CARDS AE, DC, MC, V
CHILDREN welcome if well behaved
DISABLED no access
PETS welcome if well behaved, but not allowed in public rooms or bedrooms
CLOSED Nov to end Mar
PROPRIETORS Brian and Lindy O'Hara

IRISH REPUBLIC

SHANAGARRY, CO CORK

BALLYMALOE HOUSE
~ CONVERTED FARMHOUSE ~

Shanagarry, Midleton, Co Cork
TEL (021) 4652531 **FAX** (021) 4652021
E-MAIL ref@ballymaloe.ie **WEBSITE** www.ballymaloe.ie.

THIRTY BEDROOMS NORMALLY rules out a hotel for this guide, but we cannot resist this amiable, rambling, creeper-clad house – largely Georgian in appearance but incorporating the remains of a 14thC castle keep – set in rolling green countryside. Visitors in 1998 were 'immensely impressed' and found the staff 'as well-drilled as an army, but jolly, with abundant charm'.

The Allens, who have been farming here for over 40 years, opened as a restaurant in 1964 and started offering rooms three years later. Since then they have added more facilities and more rooms – those in the main house now outnumbered by those in extensions and converted out-buildings.

Despite quite elegant and sophisticated furnishings, the Allens have always managed to preserve intact the warmth and naturalness of a much-loved family home. But not all visitors agree: one reporter judged that Ballymaloe was becoming rather commercialized. Even that reporter, however, was impressed by the standard of food. Mrs Allen no longer takes an active role in the cooking. It is now Rory O'Connell who prepares the Classic French and Irish dishes alongside original dishes, all based on home produce and fish fresh from the local quays. (Sunday dinner is always a buffet.) Just as much care is lavished on breakfast, and the famous children's high tea.

~

NEARBY beaches, cliff walks, fishing, golf.
LOCATION 20 miles (32 km) E of Cork, 2 miles (3 km) E of Cloyne on the Ballycotton road, L35, ample private car parking
FOOD breakfast, lunch, dinner
PRICE €€€–€€€€
ROOMS 33 double and twin, 31 with bath, 2 with shower; all rooms have phone
FACILITIES 3 sitting rooms, conference/TV room, conservatory, library; tennis, golf, swimming pool **CREDIT CARDS** AE, DC, MC, V **CHILDREN** welcome
DISABLED access easy; some specially adapted rooms
PETS not accepted **CLOSED** Christmas **PROPRIETORS** I and M Allen

HOTEL NAMES

HOTEL NAMES

HOTEL NAMES

Hotel Names

HOTEL LOCATIONS

Hotel Locations

HOTEL LOCATIONS

HOTEL LOCAT